Upper Perené Arawak Narratives
of History, Landscape, and Ritual

Upper Perené Arawak Narratives of History, Landscape, and Ritual

ELENA MIHAS

With Gregorio Santos Pérez
and Delia Rosas Rodríguez

UNIVERSITY OF NEBRASKA PRESS, LINCOLN AND LONDON

RECOVERING
LANGUAGES LITERACIES
OF THE AMERICAS

This book is published as part of the Recovering Languages and Literacies of the Americas initiative. Recovering Languages and Literacies is generously supported by the Andrew W. Mellon Foundation.

∞

Library of Congress Cataloging-in-Publication Data
Mihas, Elena.
Upper Perené Arawak narratives of history, landscape, and ritual /
Elena Mihas; with Gregorio Santos Pérez and Delia Rosas Rodríguez.
pages   cm
Summary: "A comprehensive bilingual collection of Ashéninka Perené Arawakan oral literature, including traditional narratives, ethnographic accounts of old customs and rituals, contemporary women's autobiographical stories, songs, chants, and ritual speeches"—Provided by publisher.
Includes bibliographical references and index.
ISBN 978-0-8032-4537-2 (cloth : alk. paper)
ISBN 978-0-8032-8564-4 (paper : alk. paper)
ISBN 978-0-8032-6529-5 (epub)
ISBN 978-0-8032-6530-1 (mobi)
ISBN 978-0-8032-6528-8 (pdf).
1. Ashaninca Indians—Peru—Perene River Valley—Social life and customs. 2. Ashaninca Indians—Peru—Perene River Valley—Rites and ceremonies. 3. Perene River Valley (Peru)—Social life and customs.
4. Ethnology—Peru—Perene River Valley. 5. Campa language—Peru—Perene River Valley—Texts. 6. Oral tradition—Peru—Perene River Valley. 7. Folk literature—History and criticism. 8. Narration (Rhetoric). 9. Discourse analysis. I. Santos Pérez, Gregorio. II. Rosas Rodríguez, Delia. III. Title.
F3430.1.A83 M54 2014
305.898'39—dc23
2014030510

Set in Huronia by Tseng Information Systems, Inc.
Designed by Ashley Muehlbauer.

For my husband, Peter Andrew Mihas

Ayenkitsarini opoña ovairopaye aipatsiteka, aisaitzi amitapintajeetari: Iyenkitsari irashi asheninkaite saikatsiri katonko parenini.

—Gregorio Santos Pérez and Delia Rosas Rodríguez

CONTENTS

ILLUSTRATIONS

FIGURES

MAPS

ACKNOWLEDGMENTS

I am very grateful to the thirty Ashéninka Perené narrators for their invaluable contribution to this book. Their expertise, enthusiasm, camaraderie, and good-humored attitude in the face of occasional setbacks made the whole process an extremely enlightening and rewarding enterprise for me. My warmest thanks go to Gregorio Santos Pérez and Delia Rosas Rodríguez, the editors of native texts and team leaders whose doggedness and clear understanding of the project's goals enormously sustained our teamwork. I also acknowledge with gratitude other book contributors: Raul Martin Bernata, Victoria Manchi de Martin, Ines Pérez de Santos, Moises Santos Rojas, Elías Meza Pedro, Ruth Quillatupa Lopez, Daniel Bernales Quillatupa, Bertha Rodríguez de Caleb, Abdias Caleb Quinchori, Victorina Rosas de Castro, Gerardo Castro Manuela, Julio Castro Shinkaki, Paulina García Ñate, Alberto Pérez Espinoza, Elena Nestor de Capurro, Fredi Miguel Ucayali, Luis Mauricio Rosa, Manuel Rubén Jacinto, Cristobal Jumanga Lopez, Abraham Jumanga Lopez, Otoniel Ramos Rodríguez, Clelia Mishari, Livia Julio de Quinchori, Frida Thomas Huamán, Almacia Benavidez Fernandez, Luzmila Machari Quinchori, María Virginia Lopez, and Carmen Pachiri Quinchori. I also thank Dora Meza de Santos for invaluable assistance during our trips to remote communities.

1. (*top left*) Gregorio Santos Pérez with his wife, Dora
2. (*top right*) Daniel Bernales Quillatupa
3. (*middle left*) Ines Pérez de Santos and Moises Santos Rojas
4. (*middle right*) Elías Meza Pedro
5. (*bottom left*) Ruth Quillatupa Lopez
6. (*bottom right*) Delia Rosas Rodríguez with her grandchild and Bertha Rodríguez de Caleb

7. (*top left*) Bertha Rodríguez de Caleb
8. (*top right*) Victorina Rosas de Castro with her child
9. (*middle left*) Abdias Caleb Quinchori
10. (*middle right*) Julio Castro Shinkaki
11. (*bottom left*) Gerardo Castro Manuela with his son and
Abdias Caleb Quinchori
12. (*bottom right*) Paulina García Ñate

13. (*top left*) Elena Nestor de Capurro with her daughter, Gloria
14. (*top right*) Fredi Miguel Ucayali
15. (*middle left*) Victoria Manchi de Martin, Raul Martin Bernata, and Luis Mauricio Rosa
16. (*middle right*) Alberto Pérez Espinoza
17. (*bottom*) Manuel Rubén Jacinto with his wife

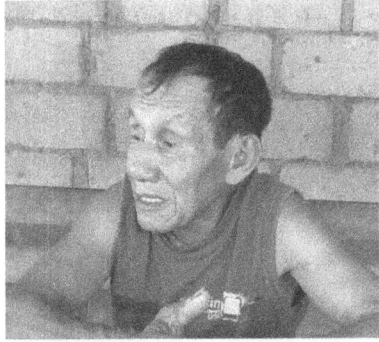

18. (*top left*) Cristobal Jumanga Lopez
19. (*top right*) Abraham Jumanga Lopez
20. (*middle left*) Otoniel Ramos Rodríguez
21. (*middle right*) Frida Thomas Huamán
22. (*bottom*) Luzmila Machari Quinchori

23. (*top left*) María Virginia Lopez
24. (*right*) Livia Julio de Quinchori
25. (*middle left*) Carmen Pachiri Quinchori
26. (*bottom left*) Almacia Benavidez Fernandez

I also extend my sincere gratitude to Héctor Martin Manchi, the president of CECONSEC (la Central de Comunudades Nativas de la Selva Central); Osbaldo Rosas Rodríguez, the chief of Bajo Marankiari; Fredi Miguel Ucayali, the chief of Pampa Michi; and Frida Thomas Huamán, the chief of Pumpuriani, for their cordial support and assistance. Special thanks are due to Daniel Bernales Quillatupa (Aroshi) for creating beautiful illustrations, to Delia Rosas Rodríguez for donating images of Ashaninka warriors embroidered on her handmade cloth, used on the book's cover, and to Adella Edwards for making three detailed maps of the area.

I am grateful to the granting agencies—the Firebird Foundation for Anthropological Research, the National Science Foundation (DDIG #0901196), and the Endangered Languages Documentation Programme (SG 0002)—for their support. I also thank Sasha Aikhenvald and Bob Dixon for their financial assistance.

I appreciate a great deal the kind encouragement and insightful feedback on the manuscript that I received from two anonymous reviewers, from Sasha Aikhenvald, and from Bob Dixon, and the copious proofreading comments from Brigitta Flick and Pete Mihas, my husband, whose willingness to be my sounding board and unwavering support made the work on this project so much easier.

INTRODUCTION

Objective, Method, Data, and Structure

This book is a result of sixteen months of linguistic fieldwork among Peruvian Upper Perené Arawaks from Chanchamayo Province, Peru, spanning a period of five years. My first, short visit to Chanchamayo Province occurred in 2008, followed by a series of long-term fieldwork periods in subsequent years. The research project began with a utilitarian purpose of fulfilling the requirement for a doctoral degree in linguistics but eventually morphed into an ethnographic-documentary study that attempts to provide a broad perspective on the Ashéninka Perené world as described by the indigenous speakers. The text selections in this anthology constitute a self-portrayal of the natives' ways of thinking and living, both in the past and present.

This study also takes into account existing ethnographies of indigenous Amazonian people, including academic publications about Ashéninka/Asháninka subsistence patterns; social, religious, and cultural life; and ecological adaptation (e.g., Anderson 2000; Bodley 1970, 1972, 1973; Chevalier 1982; Elick 1969; Gow 1991; Hvalkof 1989; Lenaerts 2006b, 2006c; Narby 1989; Rojas Zolezzi 1994, 2002; Santos-Granero 1998, 2002a, 2002b, 2004a, 2004b; Santos-Granero and Barclay 1998; Sarmiento Barletti 2011; Varese 2002; Veber 2003, 2009; Weiss 1973, 1974, 1975). These accounts offer critical insights and anchoring reference points, necessary for providing the sociocultural context for the Upper Perené narratives and placing the collected texts within pan-Amazonian symbolic discourses. It should be noted that the speakers of Ashéninka and Asháninka varieties are often thought of as a culturally homogenous group, which must have made acceptable the academic convention of writing the two names with the slash, Ashéninka/Asháninka.

This ethnographic-documentary work is decidedly text focused, comprising fifty-eight native texts with accompanying translations and detailed commentary. As such, its research framework is closely aligned with the discourse-centered approach to language and culture (Sherzer and Urban 1986; Sherzer 1987) in that it treats Upper Perené language in use as reflective (and constitutive) of the native society's events and practices (see Basso 1985, 1987, 1995; Graham 1995; Oakdale 2007; Sherzer 1990, 2004; Urban 1991; Uzendoski and Calapucha-Tapuy 2012). The anthology's ethnographic texts, which "constitute a society's verbal life" (Sherzer 1987:306) emerging within a range of documented speech behaviors, are used as leads for an exploration of the broadly defined themes of Upper Perené native history, landscape, and ritual symbolism.

The documentary project's main objective of making public minimally cleaned-up data has been attained inasmuch as the material in this collection has been gathered, transcribed, and translated by several Upper Perené Indian authors themselves. In addition, the content of the volume was discussed by the contributors, their family members, their neighbors, and the cadre of tribal governance multiple times, to ensure general approval of the project's ultimate product. This book is a collective effort by many Upper Perené Arawaks; the contributors' names prominently appear at the beginning of each text and their pictures appear in the acknowledgments section. The published material comes as close to "the real history" and "direct publication by Indians themselves" (Lévi-Strauss 1978:37) as could be done in the current community context.

With regard to the research methods, I relied on close observation, interviews, and documentation, which included audio and video recording, transcription and translation of collected materials, and archiving data with local research organizations and international digital archives. The purpose of my fieldwork among Upper Perené Arawaks was to study their language and culture. Over the course of the project, I filled five thick notebooks with copious notes on what I observed or overheard and what people told me. I also asked my primary language consultants to help me build a multigenre corpus of audio and video recordings of Ashéninka Perené speakers from various native communities. The fifty-plus-hour corpus includes recordings of over fifty speakers from twelve villages, typically made in their homes. About a third of the collected texts have been transcribed in Ashéninka Perené and translated into Spanish.

These recordings were commonly made in group settings, as loosely structured interviews in which speakers were asked to share their perspective on a suggested issue, such as landownership, horticultural techniques, herbal healing, sorcery, or shamanism, to name a few, in the presence of their family members or neighbors. The audience would sometimes ask questions to clarify certain points or give their input on the matter discussed. It was not uncommon for the interlocutors to stray from the main subject and engage in an issue of more pressing concern to them. Such interviews were recorded with many speakers on a regular basis, during a number of fieldwork seasons, which gradually alleviated the speakers' initial tension and discomfort in the presence of the recording equipment and linguist outsider.

Language difficulties were a concern at the initial stage of fieldwork, since my knowledge of Ashéninka Perené was basic and I needed a great deal of direction and language interpretation from my primary language consultants in my work with other speakers. As my language skills got better, I assumed more responsibilities within the language-consultant team and documentary project as a whole and began working with speakers without mediation, using both Spanish and Ashéninka Perené. The rule we adhered to during our recording sessions, followed religiously, was expressed by the phrase *Piñaavaite añaaniki!* (Speak our language!). Eventually my comprehension level became advanced enough for me to be included in speakers' conversations, although my speaking ability still lagged behind and I relied on Spanish to drive home my point. The speakers I worked with were comfortable conversing with each other in my presence and were fond of quizzing me on the language. At some point they began to introduce me to others with the phrase *Oyotziro añaani* (She knows our language). I was often addressed by males as *chooki* (sister) and by females as *entyo* (sister), two kinship terms that refer to the ego's siblings.

The anthology's texts, which amount to about four hours of recording time, were transcribed in Ashéninka Perené and translated into Spanish by three primary consultants, Gregorio Santos Pérez of Villa Perené, Delia Rosas Rodríguez of Bajo Marankiari, and Daniel Bernales Quillatupa of Bajo Marankiari, who were "felt to be better models of . . . speech than others" (Bloomfield 1927:439). The accuracy of transcriptions and translations was checked by other consultants at least once, and in many cases, twice. The English translations are my own, based on my study of Ashéninka Perené and Spanish interpretations by my language consultants. Verification of the accuracy of English translations, if needed, can be easily performed, since most of the original recordings are annotated and archived in three digital archives: Archive of Indigenous Languages of Latin America (AILLA), University of Texas at Austin; Endangered Languages Archive (ELAR), SOAS, University of London; and the Language and Culture Research Centre archive, James Cook University,

Queensland, Australia. The archives provide unrestricted access to the deposited collections.

Selection of texts for this anthology presented a challenge, considering the sheer number of recorded performances, which exceeds two hundred. Two factors were influential in the decision as to which texts were to make the cut: the speakers' recommendation, and the availability of comparable published materials in Ashéninka Perené with translations in English. When making the decision about what should be included I consulted those speakers who significantly contributed to the documentary project, some of them being in a leadership position in the community. Most of them are truly concerned about the erosion of traditional ways of living and are alarmed by the disregard of linguistic and cultural heritage that is characteristic of the younger generations. The need to maintain the old customs and traditions, seen as a way of staying true to the native identity, is emphasized in many collected texts, sending an important message to the narrators' younger kinfolk.

This book would not be possible without a first of its kind, bilingual Ashéninka Perené–Spanish publication that came to fruition at the speakers' initiative and with grant support from the Endangered Languages Documentation Programme. This storybook, titled *Añaani katokosatzi parenini* (The language of Alto Perené; Mihas 2011), consists of eighty-three Ashéninka Perené texts, with translations in Spanish. The book was intended to serve the needs of bilingual teachers, parents, and schoolchildren. After the precedent was set, the speakers suggested that a future Ashéninka Perené–English text collection should honor the native community's wish to make public texts that offer native perspectives on local history and cultural traditions. A few texts from the Mihas 2011 publication also appear in this book. The scope of issues broached and the method applied in both books is very similar: narrators consistently make multiple references to spiritual forces and rituals and landscapes associated with them. They place special emphasis on explaining the meaning of the events and situations described and pointing to their causes.

This book is an opportunity to make public individual indigenous accounts of local history, some of which have been passed down from grandfathers to their grandchildren as part of the family tradition (Vansina 1985:17–18). The surviving grandchildren are now in their seventies. Their stories, once recorded and written down, have become "permanent … testimony" (Vansina 1985:63), reaching as far back as the mid-nineteenth century. In view of the dearth of published multithemed Ashéninka Perené accounts accompanied by translations into English, it was an especially compelling task to include illustrations of spiritual, mortuary, and cannibalistic aspects of past indigenous cultural practices, a gap that this comprehensive anthology aims to fill. This anthology considers essential the documentary requirement and includes texts that may perhaps cast native culture in an unfavorable light, such as narratives about killing and eating children or executing women alleged to be witches.

The book consists of three thematic parts: history, landscape, and ritual. Each part includes performances recorded from various speakers and centers on the original texts, accompanied by English translations and detailed notes and prefaced by a general introduction that draws on both my fieldwork notes and scholarly ethnographic accounts by other students of Amazonian peoples. The first part, "History," explores themes of resistance, armed violence, indigenous displacement, slavery raids, endo-warfare, implantation of Adventist religion, and persecution of witches. The second part, "Landscape," deals with the places and spaces central to Ashéninka history, namely Tziviarini (the Salt River), Ashiropanko (the Iron House), and Manitzi-panko (the Jaguar House; La Boca del Tigre in Spanish). The final part, "Ritual," is concerned with performances involving ritual specialists (shamans and herbalists) and mundane rituals practiced by ordinary folks.

In terms of genre, this ethnographic collection makes distinct-ions among narrative, song, chant (a repetitive song performed by more than one person), and oratory. These four are distin-guished in the Ashéninka Perené language: narrative is *kinki-tsarentsi*, song is *pantsantsi*, chant is *vishiriantsi*, and oratory is *kamenantsi* (literally "advice," "instruction"). Ashéninka Perené speakers do not differentiate between mythological and his-torical tales, both types being lumped into the category of *kin-kitsarentsi* (narrative; *cuento* in Spanish). Only a few recorded Ashéninka Perené myths are included here because of space limitations and because there is an ample body of work detail-ing pan-Kampan mythological themes (Anderson 2000; Weiss 1974, 1975; Santos-Granero 1998; Rojas Zolezzi 1994; Torre López 1966; Kindberg et al. 1979; Varese 2002). Most selected texts are reminiscences of past events or accounts handed from grand-fathers to grandchildren as part of a personal family tradition. Some texts are eyewitness accounts.

The ritual songs presented here used to be sung while danc-ing and playing panpipe music. Oratory is represented by a col-lection of "lectures" or traditional advice given to an intimate audience of boys and by incantations or prayers directed to spiri-tual forces, written down from memory by the language con-sultants.

HISTORICAL BACKGROUND AND CURRENT SOCIOECONOMIC SITUATION

Ashéninka Perené, also known as Upper Perené or Alto Perené in scholarly literature, is a highly endangered Amazonian Arawak language, spoken by approximately one thousand speakers in Chanchamayo Province in central-eastern Peru. The extant ethnic population exceeds fifty-five hundred people (Lewis, Simons, and Fennig 2013).

The speakers refer to themselves as *katonkosatzi* (upriver people) or *parenisatzi* (river people). Another autodenomination is *ashaninka* or *asheninka* (our fellow man). In Spanish orthography, the middle vowel in the language name is marked by the diacritic acute symbol. Most literate Ashéninka Perené speakers dislike the use of the diacritic in writing, especially in the term "Ashaninka," and so this collection does not use the diacritic.

When speakers use Spanish to describe themselves, they say "Ashaninka del Alto Perené" (Ashaninka from the Upper Perené River). In this book, the terms "Ashaninka" (note the absence of the diacritic), "Ashéninka Perené," and "Upper Perené Arawaks" are used interchangeably.

The term "Ashéninka (or Ashéninca) Perené" is commonly employed in scholarly literature (e.g., Aikhenvald 1999:68, 2012:35, 351; Anderson 2000:42–45). This designation has been introduced by linguists from the Summer Institute of Linguistics (see the SIL online language database, www.ethnologue.com). Another common term is "Ashéninka del Alto Perené," preferred by Peruvian linguists (e.g., García Salazar 1997; Heise et al. 2000; Romani Miranda 2004).

The language is considered to be closely related to other members of the Northern branch of the Kampan (aka Campa) subgrouping of Arawak, composed of varieties of Ashéninka

(Pichis, Ucayali, Apurucayali, Pajonal), Ashaninka (Tambo-Ene), and Kakinte (also spelled Caquinte; Michael 2008:218). Map 1 shows the location of Ashéninka Perené neighbors. The Upper Perené River is flanked by the settlements of Yanesha in the northwest, Ashéninka Pichis in the north, Ashéninka Gran Pajonal in the northeast, and Asháninka Tambo-Ene in the east and south. Map 1 also illustrates other areas inhabited by speakers of Kampan languages: Ashéninka Apurucayali, Kakinte, Machiguenga, Nanti, Nomatsiguenga, and Ucayali-Yurúa. A cluster of Panoan-speaking populations is found in the map's north section, and the Arawak-speaking Piro (Yine) are in the west section. The area of Quechua-speaking Andean highlanders is located to the east of the Perené valley.

There are thirty-six Ashéninka Perené settlements, all located in the Upper Perené valley, at the foot of the central eastern Andes and on the western fringe of the Amazonian jungle. Approximately half of the villages are hidden in the hills on both sides of the Perené River, while the rest are located on the Perené valley floor. The hillside villages are connected by narrow gravel roads or footpaths that can accommodate a motorbike or a passenger vehicle. The villages on the valley floor typically lie close to the central highway that runs from Lima to Satipo. The most populous settlements along the highway are Pampa Michi, Santa Ana (which has become a mestizo town), Bajo Marankiari, and Pucharini. During the last twenty years, Pichanaki has been transformed from a small Ashéninka Perené settlement on the Pichanani River into a major mestizo-populated urban center and bustling commercial hub for organic green coffee producers of the Perené valley. Map 2 illustrates the location of Upper Perené settlements. The names of the communities are spelled in agreement with the conventions used in the *Atlas de comunidades nativas de la Selva Central* (Benavides 2006).

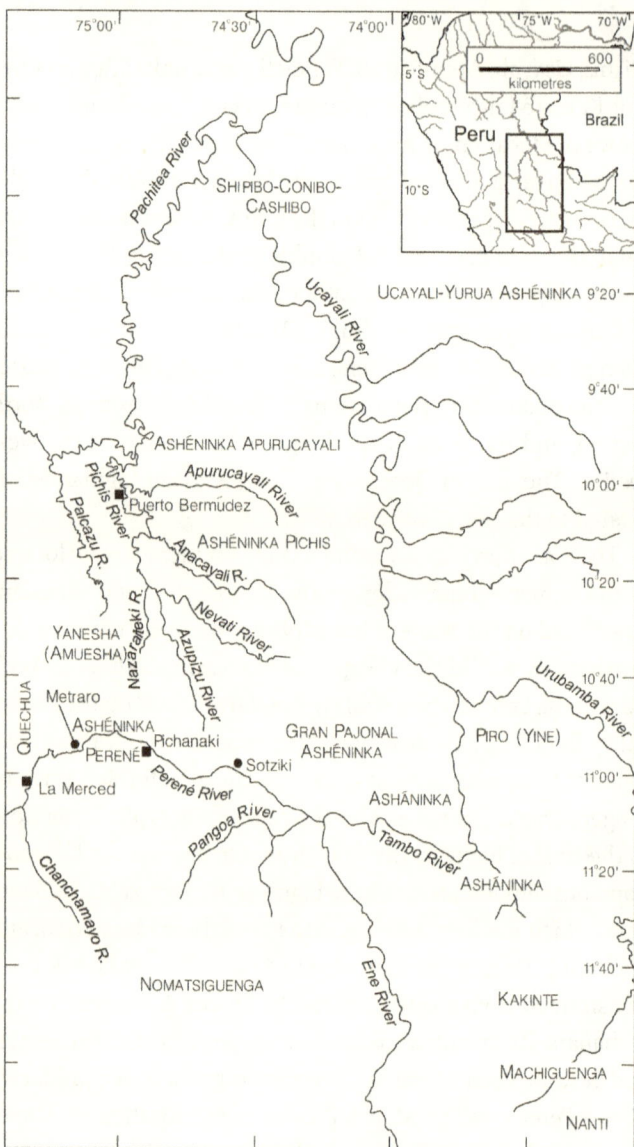

1. Area inhabited by speakers of Kampan languages and other neighboring groups. By Adella Edwards.

The Perené River, formed at the confluence of the Chanchamayo and Paucartambo Rivers, flows in a southeasterly direction at elevations ranging from four hundred to six hundred meters above sea level. The Perené empties into the Tambo River where it joins the Ene River. The junction is located ten kilometers downstream of the village of Puerto Ocopa. For some of its length, which is 165km, the Perené cuts through narrow, towering canyons, but for the most part the meandering river flows through flat, open land. At some locations the river has moderate-sized floodplains shaped by annual floods that occur during the rainy season, which lasts from November to April. The Upper Perené River is notorious for its turbulent currents and whirlpools in its main channel.

The valley hillside, which is referred to as *ceja* (eyebrow) (Lathrap 1970:34), once had extensive areas of tropical premontane forests occurring roughly from five hundred to fifteen hundred meters above sea level, much of which has long been deforested and is now used in slope-farming systems.

Arawak-speaking hunter-gatherers have been present in the area for a long time, possibly for millennia (Aikhenvald 2013; Hornborg and Hill 2011:13; Lathrap 1970:177). Their subsistence economy combined hunting, fishing, gathering, and horticulture (Rojas Zolezzi 1994:85). In the past, hunting with a bow and arrow was a major male occupation. The common hunting method was to build a hunter's shack (*ivankoshita*) out of palm fronds, then wait for the game to approach and shoot it at close range. The valued game animals included *samani* (paca; *Coelogenus paca*), *kintori* (tapir; *Tapurus americanus*), *kitairiki* (collared peccary; *Tayassu tajucu*), and *shintori* (white-lipped peccary; *Tayassu pecari*). The most prized game birds were turkey-like *tsamiri* (razor-billed curassow; *Mitu mitu*) and *sankatzi* (Spix's guan; *Penelope jacquacu*), as well as the smaller

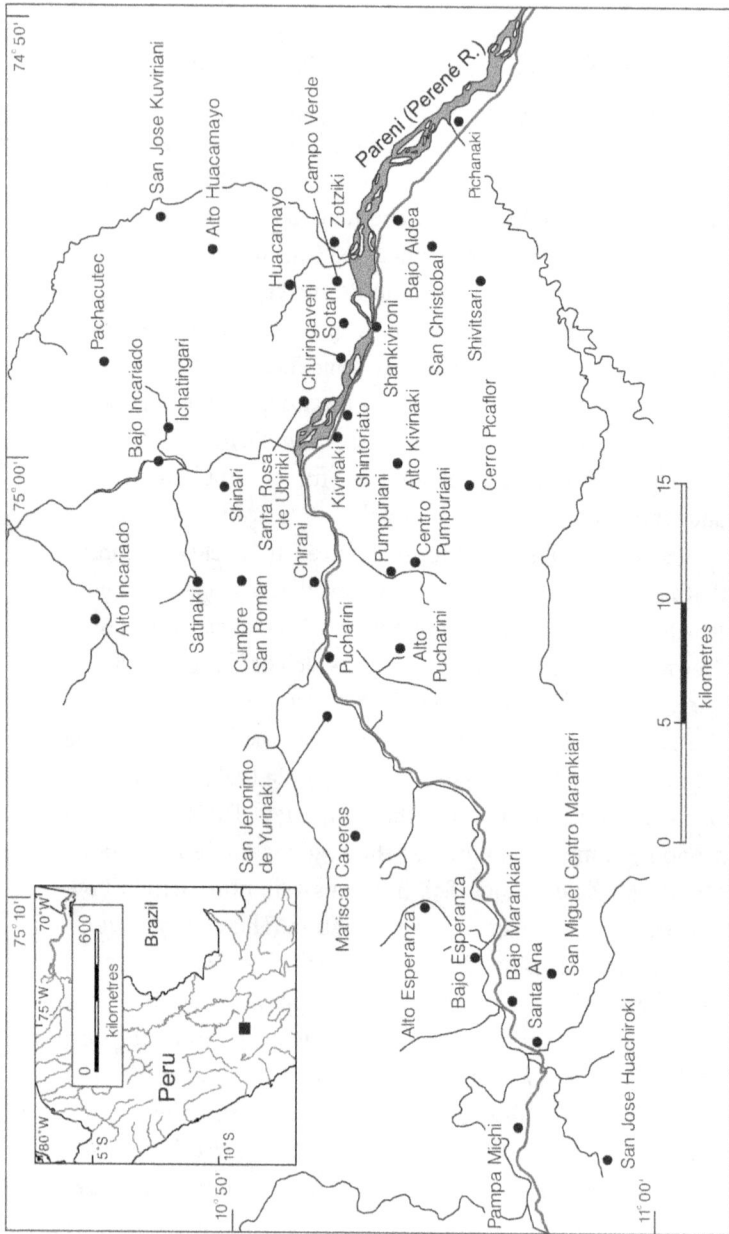

2. Upper Perené Ashaninka settlements. By Adella Edwards.

birds *kentsori* (gray tinamou quail; *Tinamus tao kleei*) and *kon-tsaro* (dove species; *Leptotila verreaxi* or *rufaxila*).[1] In modern times, game animals and birds have become so scarce that they have ceased to be a major source of protein for the local population, and game is no longer hunted.

Unlike hunting, fishing has remained a major subsistence pursuit, regularly practiced by both men and women. The so-called hydrocentricity of Upper Perené Arawaks' socioeconomic ecologies is associated with their "deeply entrenched and indissoluble connection to riverine ... environments" (Hornborg and Hill 2011:10), which is evident in the consistent exploitation of water features. There are two manual techniques used to catch fish. The manual type of fishing is possible only in the dry season, when the water is clear. In shallow water, catching fish by hand is done by turning over stones and quickly grabbing a small fish species, *jetari* (*carachama*; *Aphanotorulus unicolor*). Another technique simulates the way bears catch fish, as a person crouches in the water with his or her body fully submerged, with eyes wide open, in search of the fish species *chenkori* (*huasaco*; *Hoplias malabaricus*).

In addition, fish are caught in the river with the help of special paraphernalia. Male fishermen can use arrows to pierce fish in the water, for example, *shima* (*boquichico*; *Prochilodus nigricans*), which requires special skill. Men, women, and children commonly catch small fish with a hook, for example, *kovana* (*lisa*; *Leporinus trifasciatus*) and *shiva* (anchoveta; *Knodus breviceps*). This type of fishing is possible during the whole year and is done in the water pools with slow-moving or stagnant water called *osampana* or *osanteña*.

In the water pools, people also fish with a hand fishnet, *kitsari*. Small water streams called *nijaateni* are suitable for fishing with fish traps called *shimperi* (a fence fabricated from a woven plant mat attached to wood planks), or *tsiyanarentsi* (a conical trap with a wide funnel-like opening), which is done in combination with the application of vegetable poison *vako-(shi)* (*huaca*; *Clibadium remotiflorum*) or *koñapi* (*barbasco*; *Lonchocarpus nicou*). Catching fish with the *shimperi* requires creating a small dam of stones, constructed in the area where the stream pool empties into the stream, so that an artificial "waterfall" is created. The *shimperi* or *tsiyanarentsi*, positioned below the dam, prevent fish from swimming into the stream's current. The small brooks and streams are also places to look for *pomporo* (land snail; *Strophocheilis popelairianus*), *totziroki* (*churo*, aquatic snail; unidentified), and *kito* (*camaron*, a crustaceous species; *Macrobrachium amazonicum*).

Horticulture used to be of the swidden, slash- and-burn type, with one plot of land, called *ovaantsi* (*chacra*) being planted and another, called *ovaantsiposhi* (*purma*), left fallow. Males would do the arduous and time-consuming tasks of clearing the land and planting polycultural cultigens, while women would weed and harvest the crops. Due to the rapid deterioration of soil quality caused by the extensive method of its exploitation, the *ovaantsi* had to be abandoned within a few years of its use for long-term fallowing, and the family would look for another plot to clear.

Nowadays, all land suitable for cultivation in the Upper Perené valley is taken, and the native population has switched to "permanent, fixed-field agriculture" (Whitten 1985:31). To maintain soil fertility, fertilizers and crop rotation are used. The indigenous crops best suited for soils in the humid tropical climate are *shinki* (maize; *Zea mays*), *machaki* (beans, various genera), *koritzi~koritya* (sweet potato; *Ipomoea batatas*), *inki* (groundnuts/peanuts; *Arachis hypogaea*), and a variety of tubers, such as *mavona* (yam; *Dioscurea trifida*), *shoñaki* (sweet cornroot or dale dale; *Calathea allouia*), *impari* or *pitoka* (taro; *Xantho-soma sagittifolium*), *poi* (yam-bean; *Pachyrhizus erosus*), and the staple crop *kaniri* (sweet manioc; *Manihot esculenta*), "one of the most productive and least demanding crops ever developed by man" (Lathrap 1970:44). Sweet manioc is also known as yuca or cassava. A variety of other plants were originally grown for household needs, but now they are planted essentially for commercial purposes: *pariantzi-parentzi* (plantains; *Musa species*), *mapocha* (papaya; *Carica papaya*), *tzivana* (pineapple; *Ananas comosus*), and *potsotzi* (annatto; *Bixa orellana*). Some families plant commercial crops of *kajai* (coffee; genus *Coffea*) and *kimito* (cacao; *Theobroma cacao*). Upper Perené farmers either directly sell the harvested crops at local or regional markets or contract with wholesalers from Lima.

In the old times, gathering was a regular activity, popular with both sexes. The documented corpus provides evidence that *shitovi* (mushrooms), all sorts of *chochoki* (wild fruit), and *incha-shi* (medicinal plants) were routinely collected during daytime walks into the forest. The following wild fruits were harvested, depending on the time of the year: *shevantyoki* (*uvilla*; *Pouroma cecropiifolia*), *intsipikiritoki* (*naranjillo*, or little orange; *Solanum quitoense*), *maasheroki* (granadilla; *Passiflora ligularis*), *tsirintsiki* (*uvas del monte*, or mountain grapes; unidentified), *shaaki* (*ungurahua*; *Oenocarpus bataua*), and *meronki* (*chimiqua*; *Perebea chimicua*). Nowadays, gathering pursuits are largely forgotten. Even older-generation individuals struggle to identify the wild fruits they collected in their youth. Adult speakers in their forties and older still maintain a robust knowledge of medicinal plants (see Lenaerts 2006c; Luziatelli et al. 2010), but forest walks for the purpose of herb gathering are mostly practiced by herbal specialists and healers.

The Upper Perené kinship system is characterized as ego-focused and nonunilineal (cognatic), that is, it includes a person's kin, beginning with his or her father and mother, without emphasis on patrilineal or matrilineal descent. Genealogies are shallow, consisting of three to four generations. It is not uncommon for Upper Perené Arawaks to lack knowledge of their great-grandparents, and even their grandparents (see Bodley 1970:65).

Upper Perené Arawaks are endogamous in that they tend to marry within the Kampan group and beyond, but within the geographical boundaries of the Perené valley. My observations show that the pool of potential mates comprises Yanesha, Ashaninka Tambo-Ene, Ashéninka Pichis, Machiguenga, Nomatsiguenga, Shipibo, and Andean Quechua-speaking highlanders. Marriages with mestizos are common as well, but newlyweds are often asked to leave the community, out of fear that a mestizo spouse could make land claims damaging to the community or, in the case of a mestizo husband, sell his property rights to outsiders. An example of a native community governed by this rule is Pumpuriani, whose chief, Frida Thomas Huamán, vigorously defends the villagers' land rights.

Two group terms capture the main distinctions made with regard to fellow speakers: *no-shani-nka* [1SG.POSS-be.same-NMZ] (my kindred/family), applied to an "overlapping network of kinsmen" (Bodley 1970:66) of sometimes twenty-five or more people, and *a-shani-nka* [1PL.POSS-be.same-NMZ] (our fellows), which includes all Kampan populations.

Polygyny once was common among headmen, but nowadays it is very rare. Overall, excessive pursuit of women and multiple sexual hookups are frowned upon, being described as *ochaa* (lack of sexual restraint; in Spanish, *fornicación*). Adoptions were routine, especially in the old times of high adult mortality. For adopted kin, the verbs *tsika* (adopt) or *pira* (domesticate) are used, for example, *otsikatana* o-tsika-t-an-a [3NMASC.S-adopt-EP-DIR-REAL] (she adopted [her]).

Marriage preferences used to be based on two major subdivisions in kinship relationships: "nuclear-like" kin and "classificatory" kin, the latter forming a pool of potential mates. According to Rojas Zolezzi (1994:88), the Upper Perené kinship system is of the Dravidian type. It distinguishes between "cross-cousins" and "parallel cousins," based on the perception that siblings of the same sex are be much closer than siblings of the opposite sex. For example, female ego's father's brother, *pavachori* (nonvocative form *niritsori*), and mother's sister, *nanaini* (nonvocative form *nonirotsori*), are regarded as potential parents; their children are both "parallel cousins" and potential siblings. In contrast, father's sister's children and mother's brother's children are "cross-cousins," seen as potential mates. Mother's brother, *koko* (*nokonkiri*), is referred to as potential father-in-law, while father's sister, *aiyini* (*nayiro*) is referred to as potential mother-in-law (Bodley 1970:56; Chevalier 1982:259–65; Rojas Zolezzi 1994:88–91). Among the present-day Upper Perené Arawaks, this system is completely disregarded. In fact, some scholars question whether the cross-cousin marriage was ever a "preferential" marital arrangement among Ashéninka/Ashaninka populations. For example, cross-cousin marriages constituted less than 1 percent of the eight hundred marital unions in Bodley's survey in the Ashéninka Pichis and Ashaninka Tambo areas in the 1960s (Bodley 1970:71).

The indigenous pattern of social organization was based on small, dispersed settlements, *nampitsi*, of self-sufficient extended families under the nonhereditary leadership of a local headman, called *jevari* jev-a-ri [lead-REAL-REL] (leader) (Lehnertz 1974:31). Currently this pattern has been replaced with nucleated settlements built around a school (and often a church). These are called in Spanish *comunidad nativa* (native community). In Ashéninka Perené, a speaker will refer to his or her native community with *noyomonirateka* no-yomonira-te=ka [1SG. POSS-community-POSS=DEM] (my community) or *nonampi* nonampi [1SG.POSS-community] (my settlement).

In the old times, social power was vested with three important institutions: the *pinkatsari* (regional leader), *ovayeri* (warrior), and *sheripiari* (shaman) (Rojas Zolezzi 1994:224; Vilchez 2008). The headman, called *pinkatsari*, was a recognized leader of higher authority, in comparison with a *jevari* (local leader). The *pinkatsari* was a supreme leader in that he was known to possess common wisdom and knowledge of the forest and to be a good hunter and warrior, but most of all, he demonstrated a great power of persuasion in his public speeches (Rojas Zolezzi 1994:225). The *pinkatsari* was also expected to have a good knowledge of *ivenki* (magic plants), community rituals, the movement of the stars and planets, and changes in the seasons so as to be able to give advice on matters of planting, harvesting, and other subsistence pursuits; his prestige and eloquence were put to test during the resolution of internal conflicts within the area of his control (Rojas Zolezzi 1994:226).

Currently, the tribal chief's role has changed to that of being a strategist who facilitates or sometimes determines the socioeconomic orientation of his community in the market economy and that of being a liaison or legal representative of the *nampitsi* in its dealings with the outside world of the state, private businesses, and political organizations. For example, on behalf of his community, Fredi Miguel Ucayali, the chief of Pampa Michi, negotiates with travel agencies to arrange for a regular flow of tourists from Lima, who buy native crafts and bring money to the village. The tribal chief of Bajo Marankiari, Osbaldo Rosas, oversaw the construction project of building a few cabins on the Playa Remanso, the Perené riverbank. The cabins are now advertised on the community's website as a tourist destination.

The vanished institution of *ovayeri* ov-a-ye-ri [kill-EP-DIST. REAL-REL] (the one who kills, or warrior) served the function of the swift rebuttal of a territorial threat posed by an enemy. Note that the verb root *ov* can express either the meaning of eating or the killing sense, but verbs are distinguished on the basis of the reality status endings that signal their membership in different lexical classes. The verb "eat" belongs to Class A, for example, *ivaka* i-v-ak-a [3MASC.S-eat-PERV-REAL.A] (he ate), whereas the verb "kill" is from Class I, for example, *ivaki* i-v-ak-i [3MASC.S-kill-PERV-REAL.I] (he killed).

The *ovayeri* were recognized as such on the basis of their experience in combat and the number of people they killed (Rojas Zolezzi 1994:230; Macera and Casanto 2009). The *ovayeri* were propelled to the leadership role during times of military conflict with *kisanintantzinkari* kis-a-nint-ant-tzinkari [be .angry-EP-DIM-EP-CUST-NMZ.MASC] (those who are angry, or enemy). The enemy were Panoans (Shipibo, Conibo, Cashibo) and the Arawak-speaking Piro (Yine) (Rojas Zolezzi 1994:228). These antagonistic groups were called *ovantzinkari* ov-ant-tzinkari [kill-CUST-NMZ.MASC] (those who kill, or killers). The enemy status was also accorded to the Kampan populations of the valleys of the Tambo, Ene, and Ucayali Rivers or of the uplands of Gran Pajonal (Great Grasslands). In colonial times, Spaniards and colonists fell into the enemy category as well. Part 1, "History," includes the text *Tsika okantakota ovayeri-tantsi* (About the Craft of War), by Daniel Bernales Quillatupa, about the *ovayeri* training and their code of behavior.

Arguably, it was the shaman, called *sheripiari* sheri-pi-a-ri [tobacco-convert-REAL-REL] (the one who is intoxicated by tobacco) (Shepard 2002:210), who was the central figure of the Upper Perené social organization (Varese 2002:162). The exact meaning of each morpheme and their English equivalents are still being debated by academics. Native speakers translate the term into Spanish as *él que chupa tabaco* (the one who consumes tobacco). In drug-induced nocturnal flights, shamans resolved conflicts with the outside world while mediating between the supernatural owners of the forest and the river and the souls of dead people; they also resolved interpersonal conflicts while diagnosing and treating sick people. In a shamanistic trance, a shaman "saw" the disease-causing minor infractions or evil deeds committed by his folk and identified ways of redressing the harm done. Part 3, "Ritual," presents an in-depth discussion of Upper Perené shamans' mystical powers and their impact on the community's life.

In spite of the loose social structure, solidarity and social networks were created "through marriage ties, residence rules, ritual gatherings, commerce, and political alliances" (Santos-Granero 2002a:30). Long before Upper Perené Arawaks came into contact with Spaniards, they had repelled constant attempts "at invasion and annexation" (Descola 1992:121) by Quechua-speaking populations from the Andean highlands (Varese 2002:40). Upper Perené Arawaks controlled salt extraction and trading networks with their Arawak and non-Arawak neighbors, including Panoan populations of Conibo, Cashibo, and Shipibo (Tibesar 1950; Brown and Fernandez 1992:177). There was also small-scale trade with the Inca Empire (Benavides 1986:33; Varese 2002:39).

Among the adjacent ethnic groups, Amuesha (Yanesha), located to the northwest of the Upper Perené valley, historically have been the Upper Perené Arawaks' closest ally and friend. Weiss regards them as "virtually identical with the Campas in their material culture" (1975:232). Mixed Campa-Yanesha settlements and marriages are a long-standing tradition. The Upper Perené pagan worship of the stone divinity Yompiri and sacred fires is attributed to the influence of Yanesha (Santos-Granero 2004a; Weiss 1975:272–73).

In contrast, the Kishiisatzi (Pajonal Campa; Pajonalinos in Spanish) were fearsome neighbors who occupied a vast territory of the Gran Pajonal, to the northeast of the Perené valley. In general, all Campa men were characterized as "master bowmen and . . . courageous and ferocious warriors" (Weiss 1974:386), but the aggressiveness and warfare skills of Kishiisatzi were unmatched. Upper Perené language consultants would always emphasize the superior athleticism, ruthlessness, and outstanding scouting and shooting skills of their Kishiisatzi neighbors. On the basis of his ethnographic study, Varese indicates that war expeditions of Pajonalinos involved "kidnapping of women, family revenge, and territorial defense against members of other linguistic groups or members of one's own tribe"; in the rubber boom period, Pajonalino raids into the Perené valley were "stimulated" by the slave trade (2002:21–22).

However, the most formidable threat loomed from the Arawak-speaking Shimirentsi (Piro) and Panoan Conibo residing in the Ucayali River basin. Both were called *ovantzinkari* (killers). Language consultants translate the word into Spanish as *asesinos* (assassins). These Amazonian peoples were culturally very close, "while [they] differed markedly from Campa/ Machiguenga" (Gow 1991:32). Crucially, for both Piro and Conibo, wealth came from war expeditions, and both were notorious for raiding Campa settlements. Conibo warriors were recognized as "renowned pirates and slave traders" (Santos-Granero 2009b:24). Each Conibo raid was a well-planned and masterfully executed military affair, aimed at capturing slaves and taking booty. Raided villages were burned down and their male defenders were killed (Santos-Granero 2009b:56–61). Piro and Conibo often served as missionaries' guides, using the opportune moment to pillage Campa villages and take women and children as slaves (Amich 1854:98, 100).

Missionizing attempts, initiated by Jesuits in the late sixteenth century, turned into a sustained evangelizing campaign in the mid-seventeenth century, when a network of short-lived missions, called "ephemeral occupation attempts" by Santos-Granero and Barclay (1998:21), was established by Franciscan friars in the Chanchamayo-Perené area. Accompanied by raging epidemics among converts and constant bloody revolts and uprisings, the biggest under the leadership of Juan Santos Atahualpa in 1742, the missionizing effort came to a halt in the mid-eighteenth century (Lehnertz 1974:149–50; Métraux 1942; Tibesar 1952). The Ashaninkas' violent repudiation of the imposed Franciscan order was directly motivated by the friars' condemnation of the indigenous lifeways, such as polygyny, use of ethnomedicine for healing purposes, coca chewing, and manioc beer drinking (Veber 2003:192; Varese 1996:61). Other factors of a spiritual order played a prominent role in the failure of missionization. Veber points out that the primary objective of the resistance movement was "purification" and restoration of the "physical and mental health of the people" (2003:195). The indigenous rejection of mission life was also predicated on "epidemics, corporal punishment, the uncongenial discipline of mission life, assertions of control over Indian children, and relentless hectoring by monks" (Brown and Fernandez 1992:181).

When the Upper Perené area was eventually reconquered by the Peruvian military a century later, a steady flow of Andean colonists followed. Their settlement had been encouraged by the friars and the state, with the objective of stabilizing the area around the missions, but the colonist influx greatly increased after the recapture of the region by the military. In addition, the massive importation of European, Asian, and non-Andean Peruvian immigrants, initiated by the Peruvian state, made irreversible the concomitant displacement of the native population. By 1890 most of the Ashaninkas who inhabited the Chanchamayo and Paucartambo valleys and had survived the military "pacification" and armed scuffles with the colonists were displaced (Santos-Granero and Barclay 1998:234). Bodley (1972:222) reports that fourteen thousand "agriculturalists" had arrived in the Chanchamayo valley by 1907; in 1927 eighteen hundred more colonists were settled there.

The establishment of the British-owned Peruvian Corporation in 1891, with its headquarters in Pampa Whaley, heralded an era of the forceful, profound conversion of the Upper Perené valley into a market-oriented coffee-growing region. The Peruvian Corporation occupied over five hundred thousand hectares of what used to be communal Ashaninka land, turning it into *cafetales* (coffee plantations) and *pastizales* (pastures). The area invaded by the corporation became known as the Perené Colony (Barclay 1989). Ashaninkas were allowed to stay on the condition that they work for the company. About five hundred indigenous workers were employed by 1913 (Bodley 1972:222; Brown and Fernandez 1992:184; Chevalier 1982:210).

In the context of the military invasion, colonist occupation, and native population decline, few nonviolent options for defense of land rights were left for the dispersed and demoralized native population. One was through participation in the Perené Colony's land partitionings. To ensure that the indigenous population remaining on the company's land (especially those who lived close to the company's headquarters in Pampa Whaley) was concentrated in a nucleated settlement, making them available to serve as subcontracted coffee producers, in the late 1940s the company allotted fifteen hundred hectares in the Río Vayós area to one hundred Ashaninka families. Ashaninkas came into possession of small lots in the community of Mariscal Cáceres, an average 8.8 hectares per family, in comparison with an average 37.8 hectares per Andean landowner (Santos-Granero and Barclay 1998:236).

Another way to resist eviction from the land was to buy an individual lot from the Peruvian corporation. Some Ashaninka families residing in Marankiari, Pumpuriani, Pucharini, and a few other villages followed this route in the 1950s. To obtain guaranteed access to the ancestral land, Ashaninkas also sought affiliation with the missions of the Seventh-Day Adventist Church (e.g., the Metraro mission), which was acting on their behalf within the Perené Colony in the 1920s and 1930s. Later on, many Indian Adventists chose to move to areas with less colonization pressure, for example, to the Pichis valley (Narby 1989:65). In the 1970s and 1980s the remaining Upper Perené Arawaks took advantage of the 1974 Native Communities Law (Decree Law 20653) to establish native communities, which were granted land titles. Due to the unprecedented colonization pressure, in 1989 the newly formed Upper Perené native communities constituted only a fraction (23 percent) of the total number of registered *comunidades nativas* in the region of Selva Central, which encompasses Chanchamayo, Oxapampa, and Satipo Provinces (Santos-Granero and Barclay 1998:245).

To ensure their survival, the Upper Perené Ashaninkas made a conscious choice to participate in the cash economy by turning to the production of extensive crops of *naranka* (citrus fruit), *pariantzi* (bananas), *tzivana* (pineapple), *kimito* (cacao), and *kajai* (coffee). Currently the native population is well integrated into the regional market economy as agricultural producers or seasonal laborers. For local indigenous populations, commercial agriculture is reported to be a critical means of obtaining cash and access to market goods (Santos-Granero and Barclay 1998:254). The rapidly increasing degree of household market incorporation and dependence, with concurrent orientation of native communities toward commercialization, has had a significant impact on the views of those in individual households (Narby 1989; Peralta and Kainer 2008). The dynamic of cultural change appears to be directly stimulated by "the fervor to develop and the allure of money and market goods" (Henrich 1997:340, 348), evidenced in many recorded texts from the Ashéninka Perené corpus.

Undeniably, the cumulative effect of colonization-related agents of change has fueled the current entrepreneurial spirit and material aspirations of the Upper Perené Ashaninkas. Among such agents of change are exposure to the metal tools and iron-tool manufacturing technologies supplied by Franciscans, the individualistic Adventist work ethic, and the example of "civilized" Andean colonists making the best of their access to Western goods (Santos-Granero and Barclay 1998:243). Nonetheless, native sociocultural reproduction remains fairly strong in spite of the unyielding pressure exerted by the Peruvian state, the colonist society, and Seventh-Day Adventist missions (Martel Paredes 2009; La Serna Salcedo 2012).

BELIEFS

Ashaninka society has a high degree of certainty about its own ways, which, in combination with its "unassailable self-assurance" (Hvalkof 1989:144), may account for the autochthonous cultural tenacity noted in many scholarly studies (Weiss 1975:234; Elick 1969:235–37; Bodley 1970:183). The texts collected here reflect the intransigent Ashaninka cosmos, including their distinctive beliefs and ideas about humanity and divinity. The premises of Ashaninka ideas about the world and themselves are rooted in the indigenous Amazonian conceptual frameworks of "animism" (Descola 1992) and "perspectivism" (Viveiros de Castro 1996, 1998). In particular, animistic indigenous thought embraces an idea that "natural beings possess their own spiritual principles and that it is therefore possible for humans to establish with these entities personal relations," that these entities "have human dispositions" and "behaviors" (Descola 1992:114).

According to Viveiros de Castro (1998), perspectivism, as a projection of animism, is the indigenous theory about the way human and nonhuman beings see themselves and others. For example, from an Ashaninka point of view, humans see themselves as humans, animals as animals, and spirits as spirits. However, they also believe that animals (especially predators) and spirits see themselves as humans and humans as animals (prey). Thus the point of view (or perspective) makes the difference between the bodies understandable only from the outsider's viewpoint (Viveiros de Castro 1998:478). This dependence on the other's view of oneself for one's own body image entails an assumption of bodily temporality, instability, and transformability.

Moreover, indigenous ontology insists that ex-humans lost their human form due to a voluntary or involuntary bodily metamorphosis that is "taken for granted and thus is seldom singled out for comment" (Wilbert and Simoneau 1992:31). Most often, people are transformed into animals, which is not surprising considering that in hunting societies animals are "the strategic focus of the objectification of nature" (Descola 1992:115).

The Ashaninkas possess a deep-seated belief that humans are perpetually hunted by demonic entities that practice elaborate killing methods on Ashaninka individuals. These convictions are rooted in a conception of the universe as consisting of two "mutually antagonistic" ontological "domains" (Descola 1992:121). The domain of "positive value" includes Ashaninkas, genetically related Kampan ethnic groups, certain animal and plant species and their masters, and divinities such as Pava and Tasorentsi, while the "negative value" domain is comprises the outsiders (*chori* [Andeans] and *virakocha* [whites]), some animal and plant species, and spiritually evil entities, grouped under the term *kamari*, including *kamari matsi* (demonic human witches) (Descola 1992:121; Weiss 1975:282–308). Among the "negative value" entities are *matsi* (a human witch), which feeds on the flesh of unsuspecting victims when they are asleep; the demonic *peyari* (a forest bone spirit in the form of a game animal, usually a deer), which kills males by an act of copulation; and *kiatsi* (a siren-like river creature in the form of an anaconda or an armadillo), which kills by wrapping her prominent antenna-like whiskers around the individual's lower limbs and dragging him into the water depths, to name a few.

In spite of long contact with outsiders and the sustained and intensive Christianization of Upper Perené Arawaks since the 1920s, the indigenous ontological beliefs remain "an extraordinarily resistant cultural bloc" (Lenaerts 2006a:554). This is evidenced in the fundamentally unchanged ritual production, which may exhibit elements of "mimetic appropriation" of Christian symbols, with the obvious purpose of using "the Other's" "powers for their own benefit" (Santos-Granero 2009a:488). For example, expert herbal healers, including my two language consultants, may use "mimetic" symbolic gestures (a sign of a cross) and ritual objects (a candle) while treating a patient. Nonetheless, those are elements of cosmetic nature, which essentially adorn the rock-solid foundation of indigenous ontology.

NARRATORS

The texts chosen for this anthology are grounded in the actual performances of thirty Ashéninka Perené speakers (fifteen women and fifteen men), most of whom were contracted as language consultants for the entire duration of my fieldwork periods. All were paid the hourly rate of a Peruvian schoolteacher (eight to twelve, in some cases fifteen, Peruvian soles), with the payment made at the end of each meeting. The book contributors come from nine villages (Bajo Marankiari, Pampa Michi, Santari, Ciudadela of La Merced, Mariscal Cáceres, Pucharini, Pumpuriani, Churingaveni, and Pampa Silva/Villa Perene). Of those, the youngest consultants are Frida Thomas Huamán and Carmen Pachiri Quinchori, both born in 1976, and the oldest are Julio Castro Shinkaki (born in 1928) and Livia Julio de Quinchori (whose exact age is unknown, but her relatives believe her to be a centenarian). All narrators, except Elena Nestor de Capurro, are fluent bilinguals. Six consultants have good education; five men are college-trained bilingual teachers, and one woman finished high school. Others either have basic literacy skills or are illiterate. Most of the consultants' households combine commercial and subsistence agricultural production. A few have jobs in the public education sector. Many consultants from Bajo Marankiari and Pucharini are members of the Seventh-Day Adventist Church. It has become customary that most consultants from Pampa Michi, Bajo Marankiari, and Pampa Silva/Villa Perené would meet with me regularly in their homes during my annual fieldwork seasons.

The history of the language consultant team begins in 2009, with the establishment of its core, which includes Gregorio Santos Pérez and his wife, Dora Meza, Delia Rosas Rodríguez, Raul Martin Bernata, and Daniel Bernales Quillatupa. I met Gregorio

Santos Pérez, fifty-three, through a mutual acquaintance in 2009. Gregorio was raised in Bajo Marankiari, where his parents still reside, and moved to Santa Ana less than twenty years ago. A bilingual teacher who was trained by SIL missionaries and has the equivalent of a master's degree in elementary education, Gregorio stands out due to his many talents and passion for language work. He is an excellent narrator, a skillful transcriber and translator, and a thoughtful analyst of his language's grammar. My linguistic work has greatly benefited from Gregorio's hypotheses and interpretations. In the past, Gregorio traveled extensively in the area, due to his various teaching assignments. Nowadays he makes short trips, either at my request or on his own initiative, to Upper Perené communities to record and write down speakers' narratives. We have become good friends, forging a truly collegial intellectual partnership. Gregorio belongs to a small group of local bilingual teachers who have been advocating for official recognition of their mother tongue by the Peruvian state, so far unsuccessfully. Gregorio's wife, Dora Meza de Santos, a homemaker, was been my guide and companion on many trips to remote Upper Perené villages in 2012–13. Dora was born in Mariscal Cáceres, but at an early age, after her mother's death, she was sent to the mestizo town of Santa Ana to be schooled in Spanish. Two of the couple's eight children (the oldest) are fluent in the Ashéninka Perené language; others are semipassive or passive speakers. The four selected texts recorded by Gregorio are his recollections of ritual practices associated with taking a wife and fishing, along with two other stories he heard from his mother and a fellow woman, one of which deals with intertribal violence and the other a story about the forest spirit *peyari*.

Delia Rosas Rodríguez, forty-six, is another major contributor to the project. She was among the first female language consultants; I recruited her in Bajo Marankiari in 2009 while I was walking door-to-door in search of Bertha Rodríguez de Caleb, the chief's mother, recommended to me by Gregorio Santos. A meticulous and skillful transcriber of the collected texts, Delia did a lot of behind-the-scenes work to ensure that the book project came to fruition. Delia has good Spanish literacy skills and is a quick study. In 2010 she learned how to use the digital recorder, video camera, and laptop and, at my request, did video and audio recordings of seven Ashéninka-speaking villagers and transcribed and translated most of the recorded texts. Thanks to her impeccable work ethic, intelligence, reserve, and competitiveness, Delia has moved to a position of leadership within the team, which is not always taken well by males. Delia was born in Bajo Marankiari and has resided in the village most of her life. As a teenager, she traveled to Lima in search of work. In Lima she finished high school and did one year of college coursework, and she also worked as a house maid for a number of years. Nowadays Delia runs a small business from her house, selling snacks, bottled beer, and canned light drinks to the villagers. She has two daughters; the older daughter is fluent in the language, the younger is a passive speaker. Two texts by Delia are included in this anthology. One is a chief's speech on the occasion of a villager's death, which she heard as a young woman, and another is a prayer to the stone divinity that Delia wrote down on the basis of her mother's and stepfather's recollections.

My first Ashéninka Perené language teacher, Raul Martin Bernata, sixty-one, has lived most of his life in Pampa Michi. As a retired paramedic, he possesses an advanced knowledge of medicinal plants. Raul knows many native myths and is well-versed in Ashaninka history. His weather-beaten notebook contains dozens of myths scribbled in elaborate Spanish. Initially we would meet a few times a week, but after our team's membership dramatically increased, we switched to one weekly meeting. During his attempts to recruit language consultants in Pampa Michi, Raul often expressed to me his disappointment at the entrepreneurial aspirations of his fellow villagers who rejected his offer to collaborate on the language project. The reason, he explained to me, is unrealistic expectations of high monetary gains, which the documentary project has never promised to deliver. Raul's wife, Victoria Manchi de Martin, fifty-four, is the mother of eleven children and a skilled artisan who creates handicrafts for sale, using traditional techniques and materials. Victoria is a proficient native-language speaker from the Bajo Marankiari provenance. She has regularly participated alongside her husband in discussions of the native language's use, its grammar, and its lexicon. Raul's contribution to the anthology is a myth about the origin of the landmass in the middle of the Perené River, located across from the village of Villa Progreso. Victoria and Raul were also the enthusiastic audience for Elena Nestor's and Luis Mauricio Rosa's performances.

Daniel Bernales Quillatupa (Aroshi), fifty-one, is one of the principal contributors to the book project. As an employee of the local Department of Education, he had overseen the work of bilingual teachers in Chanchamayo Province for nearly a decade before being promoted to the position of bilingual specialist in the adjacent Satipo Province. Currently he is a coordinator with the Programa de Educacion de Logros de Aprendizaje (PELA) at the Ministry of Education in Lima. Born and raised in Bajo Marankiari, educated in an SIL-run college, Daniel has excellent Spanish and Ashéninka literacy skills and a vast knowledge of indigenous culture. Daniel is also a talented artist, and he drew illustrations for this book. The nature of his work was such that he was away on business trips during the week, so he mostly worked independently, recording other speakers and transcribing and translating the recorded texts. As a high-ranking state employee, Daniel is in favor of the use of the pan-regional "normalized" alphabet for native languages introduced by the Peruvian Ministry of Education in 2008. In contradistinction, other consultants, along with tribal and political authorities, prefer the alphabet designed specifically for the Upper Perené population. Despite the disagreement on the Ashéninka Perené alphabet design, Daniel has contributed five selections to this text collection: a description of the menarche rite; two accounts by his grandfather, one about shamanistic training and one about warrior training and lifestyles; traditional advice given by his father and mother when he was a child, written from memory; and two incantations, about how to chase away rain and how to have a good fishing expedition, which he heard from his kinfolk in his youth. The selections are spelled according to the writing conventions approved by the 2013 language consultant meeting.

The mother of Daniel Bernales Quillatupa, Ruth Quillatupa Lopez, seventy, is a very articulate and talented narrator who commonly injects her philosophical comments into narratives and conversations. I had only sporadic contact with Ruth, since it had been resolved early on that her son, Daniel Bernales, was better suited for making extensive recordings and transcriptions of Ruth's speech. Born and raised in Bajo Marankiari, Ruth possesses a vast knowledge of local history and past customs. Ruth has a quick wit and a critical mindset, along with a nostalgic view of the traditional Ashaninka lifeways, evident in her reminiscences of the salt extraction and the witnessed persecution of alleged witches. In addition to these two narratives, she contributed a story about how her fellow men came into possession of fire and one about the origin of Manitzipanko (the Jaguar House), the cave located in the towering canyon of the Perené River, eleven kilometers downstream from Santa Ana.

Elena Nestor de Capurro, seventy-four, has lived all her adult life in Pampa Michi. She is illiterate and essentially monolingual. In my last two fieldwork seasons, Elena frequently mentioned to me that her collaboration is largely motivated by the desire to be in the book, saying *pisankinatakotena* (write about me) and that she expects me to bring her a copy, *pamakinaro sankinarentsika* (bring me the book). To Elena, publication of her contributions is a matter of creating a memorable legacy for her family and being acknowledged by her fellow men as a bearer of the long-standing storytelling tradition. Elena is an incredibly talented performer who has a knack for impersonating the characters in her profoundly entertaining stories, exemplified by the selected story about the creatures inhabiting the Pampa Michi hills. Her knowledge of native songs and dances is unmatched. Elena's ritual song "*Mavira*", presented here, was sung at the end-of-the-year festival in Pampa Michi. Elena is the widow of the former chief and founder of the native community of Pampa Michi, Augusto Capurro Mayor Kinchori. After his death, their daughter Gloria Nuria became prominent in the community as its representative in the regional governance system.

Luis Mauricio Rosa, sixty-three, is a fine narrator who knows a great deal about Ashaninka history and traditional skills. A nice and unassuming man, he tends to respectfully agree with his brother-in-law, Raul Martin, when we have group discussions in Pampa Michi. However, when no authoritative figure is present, Luis comes to life, providing insightful input on language issues under consideration and narrating stories whose elaborate plots and entertaining dialogues impress other speakers. Luis lives alone in the remote village of Santari, in the hills overlooking Santa Ana. He is constantly on the move in search of jobs. Luis often visits with his sister and brother-in-law in Pampa Michi. His specialty is construction of houses with thatch-woven roofs, which requires a unique skill. His expertise is in demand since the numbers of knowledgeable builders are dwindling. Luis's contribution to this anthology is two stories, one about the origins of Ashaninka burial practices and another about the *mavira* festive ritual practices.

Fredi Miguel Ucayali, forty-eight, is the current chief of Pampa Michi. He lost his parents early in his life and was raised by his grandparents. Fredi started but didn't finish the college coursework necessary to become an elementary school teacher, but he was able to land teaching jobs in bilingual rural schools. He became politically active in his thirties and ran for the chief's office in Pampa Michi. During the early phase of the language project, the chief's deep-seated distrust of outsiders prevented him from establishing a working relationship with the language consultant team associated with a gringa (white woman), but eventually Fredi relented. Fredi's hobby is collecting framed pictures of himself, which he hangs on the outside walls of his house. Once I asked the chief what he would like me to bring him as a gift next time I come back, and he requested his framed portrait. Fredi is an articulate and effective orator who strongly advocates for traditional Ashaninka values. He is also knowledgeable about herbal healing and provides services to both his fellow men and mestizos as a *curandero* (healer). Fredi's recollection of his grandfather's story about the military conquest of the Upper Perené area in the second half of the nineteenth century is a riveting addition to this anthology.

Bertha Rodríguez de Caleb, seventy-two, is a gold mine of cultural information about her fellow men's ways of living. Bertha was born and lived most of her life in Bajo Marankiari, although as a young woman she resided for a while in the small community of San Pablo, not far from Puerto Bermúdez, in the Pichis River area. Her first husband died from cholera at twenty-six, and the widow with three children had to scratch out a living while bouncing from one native community to another. The soft-spoken and slightly built Bertha has a gentle disposition and is always willing to walk the extra mile to do her language-consulting job right. She was one of the first women to agree to participate in the documentary project. Bertha has six children; three of them live in Bajo Marankiari. Her youngest child, Osbaldo Rosas Rodríguez, is the current chief of the village. Bertha's eyewitness account of the ritual for mass-cleansing of alleged witches in the village of Nazaraiteki (San Pablo), a story about the establishment of the village of Bajo Marankiari, a commentary on the local headman Apinka, and a ritual song dedicated to the solar divinity Pava provide illuminating glimpses of the history of her people.

Bertha Rodríguez de Caleb's daughter, Victorina Rosas de Castro, fifty-three, and her husband, Gerardo Castro Manuela, fifty-five, were both born in Bajo Marankiari. Victorina is a skilled crafts maker and the mother of six children. The flamboyant and articulate Victorina excels when she performs as a narrator or as an analyst of her mother tongue. In one of our conversations she admitted to me that her biggest regret is not having finished college, although she briefly attended two teacher training institutions; she would have made an excellent teacher. My contact with Victorina's spouse, Gerardo, was limited due to his frequent absences from the community. Gerardo is a former chief of Bajo Marankiari and a retired bilingual teacher. He was educated in an SIL-run teacher-training college and worked for many years as a bilingual teacher in elementary schools in Ashéninka-speaking communities. He still signs up for occasional teaching jobs in remote communities. Gerardo has a comprehensive knowledge of indigenous history. This book includes Victorina's rendition of her mother-in-law's capture by Ashaninka slave raiders and Gerardo's story of a local temple-forge called Ashiro-panko (the Iron House).

Gerardo's father, Julio Castro Shinkaki, eighty-five, is a transplant from the *kirinka* (downstream) area and was one of the founders of the village of Bajo Marankiari in the 1930s. In spite of his advanced age, he is economically independent, toiling on his *chacra* most of the day, although recently he has been having memory problems. Julio is perhaps the last standing witness to the process of radical changes in the Upper Perené physical and sociopolitical environment of the last seventy years. Julio's insights into the indigenous place-naming practice and the history of some place-names are central to the "Landscape" section of the book.

Ines Pérez de Santos, sixty-nine, was born in Bajo Marankiari and lived most of her adult life in the village. Her older son, Gregorio, introduced me to Ines in 2009, offering an opportunity to videotape his mother's healing techniques. Since then I have been a frequent visitor in her house. As the principal breadwinner of the family, Ines provides room and board to her youngest sons and a daughter, their numerous children, and occasional visitors and patients. Both Ines and her husband, Moises Santos Rojas, seventy, who is a thoughtful and thorough interpreter of his kinfolk's past life experiences, earn their living as herbalists. Ines has a broad network of clients who recommend her services to others and spread the word about her superior skills in folk medicine. Ines and Moises are active members of the Seventh-Day Adventist church in Bajo Marankiari and often make allusions to biblical commandments in their narrations. Ines is an articulate and captivating narrator and a language expert whose judgments on grammar issues and comments on cultural events and artifacts are taken by others with deference. The couple's selected reminiscences of encounters with shamans and alleged witches, along with comments on *ovayeri* (warriors), the *mavira* festival, the masters of animals, *maninkaroite* (invisible women), and evil spirits are included in this anthology.

Alberto Pérez Espinoza, sixty-seven, is Ines's brother. He is an excellent fisherman and a smart gatherer of plant and aquatic life that could be used as food. Alberto spends his days on the river, fishing and gathering, and in the evenings he helps his wife, Bertha Yupanki, with making traditional handicrafts. Alberto is an artful narrator who enthusiastically shares his knowledge of traditional stories. His narrative about the origin of sweet manioc is included in this collection.

Abdias Caleb Quinchori, seventy, the husband of Bertha Rodríguez, was elected chief of Bajo Marankiari in the past. At present, he toils in his vegetable garden and makes brooms, fire fans, and other household objects for sale. Abdias served on the project's editors' team and also recorded a number of stories for the project. His source of knowledge comes from the family oral tradition. One of his grandmother's stories about ritual cannibalism, a commentary on the local strongmen Apinka and Marinkama, and his reflections on the cause of his infirmity are included in this book.

Paulina García Ñate (she is not certain of her date of birth but guesses that she is in her early seventies) is a talented singer and a knowledgeable consultant. Paulina's roots are in Alto Koyani, a small community with deeply rooted native ritual practices in the Pichanaki uplands. Although she has lived for decades in Bajo Marankiari, villagers always stress the fact that she hails from a different location and is not a member of the local Adventist community. Paulina lives with her daughter and grandchildren close to the beach and makes her living by selling peanuts and other produce harvested from her small vegetable garden, which she maintains in the floodplain area of the river. Paulina joined the consultant team on her own initiative in 2009. Her main contribution to the project was recording songs and providing detailed explanations of occasions on which they are sung. Four of her ritual songs are included: two give thanks to the solar and lunar deities, and another was sung by a ritual specialist during the shamanistic treatment of his patient. Paulina heard the song from her shaman grandfather when she was a young girl. Paulina's fourth song, about *ovayeri* (warriors), also is a childhood memory of her home village's ritual practices.

Cristobal Jumanga Lopez (deceased in 2012 at the age of sixty-two) and his brother Abraham Jumanga Lopez, seventy-three, were born in the Adventist mission of Nevati, in the Pichis River basin. Their adult years were spent in Pucharini, where the brothers' families currently reside. The families' main occupation is growing cash crops. The Jumanga family is known for its political clout, earned during the years of Abraham's son's service as the chief of Pucharini and his son-in-law's term as president of CECONSEC (la Central de Comunidades Nativas de la Selva Central), the main political organization in the area. Both brothers are distant relatives of Dora Meza de Santos, who was instrumental in their recruitment. The brothers' recordings were made in the summer of 2010, outside their family compound in Pucharini. The younger Cristobal was the more reserved and articulate of the two. He knew hundreds of traditional stories. Being a seasoned storyteller, he possessed the talents of a fine performer. Told in his inimitable high-pitched voice, at a brisk pace, his witty and imaginative stories held his audiences in rapt attention. One story included in this collection describes the bodily transformations of three brothers performed by the solar divinity Pava. Another story is based on Cristobal's grandfather's account about a temple where the sacred fire was worshipped, located in the headwaters of the Perené River.

Cristobal's feisty and vivacious brother Abraham contributed a commentary about place-naming practices. Abraham insists that many place-names in the Upper Perené area owe their origin to an Ashaninka woman called Tzivi (Salt person), who later was transformed into tiny beads of salt.

Manuel Rubén Jacinto, seventy, is a well-respected Adventist church leader in Pucharini. His parents come from the highlands of the Gran Pajonal. He was born in Chivanari, in the Upper Perené valley, and lived nearly all his life in Pucharini. My interactions with Manuel occurred on a few occasions when I visited the community in 2011 and 2013. Manuel is a thoughtful and knowledgeable storyteller. His historical account about the Gran Pajonal warrior Marinkama and his lost battle in the Upper Perené valley is included in this book. Manuel's story was recorded in 2011, outside Cristobal Jumanga's house in Pucharini.

Frida Thomas Huamán, thirty-seven, is the current chief of the small native community of Pumpuriani, located in the uplands of the Perené valley. I met Frida in 2012 when Dora Meza de Santos and I were canvassing the village in search of elders willing to share with us their memories of old customs and traditions. In contrast to the lukewarm reception from other villagers, the chief was quite enthusiastic about the opportunity to participate in the book project. The energetic and assertive Frida, who was born and raised in the village, is an ardent supporter of Ashaninka land rights and intends to keep her village free of outsiders by not allowing the settlement of married couples with a non-Ashaninka spouse. This collection contains the transcript of Frida's explanations of her deceased grandfather's shamanic healing practices, recorded in 2012, outside her house in Pumpuriani.

Luzmila Machari Quinchori, forty-six, is a professional healer from Pumpuriani who specializes in *chonkantsi* (steam bath treatment). She was trained to administer steam bath treatments in Puerto Bermúdez, in the Pichis valley, and earns her living by receiving patients in the Pumpuriani area. Accompanied by Dora Meza de Santos, I made a few recordings of Luzmila after the Pumpuriani chief had recommended her as a good pick for a consulting job. In the 2012 recording, *Antavairi aavintantzin-karo* (Healer's work), Luzmila shares her perspective on the disease epidemiology and restorative effects of steam bath treatments.

María Virginia Lopez, seventy-three, was born in Mariscal Cáceres. She is a well-reputed healer, trained in Puerto Bermúdez. I ran into María by accident when Bertha Rodríguez de Caleb hired her to administer a steam bath treatment in her Bajo Marankiari house. When the 2010 recording of María's steam bath treatment was made, she was living in the native community of Ciudadela in La Merced. Currently her whereabouts are not known. This collection includes the transcript of a steam bath treatment that she administered to Abdias Caleb Quinchori, a resident of Bajo Marankiari, at his house, in the presence of his family members.

Carmen Pachiri Quinchori, thirty-six, is a crafts maker who lives in Ciudadela, the multilingual native community of La Merced. Ciudadela residents largely make their livings by sales of crafts or herbal remedies and heavily depend on tourist traffic. Crafts making is a tough business for Ciudadela's Ashéninka families, including Carmen's, due to stiff competition from the nonlocal Shipibos, outstanding artisans and assertive vendors of traditional crafts who live next door. Carmen became interested in the book project during one of my visits to the community in 2012, when I was working with a speaker of Ashéninka Pichis. In the spring of 2013 we met on a regular basis to make recordings of Carmen's stories, many of which she heard as a little girl from her grandmother, Livia Julio de Quinchori, from Mariscal Cáceres, who essentially raised her. Carmen is married to a Machiguenga native, Percy Bustamonte Quinchimori, the current chief of Ciudadela. They have three children; the oldest is a fluent speaker of Machiguenga. Carmen's story about *kiatsi*, the demonic owner of the Perené River, is included in the collection.

Almacia Benavidez Fernandez, seventy-two, of Pokinkaro, was recommended to me as a successful Ashéninka healer by her gringo apprentice, a former librarian of Polish extract who had worked with her in the hope of mastering the basics of herbal healing. He thought that she might be interested in talking about her profession on camera. However, when I was introduced to her in her home in La Merced in the spring of 2013, Almacia was clearly more attracted to the idea of sharing her vast knowledge of myths, which she had picked up from her centenarian mother, who lives in the Puerto Bermúdez area. One of Almacia's stories about the Armageddon-like earthquake and flood in the Pichanaki area is part of this anthology.

In this book I also used texts that were independently recorded and transcribed by my primary consultants. The data providers for the texts collected by Daniel Bernales Quillatupa included his mother, Ruth Quillatupa Lopez, and his longtime friend and colleague Otoniel Ramos Rodríguez, fifty-two, from Churingaveni. Gregorio Santos Pérez collected data from his father-in-law, Elías Meza Pedro, sixty-eight; Clelia Mishari, seventy-three; and Livia Julio de Quinchori (age unknown), from Mariscal Cáceres. The selected stories by these authors include a commentary on the place-name Pichanaki (Otoniel Ramos Rodríguez), reflections on ritual practices of giving thanks, and commentary on the strongman Apinka (Clelia Michari, Livia Julio de Quinchori, and Elías Meza Pedro). Elías Meza Pedro's story *Imoro Naviriri* (The Naviriri Hole), about a deep indentation in the form of a crater, found in the uplands of Metraro, not far from Mariscal Cáceres, was recorded and transcribed by me, during my trip to Mariscal Cáceres in 2012.

STORYTELLING TRADITION AND ITS VITALITY

The Ashéninka Perené storytelling tradition is rigorously constrained by the orally transmitted repertory of native texts. Descriptions of the ancient past are basically mythological accounts perpetually recycled among Upper Perené storytellers. The myths exhibit a considerable degree of variability, but the common threads involve plots, occasions, themes, and characterizations, vividly revealed in the traditionally narrated adventures of the culture hero and trickster Naviriri the Transformer and his grandson Poiyotzi (sometimes called Kirii) and in numerous folk stories. According to Weiss, it is inevitable to collect "various, partially overlapping fractions" of a group's heritage materials (1975:227). A great deal of variation in the details of the recorded traditional stories is to be expected, due to the oral nature of the transmission mechanism. Nonetheless, the invariant core of traditional accounts is firmly anchored in the landscape features associated with a described event. For example, the well-known place of Naviriri's death, Imoro Naviriri (the Naviriri Hole), is located not far from Mariscal Cáceres; the cave in which a shaman-turned-cannibal was shut away, called Manitzipanko (the Jaguar House; its Spanish equivalent is La Boca del Tigre, "the Tiger's Mouth"), is eleven kilometers downstream from Santa Ana.

Historical accounts of modern times are more overlapping in their scene settings, sequencing of episodes, plots, and characterizations, perhaps due to the accuracy of personal testimony, which remains relatively unaltered by oral transmission within the short time span of the tradition. Although it is common to see "expansion or contraction of descriptions, omission or addition of detail" (Vansina 1985:53), it is unusual to find in the collected corpus eyewitness accounts fused with hearsay evidence. Historical accounts of modern times are always specific with regard to the physical location of the reported event. Minimally, event locations are described with the help of terms of the absolute orientation system that designates the riverine horizontal axis as *katonko* (upstream) and *kirinka* (downstream) and the mountain's vertical axis as *tonkari* (up) and *otapiki* (down).

Delivery skills vary from performer to performer. Performance features are more often observed among male narrators, who make use of facial expressions, gestures, rising intonation, louder voice volume, and higher pitch at the climactic moments, while females tend to speak in a casual manner, in a subdued and measured voice, without explicit dramatization of the described events. Pointing and descriptive gestures, wherein hand movements schematically depict the reported action, are often employed during the performance to clarify the point.

A notable performance feature is the pervasive use of ideophones, that is, single expressive words that depict the speaker's sensory experiences (Nuckolls 1995). There are over 150 ideophonic expressions in the Upper Perené language variety, evoking perceptions of hitting, cutting, light being emitted at regular intervals, daylight gradually advancing at sunrise, smoke from the fire billowing into the air, body ache, and many other actions and states (Mihas 2012). A unique function of ideophone use is the heightened "involvement" of the interlocutor, resulting in his or her better understanding of the narrator's message (Nuckolls 1992). Ideophones are called "foregrounding" devices in discourse, in that their expressivity and artistic delivery are bound to keep the audience engaged. An alphabetically organized list of Upper Perené ideophones used in this collection is located in the appendix.

Ideophone and depictive-gesture coupling is a pervasive performance feature, aimed at evoking a particular imagistic scene in listeners' minds. Apart from the ideophonic-gestural depiction, the narrator's performance typically includes the speaker's gaze focused on his or her own hands (Mihas 2013).

Other factors affecting the performance are the setting and receptiveness of the audience. A blaring TV or boom box in the vicinity will dull any performer's enthusiasm very quickly. Or domineering individuals from the audience, who condescendingly interject with unsolicited corrections, will have a stifling effect on the performer. On the other hand, friendly feedback and quick questions are appreciated. The audience's feedback comes in the form of the validation responses *je* (yes), *aja* (affirmative reaction to the interlocutor's statement), *tema ari* (is that so?), and *aritakitaima* (maybe, perhaps); the expressions of doubt *irotakitaima* (is that right?) and *omaperotatya* (is that true?); expressions of surprise (*iye* or *iyo*) and of compassion (*atyama, iyama, ñaamisa*); and the refutation expressions *te* (no), *te, kaari* (no, this is not so), and *tetya* (not at all.)

The conventional structures of both traditional stories and historical accounts include the opening formula *nonkinkitsata-kotero* (I will tell about) and the closing formulas *ari okaratzi* or *ari ovirapaki* (that's all). Other common stylistic devices are the temporary adverb *iroñaaka* (now, at present), which often indicates the end of a sustained episode; the sequencing adverbs *opoña* or *ipoña* (then, afterward); the contemporaneous adverbial forms *ikanta* or *okanta* (in the meantime); interjections; and the reportatives *ikantzi* (they say), *ankante* (we'll say, so to speak), and *akantavetakiri inkaranki* (as we said before). These structures typically lard the performance of Ashéninka Perené narrators.

Contemporary oral literary traditions have been in decline among Upper Perené Arawaks. Traditional storytelling is falling into disuse because of an accelerated shift to Spanish. The waning of oral performances is also linked to Adventist spiritual restrictions that prohibit some forms of entertainment, including weekend beer parties. In the past, oral performances were regular informal events carried out at beer parties among adults, which included dancing, singing celebratory chants, and telling stories (Weiss 1974:397). Stories were also narrated to children before bedtime (Anderson 2000:59). Women sang lullabies to babies as well as ritual songs honoring the sun and the moon (Weiss 1975:470). On formal occasions, such as tribal gatherings in the communal house, speeches were made and chants were performed. Shamanistic curative performances were known to include ritual singing (Weiss 1973:44–45). Currently, some extant literary oral traditions are still maintained on an individual basis in more traditional households, but native public discourses have become commodified and are displayed mainly for tourist consumption, when village leaders orate and chant and dancing groups of women or youth perform before tourists.

EXPRESSION OF INFORMATION SOURCE AND THE NARRATOR'S VIEWPOINT

Among Upper Perené Arawaks, it is expected that the information source will be identified explicitly when giving an account of past or present events. The sensory channel (visual, acoustic, tactile, "gut feeling") engaged in the process of the lived sensory experience is invariably specified when a piece of information is shared with an addressee. The means that speakers use for this purpose are the lexical verbs *ñ* (see), *kim* (hear/taste/smell/ sense), and *yoshiri* (sense, intuit) and the bound marker *-amampi* (have intuitive suspicion that something bad is going to happen). The parenthetical verb *koñaaro* (appear clearly) is used in accounts of visions, whether experienced in a dream or in an awakened state. The hearer-eyewitness parenthetical *ñaakiro* (you've seen it) refers to the addressee's visual past experience, which was shared with the speaker.

Verbal reports are accorded a significant role in social interaction; they directly specify the source of information via the quotative verb *kant* (say), as in *ikantzi/okantzi* (he/she says). The reportative parentheticals *ikantziri/akantziri* (they say) and *no-kantziri* (I say) are also commonly used, the former making reference to the collective experience of the unidentified source, the latter referencing the speaker's concrete personal experience. In the case of absence or paucity of personal sensory experiences, a variety of other devices are utilized to express the speaker's uncertainty about the accuracy of the volunteered proposition, such as the verb *kimi* (seem) and clitics encoding doubt, general expectations, and assumption (*=ma*, *=tyami*, and *=ratya*, respectively).

The parentheticals are manipulated as a stylistic device. For example, the parenthetical verb *ñaakiro* (you've seen it) has a dramaturgic effect, serving as an invitation to the addressee to relive anew the reported event. The use of the parentheticals *ikantziri/akantziri* (they say), especially when used without the marker of assertion *=kia*, creates a distancing effect when the speaker does not guarantee that the statement is accurate.

Information flow is not restricted in Ashéninka Perené society. Regardless of the recipients' social status, information is marked for source and exchanged in the same fashion. For example, the abovementioned inventory of tools for marking the information source applies to ritual incantations addressed to supernatural beings like Pava (solar deity) or Tasorentsi (a powerful figure endowed with supernatural powers).

At the core of all information-source meanings is the speaker's viewpoint. In particular, objective or credible information sources are those over which the speaker has exclusive authority, which are directly experienced. These are encoded via the perception verbs, the parenthetical self-reportative *nokantziro*, the parenthetical verb *koñaaro* (appear clearly in a vision), and the intuitive suspicion marker *-amampi*, which directly attaches to the verb root. In contrast, subjective or noncredible information sources are those for which the speaker is not responsible, which are not directly experienced. These are encoded by the grammatical markers of inference, assumption, and general expectation (*=ma*, *=ratya*, and *=tyami*, respectively), the hearsay parentheticals *ikantziri/akantziri* (they say), and the verb *kimi* (seem).

ORTHOGRAPHY

Ashaninka is an official language in lowland Peru where Kampan languages are spoken. A standardized pan-regional alphabet was approved in 2008 by the Peruvian Ministry of Education for the Ashéninka/Ashaninka bilingual schools; it uses the grapheme ⟨b⟩ for the bilabial approximant /w/ and the grapheme ⟨t⟩ for two different phonemes, the alveolar stop /t/ and the alveolar affricate /ts/. However, Upper Perené speakers, following the previous writing tradition, are accustomed to using the grapheme ⟨v⟩ rather than ⟨b⟩ for the bilabial approximant /w/ and the grapheme ⟨tz⟩ for the unaspirated alveolar affricate /ts/. The texts presented in this collection rely on the writing conventions used by the literate native speakers and approved at a language consultant meeting in April 2013.

The palatal glide is considered here to be an allophone of the non-stress-bearing high front vowel when it occurs in the same syllable with /a/, forming the rising diphthong [ja] (Hualde 2005:54). In writing, the glide is expressed as ⟨i⟩, e.g., *piarentsi* (manioc beer).

The assimilatory palatalization process is restricted to the alveolar stop /t/ and nasal stop /n/ in contexts where they are followed by the diphthong /ia/. The resultant palatalized allophonic segments are encoded in the following way: the combination ⟨ty⟩ marks the alveo-palatal stop, while the symbol ⟨ñ⟩ marks the palatal nasal stop. Note that both the alveo-palatal stop and the palatal nasal stop are phonemic in the language.

VOWELS

i   Spanish i; when followed by a, becomes the palatal glide [j], as in *riachuelo* (small river)

ii   elongated i

e   close to Spanish e; can be articulated in the range from Spanish i to Spanish e

ee   elongated e

a   Spanish a

aa   elongated a

o   articulated in the range from Spanish o to Spanish u

oo   elongated o

CONSONANTS

p   Spanish p

t   Spanish t (unaspirated)

k   Spanish k

ty   similar to the first consonant in English *tune*

ts   aspirated affricate, similar to the word-final consonant in English *hats*

tz   unaspirated affricate, similar to the middle consonant in English *pizza*

ch   Spanish ch

sh   English sh

s   Spanish s; when followed by i, can be articulated as a voiceless alveolar sibilant which has a whistling quality, but similar to sh

j   English h

m   English m

n   English n

ñ   Spanish ñ

v   Spanish v, as in *viuda* (widow)

r   Spanish r, as in *frio* (cold)

y   English y, as in *boy*

ABBREVIATIONS

1	first person
3	third person
-	symbol for an affix boundary
=	symbol for a clitic boundary
A	subject of transitive verb
ADV	adverbial
AUG	augmentative
CL	classifier
CUST	customary
DEM	demonstrative
DIM	diminutive
DIR	directional
DIST	distributive
EP	epenthetic
HAB	habitual
IMP	impersonal
IRR	irrealis
LOC	locative
MASC	masculine
NMASC	nonmasculine
NMZ	nominalizer
O	object of transitive verb
PERV	perfective
PL	plural
POSS	possessive
PROG	progressive
REAL	realis

REAS	reason
REL	relativizer
S	subject of intransitive verb
SG	singular
STAT	stative

SYNOPSIS OF TEXTS

The texts presented here address the following themes:

Texts 1–4: Mythic beginnings of primordial times.

Texts 5–13: The dramatic developments of modern times, inter- and intratribal violence, armed resistance to the colonizers, and the slave trade.

Texts 14–15: The conversion of the displaced and demoralized Upper Perené Arawaks to the Adventist strain of Christianity, and the persecution of witches.

Text 16–18: Upper Perené landmarks associated with the worship of sacred fires.

Texts 19–20 Tziviari (The Salt Hill), a well-known Upper Perené location where salt used to be extracted by many Kampan and non-Kampan pilgrims.

Texts 21–23: Renowned Upper Perené landmarks with mythic origins.

Texts 24–25: Place-naming practices of Upper Perené natives.

Texts 26–34: Spiritual beings who inhabit the environs of the Upper Perené homeland.

Texts 36–37: Place rituals, exchange rites, and ritual use of *ivenki* plants.

Texts 38–40: Prayer, incantation, and ritual behaviors.

Texts 41–44: Upper Perené calendrical rites.

Texts 45–47: Feasting and festival rites.

Texts 48–50: Rites of passage.

Texts 51–58: Affliction rituals, particularly shamanistic interventions, and the role of the herbal healer in treating afflicted fellow men.

1

History

For Upper Perené Arawaks, history is firmly situated in the temporal frames of concrete events enacted by agentive entities and is localized within a certain space. To be credible, the Ashaninka conception of history does not demand continuity and exactness in the spatiotemporal localization of happenings in the world. Nonetheless, history is ordered in a certain way. In the narratives collected here, history reveals a sort of dichotomous architecture. It is divided into two main space-time periods, the remote past and modernity, expressed in the language by the temporal words *pairani* (ancient times, long ago, in the past) and *ironaaka* (now, at present) (see Rojas Zolezzi 1994:110). When there is talk about the past, a boundary will often be drawn between *pairani* (long ago) and *ironaaka* (now), emphasized by the speaker.

Depending on the context, *pairani* and *ironaaka* can have additional interpretations. For example, *pairani* can refer to fairly recent times, meaning "a few/ten/twenty . . . years ago. The ubiquitous *ironaaka* typically functions as a "neutral connector . . . [when] the speaker wants to identify the separateness" of a part of the sentence (Danielsen 2007:397). When found on the boundaries of nominal and verbal phrases, the temporal word *ironaaka* (now) signals a transition to another unit of thought.

The time depth of Upper Perené historical knowledge is rather shallow. In the documented orally transmitted historical accounts, narrators typically mention their grandfathers' generation as the source of the directly witnessed or experienced event.

The Upper Perené oral tradition structures spatiotemporal frames of the recorded narratives in the following way: *pairani* (the remote, mythic past) and the modern times of *intanakarori* (village founders) and *nocharinitepaye* (our grandfathers) with the revolutionary *tiempo de la Peruvian Corporation* (the period of the Peruvian Corporation) being the point of the most sweeping socioeconomic changes. In its abbreviated version, the last term may resurface as *en el tiempo de la Peruvian* or *en el tiempo de la compañía* (during the company's times). The bipartite division of Upper Perené space-time has fluid boundaries, since critical characteristics of the old times are still present in the early modern times, such as sudden bodily transformations and shamanistic mediation with the outside world of spirits.

The *pairani* (remote past) period in the Upper Perené texts is the "undifferentiated world that existed prior to the separation of humans and animals into distinct categories of being" (Hill 1993:60–61). When texts describe events within the mythic space-time, they begin with the following characterization of the main protagonist: *ovakera yatzirivitani pairani* (when he was a human in the ancient times). The mythic past times also witnessed numerous transformations of humans into nonhuman beings, such as plants, animals, insects, or rocks, resulting in the eventual separation of the human and nonhuman worlds. During the past mythic times, Upper Perené Arawaks acquired their crafts, cultigens, rituals, and access to fire. The "undifferentiated" human-nonhuman times of the mythical past are also described in the oral tradition of Ashaninka Tambo (Campa, Arawak; Weiss 1975), Wakuénai (Baniwa, Arawak; Hill 1993), Amuesha (Arawak; Smith 1977), Shipibo (Panoan; Roe 1988), and Curaray Runa Quichua (Quechua; Reeve 1985, 1993–94).

The transition to the modern period is defined by markedly elevated warfare, large-scale migration, and "cultural decline and slow physical agony" (Varese 2002:86). This period epitomizes what Fishman calls "dislocation": "population diminution"

due to minority-language speakers' forced or voluntary migration, "poverty," and "cultural suicide" due to the dictates of colonist market economy and culture (1991:55–65). Social memories
of many Amazonian societies registered the fact that rubber-
boom barons acted as major dislocating agents (Gow 1991:62;
Hill 1993:61). In contrast, in the Upper Perené valley it was the
British-owned Peruvian Corporation, brought in on the heels of
the mid-nineteenth-century military conquest, that had a profoundly "dislocating" impact on the indigenous population.

The turbulent times from 1891 to 1965 in Upper Perené texts
are designated in Spanish as *en el tiempo de la compañía/Peru-
vian Corporation* (during the times of the company/Peruvian
Corporation). In particular, the period of transition to modernity is essentially drawn at the onset of the massively dislocating event, associated with the mid-nineteenth-century military
invasion by the Peruvian army, with the resultant flight and displacement of the indigenous population and the irrevocable
and unstoppable spread of the colonist agricultural economy,
in tandem with the ever-increasing presence of *chori* (Andean
settlers) and *virakocha* (nonindigenous outsiders). Both groups
are talked about with palpable enmity, although *chori* are spoken of with hardly concealed disdain, whereas *virakocha* are
both feared and hated. Supernatural agents and quasi-legendary
events are often referenced in Upper Perené historical narratives, describing the beginning of modernity.

The *iroñaaka* times are associated with the establishment
of Upper Perené nucleated settlements, organized around a
school, by *intanakarori* (village founders) and *nocharinitepaye*
(our grandfathers). The nucleation process began in the 1920s,
after the arrival of the North American Adventist missionary
Fernando (Ferdinand Anthony) Stahl. Some of the nucleated

settlements originally emerged as Adventist mission posts and later were registered as native communities, after the enactment of the 1974 Law of Native Communities, which gave Ashaninkas legal entitlement to land.

In other oral Amazonian traditions, the division of space-time is more comprehensive. For example, among Ashaninka Tambo, six temporal periods are distinguished: the *perani* (mythic times), *el tiempo de los antiguos* (the ancestors' times), *el tiempo de la esclavitud* (the slavery time), *el tiempo de los gringos* (the missionaries' time), *el tiempo de la subversión* (the internal war time), and *el tiempo de la civilización* (the time of civilization) (Sarmiento Barletti 2011:chap. 2).

In the tales of the Ashaninka neighbors Shipibo (Panoan), from the Ucayali River valley, the temporal continuum is reported to be divided into three spatial frames: the remote mythic time, called *moatian icani* (time of Noah); the middle time *moatian ica* (or *ini*) (time of the Incas); and *moatian* (the grandfathers' time), which approximately spans the period of the last fifteen generations (Roe 1988:111). The transitional middle period of the Incas overlaps with mythic and modern times in that although it makes references to mythic events and characters, it also contains elements from the Shipibo historical past.

In what follows, a brief characterization of the Upper Perené Ashaninka ancient past and modern times will be given, as they are remembered by the Upper Perené Arawaks, with each period having its distinctive events and heroes.

The remote past is linked to the world of bodily transformations and to its principal agents of change, the solar divinity Pava and the capricious and unpredictable Naviriri Piantzinkari (Naviriri the Transformer), who would on a whim turn people into animals, insects, plants, or material objects. The exploits of Naviriri and his grandson Poiyotzi (also called Kirii) terrorized the native population, and eventually they were both killed by their own fellow men.

The other transformer, the solar divinity Pava, is credited with creating the whole animated cosmos via a series of transformations. Pava is not to be confused with "the God of another world and another language," furnished by missionaries; although Pava does bear "veneers of the Christian God" (Lenaerts 2006a:546), the critical distinction lies in Pava's method: nothing is created from scratch, but all is transformed from one form into another (Weiss 1975:266). This point is illustrated by Cristobal Jumanga's narrative *Pava vitsikirori kipatsi* (Pava, Who Made the Earth), in which the solar divinity transforms his human offspring into fish species. An act of bodily transformation is achieved through the magic blowing of breath through the mouth with pursed lips, followed by the ritual formula *afuu* (be it).

In addition, sudden bodily transformations also occurred due to the punishment administered by shamans or as the result of shaming by fellow men or self-inflicted shame. At other times, spontaneous self-transformations transpire for no obvious reason. The bodily transformations are permanent and irreversible, except shamanic "temporary disembodiment/re-embodiment" conversions, during hallucinatory trances, into jaguars or other animal species (Lenaerts 2006c). For example, the text *Pichanaki* by Otoniel Ramos Rodríguez (in part 2) reports on a shaman who would transform into a jaguar and crush people with a rock during his nocturnal dream flights; Ruth Quillatupa Lopez's narrative *Manitzipanko* (The Jaguar House; in part 2) is a story about the jaguar-shaman devouring people in the Upper Perené area. Part 1, "History," contains two texts that illustrate spontaneous nonshamanic transformations as well. In Alberto Pérez Espinoza's *Okoñaatantakari kaniri* (How Sweet Manioc Appeared), the mythological benefactor *tsinaro* (grasshopper), who gave the sweet manioc cultigen to a young Campa girl, self-transforms into a grasshopper after having been seen by the girl's mother.

According to Ruth Quillatupa Lopez (*Okoñaatantari paa-mari* [How Fire Came into Existence]), the fire was first obtained by a widowed Ashaninka woman from the *chorito* (blue-headed parrot) woman, who was a messenger from the dead. The dead people's gift of fire didn't last long. Only after the widow was taught by the *patyankori* (squirrel) man to rub a piece of cotton against dry wood did the Ashaninkas gain control over fire. Although the narrator does not elaborate on the fate of the Squirrel man, the Blue-headed parrot woman self-converted into a bird with a red spot under its tail feathers, after having been burned by the widowed woman's fire. The transformation occurred when she stealthily extinguished the fire, not willing to share it with other humans.

The ancient past was a turbulent time of regular engagements with multiple lethal threats posed by the aggressive creatures inhabiting the forest, the hills, and the river. This subject is extensively discussed in part 2, "Landscape," with its focus on the stories of human struggle against evil spiritual beings such as *kamari* kam-a-ri [die-REAL-REL] (demon) and other powerful entities, known under the generic term *ashitarori* ashi-t-a-ro-ri [own-EP-REAL-3NMASC.O-REL] (the masters or owners of the place) (or *ashitariri*, depending on the gender class of the protected species).

The primordial past was the prime time of shamans, or *sheri-piari*. Shamans were the ultimate mediators between the outside world of spirits and dead humans and the local community that they served. The challenge of their job was "to mend what might be called rifts in a cosmic network" (Whitten 1985:88). Currently there is no known old-school shaman left in the

Upper Perené area. Those who claim to be shamans, according to locals, are fakes, since they do not consume tobacco, an old psychedelic drug of Upper Perené ritual specialists. Nonetheless, memories of past shamanic "rescue missions" are still alive and are passed on within families. In people's recollections of those memorable events, shamanic activities involved tracking down and finding ways of neutralizing a murderous evil entity, for the sake of the community's safety. Some speakers comment that the presence of evil spirits has significantly decreased due to the relatively dense population of the area, associated with the well-established colonist economy. As a result, shamanic services might have become of less value. Shamanic practices will be dealt with in part 3, "Ritual."

This presentation of the native understanding of the historical past would be incomplete without mentioning the name of the man who is known among locals as Api Inka (Seer Inca), or in casual speech, Apinka. Most Upper Perené Arawaks subscribe to the belief that Juan Santos Atahualpa, or Jova Santoshi Ataaripa, or Apinka Ataaripa, is a major historical figure of the old times (Macera and Casanto 2009).[1] In scholarly analyses of Apinka's outstanding guerilla campaign against the Spaniards—which resulted in the total expulsion of the Spanish colonizers from the Ashaninka land in the mid-eighteenth century—it is assumed that Apinka's military success might have been due to his followers' messianic proclivity, that is, visions of a new social order established by a god's messenger, inasmuch as Apinka presented himself as such (Métraux 1942; Michael Brown 1991; Brown and Fernandes 1992; Santos-Granero 2004a; Varese 1996, 2002).

Other scholars downplay the pan-Ashaninka messianic element in the 1742–52 rebel movement, pointing out that Apinka's major source of followers was Quechua-speaking highlanders,

with small populations of Upper Perené Ashaninkas and Amue-
shas from the Chanchamayo valley involved in the revolt (Lehnertz 1974:134). Skepticism is also fueled by a lack of documented
prerevolt millenarian rituals among Campas (Veber 2003:187).

The 2009–12 Upper Perené documentary corpus contains
three Apinka stories, which are mute with regard to indigenous
messianic aspirations. The Apinka texts exhibit a bipartite distinction in the stories' plotlines, along with the main character's qualities. It is argued that mythic thought has a propen-
sity for going astray, engendering contradictory myths within a
single community (Lévi-Strauss [1964] 1992:2–3). Folklore is also
known to alter the cultural hero's function or character value
with its opposite (Lévi-Strauss 1955:442). Additional evidence
from interviews with native speakers also reveals a two-way dis-
similarity in the native reconstruction of the Upper Perené historical past.

The first Apinka of the Upper Perené narratives is a multi-
layered composite, possibly related to the Inca or Pachakama
of Quechua-speaking highlanders, who traveled a lot and introduced locals to natural resources and ways to exploit them (Martel Paredes 2009:42; Lenaerts 2006a:547). The other Apinka is
an influential tribal chief from the area of Metraro and Mariscal
Cáceres (see Martel Paredes 2009:43). The second Apinka can-
not possibly be traced back to the times of the Juan Santos Atahualpa rebellion in the 1740s, since native family tradition describes the Apinka-centered events' midpoint as being in the
nineteenth century.

According to the narrator Luis Mauricio Rosa, an itinerant
god called Pava Apinka (God Apinka) taught the Upper Perené
Ashaninka traditional crafts and skills and before his death ad-
vised his fellow men to bury each other in the ground. This story
represents a Christian strain of missionized Ashaninka mythic

thought revealed in the characterization of Apinka as a kind and loving character, on a mission to help people. Apinka is shown to introduce Upper Perené Arawaks to occupational activities and natural resources. When Apinka is buried — alive, as it turns out — his coffin is unearthed, and he goes to heaven leaving a commandment to bury the dead in the ground. The text was recorded in the narrator's sister's home in Pampa Michi, in 2009.

Two other stories of the brutal *pinkatsari*, known under the name of Apinka, are the complete opposite of the "loving and helpful Apinka" myth. In particular, Bertha Rodríguez de Caleb's family tradition describes Apinka as a miserly ruler from the uplands of Metraro who was buried there, along with his gold. Bertha's source was her grandmother, who lived in Apinka's village and worked for him until his death. The 2010 recording of Bertha and her husband, Abdias Caleb Quinchori, made in a relative's home in Bajo Marankiari, contains striking comments about the avarice and despotism of the headman. The narrators emphasize Apinka's calculated policy of depriving people of food, which led to severe malnutrition and starvation of those living in his *nampitsi*. After the military takeover of the Perené valley in the mid-nineteenth century, Apinka's gravesite was desecrated and the gold found there was stolen by Spaniards.

The narrators also contend that Apinka had a brother, called Marinkama, a blacksmith who established a local forge known as Ashiropanko (the Iron House) and who trained a group of celibate youths as his apprentices. Marinkama performed priestly duties in the temple-forge, being in charge of the forge's sacred fire. Marinkama's grave is reported to be located in the hills adjacent to Bajo Marankiari.

The subject of Apinka's life and death is also discussed by the Kishitariki (present-day Mariscal Cáceres) resident Elías Meza Pedro, with his son-in-law Gregorio Santos Pérez and his

old-time neighbor, Livia Julio de Quinchori. In the 2011 recording, titled *Apinka*, Elías Meza Pedro states that Apinka instilled
great fear in Upper Perené Arawaks. Folklore remembers him
as a distant, ruthless, and despotic killer. Apinka, with the help
of his *aminantatsiri* (guards; literally, amin-ant-atsi-ri [watch-
CUST-STAT-REL] [those who are on the lookout]), kept natives
in wretched misery and punished disobedience by beheading
the alleged wrongdoer. Narcissism was his principal personality
trait, as shown in the text, since he forced those who would
come to see him to address him on their knees. The headman
was eventually killed by an Ashéninka warrior from Gran Pajonal. The text was recorded by Gregorio Santos Pérez in the home
of Elías Meza Pedro in Mariscal Cáceres.

Placed within the documented native historical knowledge,
Asheninka Perené renditions of past events involving the cultural hero Apinka are silent with regard to the putative "millenarian fervor" (Michael Brown 1991:392). In spite of the sustained community-based documentation effort, pertinent evidence is unlikely to be forthcoming in the future due to the
rapidly shrinking speaker base and declining oral tradition.

Modern times have been punctuated by three fundamentally disruptive events: the mid-nineteenth-century military conquest, the existence of the Peruvian Corporation on tribal land
from the 1890s through 1965, and the appearance of Fernando
Stahl, the Seventh-Day Adventist missionary in 1921. These
events are commented on by many people in the collected texts.

In contrast, the 1879–1912 rubber boom and the Peruvian internal conflict that began in 1980 and is still ongoing did not profoundly affect Upper Perené populations, which are geographi-
cally located on the periphery of the rubber-extraction territory
and the conflict zone. In Upper Perené historical accounts, these
events appear to be either inconsequential or too sensitive to be

a speaking point. Specifically, other than occasional mentions of a father's or grandfather's long absences because he had gone far away to cut *shiringa* trees (*Hevea brasiliensis*), the Upper Perené documentary corpus contains virtually no record of the rubber boom's effects.

The terror activities by the antigovernment guerilla organizations Sendero Luminoso (Shining Path) and Movimiento Revolucionario Tupac Amaru (MRTA, or Tupac Amaru Revolutionary Movement) were not elaborated on in conversations or narratives due to the speakers' visible lack of interest in the subject, or perhaps their unwillingness to discuss it. On a few occasions, I heard brief remarks on terror-related incidents regarding violent deaths, destruction of property, and pilfering of food supplies. I was told that during the decades of terror, rape and abduction of Upper Perené young girls and women (some as young as six years old) were common, and the brutality of *senderistas,* called *kityonkari* (the reds), was stressed. In contrast, Ashaninkas from the Tambo and Bajo Urubamba Rivers, who joined forces with the subversives and spent years in their camps, are reported to comment on the subject with regularity and forthrightness (Sarmiento Barletti 2011:71–72).

The beginning of modern times was marked by the mid-nineteenth-century military conquest of the native territory and concomitant indigenous resistance to the army's advance into the ancestral land. The massive scale of the military conquest and colonist penetration overwhelmed Ashaninkas, but they continued to respond with classical guerilla warfare by regularly carrying out surgical strikes on the military and colonists, in various locations, always making surprising appearances and quickly withdrawing afterward into the jungle.

The collected oral accounts have not retained names of Upper Perené warriors from those early modern times. However, one of the most frequently cited *ovayeri* (warriors), is Marinkama, a charismatic and accomplished headman from the highlands of Gran Pajonal who reportedly came with his brother and other companions to the Upper Perené valley, responding to his local brothers-in-arms' plea for help (Veber 2009:133, 179). According to native sources, Marinkama actively participated in skirmishes with the military and Andean colonists in different parts of the Chanchamayo and Perené valleys in the 1840s.

This chapter features two texts in which Marinkama's name is either implied or directly mentioned. The first account, *Yookantapakairi virakocha* (How the Whites Threw Us Out), by the current chief of the native community of Pampa Michi, Fredi Miguel Ucayali, was recorded in Fredi Ucayali's home in the spring of 2012, as part of a long interview about the past and present periods of Ashaninka history. Fredi Ucayali heard this particular story of the military defeat of allied indigenous forces in the Upper Perené valley from his grandfather, who raised him and to whom he owes his vast knowledge of the Ashaninka past as well as traditional customs and crafts. Map 3 illustrates Fredi Ucayali's description of the Peruvian military conquest and the retreat path of Ashaninka people in the 1840s.

The Gran Pajonal warrior Marinkama was also involved in another unsuccessful and undated battle against the Peruvian military, in the downriver area called Natsitonini (the Stream of Bones). Manuel Rubén Jacinto, one of the esteemed elders of the Seventh-Day Adventist Church in Pucharini, in the text *Natsitonini* (The Stream of Bones), describes Marinkama's strategic mistake—he struck alone, without waiting for reinforcements from the local chief and was overcome by the enemy. The narrative was recorded in the summer of 2011 in Pucharini, at the house of the narrator's relatives, the Jumanga Lopez brothers.

3. Historical landmarks in the "contested" Upper Perené landscape. By Adella Edwards.

Manuel Rubén Jacinto's parents, descendants of warriors from Gran Pajonal, were the original source of the story.

Native personal memories and oral tradition unequivocally point to the historical prominence accorded to the institution of *ovayeri* (warriors) in Ashaninka society. Since early youth, *ovayeri* were rigorously trained in the acrobatics of dodging arrows as well as in archery marksmanship, stealthy enemy stalking, and utmost physical endurance. They were also trained to skillfully use the magic herbs *ivenki* (piripiri; *Cyperus piripiri*) in order to aim with precision, protect themselves from the enemy's arrows, and quickly recover from wounds (Rojas Zolezzi 1994:230). In addition, to acquire a warring spirit and to covet combat, the magic plant *pinitsi*, called *tilo* or *pusanga* in Spanish, was administered into the eyes of the warrior. The career of *ovayeri* was respectable but woefully short due to warriors' high mortality rates in combat. The profession's perk was an opportunity to take the enemy's belongings and to kidnap women, with both activities described by the verb root *koshi* (rob). Like chiefs, warriors were known to take many wives (Macera and Casanto 2009).

The specifics of *ovayeri* training in the Upper Perené area are provided by Daniel Bernales Quillatupa in his text *Tsika okantakota ovayeritantsi* (About the Craft of War). As a boy, Daniel heard his grandfather's stories about *ovayeri*, and he wrote them down from memory at my request, in the spring of 2012. Daniel's grandfather participated in the *ovayeri* annual boot camps that were conducted in the summer, when *savoro* (wild cane; *Gynerium sagittatum*) begins to sprout and large stretches of sandy beaches along the Perené River become exposed. The annual gatherings on a sandy beach were organized by Daniel's grandfather's father, who was a local chief.

When native settlements were raided by *ovayeri*, the headman and his male relatives were the first target. If male defenders survived the raid, they would pursue the kidnappers, but these reprisals were generally ill-fated. The males would be either killed during the raid or ambushed and killed during the postraid chase. Tribal endo-warfare eventually reached "gigantic proportions" (Chevalier 1982:200). Upper Perené Ashaninkas were especially fearful of their neighbors from Gran Pajonal (Weiss 1975:237), notorious for their brutality and superb mastery of the bow and arrow.[2] The text *Apapanani* (The Brook of Liver Parts) is a recollection of the bloody endo-warfare in which Upper Perené and Gran Pajonal Arawaks were steeped in early modern times. The narrator, Gregorio Santos Pérez, heard the account from his mother many years ago, when the family was fishing in the area of the reported bloodshed. The narrative was recorded in 2011, outside the narrator's house in Villa Perené.

Ovayeri had their songs, according to native lore. Vansina calls the messages transmitted by this sort of song "precious . . . snippets of historical information" (1985:93). *Ovayeritantsi* (the craft of war) was immortalized in the chant recorded by Paulina García Ñate in 2010, in the village of Bajo Marankiari. The chant is called *Ovayeri inoshikantarori kooya* (When Warriors Kidnapped a Woman). The chant has a repetitive chorus, *chanaina*. As in other Upper Perené chants, the "vocable" *chanaina* resembles a native word but has no meaning (Beier 2002). In the chant, it serves as a substitute for the word *tsinani* (young girl). The chant is performed by men standing in a circle with their arms intertwined and rhythmically stepping forward while thrusting their upper bodies toward the circle's center. The old-time warrior chanting lore is still maintained by a few older-generation natives of Bajo Marankiari, having been completely forgotten in other villages.

Modern times are also associated with the slave trade, conducted by roving bands of Ashaninka *ovayeri* and raiding groups

of non-Ashaninka tribes called *ovantzinkari* (killers), who specialized in kidnapping women and children and killing the captives' male relatives within the territory of their own tribes and
beyond. Started after the military conquest of the region in the
mid-nineteenth century, these raids, called in Spanish *correrías*
(runs), generated a stable traffic of slaves. In the context of a
greatly constricted labor market on the one hand and lost indigenous ironworks technologies and severed trade ties with neighbors on the other, the slave trade supported the colonist economy and satisfied the native demand for material goods such as
rifles, cartridges, pots, fabric, and blankets.

The captured women and children were sold to colonists of
Andean or European ancestry and subjected to unrelenting and
brutal exploitation. Treated as subhuman things, the captives did
housekeeping, tended to domestic animals, and worked in vegetable gardens. The large-scale system of slave trafficking was so
tightly embedded in the colonists' socioeconomic existence that
it was regarded as "normal" even in the early twentieth century
(Veber 2009:34). Cases of slave trafficking of children were recorded until the early 1960s (Weiss 1975:233; Brown and Fernandez 1992:187).

The text *Ovayeri inoshikantzi eentsi* (The Warriors Kidnapped Children," by Ines Pérez de Santos, is a poignant commentary on the defensive techniques used by the villagers to
protect their young from child kidnappers. In her recorded reminiscences, Ines Pérez de Santos attributes the luck of staying
alive to the rules she unfailingly adhered to as a child: be quiet,
stay close to your parent or other adult relative, and hide at the
slightest sign of threat. Many families had constructed hiding
places for their children. The narrator recalls hiding under a low-
level wooden bed with five other young girls, in a makeshift hole

that resembled a shallow grave. Often the girls had to stay half-buried in the hole overnight.

The text by Ines Pérez de Santos also discloses the kidnappers' names and backgrounds; many were from the neighboring community of Alto Marankiari, and some were even the narrator's relatives. The commentary was recorded in the spring of 2013 in Bajo Marankiari, when the narrator, her husband, Moises Santos Rojas, and I were perusing an elementary school textbook that contained hand-drawn portraits of local *ovayeri*.

Another perspective on child kidnappings is presented in *Nonkinkitsatakotero nayironi* (I Will Tell about My Deceased Mother-in-Law), by Victorina Rosas de Castro. It is a chilling story of the narrator's mother-in-law's enslavement, personally related to her by the slave-trade victim. At about age seven, the mother-in-law was kidnapped from her parents' house in the Río Negro area, when her father and mother went fishing. The girl was brought by the kidnappers to La Merced, then shipped to Tarma, then to Lima. Eventually she returned with her masters to the Chanchamayo valley and escaped to freedom only when she was in her thirties. The narrative was recorded in 2010, at the narrator's sister's residence in Bajo Marankiari.

Apart from the gory violence of "gigantic proportions" (Chevalier 1982:200), modern times are also defined by the adoption of Christian beliefs and the abandonment of pagan views and rituals. Those Ashaninkas who take a negative view of the implantation of Christian beliefs lament the passing of the time when the solar divinity Pava and the masters of the plants were recognized by all and honored in the ritual thanking ceremonies. That contemporary Ashaninkas do not pay respects to the true Ashaninka divinity, Pava, is for some a clear demarcation line dividing the old and modern times. In contradistinction, to other Ashaninkas the past state of ignorance, expressed by *te noyote Pava* (we didn't know God), is seen as an obstacle to overall Ashaninka enlightenment and entry into a so-called civilized state. This perspective is evident in *Tsika okanta nosaikantakari Marankiaroki* (How We Settled Down in Bajo Marankiari), by Bertha Rodríguez de Caleb, who attributes to *amakirori ñaantsi* (the one who brought the Word)—that is, Fernando (Ferdinand Anthony) Stahl, the Seventh-Day Adventist missionary from the United States who evangelized in the Upper Perené area from 1921 to 1928—the ultimate agency in the betterment of Ashaninka well-being. The narrative was recorded in 2009 in the narrator's daughter's home in Bajo Marankiari.

In conjunction with Bertha Rodríguez de Caleb's praise of the Adventist mission, it should be noted that the enthusiastic support of the Adventist missionary Fernando Stahl by the Upper Perené valley indigenous population is well documented (e.g., Bodley 1973; Santos-Granero 2002b, 2004b; Stahl 1932; Veber 2009:37). Academic sources vary in their assessment of the basis for this unexpectedly vigorous embrace of the Adventist strain of Christianity. Simply put, it is either explained by the inherent messianic disposition of Upper Perené Ashaninkas or it is attributed to the sympathetic nature of Adventist missionizing, which promised an end to the colonist invasion due to the imminent destruction of the white world (Bodley 1970:111; Veber 2009:37). The indisputable fact is that Adventist mission posts provided an opportunity to stay on the ancestral land and a timely refuge inside the mission compounds for Upper Perené Arawaks who had been displaced, weakened by epidemics, and demoralized (Santos-Granero and Barclay 1998:238).

There was an additional factor at play. According to native speakers' oral accounts, Stahl pushed for the establishment of schools, as it was the case in the first Upper Perené mission of

Metraro, and he emphasized the importance of native literacy.[3] Based on my observations, Upper Perené Arawaks highly value education (see Killick 2008; Sarmiento Barletti 2011:chap. 12). When placed in the context of the indigenous quest "to appropriate the Other"—in this particular situation, in the context of a need to gain access to the knowledge that makes the Other so powerful (Santos-Granero 2002b, 2009a)—the success of the Adventist mission is hardly surprising.

The grip of Seventh-Day Adventist missionaries on Upper Perené Arawaks was perhaps magnified due to the missionaries' mediation with the Peruvian Corporation, locally known as the Perené Colony, from the 1920s through the 1940s. The London-based coffee-producing company, which received five hundred hectares of Ashaninka tribal land in the Perené valley as part of the Peruvian government's debt settlement, was in dire need of a stable and reliable labor force and welcomed Fernando Stahl's proposal to establish a mission post in Metraro, hoping to profit from this arrangement (Barclay 1989:124–25). In 1922 Stahl received three hundred hectares from the company in the Metraro area, which became one of the first nucleated indigenous labor settlements within the Perené Colony (Santos-Granero and Barclay 1998:238). When the shortage of food and epidemics forced Ashaninka families to leave the colony, they founded other mission villages in the Perené valley, including Bajo Marankiari. The Adventist converts' peregrinations are described in the Bertha Rodríguez de Caleb text *Tsika okanta nosaikantakari Marankiaroki* (How We Settled Down in Bajo Marankiari).

Accusations of sorcery, a common phenomenon in Amazonia (Whitehead and Wright 2004), and punishment meted out to the alleged sorcerers is a "dark" subject that was commonly brought up by native speakers in their characterizations of the recent past. Many narrators witnessed the incidents that would result in the execution of the alleged witch. Although identification, forced "purification," and punishment of witches are directly linked to their shamanic practices as religious specialists, to be addressed in detail in part 3, "Ritual," it was deemed necessary to include at least one witness account of this sort in the book's "History" section. The rationale for including it in the overview of the recent historical past was to abide by the project's documentary objective and to provide a full-bodied picture of modern times.

Scholarly studies of sorcery in Chanchamayo Province indicate that the issue became extremely enlarged only in the late nineteenth century (Santos-Granero 2002b, 2004b). Although its intensity and lethality have abated—now accused witches are either asked to leave the community or physically avoided—sorcery continues to preoccupy native speakers' minds. The illustrative case described by Bertha Rodríguez de Caleb in *Tsika okanta noñaakoventakiri matsipaye* (How I Witnessed Events Involving Witches) documents in minute detail the nature of multiple accusations and the massive cleansing procedure of the alleged witches at the Adventist mission post of San Pablo (Nasaraiteki). The village was founded by converted Upper Perené Arawaks who relocated to the Pichis valley in pursuit of a better life. The incident occurred in 1961, when the narrator was residing in this village with her family. The recording took place in 2010, in the narrator's daughter's house.

ONE

Pava vitsikirori kipatsi

(Pava, Who Made the Earth)

Cristobal Jumanga Lopez

[1]Ankinkitsatakoteri aparoni. [2]Ikantakota pairani acharinite ikinkitsatakotziri ikantziri pava. [3]Maatsi pava pairani ashitariri, vitsikirori kipatsi iroñaaka. [4]Maatsi mava itomi, osheki ivari iririntzipaye paita ankantakote iyora shima, jetari, poña iyora paitari shaa. [5]Ikantzi osheki ivari ishaninkapaye. [6]Ikantavitari inavita ashitariri, "Notomi, aitaki pivakari pirintzitepaye."

[7]Aikiro ijatatzi iva. [8]Poña ikantzi, "Tsika nonkanterika neentsiteve?" [9]Poña ikinkishiriaka pava, ikantzi, "Novashiñiirita." [10]Ivitsikakiniri aparoni iviari, ipakiri, ikantziri, "Notomi, piri."

[11]Iraki, ipakiri pashini, pashini ipakiri, ikaratzi mava. [12]Ari okaratzi ipakiri, shinkitaka, ikimita iroñaaka tampatzika. [13]Ikantziri, "Notomi, pimaye." [14]Maajeetaki.

[15]Poña ikinkishiriaka pava ikantzi, "Tsika nompiirika iroñaaka yoka notomipayeka? [16]Iyoka nintavakia nompiavakiri shaa vantana, ikanta antarite iraikipaye, oshitovapintsakiyetaki iraiki, okanta ivantayetaka." [17]Inoshikakiniri, itsopakiniri, iminkiakiniri aka, ishetakikika, irotaki ishetakitajari. [18]Poña itasonkakiri, ikantakiri, "Afuu, shaa pimpiya

iroñaaka. [19]Samapakana pivari pirintzite, iroñaaka pivajiari mani, katsitoripaye, irotaki pinkiyantyarori pishetaki, arive." [20]Poña ivasakiriajiri. [21]Itzimpatakiniri iroñaaka ivante, itzimpatsovakitakiniri, añaajeetziri shaa iroñaaka saikatsiri kirinka, añiiriri ikantatsovakitzita. [22]Pava tzimpatakiniri pairani, okantzi ñaantsi iroñaaka, pava tzimpatakiniri, ikantzi, "Afuu, shaa pimpiya." [23]Ipiakiri pava.

[24]Poña yaminaki nariatya shima, ipitariatzitaka. [25]Ivasakiriajiri, ikantzi, "Notomi, pintzinai."

[26]Yaminakiniri itsarateki, iñaakiro ivatsa atziri, yatzirivatsate, ivakeniri jaka. [27]Añiiri shimaranki akaranki iitokiranki, ñaakiro yatzirivatsate. [28]Ivari atziri, ivakiniri aka. [29]Ari ikimitakiri jetari, ivakiniri aisatzi jaka. [30]Ijataki pava ikantziri, "Irotaki osheetye, notomi. [31]Pimpiirinte, tsame pijate pinkaatya, pimpishinkiriajiata, shinkitakami, pimpishinkiriajiata."

[32]Iri intakaro pava, itsitziyaki nijaaki, *tsapon*, inoshikaki mapi okaakitapaki otsapiaki. [33]Poña ikantakiri itomini, "Notomi, pimitatyera avirokakia iroñaaka, nokimitaka naaka nomitaka." [34]Mitanaka shima, itsitonkapakaro iroñaaka mapi ivanteki. [35]Irotaki añaantariri shima ipiatonokivaita irirori ikantatonokivaita.

[36]Poña ikantakiri, "Afuu, aviroka pimpiya shima, ari pisaikatye nijaaki ivajiamita pirintzitepaye, okaratzi pivakari avirori."

[37]Ari ikimitari jetari. [38]Mianaka jetari, ari itsirikapaka mapiki. [39]Iro añaantariri ikantatonatzita jetari.

[40]"Ari pinkimitajiari pimpiajia jetari, ari pinkiaji mapitapiki, pirintzite okaratzi pivajeetari pairani. [41]Ari yaminajimi, ivajiami avirori."

[42]Ari otsonka, opiapaja iroñaaka okaratzi ivakari pairani. [43]Avajari shima iroñaaka, añaantari akovityeri avari shima, jetari. [44]Ari otsonkapakari kinkitsarentsi.

¹We will talk about somebody. ²Long ago our elders told about him, they called him Pava. ³There was Pava who was their lord, who made the earth. ⁴Pava had three sons, and they were eating their brothers, as we shall say, *chupadoras* (small fish species), *carachamas* (fish species), and then those called anteaters. ⁵They say, they ate a lot of their fellow men. ⁶The father was saying to them in vain, "My sons, it is enough that you have been eating your brothers."

⁷They continued to go [hunting] and eating [humans]. ⁸Then Pava said, "What shall I do to my children?" ⁹Then Pava gave some thought to it and said, "I will entrap them." ¹⁰He made a drink, gave it to one son, and said to him, "Have a drink, son."

¹¹He drank, and Pava gave it to another, the other son drank it; he gave it to all three. ¹²He gave it to all of them, and they got drunk, [when] it was around midday. ¹³Pava said to his sons, "Sleep, my sons." ¹⁴They fell asleep.

¹⁵Then Pava gave it some thought and said, "What shall I transform these sons of mine into? ¹⁶I will begin with this one, I will transform him into an anteater, because he has big teeth, his teeth protrude forward, he eats with them." ¹⁷He pulled his son's teeth, pulled them out with the roots, and inserted them here, into his nails, these are the nails the anteater has had since then. ¹⁸Then he blew on him and said, "Afuu, you will turn into an anteater now. ¹⁹I'm fed up with you eating your brothers, now you'll eat bullet ants, small ants, with these nails you will dig for them well."

²⁰Then Pava made his son wake up. ²¹He elongated his mouth, he elongated his snout, [that's why] we see anteaters downstream, we see that they have long snouts. ²²Pava elongated them, as the Book [the Bible] says, Pava elongated the snout and said, "Afuu, you will turn into an anteater." ²³Pava converted him.

²⁴Then he saw that Chupadora was lying with spread-eagled legs. ²⁵He made his son wake up and said, "My son, get up."

²⁶He looked in his son's bag and saw the meat of a person, human flesh, and he placed it here [points to his forehead]. ²⁷[That's why] we see it on Chupadora's head here, you've seen it, human flesh. ²⁸His son ate people, and Pava placed the meat here. ²⁹He did the same to Carachama, he also placed it here [points to his forehead]. ³⁰He went [up to his son] and said, "It is getting dark, my son. ³¹Get up, let's go and bathe, you'll sober up, you are drunk, you'll sober up."

³²Pava began [bathing in the river], he dove into the water, *tsapon* (the splashing action produced by a heavy object), and pulled out a stone near the riverbank. ³³Then he said to his son, "My son, now you'll jump too, like I jumped." ³⁴Chupadora jumped and smashed his mouth against the stone. ³⁵That's why we see Chupadora with the transformed mouth, it has a massive mouth.

³⁶Then Pava said, "Afuu, you will convert into a *chupadora*, you will live in the water, and your brothers will eat you, exactly like you ate them before."

³⁷Pava did the same to Carachama. ³⁸Carachama jumped and stuck to the stone. ³⁹That's why it has a thick mouth now.

⁴⁰ "You'll transform into a *carachama* and will stay under the stones. ⁴¹Your brothers, whom you ate before, will be looking for you to eat you."

⁴²So it ended, all [the food supply] vanished, what they [the brothers] ate long ago. ⁴³We eat fish, but there is lack of *chupadoras* and *carachamas*. ⁴⁴This is where my story ends.

TWO

Okoñaatantakari kaniri

(How Sweet Manioc Appeared)

Alberto Pérez Espinoza

[1]Nonkinkitsatakotero aparoni kooya mairentzinkaro, imairentaitziro ovankoshiki. [2]Pairani tekatsi kaniri. [3]Kaatsi kaniri, ijatzi iri yaminayetzi intaina, itsipatanakaro iina, ipokaji sheeteni. [4]Ari ikantatya kitaiteriki, yamayetaji kapicheeni ivavaityari tsika opaityarika ivarite.

[5]Aparojatzini iroñaaka ishitovashitakiro tsinaro, antarite tsinaro. [6]Yatziritzimotakiro kooyara ipankoshitzirira ovankoshiki. [7]Yatziritzimotakiro, yamaki kaniri. [8]Antaro imotyatsatetzi. [9]Ikantziro, "Kooya, paatzikena aka nomotyakika."
[10]Aatzikakiri, shitovanaki kaniri, akishirintsipaye.

[11]Arika ijate iri antamiki, ari ikantatya ipokapintzi.

[12]Iroñaaka piyanaja kitaiteriki. [13]Iniro otsipatari oimi ojajeetzi amini ovarite ovajeetyari, ikantziri pairani, tekatsi kaniri. [14]Ari ikantatya ipipiyata, ipokaji pashini kitaiteri, yamaji kaniri. [15]Aisatzi ikantapaji, "Paatzikajena," shitovanaji kaniripaye, kaniri, okaratzi iroñaaka ivaitari kaniripaye.

[16]Poña pashiniki kitaiteri, aisatzi ipiyaja, yamaki iroñaaka ovatzi impankiyeteri, onkantya ivajeetyari. [17]Iroñaaka jaitetzi iniro aminaji ovaritepaye antamiki. [18]Ojatzi intaina iniroraja. [19]Te ojate, osaikaki omanaka oñaantyari iroñaaka amatsiri iyaniri. [20]Omanaka. [21]Opiyaka, opiyaka. [22]Ari opianaka

iyaniri, tekatsitaji kaniri iroñaaka. ²³Kantzimaitacha ipankitanaki ovato, shookamashini kaniri iroñaaka.

²⁴Poña okantziro ishinto, "Kooya, paitakama pokatsiri amayetzirori kaniri?" ²⁵Te onkinkitsate. ²⁶Ikantakiro, "Airo pikamantziro piniro, arika pinkamantaki, ari ompiajia kaniri, tekatsi avajia."

²⁷Te iroñaaka, ipankitakira, tzimaki aajatzita kaniri.

²⁸Ojataki iroñaaka, okantakiro ishinto, "Nojatatye antoo antamiki." ²⁹Amatavitakiro ishinto, manaka. ³⁰Poñaashitaka, opiyaja oñaapatziri shiramparira, ikinkitsatakavaitziro ishinto. ³¹Ari opianaka kaniri. ³²Te impokaje shiramparira, pianaja tsitsiri, jataji yatzirivitakara ovakeraini.

³³Poña ipokaji oimi iponaajara antamiki. ³⁴Yaminavitapajari kitaiteriki, te impokaji, tekatsitaji kaniri, tekatsi ivajia. ³⁵Ikantziro iina, "Paita pimishiyantakariri shirampariranki amapintatsiriranki kaniri? ³⁶Iroñaaka kaatsi avajia." ³⁷Ipasavaitakiro iina. ³⁸Ikantziro, "Aviroka kantakashitakaro, te añaajiri shiramparirianki amapintatsiri iyaniri."

³⁹Ari okaratzi nokinkitsatakaimiri, pasonki.¹

I will tell about a young woman in seclusion who was placed in a menarche hut. ²In the old times, there was no sweet manioc. ³There was no sweet manioc, and the father would go out to look for food in a distant area, together with his wife, and both would come back home in the darkness. ⁴So it was every day that they would bring a little bit of something to eat.

⁵One day a grasshopper, a big grasshopper appeared. ⁶He turned into a human being in front of the girl, in the secluded area of her menarche hut. ⁷He turned into a human being and brought her sweet manioc. ⁸He had a big rounded stomach. ⁹The Grasshopper man said to her, "Woman, step on my stomach,

here." [10]She did, and sweet manioc, lots of grilled sweet manioc came out.

[11]When her father would go to the forest, the Grasshopper man would always come. [12]The Grasshopper man would return during the day. [13]The mother together with the father would go to the forest to look for food so that they all could eat, as it was said, there was no sweet manioc [in the old times]. [14]So it was, the Grasshopper man would always come back and bring sweet manioc. [15]He would say, "Step on me," and sweet manioc would come out, which has been eaten since then.

[16]Then, one day he [the Grasshopper man] came back and brought seedlings of sweet manioc, so that they could plant them and eat the crop. [17]Now, the girl's father went to the forest to look for food. [18]The mother went far away. [19]But she didn't go: she stayed and hid to find out who brings sweet manioc [to them]. [20]She hid. [21]She would come back repeatedly [to the menarche hut]. [22]Sweet manioc disappeared, there was no manioc. [23]Nonetheless, they planted it, and it sprouted.

[24]She asked her daughter, "Woman, who comes to bring sweet manioc?" [25]The daughter didn't tell her. [26]The Grasshopper man had told her, "Don't advise your mother; if you advise her, sweet manioc will disappear, there will be nothing to eat."

[27]Nowadays, it doesn't [matter because] when they planted it, sweet manioc came into existence.

[28]The mother went up to the daughter and said to her, "I will go far away to the forest." [29]She deceived her daughter and hid. [30]Afterward, she returned [to the menarche hut] and saw a man who was conversing with her daughter. [31]This is how sweet manioc disappeared. [32]He didn't return, that man, because he turned into a grasshopper and went away, [but] he had been a person before.

³³Then the woman's husband came back from the forest. ³⁴They looked for the Grasshopper man, but he didn't come, and there was no manioc, and nothing to eat. ³⁵He said to his wife, "Why did you drive away the man who was always bringing sweet manioc? ³⁶Now there is nothing to eat." ³⁷He beat up his wife. ³⁸He said to her, "You are guilty, because now we don't see the man who was always bringing sweet manioc."

³⁹This is all that I have told you, thanks.

THREE

Okoñaatantari paamari

(How Fire Came into Existence)

Ruth Quillatupa Lopez

[1]Iroñaaka nokinkitsatakotavakero okanta pairani otzimantakari avaamaritepaye. [2]Iroñaaka aparoni ashaninka ikamaki oime, pairani te añeero posporopaye. [3]Iroñaaka osaikavaitzi ashinonkavaita apaniroini. [4]Oñaatziro aparoni chorito opokaki, osatevoinataro omantsaki. [5]Iroñaakakia opokapaji, okantziro, "Otyankatyana isha, okantzi, 'Paanakiniro paamari, antaroite ashinonkaka.'" [6]Iroñaaka okantziro, "Niroka, otyankakemi pósporo poisantajiarori paamari. [7]Airo pitsivakero, ari pikantaitatyeyani poishero, otsivakapitsatzimikari."

[8]Irotaki iroñaakaja oisakiniro paamari. [9]Ari okasavaiveta oyaniri, antzi oviari, atzirintakarira ivaitzirira, iroñaaka oviari, eh, kirankaitaitaki, okasavaitakirira kirapetokirini oyaniri.

[10]Okanta, okanta iroñaaka ipokashitakiro antarite pakitsa. [11]Okantziri otomira, "Ñaakero, chapinki nokantzimi, ari asaikaki kameetsa. [12]Iroñaaka tsika okanta avavaitaja?" [13]Iroñaakaja otsivakajero ovaamaritera.

[14]Poñaashitaka ipokashitakero patyankori. [15]Pokake iroñaaka inijakero, yamakiniro inchakii. [16]Oñaakiri ikinapaki kityonkari iitsari, te oñaapinterita. [17]Iroñaaka ipokakera, ikantzirokia, "Airo pimasontotzi ashaninka, pichenkite mapi, ari omorikaki. [18]Pintye ampee, aririka pinteyake ampee,

paroviro, poñaashitaka paake inchakiira potsotzi."¹⁹Irotaki inijairi. ²⁰Ikantzi, ²¹"Incharanki, pamini, ari piyoteri." ²²Yaake, yaavitatakiro, ikantziro, *shoki, shoki, shoki, shoki, shoki!*²³Paamaritanaki iroñaaka irora ampeera, irotaki ovaamaritetajari.

²⁴Iroñaaka irora ovakirora chapinkiranki choritora ovaamarite, irotaki añaantarori choritoranki aka, omorikiranki itapinomaki, irotaki ovaamarite. ²⁵Iroñaaka patyankori, "Tsame amirokavaki." ²⁶Ikantakiro ampeeki, iñaatziro omorikanaki.

²⁷Irotaki oyotantayetarori aparopaye ashaninkapayera iroñaaka.

¹I will tell you how fire appeared in the old times. ²There was one fellow woman, her husband died, and they didn't have matches in the old times. ³Someone saw her suffering. ⁴The widow saw the Blue-headed parrot woman come, with her head being covered with her *cushma* (traditional robe). ⁵The Blue-headed parrot woman came and said, "I was sent by your grandmother, and she said, 'Take this match to her because she is suffering a lot.'" ⁶So the Blue-headed parrot woman said to the widow, "Here it is, she sent you matches to make a fire. ⁷Don't put it out, you should keep it burning, so that no one extinguishes it."

⁸She lit a fire for her. ⁹So the widow boiled her manioc and made manioc beer, and because the fire was from someone who used to be a person, who was killed, the food was reddish, and the pieces of cooked manioc were red.

¹⁰Some time passed, and the Big-hawk man came. [When the Big-hawk man came, the Blue-headed parrot woman put out the fire because she didn't want other people to use it.] ¹¹The widow said to her son, "You've seen it, recently I told you that we were fine. ¹²How are we going to eat now?" ¹³Her fire was extinguished.

¹⁴Then the Squirrel man came. ¹⁵He came to teach the widow and brought wood sticks. ¹⁶The widow saw the Squirrel man walk, dressed in a red *cushma*; she had never seen him before. ¹⁷When he came, he said to her, "Don't be dumb, our fellow woman, you have to strike the stone [with another stone], and it [the cotton] will burn. ¹⁸You will spread a thick piece of cotton fabric, dry it in the sun, and then take an annatto stick." ¹⁹This is what he taught her. ²⁰He said, ²¹"Well, look, this is how you will learn." ²²He took a stick, put it between his feet, and rubbed the stick with his hands, *shoki, shoki, shoki, shoki* (rubbing action). ²³The cotton [which was positioned below the stick] caught fire [from the hot stick]; it was what lit the fire.

²⁴That's why we can now see a red area here that the blue-headed parrot species has [under its tail feathers]—it was the flame of the fire that burned it. ²⁵The Squirrel man said, "Let's rub it [again]." ²⁶He did it with cotton, and the wood went aflame.

²⁷That's why some of our fellow men know it [how to make fire].

FOUR

Pava Apinka

(God Apinka)

Luis Mauricio Rosa

[1]Nonkinkitsatakoteri pava Apinka, ikanta pairani ipokanaki pava Apinka, isaikaveta aka. [2]Isaiki, iyomitakantanakiro okaratzi avarika, avari, amonkotzi, okaratzi antzirika iroñaaka, maaroni. [3]Poñaaka ikinavaitzi, iyomitantakiro maaroni okaratzika aka kipatsi. [4]Iro ariitzimotapakiri inkamantyari, iñaakiri pava ikantaitziri Apontsiki, iyanini atziri ikaratzini aka. [5]Iyoka ikantaitziri pava Apontsiki, matsi inatzi, matsi, itsikatakari pava Apinka, ipiratakari. [6]Yamonkotzi, yamonkotzi, yamonkotzi, isamapakari. [7]Ipoñaaka isamapakarija, isamavetapakari pava Apinkaja, yamonkatajiniri kapichiini. [8]Ipavetajari, ookantapajari jaka iniyorinteki. [9]Yamonkarira ishiko, yaaki, ityavantetakaro, ari okantanakiri, ikamarankanaki, *ajak, ajak, eje, eje*. [10]Ikantzi, "Pamakina irora iroka kitamarori, noshetyari aka." [11]Ishetaka, ishetaka, ikanta, ikanta, kamaki. [12]Kamakiraja ikantzi, "Naaka te nokame, airo nokamapirotzi, nojatatye, nojate jenoki, naye irora pañaantajiari avirori. [13]Airo pikinkivaritanta, nojatatye." [14]Jaitetaki, aaj, koraketaintsi pashini jevatakantzirori. [15]Ikitatya atziripaye, ikantzirija, "Kamaki yoka, tsame akitateri, shitzitaki. [16]Arika ishitzitanakirika, airo akantaji ankitatajiri

intsompainta." ¹⁷Poña ikitaitakeri pava Apinka intsompainta.
¹⁸Irotaki ityakovetakarira, ityantyariri maaroni, ikaimanaki
pava Apinka, "Pivitamoriakotaina, uj!"

¹⁹Ikiyajeevetaja, *chek, chek, chek, chek,* ikiyajeeveta, *chek,
chek.* ²⁰Iro iviravetaja inijantapajiari, iro yaminajeetantapajiari,
se quedó seco, ari ikamanaji pava Apinka, piyanaja, piyanaja,
ikamanaji. ²¹*Pero* te ikamaperote, ijajatzi, jataji jenoki. ²²Ikanta-
naki, "Ari pinkantaitatyeya, pintyavakaiya avirori. ²³Pikama-
kirika, pikitatavakaiya intsompainta."

²⁴Ari okantari, ikantanaki ashitairi, okanta iroñaaka.
²⁵Akamakirika arori, akitatavakakai intsompainta. ²⁶Iro
yookanakiri ashitairi, iñaani. ²⁷Iroñaaka akantzi, "Ookashi-
tyari, jenkarini shitzirini ishitzinka." ²⁸Airo ashintziri, ari
okantari, arika ashitzitanaki, airo okantaji akitatavakajia.
²⁹Aritapaki.

¹I will tell about god Apinka, how he came and stayed here in
the past.

²He was living here and he taught [us] everything: to eat [cer-
tain foods], to chew coca, to do all that we do these days, everything. ³After he taught us everything that there was in this land,
he traveled. ⁴A day arrived when Apinka was about to die, and
he saw a god called Apontsiki, a person of short stature. ⁵He was
called god Apontsiki, and he was a witch, a witch whom god
Apinka adopted, who became his pet.

⁶God Apinka chewed coca for a long while, then he got
bored. ⁷After he got bored, he chewed coca leaves a little bit.
⁸God Apontsiki gave Apinka coca, [because] his throat hurt him.
⁹When Apinka was chewing his powdered lime, which he had
taken out and thrown in his mouth, he began vomiting, *ahak,
ahak, ahak* (vomiting action).

¹⁰He said, "Bring me a piece of white cloth, I will wipe it off

here." [11]He kept wiping it off and then died. [12]When he died, he said, "I didn't die, I won't truly die, I am going, I will go to heaven, I will obtain that for you to live too. [13]So that you don't get old, I am going."

[14]He was gone, but another leader was coming. [15]They were going to bury dead people and said, "Oh, this one is dead, let's bury him, he stinks. [16]If he stinks [a great deal], we won't be able to bury him in the ground." [17]Then they buried god Apinka in the ground. [18]When they had completely filled the grave with soil, god Apinka groaned, "Turn me over [in my coffin]!" [He was buried face down.]

[19]They excavated the grave again, *chek chek* (action of digging out soft soil). [20]When they had nearly reached the level where he was buried and were about to see him, it was dry there, but he died again, he became dead again. [21]Nevertheless, he didn't truly die, he went to heaven. [22]He said, "This is what you will do: you'll bury each other. [23]When you die, you will bury each other in the ground."

[24]This is what our Lord said, this is how it is [done] at present. [25]When we die, we bury each other in the ground. [26]This our Lord left to us, his word. [27]Now we say, "Let's dispose of him, it gives off stinking odor, his stinking body." [28]We won't be together, so it is, when we stink, we won't be buried. [29]Here it ends.

FIVE

Apinka

*Bertha Rodríguez de Caleb and
Abdias Caleb Quinchori*

[1]–Ankinkitsatakoteri ikantakota Apinka. [2]Iñaavakiri,
iñaaitavakiri arika orave iya, impaiteri ivarite iyoyetaitziniri
osheki ivari. [3]Iroma ikarajeetaiyenira iratziritera impaiteri
kapicheenipatsaini, aparoni piratoki. [4]Itsonkiro kaniri, vatsatsi
arika impaitakiri, ontzimatye iyari orave, inkimpoya-
vaitero pashiniki kitaiteri, irora aparoni *semana* itsonkatan-
taiyeni ivarite. [5]Ari okantakoyetziri kamayetaintsiri osaropaye
irori. [6]Ari okaratzi akimakotziriri ikantakota iyora Apinka.

[7]–Nosaroni okantzirori, "Nosaikimotakiri naari ivankoki
Apinka, nopishivantakiri, nokotsivintziri." [8]Aajatzi okantzi
pairani arika irovanajiarika, impaitakiri osheki kaniri,
impaitakiri antarite vatsatsi, irima iratziritepaye irovakia
kapicheeni vatsatsi, opoñaanaka osheki iyaniri. [9]Irovakia
kapicheeni irojatzi intsonkantakiaro iyaniri, ivajeri ivatsatsite
apapakoroni kitaiterikipaye. [10]Arika okantziri nosaroni
oñiiri irori osaikimotantakariri irojatzita ivankarotapaki;
antaroperotaki oñaakiri irojatzi inkamantakia iyoka Apinka.

[11]Ikamakira, oñaakiri iroka, okantzi, yaitanakiri Kishitariki, ari ikitaitakiri, yaitanakiniri osheki iirikite, ishiyetari javo
ikarayetzira. [12]Okantzi, itaromaitakiniri, ikiyashitakiri irojatzi
oviraka niyankira. [13]Inkiyakero intsompoiki oviraka niyanki
omorora inareetakiri, iroñaaka inariakiriri irirorikia jeñokini.

¹⁴Iritaki ishitashitakiri iirikite. ¹⁵Aka tonkariki, oinijavitanaro, okantzi, Kishitariki, nokantzi, ari ikitaitakiri iyora Apinka, ovakerani ikamaki. ¹⁶Te ayotakoteri iroñaaka saikatsirika terika yaakeritaima aminayetziririra kiriki.

¹⁷–Ishipañoripaye?

¹⁸–Ikiyakotainiri, ikoyeyetainiri. ¹⁹Irima irirentzi kitatainchari tyonkarikiniki ipaita Marinkama, irirentzi Juan Santos Atahualpa, Apinkatatsiri, akantziri añaaniki Apinka, Inka Juan Santos Atahualpa.

²⁰–Kaacharinta, Marinkama irotaki anta okantavitakari Ashiropanko, ivetsikiro kotsiro, ivetsikiro shacha, ivetsikiro iveratotepaye, kovitzi ivantayetari, ivantari. ²¹Poñaanakakia noshaninkapaye poñaachari kirinka amatsiri ivitzipaye, tsimeri vaneenkantzi, ikampiatzirori ivetsikanipaye, iyoka poñiinkaripaye. ²²Yame ivitzi, vaneenkantzi, ikampiatziro saviri, shacha, kovitzi, iveratote ipayetziri, irotaki ikampiatzirori ivetsikirika. ²³Kameetsa ivaneenkatziro ivanko itsipatairo vitzitsipaye, vaneenkantzi. ²⁴Ari ikantari.

²⁵Iroñaaka ivankari antavaijeetatzirira, ikoyejeetatziri ivankari, kaari ñeeroni kooya; ivankaropaye irori kaari ñeerini shirampari o omayempiteri, ojateta kameetsa antavairi. ²⁶Iroma arika oñaapairi shirampari kooya, shirampari irirori iñaakerorika kooya, yantavaijeetzira, arika intaakero airo oshitove kameetsa, okaratzi irantavairira. ²⁷Ari okantari ovakerani aka osaikinta tsika ipaitaranki antakantayetzirori iririntzi Apinkatatsiri, ipaita Marinkama. ²⁸Ari ikitatari iroñaaka tonkarikinta. ²⁹Ari ikitatari iririntzi.

³⁰Ari okantari ovakerani aroka irojatzitaima opiantanaka. ³¹Ipokapakera yora virakochapaye, yaapitsatantakariri iirikite, ari itsonkari, ipiapaka, te ayotanajero tsika ikantanairi iirikite. ³²Ari ovirapakari. ³³Ari ovakerani ikantzi irirori, ikantavitakari, ikantzi, "Eero pikoshitzi, eero pimayempitzi, eero pipiyatsata,

tsame antavaite!" [34]Kooyapaye ovametziro okirikakairo, irotaki ante arori. [35]Ari ikantari ashaninka, irojatzi ipokantakia iyoka virakochapaye, kitamarantzipaye, ari ovirapakari, itsonkayetantakariri, ipiantakaririka iroñaaka. [36]Yaaitapaintziri irirori, yoisoyetanakiri, ari overapakari.

[37]Te noyotanajero overanaka ojatanakinta, ari ovirapakari, ari ovira. [38]Okamantanaro naari nosaro osaikimotzirora ovakera eentsitapakini, ivankarotantakari irojatzi oñaakeri ikamaki.

[39]Ari itsonkapakari. [40]Ari ikantari iroñaaka añaaventziri iroñaaka Apinkatatsiri.

[1]–We will tell about Apinka. [2]When people saw him, when he would eat, he would be given food, and they would serve a lot of food to him. [3]In contrast, when all his people would gather to have a meal, he would give them meager amounts of food, on one plate. [4]They finish yuca, and if he gives meat to them, they have to save the [rationed] food for the next day, to last for a week. [5]So her deceased grandmothers told us about him. [6]This is what we heard about Apinka.

[7]–My deceased grandmother told me, "I lived in Apinka's presence in his house and cleaned and cooked for him." [8]She also said that in the old times, he was given a lot of yuca and a lot of meat, but his people ate meager amounts of meat and a lot of yuca. [9]They ate little meat; when they eat it with yuca, they eat their [rationed] meat for five days. [10]This is what my grandmother said, she saw Apinka when she was growing up, and when she became a young woman, she saw him die.

[11]When he died, she said that she saw him being taken to Kishitariki [Mariscal Cáceres], and he was buried there, together with his mass of gold, which looked like soap bars. [12]She said they placed the gold orderly for him, until they filled the grave

halfway. ¹³They kept filling the grave with the gold until they reached the middle of the grave, where they laid Apinka on top of it. ¹⁴His gold was spread in the grave. ¹⁵She explained it to me that Apinka was buried over there, in the uplands, she said, in Kishitariki [Mariscal Cáceres], when he died. ¹⁶We don't know whether the gold is there, or it might have been taken by those who were looking for it.

¹⁷–By Spaniards?

¹⁸–They dug it out and took it. ¹⁹But his brother, called Marinkama, is buried close by, in the hills, the brother of Juan Santos Atahualpa, Apinka, we say in our language, Apinka.

²⁰–Where this smoke is, this is where Marinkama, over there in what is called Ashiropanko (the Iron House), made machetes, axes, dishes, and pots for eating. ²¹My fellow men from the downstream area would come and bring feathers, feathers of beautiful birds, and the visitors would exchange them for fabricated things. ²²They were bringing feathers and colorful things and exchange them for machetes, axes, pots, and dishes, which they gave to them; this they exchanged for what they fabricated. ²³They adorned their homes nicely with colorful things and feathers. ²⁴So it was this way.

²⁵Young people who worked [at the forge] were selected; those who wouldn't see women or girls, and girls [who] wouldn't see young men or be promiscuous, so that they would work properly. ²⁶But when a woman sees a man, and a man sees a woman, when they work there, when they melt iron, it wouldn't turn out well, all that they were making. ²⁷So it was this way when Apinka's brother lived here, the one who made them work. ²⁸He is buried in the hills. ²⁹There his brother is buried.

³⁰So it was this way until it was lost. ³¹When outsiders came, they took away the gold, it all ended, it disappeared, and we don't know where Apinka's gold is. ³²This is where it ended. ³³He

would say in the past, "Don't steal, don't fornicate, don't disobey, let's work!" ³⁴Women learned to weave fabric, this is what we would do. ³⁵So they were this way, my fellow men, until outsiders and whites came who ended it all, so that it would all disappear now. ³⁶They took him, he was trussed up, it all ended.

³⁷I don't know where I am going with this, this is all. ³⁸My grandmother informed me about it, since she lived in his presence when she was a child, and when she was a young woman, she saw him die.

³⁹Here it ends. ⁴⁰So it is, what we are saying now about this Apinka.

SIX

Apinka

Elías Meza Pedro, Gregorio Santos Pérez,
and Livia Julio de Quinchori

[1]–Pikimakoventziro pairani aviroka pava Apinka?
[2]–Te noyote naari.
[3]–Ovakera peentsitapakini?
[4]–Ovakera neentsitapakini pairani mikiyashiranki ovakira noñaapakiri ivira yairishetotsitapakaini, ivira aka. [5]Noñaajirika naari noshiritajiari Apinka? [6]Kamayetaji intakantayetarori ashitarori inampi jaka.
[7]–Kamayetaji?
[8]–Kaatsitaji iroñaaka. [9]Nopokaki ovakira neentsivaitzini, tsika noyotajiri naari Apinkakia?
[10]–Tsika piñaapakirika pitsipavitari inavita kaminkarayeni? [11]Tsika piñaakirika janta, pipoñaanta o aka piñaapakiri?
[12]–Noñaapakiri jaka, yorinasatzi inatzi.
[13]–Papá, paita ikantaitziri "yorina"?
[14]–Tema irotaki ovairo parinini ikantaitziro "yorinani."
[15]–Tema maatsitaima pairani ikantaitantarori "yorinani."
[16]–Te ayotero aroka.
[17]–Irotaki nokantapintzi naari, te noyotero naari paitataima opaitantari "yorinani." [18]Te noñiiri naari Apinka, nokimashitaja naari. [19]Piyotzimajante aviroka, tema irotaki piniro iro saikavitaincha aka, naakamaja nosaikatatzi kirinka.
[20]–Akama isaikapaintzi Apinkatatsiri, papá? [21]Tsikama isaikapaintzi pikimakoventzirika?

²²–Apinka isaiki pairani anta, intatzikironta, Zona Patria, Zona Patriatakinta, jantoo. ²³Ari isaiki pairani ikantaitziri Apinka. ²⁴Pavisanaki pairani otapikinta yorinaki, ari te piyotero?

²⁵–Te noñiiri naari Apinka.

²⁶–Irotaki ikantziriranki visantzinkari.

²⁷–Je, je, osheki ivisantzi, je, je, irive.

²⁸–Tema irotaki ikantziri asheninka, "pava inatzi", irashi ashaninka pairani?

²⁹–Je, je, iritaki, iritakitaima, iritaki ivavani asheninkapaye pairani. ³⁰Yapototzirira irirori, yora Apinka, iritaki ankantero pinkatsari, pinkatsari inatzi, maatsi osheki yatzirite. ³¹Aririka inintanaji *fiesta*, intyankeri yatzirite ijate inkovintsate.

³²–Ikantziri irora yamampavaitya?

³³–Je, je, ikantziri yamampavaitya. ³⁴Inkintayete kemari, maniro, maaroni piratsipaye, iritaki impiyotzimoitekia iyora Apinkara, impiyotzimoite. ³⁵Arika inintakante *fiesta*, ikantziri, inkanteri yatzirite, "Tsame ante *fiesta*." ³⁶Iroñaaka intyankero kooyapaye, "Pinkotsite," onkotsitake. ³⁷Arika ontsonkapakia onkotsijeetakiraja, inkaimake, inkante, "Tsame pimpoke, tsame avajeetya." ³⁸Iro kantacha eero ava osheki anta. ³⁹Ari impavitakai vatsatsi, kimotari, kantzimaitacha iroka kapicheeni ampitsai.

⁴⁰–Ampitsatye kapicheeni?

⁴¹–Intaani kaniri irotaki ayari osheki, iroma irora vatsatsi kapicheeni ampitsai. ⁴²Arika ampitsapante kimotaini, maatsi aminanatatsirirakia, "Itsainkatzi iyoka," inkaimiteri iyora ivinkatsiriterakia. ⁴³Pokanakirakia, yakanakirika, ayetapaki yatsatakotari. ⁴⁴Maatsi *puente*, areetapaka *puente*ki, poña yaanakiro. ⁴⁵Ikantakirika, "Kooya, inkantavakiri, otsainkatzi, iroka pishintaiyeni. ⁴⁶Te ontsotyero maaro pikantakantziri. ⁴⁷Ari omposhinitanakai kaniri oshamokotzitakara." ⁴⁸Ikantzi,

"Antzishi kapicheeni machaki."[49]Ari ivisaitakiro, pashini okinashitanaka, pashini okantashitanakia.

[50]–Shei.

[51]–Ovakera añaavitaroni oshiroshirontata, ivaitakiro.

[52]Aajatzi shirampari irirori. [53]Aririka onkotsivaite kemari, osheki vatsatsi, kapicheeni ampishi, kapicheeni antzishi, eero ava osheki. [54]Ari ikantari pairani.

[55]–Ari itsonkajiri ivajiarikia? [56]Apaniroinikia?

[57]–Iriro iva osheki, iritaki ovajiarini apaniroinikia, aavatsari inatzi. [58]Intaani ikantakantzirokia kapicheeni.

[59]–Pivishiri irirori!

[60]–Iriro ovachari kimota.

[61]–Oh, iyamakiave!

[62]–Vashiritenikia . . .

[63]–Ikanta irotaki itsonkia ashaninka ivisavaitziri.

[64]–Eje, imitya!

[65]–Poñaaka maatsi aparoni . . .

[66]–Pivishiri irirove!

[67]–Asheninka poñaachari kirinka, ivisaitakirikia isheninka . . .

[68]–Aj, isheninka.

[69]–Ikimakovintakiri, ikantzikia, "Kaatsima piyacharini, imaperotatya pinkatsaritzi. [70]Nojateta." [71]Pokaki. [72]Maatsi yompatzirite.

[73]–Pinkimisantaperota iroñaaka!

[74]–Ikantzirikia yompatzirite, "Nopokashitzi piyokani." [75]Ikantzirive, "Pijatatye anta, iri yotakotziro kompatziri, pijate, inkaimite." [76]Ikantziri, "Je, eero ivisavakinakia," ikimakovintzirira, osheki ivisantzi.

[77]–Iyo!

[78]–Je, pokanaki, ikantziri, "Tsikarika ikantavakimi, pimpiyatanakiari." [79]Pokaki iroñaaka, ikaratzi pokashitziriri, ontzi-

matye intyerovashitapakiari yamanirikia.[80]Ipokakira, tera yamaniri. [81]Ikantziri, "Ityankatyana piyompatzirite. [82]Nonintzi piyokani," ikantzi.

[83]Kasayacha ivisamento. [84]Ikitsatyara iitsari kitamarori. [85]Yaanakiro ivisamento, ikantziri, "Niro noyokanika." [86]Ikanta asheninkara iyotatzirora ikominki, yairikitari, *shepik*! [87]Ikantzi, tzimatsi iviani ovira aka, antarove asheninkarakia poñaachari kirinka. [88]Irojatzi ikantataitziro iroñaaka. [89]Imitsiriakiro iviamenira, yoisotantakari iviamitsara, yoisotzimaintari itapiki ivianitarokiara. [90]Ari yaaki, ishinkotakiri.

[91]–Iye!

[92]–Ikimitakantakari ashinkotziriranki sharo. [93]Ivatsikakotanakiri yashitakorokira. [94]Pokajikia iroñaaka iyora ishinkotakirira, ikantziri iyompatzirite, "Te?" [95]"Teve. [96]Ivisavitakana." [97]"Te pimpiyatanakiarikia?" [98]Ikantzi, "Te, nopiyavitanakari kapicheeni," ari ñaakiro anta ishinkotanakiri, je, je. [99]Ari ikanta, yaminakoitziri, te añiiri ishevate, ikantzi, "Paita antakiriri?" [100]Poña ikantzi, "Intsitya, naminajantaiterita." [101]Ari ikinanaki, iñaapatziri shinkotaka.

[102]–Posataki ishinkotaka.

[103]–Piyaja, ikantapaji, "Teve, ivaitakiri, ishinkotaitakiri." [104]Ikantzi, "Arima, ari ovirakia."

[105]–Itonkaitakiri kemari avirori.

[106]–Tekatsi poyetanajiarini. [107]Ipoyevitajari pashini, ikantzi, "Te." [108]Itsarovatzi, "Te." [109]Iroñaakakia yanintaajaro asheninkapaye, ivavaitakia inintakirinta iyari, ivatsivaitya osheki.

[110]–Intsitya.

[111]–Arika impaitai iroñaaka, arima avapitsantanajia, antsonkatainakiri.

[112]–Tema ari.

[113]–*Kori, kori.*

[114]–Antsonkatainakiri. [115]Ikantzi, yantakotaitzirora terika macha, yantakoshitzirora shinkipaye, piyotakoitacha macha, eje. [116]Ikantaitziri Apinka ari ovira, ishinkotaitakirira. [117]Ari otsonka.

[1]–Did you hear anything on account of Apinka long ago?

[2]–I don't know.

[3]–When you were a child?

[4]–When I was a child, I saw Miqueas [the village's founder] when he was little, of this height. [5]How can I see Apinka or think about him? [6]Those who were the founders of the village are dead.

[7]–Dead?

[8]–They do not exist anymore. [9]I came here as a child, how will I know Apinka?

[10]–Where did you meet your late husband? [11]In the village you came from or here?

[12]–I met him here, he is from Yurinaki.

[13]–Papá, why is it called "yorina"?

[14]–Because of the river's name, "yorinani."

[15]–But there should be a reason why it is called "yorinani."

[16]–We don't know why it is called "yorinani."

[17]–This is what I am saying, I don't know why it is called "yorinani." [18]I haven't seen Apinka, only heard about him. [19]You should know, because your mother comes from this area; in contrast, I am from the downstream area.

[20]–Did Apinka live here, Papá? [21]Did you hear about his presence in this area?

[22]–Apinka lived here long ago, on the other side of the hill, where [the present-day] Zona Patria is, over there. [23]There lived the one who was called Apinka. [24]You passed by the hill's low section awhile ago, where Yurinaki is, don't you know?

[25]–I haven't seen Apinka.

[26]–They say, he cut off people's heads.

[27]–Yes, he was the one who would cut off people's heads, he was the one.

[28]–Was he, as our fellow men say, a god?

[29]–Yes, he was, he was a god of our fellow men in the old times. [30]This Apinka gathered a lot of our fellow men, we will say, he was a supreme chief; he was a supreme chief who had a lot of people. [31]When he wanted a feast, he would send men to hunt.

[32]–They say, they danced?

[33]–Yes, they say, they did. [34]Men will kill tapir, deer, [and other] animals and amass the game in Apinka's presence, they will amass it. [35]When he wanted a feast, he would say to his men, "Let's have a feast." [36]He will send women to cook, and they will cook. [37]When they have finished cooking, he will call out, "Come, let's all eat." [38]Nevertheless, we won't eat a lot. [39]He will give enough meat, but we should tear off a small piece.

[40]–They were having little portions?

[41]–Only yuca we will eat in abundance, but meat—in small portions. [42]If we have a regular-size piece of meat, there are guards who will say, "This one disobeyed," and will call their chief. [43]He will come, if he responds, he will cross the hanging bridge. [44]There was a bridge there, so he arrives, and they will grab a woman. [45]They will say to him, "The woman, they will say, disobeyed, your daughter disobeyed. [46]She didn't comply with what you always say. [47]The yuca will be sweet, when there is a lot of it in the mouth." [48]He says, "If it is beans, we'll eat a little." [49]They will behead her, and other fellow men will be affected [they will be shaken by the scene].

[50]–*Shei* (expression of compassion).

[51]–One moment she was laughing, and at the next moment

she is dead. [52]Also men. [53]When women cooked tapir, there was a lot of meat, but men had little pieces, we shouldn't eat a lot. [54]So it was.

[55]–Will he have all the meat? [56]All by himself?

[57]–He ate a lot, he ate by himself, since he was a glutton. [58]He will make only us eat little.

[59]–Behead him!

[60]–Apinka ate much bigger pieces of meat.

[61]–Oh, *iyamakiave* (expression of surprise)!

[62]–It must have been a sad life for many.

[63]–It went on, as he was going to cull his fellow men by beheading them.

[64]–*Eje* (exclamation of surprise), we'll see!

[65]–Then there was a . . .

[66]–Behead him!

[67]– . . . fellow man who came from the downstream area and whose family member was beheaded.

[68]–*Aj* (affirmative reaction to addressee's statement), his family member.

[69]–He heard about [his family member] and said, "There is nobody whom I let their wrong left unpunished, although he is a supreme chief. [70]I will go." [71]He came [to Apinka's compound]. [72]He had a compadre (a trading partner) there.

[73]–Now, pay attention!

[74]–He said to his compadre, "I came because of your coca leaves." [75]He responded, "Go over there, my compadre [i.e., Apinka] knows [what to do], go and call him out." [76]The visitor said, "All right, will he behead me?" because he had heard that Apinka likes to cut off people's heads.

[77]–*Iyo* (expression of surprise)!

[78]–Yes, he came, and his compadre said, "Whatever he does

to you, don't let him get away with it." ⁷⁹He came, and every-body who comes to see him has to kneel in veneration in front of Apinka. ⁸⁰When the visitor came, he didn't genuflect. ⁸¹He said to Apinka, "Your compadre sent me to you. ⁸²I want your coca," he said.

⁸³Apinka's sword was hanging on the wall. ⁸⁴He was dressed in a white *cushma*. ⁸⁵He took his sword and said, "Here it is, my coca." ⁸⁶Because the visitor knew how to dodge in combat, he grabbed Apinka, *shepik* (action of grabbing a moving entity)! ⁸⁷They say, his bow was this thick, the bow of this fellow man from the downstream area. ⁸⁸They keep practicing with their bows at present. ⁸⁹He bent the bow, secured Apinka's hands together behind his back with the bow's string, and pushed his thick bow into Apinka's anus. ⁹⁰It pierced him like a skewer.

⁹¹–*Iye* (exclamation of surprise)!

⁹²–It pierced him like a skewer we use for roasting agouti on the fire. ⁹³He seated the dead man at the door. ⁹⁴The one who pierced Apinka returned, and his compadre asked him, "No?" ⁹⁵"Nothing [I didn't get the coca]. ⁹⁶He nearly cut my head off." ⁹⁷"Didn't you pay him back?" ⁹⁸He said, "No, I paid him back a little bit," although you've seen it, he pierced him through with his bow! (Laughing.) ⁹⁹So they saw him from afar, but they didn't see him move around, and they said, "What happened to him?" ¹⁰⁰Later one said, "Well, I'll go and take a look at him." ¹⁰¹He walked there and saw him pierced through.

¹⁰²–The roasted thing is ready to eat.

¹⁰³–He came back and said, "Not a chance of being alive, he was killed, he was pierced through." ¹⁰⁴He said, "So this might be it, so it ends."

¹⁰⁵–A tapir is killed for you.

¹⁰⁶–There was no one to continue [after Apinka]. ¹⁰⁷There

was one who tried but said, "No." [108]He had fear [that he would be killed] and said, "No." [109]Now our fellow men enjoyed themselves, they ate what they wanted until they would get satiated.

[110]–We'll see.

[111]–When food is given to us, we may [want to] save something, but we will eat it all.

[112]–Is that right?

[113]–*Kori, kori* (action of gulping a drink).

[114]–We'll finish all [food]. [115]They say, when we do some work with beans, we do it apart from corn, we pile up beans. [116]The one called Apinka was pierced with a bow, this is it. [117]So it ends.

SEVEN

Yookantapakairi virakocha

(How the Whites Threw Us Out)

Fredi Miguel Ucayali

¹Pikimavakina, noñaavintakotero okantavitani paisatziteni, tsika ipoñaaka ovakira ipokayetapaki yookantapakairi pairani virakochapaye. ²Ipoñaanaka ashaninkapaye, ovakira ikiapaki virakochapaye, yookapakai. ³Opoñaaka ikantaitziri Monovambaki, ari otzimi otzinantakari manatantsi, okanta yookantakairi virakochapaye. ⁴Okanta ashiyantakari, osheki piantakaro iñaantari, ivayetakiri pairani. ⁵Ikantarika ashaninkara, yookapakairika okanta ashiya apokaji, ariitapaka Ochovambaki. ⁶Aikiro ishiyatya, aikiro ipokatzi virakocha. ⁷Yookajai, ariitapajai Mina San Vicenteki. ⁸Apiya, aikiro ipokatzi. ⁹Ityankajaira virakochapaye, ariitajai Viitoki. ¹⁰Opoñaapaka ariitapajai San Ramonki, opoñaapaka atsatakomentotsiki Herreiria, irojatzi ariitantapakari antaro nampitsi ikantaitziri Tsiirishiki. ¹¹Isaikavitani osheki ashaninka. ¹²Ikantarika yariitapakara, aikiro ipokatzi virakocha. ¹³Ikantziri paisatziteni poñaachari intainasatzipaye, yookajai, ikantziri iroñaaka ashaninkapaye.

¹⁴Iyoka *español*payeka yariitapaka, aisatzi ikantaitziri *italianos*, yariitaka *italianos, ingleses, alemanes, europeos*, yaniitatziri *chinos, japoneses*. ¹⁵Amavitakaro Tsiirishiki, apiyavitakari, aikiro ipokatzi, aikiro ipokatzi. ¹⁶Yookajai, okanta ashiyantakari, ashiyaka. ¹⁷Aikiro apoki, ariitapaka iroñaaka ikantaitziri Pareniki. ¹⁸Atetanaka avitopaye, atetanaka ashin-

1. Upper Perené warriors fight the invaders. By Daniel Bernales Quillatupa (Aroshi).

tzipari, shiyakotakai. [19]Ariitapakaro okantaka iroka ikantaitziri virakocha ovirantapakaroka Parenini. [20]Opoña opokapaki pashini parenini ikantaitziroranki Tziviarini.

[21]Opoñaapaka apototapaka okanta opokantanakari iro-ñaaka aka pariniki, ikantaitziro Parenini. [22]Okanta ashiyakara-kia, ikantzi paisatziteni, jevavintzirorira, ikantzi, "Asaikavaki otsampishiki, asaikavaki, korakitaintsi ookajaini. [23]Korakitain-tsi osheki virakocha, aapitsatajairori aipatsite." [24]Ikantarika ikinkitsavaitzi asheninkara jevatatsirira, katziyanaka aparoni ashaninka, ikantzri, "Aviro jevari." [25]Ikantzri, "Pamine, noñaa-shita korakitaintsi ookaitajaini. [26]Nojevateta anta pariniki, notetanakia noshintzipaariki, nonkamanteritakia asheninka-paye saikatsiri parinitsapiaki. [27]Nonkanteri korakitaintsikia ookajaini, noñaashita, airo añajiro anampi. [28]Arika ivaitakai, ari ampiakia."

[29]Ikanta irirori jaitetaki, yamaatakotanaki ishintzipariki, ika-mantzri maaroni asheninkapaye saikantarori parenitsapiaki. [30]Opoñaaka tekirata avisanaki kitaiteripatsaini, añaashitakari yariitapaka ookajaini, ikantaitziri virakocha *ingleses, Peruvian*

Corporation. [31]Ariitapaka iroñaaka, imapokakai niyankiteni tsiteniri. [32]Itsonkakai, imishiyakai. [33]Ikanta isaikantapakari iroñaaka aka, anampitsiteki yantapakirika. [34]Ishekitatzira, itsonka yookajai, imishiyantakariri. [35]Okanta ashiyantakari maaroiteni, atsarovakajeetanakarini. [36]Okanta nosaikantarika iroñaaka noyomoniratekika Pampa Michikika.

[37]Airo iñaapirotami paisatziteni acharinitepaye, okanta añaantarori asaiki iroñaaka, okanta otzimantari iroñaaka asaiki aipatsite. [38]Te oshekite aipatsite okaratzi *docientos treinta ocho hectares,* tzimatsi aka, ari okaratziri asaikajeetaiyenika aka anampitsitekika. [39]Okanta airo añaapirovintaromi, añaantarori iroñaaka asaikajeetaiyeni. [40]Apasonkiteri achariniteni antaroite, okanta ikisakovintakaro aipatsite, añaantarori asaikajeetaiyeni iroñaaka. [41]Ontzimatye apasonkiteri antaroite.

[42]Iritaki ookanakairori iroñaaka, arori akinakashitanakaro, te ayote apinkatsatavakajia. [43]Okantyaranki aapatyavakaiya kameetsa, apototavakaiya kameetsa, onkantya añaantyarori kameetsa asaiki anampitsiteki. [44]Antampatzikatero, onkantya arori akimitaka ashaninkapaye maaroiteni kovachari. [45]Iroñaaka ipokashiyetapaka choripaye, iñaashintsitapakaro amantsakipaye, te ampinkatsatakairi. [46]Te, ari onkantyari, onkantya ampiyaji ikimita paisatzitepaye, apinkitsatakairo amantsaki, ayoshitya ashaninkatzika. [47]Aitaki amajiro kameetsa, antampatzitakairo okantavitani irojatzi isaikavitani paisatziteni achariniteni maaroiteni.

[1]You will listen to me: I will talk about how our ancestors lived and where they come from, considering that they were thrown out by the whites. [2]They come from the area that the whites entered; they threw us out from the place called Monobamba. [3]There was a battle, during which the whites threw us out. [4]In

order to escape, many lost their lives, a lot of people were killed long ago. ⁵Those fellow men, we were thrown out, and during the escape we came to the place called Ochobamba. ⁶We kept fleeing, and the whites kept coming. ⁷They threw us out, and we arrived at Mina San Vicente. ⁸We would return, but they would keep coming. ⁹When they pushed us out, we arrived in Vitoc. ¹⁰Then we reached San Ramon, then the Bridge of Herreiria, until we arrived at a big settlement called Tsiirishi [La Merced]. ¹¹Many of my fellow men lived there. ¹²When my fellow men arrived in Tsiirishi, whites kept coming. ¹³The ancestors called them "those who came from afar"; they threw us out, my fellow men said.

¹⁴Those Spaniards arrived, also those called Italians, English, Germans, Europeans; Chinese and Japanese came. ¹⁵We had been in charge of Tsiirishi, we made them retreat, but they kept coming, they kept coming. ¹⁶They threw us out, and we fled. ¹⁷We kept retreating and arrived at the place where begins what is called river Perené. ¹⁸We filled our canoes, our rafts, and fled. ¹⁹We reached the place, which the whites called, where the river Perené ends [river Chanchamayo]. ²⁰Then came another river, called in the past the Salt River.

²¹Then we gathered together in order to come here to this river, called Perené. ²²As we were fleeing, the ancestral chiefs said, "We will stay here on this island, we will stay; those who will throw us out are coming. ²³A lot of whites are coming, and they will take away our land." ²⁴When the chief was talking to my fellow men, one fellow man stood up and said to him, "You are the chief." ²⁵He said to him, "Look, I know that those who will throw us out are coming. ²⁶I will head over there, by the Perené River, I will get on my raft and will advise my fellow men who live on the riverbanks. ²⁷I will tell them that they are coming, those who will throw us out, and I think we won't see

our villages anymore. ²⁸When they kill us, then we'll disappear [we'll be finished]."

²⁹He took off, he went downriver on his raft and notified all my fellow men who lived along the river. ³⁰Then hardly few days had passed, when those who would throw us out arrived, called by the whites "English," from the Peruvian Corporation. ³¹They arrived and surprised us in the middle of the night. ³²They finished us, they made us flee. ³³That's why we now reside here, in this village that was built here. ³⁴Because there were many of them, they completely threw us out. ³⁵That's why we all fled, all those who had fear of them. ³⁶That's why I live here in this native community of Pampa Michi.

³⁷Hadn't our ancestral grandfathers been warriors, we wouldn't be living today on our land. ³⁸There is not much land, only 238 hectares that we have, those who live in this village. ³⁹Hadn't our ancestral grandfathers been warriors, we wouldn't live here today. ⁴⁰We should thank our grandfathers who defended our land, that's why we have a place to live. ⁴¹We should thank them a lot.

⁴²They left it to us, but we are getting astray, we don't know how to respect each other. ⁴³For we should be able to deal with each other nicely, get together nicely in order to live nicely in this village. ⁴⁴We should straighten it out, to be able to be like our ancestral fellow men, this is what we want. ⁴⁵Now Andean colonists arrived and despise our clothing, and we didn't make them respect it. No, this is not the way. ⁴⁶We should go back [to the old ways] to be like our ancestors, make them respect our clothes, should think like our fellow men did. ⁴⁷Then we'll handle it right, we'll straighten it out, the way it was when our ancestors lived.

EIGHT

Natsitonini

(The Stream of Bones)

Manuel Rubén Jacinto

[1]Irotakitaima iroñaaka nonkinkitsatero iroka ovairo otzi-shika okinika avotsi opaita Porinkishi. [2]Iroka Porinkishi koñaatatsirika airinkatantakiari anta. [3]Ankinanaki Patsirini, iroñaaka ojatanakanta kirinkaini, ari opaitari aajatzi Otsika roni. [4]Ojatanakanta kirinkaini, ari opaita pashini Tsamiri-menta. [5]Iroñaaka ampokaji jaka tonkarikika, otenkanaka ikantaitziro Potyarini. [6]Arika avisanakiro tonkariki orave Pasantaniki. [7]Janto ojatanakinta aisatzi irorave Intsipashani.

[8]Oijatanakiro irorave Natsitonini. [9]Maatsi omoro paita-chari Natsitonini, osheki irorave asheninka itonki ipiyotaka. [10]Irotaki opaitantari Natsitonini, osheki asheninka itonki opiyotaka omorokira iroñaaka nijaatenikira. [11]Irotaki opaitan-tari Natsitonini. [12]Iroñaaka jaka ojatanakira intatzikironta opaita orave Tsiirishipankani, poñaaka irojatzi oponkityata-pakanta Yurinani.

[13]Opaitantari iroñaaka, maatsi pairani ashaninka ovayeri-tachari. [14]Ari isaikiri ashaninka iroñaka ovayeritachari. [15]Ivayeriteri, akantziri, iroñaaka virakocha kisanintairi. [16]Iroñaaka jevatatsiri ari isaikiri jara, ankante, tyankiriri, kantziriri, "Pijevate." [17]Iro kantzimaitacha tzimatsi ivinitsite, terika ivinkite, yatsikashitziriri imasontovinkite, onkantya airo ivaitantari. [18]Iroñaaka ityanakaki atziripaye, ikantziri, "Tsame

amanaterita, antsonkaterita iyoka, ampiroterita iroñaaka."
[19]Aritaki ivavitakari iroñaaka.

[20]Jataki iroñaaka, kantzimaintacha tzimatsi pashini jevatatsiri iroñaaka, ipaita Marinkama. [21]Okitaitamani pokaki virakocha, ikiakotakari ivira iroñaaka antarite, antarite piratsi
iroñaaka. [22]Oirinkaka iroñaaka, yaminapakiro anta. [23]Otonkai-
tyakinta, yaminakotapakiro, ikaimapakiro iroñaaka. [24]Ityota-
paki iroñaaka, ipipitsokatakakaro ityori iroñaaka, ipipitsokatakakaro ityori iroñaaka.

[25]Pashini ikantzi, "Naaka nintyarita. [26]Nontsatsinkirita
ikintsiki." [27]Te inkanteri, yamatsatashitakari iroñaaka. [28]Ikai-
makashitakari, ikantzi, "Oh." [29]Kooya Marinkama ari intana-
kari otonkanaki itonkamento, *tok, tok, tok.* [30]Kamanaki
asheninkapaye, itzinampanakai.

[31]Poñaaka ikantzi jevatatsiri, "Intzinampakai." [32]Antaro
ivashiritanaka iroñaaka, ivashiritanaka. [33]Poña ikantzi,
"Apatatsitami inavita, arika yavisaki, naaka intavakiarinimi
nomanatavakiri, aviroka impoitatzinimi, ari pimanateri
anta, aritakimi ampirotavakiri. [34]Iroñaakama ontzimatye
intsonkaitai ivaitai."

[35]Ari okantakari iroñaaka. [36]Imanatanakara, yoijatanakiri
irojatzita iroñaaka ivantanakarori ovairo. [37]Okantziri Natsitonini terika Porinkishi otzimantakari ovayeritantsi. [38]Irotaki
ivaitanakiri iroñaaka, yoijaitanakiri ivayeriteri irojatzi kirinka.
[39]Ari okantari. [40]Ari ovirapakari iroñaaka.

[1]Perhaps I will tell about this hill's name, where the trail is, which
is called Porinkishi (plant species) Hill. [2]Porinkishi Hill, which
appears over here, is the way to go down to the jungle area.
[3]Partridge Hill goes next, where it continues into the jungle;
it is also called Hindrance Hill. [4]What goes next, located further into the jungle area, is another place, called the Curassow

Crest Stone. [5]Now, we come back here to the upriver area, this stream is called Somewhat Salty. [6]If we go further upriver, there is Grinder Hill. [7]What goes next is Inga Tree Hill.

[8]What goes further is the Stream of Bones. [9]There is a cave there, where lots of bones of my fellow men are piled up. [10]That's why it is called the Stream of Bones, because many bones of my fellow men were amassed in this cave, in the area where the stream passes. [11]That's why it is called the Stream of Bones. [12]Now, on the other side of the river Perené is Tsiriishi (plant species) Hill, which continues to the mouth of the river Yorinaki.

[13]It [Natsitonini] is called this way because there was my fellow man who was a warrior. [14]The warrior lived here. [15]He would fight, they say, outsiders who hated us. [16]He was a chief who lived here, they say, who will send [men to fight] and who will say, "Go!" [17]He had his magic herbs that he masticated to make him impervious [to the enemy's weapons], so that they couldn't kill him. [18]He will send people to fight and say to them, "Let's fight, let's finish them, we'll have a victory over them." [19]And the warriors would kill them [the enemies].

[20]He left the area, but there was another chief, called Marinkama. [21]The following day outsiders came on horseback, on tall horses. [22]One dismounted the horse and looked around. [23]He looked at the elevated area and signaled with his trumpet. [24]He played his trumpet, he turned to one side to play it, then he turned to the other side.

[25]Marinkama said, "I will begin the fight. [26]I will pierce his neck with my arrow." [27]The arrow only grazed [the target]. [28]It made him say, "Oh." [29]Marinkama's wife began to shoot from his rifle, *tok tok tok* (action of firing a rifle). [30]My fellow men died, but the enemy overwhelmed us.

[31]Afterward the other chief said, "They won a victory over us." [32]He was deeply saddened. [33]Then he said [to Marinkama],

"Had you waited longer, when the enemy passed, I would have begun [shooting] and you would have followed shooting from another side; we would have won. [34]Now it's imminent that we will be all killed by them."

[35]So it was. [36]When there was a war, the enemy pursued my fellow men, and a name was given [to the places of combat]. [37]They say "Stream of Bones" or "Porinkishi Hill," because of the war. [38]This is where my fellow men were killed, they were pursued in the war way into the jungle. [39]So it was. [40]This is where it ends.

NINE

Tsika okantakota ovayeritantsi

(About the Craft of War)

Daniel Bernales Quillatupa

[1]Pashini kinkitsarentsi nokinkitsatakoteri opaita manatantsi. [2]Ikamantana pairani aani Kovari okantakota manatantsi iñaakeri ovakera ikantzi ivankaritapake. [3]Ikantzi tzimatsi isaikimotziri aijatzi icharini, ikovi irirori isaripaye iñaaperokitajiami, okantyakia inkisakoventantyarori iipatsite. [4]Isaikinta tonkariki, yoirinkajeetzi aka, aririka intanajia irora osarentsitanaje. [5]Yoirinkajeeta jaka pareniki.

[6]Aririka intanajiaro oshookayetanaje savoro, añaashitaro aririka ookanajia antaropaye impaniki, ari onivetarori savoro oshookanaje. [7]Ikantzikia aani Kovari, aijatzi itsipatari ikarajeetzi ivankarijeetzi intsipajeetakiari iriri, isaripaye. [8]Yamanake kaniri, parentzi ivajeetyara ara, isaikajeetapakera oparaiki. [9]Aririka yareejeetakia, jevatatsirira, akantakoteri, iyora iririra iroñaaka aani Kovari, yamenapake tsikarika okameetsaitetzi, ari impiyojeetapakiari.

[10]Iroñaaka shiramparipayera antaripaye jatake yaminayetapake inchapankipaye, pashini aapaintsini irora savoroshi, impiyotapakero. [11]Pashini jatataintsini yaye irora shivitsa yoisotantyarori ivanko. [12]Aririka itsonkajeetakiro yante ivanko, ari impiyojeetyari.

[13]Iroñaaka kooyapaye onkotsitapake kaniri, pashini kooyapaye ankishite parentzi ivajeetyari. [14]Aririka osheetya-

2. Boys practice evading mock arrows. By Daniel Bernales Quillatupa (Aroshi).

nake, jatake iroñaaka ovakera intanajiaro iroñaaka osarentsitanaje tzimayetatsi iroñaaka karava, aririka inkaimanake
tsitenikipaye, jataiyanake shiramparipaye. [15]Yooteri, yaanake isamperate. [16]Ikantaitziri "sampera," irotaki savoro,
ishiviriayetakiri yoisomaitakiaro. [17]Poñaaka yootakerorika,
irotaki yamenantariri karavapaye tsikarika isatekayetakara
inchamaishikipaye. [18]Iritaki ivajeetapakiari.

[19]Aririka okitaitamanaje, irotaki jatatsini kooya ompasa-
kate, aye jetari, shavori, impitapaye ivajeetyari oparaikira.

[20]Iromakia, aririka irora osheetyanake okitaitamanairika,
ari iñaatsajeetyari iroñaaka. [21]Te iñaatsavaitashitya, iritaki
antarikonara kinkishiriakotariri eentsipaye, apaata aririka
yantaritanake, ontzimatye iriperote shirampari, inkomenkiro

chekopi, okantyatama aririka ijatake imanatya, airotsi irora
ikintantaitari. [22]Irotaki iroñaaka inijantyariri eentsipayeka
shiramparipaye. [23]Aijatzi kooya, aririka onkove oñaatsatya,
ari okantake oñaatsatya irori.
[24]Iroñaaka intsopayetaki ovakeratatsiri irora oshooke irora
savoro, aririka antaronintayetanake. [25]Itsopayetakiro, itsopake,
itsopake oshekivee, ishiyakantakero chekopi. [26]Yavitsanota-
kerorika, pashini aajatzita inkaraiyakini apite iroñaaka. [27]Inta-
nakiaro apite inkatziyake intainapaye. [28]Pashini intakiaro
iroñaaka yookimoteri savoropontsopayera, ontzimatye
inkomenkakiro. [29]Ari onkantake ishirinkanakia, aajatzita ari
inkantake imarovanake, areetarikari savoropontsopayera,
temakia katsirini. [30]Iroñaaka impiyatavakajeetakia, yooki-
motavakajeetya savoropontso. [31]Te ikisaverontyaro aririka
areevitakiari ivatsakika.

[32]Irotaki iñaatsatari iyoka eentsipaye ivankari, tema
irotake irora onkantya apaata irora airo areetaritsi chekopi,
aririka imanavetyari. [33]Iroñaaka ñaatsavairontsika, ari
onkantaki yampitero kitaiterikipaye. [34]Okitaitamanakirika,
osheetyanajerika, aririka ijate inkaatajeetya, irotaki iñaatsatari, ikantziri aani Kovari, irotaki yamitari iyoka eentsipaye.

[35]Irotakirika intanajiaro aarontsitanaje, irotaki yookana-
jero okaratzi yantajeetziri oparaikika, isaikapaintzika kapicheeni. [36]Iroñaaka iñaavajerorika opariantsinintanaje, ivitsi-
kanajia jatajeetaje janta tonkariki, isaikajeetzinta. [37]Ari
okantari, ikantziri aani Kovari.

[38]Iroñaakakia aririka irora yantarinintanake, ivankari-
peronintanake, ari onkantake iroñaaka iñaatsatavakaiya,
iñaantyaro iroñaaka yairikero chekopi. [39]Kaari tzimatsini
irora ikirikotairikira, intaani okapontsote ikapontsotanta-
vakaiya. [40]Aijatzi okimita pairani iñaatsataro savorontsovara

janta oparaikira impanikitekira. [41]Iroñaaka iñaatsatyaro chekopi kapontsotatsirira. [42]Aajatzita ari okantake yairikavakero. [43]Ari imatakero, iñaavakerorika, *shepik*, yairikavakero chekopi, ivanakero osaviki, pashini, yairikavakero okantyakia otzimantyari osheki ichekopite yashi irora manatsiririra. [44]Arika imatakero iroñaaka iyokapayeka yairikayetziro chekopira, iritaki apaata inkoyaitanakeri jatatsini janta imanatya, imanateri iyora pashinipaye irora ashaninka. [45]Tetya ikisanintavetyari.

[46]Pairani ijatatzi imanateri pashinipaye iyora atziri saikayetatsiri pashiniki nampitsi, onkantatya yaantyaniriri, ikoshitantyaniriri irishintopaye, yamajeri ishiyakaventero. [47]Iroñaaka aririka ajate irora añaatsatya, ari amaje irora ikantziri irora kiriki, *trofeo*. [48]Pairani aririka ijate imanatya, tzimatsi ikoveri. [49]Inkoshite eentsipaye, inkoshite kooya, yamajeri inampiki. [50]Ari ikantziri iyora aani Kovari.

[51]Iroñaaka ikantzi aajatzita, aririka ijatantyari imanatya, airo ijatavaishita. [52]Tzimatsi yaanakeri iyometairiri iriperantzipaye manatantatsiri, iriperantzi komenkirori chekopi, iriperantzi airikirori chekopi, te intsarovanite. [53]Iritaki opavinkeriri iroñaaka, ari ipakiri iyora ivenki paitachari parovenki. [54]Iroka parovenki omaperotatya okameentsatzi. [55]Irotaki opapiroterini iriperantzi iyoka manatantatsirika. [56]Airo okantzi onkintai chekopi, ikimitara paro, tsimeri inatzi, osheki imianita, aririka impantsai, *paro paro*, osheki imiashitaro. [57]Ari inkimityari yoka shiramparika antzirori parovenki, ari ikantari.

[58]Irotaki yaanakeri iroñaaka, ontzimatye ontzime iparovinkite, aajatzita ontzime yaanake pocharivenki. [59]Pocharivenki irotaki irora ivenki yaavintyari ikishokavakiari, aririka onkintakeri chekopi. [60]Aririka yamatsataitakiari, oshitovanakerika kapicheeni iraani, yaitzitavakiaro iroñaaka irora

pocharivenkira, yatsikanakero, *morok, morok*, inkishokakiaro.
[61]Ari avisanaki oyatsinka, airo oshitovanaje iraani, aajatzita ari
ashitanaje iroka, okintavetapakarira chekopi.

[62]Poñaaka aajatzita ikantzi iririka iriperantzi atziri ijata-
shiterira, aajatzita yaanake irora masontovenki, ipiyakoven-
tanakakari, aririka apaata iñaavetavakiari jatashitziririra.

[63]Aajatzi ontzimatye ontzime tsitenirivenki, irotaki ivenki
tsiteniritakairori kitaite. [64]Ari ominkorityapaki osheki, tsitenitanaki, pariapaki inkani. [65]Irotaki yaayetziri iyora tzimimoyetziriri shiramparira jatatsiri yovayeritya.

[66]Irorika ijate imanatavakaiya onkantya ivavakantyari,
ikantzi aanini Kovari, tzimatsi aajatzi pinitsi ikaakityari iyora
jatatsiri imanatavakaiya. [67]Iro kantacha, airo isaikanaki pankotsiki, tema imashirinkatanakia. [68]Ari okantake iviri itomi,
irishintopaye, aajatzita iina, aririka kapicheeni iñaavakero te
onkasate kaniri, te ompiri ivarite, ari inkisanakia, ari ivakero.
[69]Irotaki ikantziri aani, antzirori pinitsika, airo isaikanake
ivankoki, iro ijate janta imanatya.

[70]Aririka iroñaaka itsonkakero imanatya, yampirotakeri
maaroni ijatashitzirira, aririka impiyaje, ontzimatye ikama-
rankapaje, ontzimatye yaashitapajia pashinipaye irora inchaparitsapaye ikamarankeri. [71]Aajatzita yaashitapajia pinitsi-
paye inkaakitapajiari irojatzi onkantya avisanajeri irora
imashirinkara. [72]Ovakera iroñaaka isaikapaje ivankoki
kameetsa, airo ikisanintavaitapajero ikarajeetzi isaikajeetzi.

[73]Omaperotatya okameentsaperotzi iyotziri pairani iyora
ashaninkapaye. [74]Iroñaaka irojatzi otzimayetzi iroñaaka jaka,
iyoyetziri ashaninka, kantzimaitacha irora airo okantzi ika-
mantajairo shintsipayeni. [75]Ontzimatye iyotavakai tsika
okanta atziritzi, akameentsatzirika o terika akameentsate.
[76]Irotaki iroñaaka kaari ikamantantajai iyora, ashaninka
tzimimoyetziriri yotanitantsi. [77]Ari okantakotari ovayeritantsi, manatantsi, ikantziri ashaninka. [78]Ari okaratzi, pasonki.

¹Another story that I am going to tell is called "Combat." ²Long ago my grandfather Kovari told me about combat, which he saw when he was a young boy. ³He said, there was an old man who wanted his grandchildren to be warriors so that they could defend their land. ⁴They lived in the hills and would go down to the valley floor during the beginning of the summer. ⁵They would go down to the Perené River floor.

⁶When the giant wild cane begins to sprout, we see big areas of the sandy beaches exposed along the river, and this is what encourages the growth of wild cane. ⁷My grandfather Kovari said, young men would come together with their parents and grandparents. ⁸They would bring sweet manioc and plantains, so that they could eat there, [during the time] when they stayed on the beach. ⁹When they would arrive, the headman, who was, so to speak, the father of my grandfather Kovari, would look for a nice place, so that they would stay there together.

¹⁰Older males would look for wood poles; others would bring leaves of wild cane and pile them up. ¹¹Others would go and get vines to tie up [the parts of] the communal house. ¹²When they finish the house, this is where they will gather together.

¹³Women will cook sweet manioc, other females will roast plantains for eating. ¹⁴When it gets dark, they will go [to look for food], since when the summer begins, the *karava* species (unidentified) of frogs appear, and when they begin to croak, all males will go [to gather them]. ¹⁵They will illuminate the area, [because] they take their *sampera* torches. ¹⁶It is called *sampera* [because] it consists of the debris of wild cane, and they light it. ¹⁷When they light it, they see frogs stuck in the vegetation. ¹⁸Everyone will eat the [collected] frogs.

¹⁹The next day, women will gather small fish species of *carachama, jetari, barbon*, and centipedes for eating on the beach.

²⁰In the afternoon of the following day, everyone will begin

to play. [21]They play with a certain purpose, since older males are concerned about their children: when they grow up, they should be skilled men, should [be able to] dodge arrows, so that when they are in combat, they are not shot. [22]That's why adult males will demonstrate [these skills] to the children. [23]Women, if they want to practice, are able to practice too.

[24]They will pull out new shoots of wild cane when the shoots are big enough. [25]They will pull out a lot of them; they imagine them to be arrows. [26]They will handle them [as if they were arrows], and there will be two boys [practicing]. [27]Two [players] will begin, standing at a distance from each other. [28]One will begin throwing poles of wild cane, and the other has to dodge them. [29]He could bend over to the ground or fall down on the ground to evade the wild cane pole, because it hurts [to be hit by them]. [30]Now they switch, and the other throws wild cane [at the practice partner]. [31]They don't get angry when a wild cane pole hits the player's body.

[32]Those are the games of young boys, since in the future they will be able to dodge arrows in combat. [33]The game will be repeated every day, in the mornings. [34]In the afternoon, or when they go bathing in the river, it [throwing poles] was practiced, grandfather Kovari said, [because] it was a custom for the children.

[35]When winter begins, they stop practicing on the beach where they have stayed for a while. [36]When a pattern of rain is observed, they will get ready to go to the hills where they live. [37]It was this way, my grandfather Kovari said.

[38]When boys grow up, they will practice catching arrows in the air. [39]Not those with the pointed end, made of the *kirii* (chonta) palm tree (*Juania australis*), but those with the blunt end for practicing evading them. [40]This resembles the game of

wild cane poles, [practiced] on that sandy beach. [41]Now they practice throwing arrows with the blunt end. [42]They are able to catch them in the air. [43]This is how they handle it: when they see it, *shepik* (action of catching a moving object in the air), they catch the arrow and place it on the ground, so that one has a lot of [the] opponent's arrows. [44]When they manage to catch the arrows in the air, in the future they will be selected to go raiding, to raid other Ashaninka.

[45]They never treated each other as the enemy.

[46]In the old times, they went raiding the villages of other people, so that they could physically engage them and kidnap their daughters, and they would bring what they imagined in their minds. [47]Nowadays, when we play sports games, we bring, they say, money and trophies [as prizes]. [48]In the old times, when they raided, they had intent [what they wanted]. [49]They will kidnap children; they will kidnap women, and bring them to the village. [50]It was this way, as grandfather Kovari said.

[51]He also said that when they went raiding, they wouldn't go raiding unprepared. [52]They would take along what was taught to them by the expert shooters, expert acrobats in evading arrows, and expert catchers of arrows, who were dauntless. [53]They shared magic plants *ivenki* with them; they would give them a type of magic plant *ivenki* called "parovenki." [54]This herb is very good. [55]It was a gift from expert warriors. [56]They will not be hit by arrows, just like *paro*, the chotacabras bird (*Rufous Nightjar, Caprimulgus rufus*); it jumps a lot when it sings *paro paro* (the chotacabras's call), and jumps. [57]The man who used *parovenki* would be like the chotacabras bird, and he was.

[58]They would take it along; it was necessary to have *parovenki*, and also *pocharivenki*. [59]*Pocharivenki* is the plant that will cure when mouth-sprayed on the wound, when an arrow

has pierced the body. [60]When he is wounded, and there is bleeding, the warrior should take seeds of the plant, bite on them, *morok, morok* (penetration action), and spit them on the wound. [61]The pain will pass, there will be no bleeding, and the wound that was caused by the arrow will heal.

[62]He also said that when the brave people go raiding, they take along *masontovenki* to hypnotize the enemy, so that they fail to see the raiders.

[63]Also, they have to take along *tsitenirivenki*, which are the herbs that make the day darken. [64]Clouds begin to amass, it gets dark, and it starts raining. [65]These plants, which were thoroughly guarded, were taken along by males who were going to combat.

[66]When they go to combat to kill, grandfather Kovari said, they have the *pinitsi* (*pusanga*), which will be administered into the eyes of those who go to combat. [67]However, [after the herb is administered], a male shouldn't stay at home, because he will go into a drug-induced frenzy. [68]He could kill his son, his daughters, or his wife, if he sees that she hasn't cooked manioc or won't give him food, so he will get enraged and kill her. [69]This is what my grandfather said, that those treated by *pinitsi* shouldn't stay at home but shall go to combat.

[70]When they [have] finished combat and prevailed over the enemy, all raiders, when they go back, have to induce vomiting with special herbal roots. [71]Also, another *pinitsi* is administered into his eyes so that the warrior's frenzy passes. [72]Only then will he stay at home nicely and won't get enraged with those who reside in his house.

[73]This is true that it is good, the knowledge of our ancestral fellow men. [74]It still exists here, our fellow men know it, but it is impossible to transmit it [the knowledge] quickly [i.e., it is part of a long process of socialization into the community]. [75]They

have to know the person [to whom this knowledge is transmitted], if he is good or bad. [76]That's why they won't transmit it, [because] our fellow men guard their knowledge. [77]Such was the craft of war and combat, according to our fellow men. [78]This is all, thank you.

TEN

Apapanani

(The Brook of Liver Parts)

Gregorio Santos Pérez

[1]Iroñaaka nonkinkitsatavaki akimakovintziro okanta opaitantari nijaateni Apapanani. [2]Aparojatzini ajajeetzi notsipatanakari niri, noniro, maaroni nirintzipatsaini ankonaate amine shivari. [3]Iritaki avari arori maaroni kitaiterikipaye. [4]Akinakotanaki, amaatakotanaki irojatzi kirinkanta, ari avaatakotapaka. [5]Okantzi ina, "Aka aritaki aviriakirori. [6]Tsame avashitero tsipiri, tsipikirontsi inkiantapakiari shimapatsaini."

[7]Poñaashitakaja okantzi, "Iroka opaitatya Apapanani." [8]Nokantanaki, "Tsika opaitaka? [9]Paita ikantaitziri, ina, Apapanani?"

[10]Okantana inaja, "Kama maatsi pairani irora ipokantari ovayeripaye, ari ipiyotakiri aka irirapana atziripaye. [11]Ninkarika kinapaintsini, tsikarika impoñaapakia, ari ikintamachetziriri, intsonkateri inchekayeteri maaroni. [12]Ari ipiyoitziriri, iñaayetzi iroranki tsika opaitaranki irirapana."

[13]Nokantziro, "Ina, ninkakia?" [14]Okantzi, "Iyora kishiisatzipaye koshitziriori kooyapaye. [15]Arika impiyavintavakia, irotaki. [16]Maatsi atziri poñiinkari saikatsiri Tziviariki, kirinkaka, impokajeete aka. [17]Iñaavakapakia, irotaki inkintavakaiya. [18]Inkitavaki oshekive soraro, ankante, ovayeripaye kamatsi. [19]Shitzimainkave, ankimakiri. [20]Ivayetya tsizopaye."

[21]Nokantziro, "Ina, irotaki opaitantari Apapanani." [22]Tera

ayotatyero arori ovakira eentsitapakini. ²³Okantzi, "Jee, irotaki, notomi, irotaki opaitantari Apapanani. ²⁴Ari ipiyoitzirori
pairani asheninkapaye iyora irapana, iviyonkaripaye, isheeto.
²⁵Irotaki ipaitantaitarori Apapanani."

²⁶Irotaki, nokantziri, iroñaaka naari amaisantajiro, te ankan-
tapirotatyero. ²⁷Osaiki kirinkaininta otsipataro nijaateni, ikantaitziri Kimariani. ²⁸Osaikajinta iroñaaka ikantaitziri Eshipi-
ransa. ²⁹Aritaki osaikiri nijaateni paitachari Apapanani. ³⁰Ari
okaratapaki.

¹I will tell you about what we heard on account of the Brook of
Livers, why it is called this way. ²Once we all—my father, mother,
my little brothers—went fishing with *barbasco* (vegetable poison) in search of anchoveta. ³This was what we ate those days.
⁴We went downriver in a canoe and at some point we beached.
⁵Mother said, "Here we'll dam this area. ⁶Let's place a *quin-
cha* (rudimentary enclosure made of leaves and wooden sticks)
across the brook so that anchovetas can enter the dammed area."

⁷Then she said, "This is called the Brook of Liver Parts." ⁸I
said, "What is it called? ⁹Why is it called the Brook of Liver
Parts, Mother?"

¹⁰My mother said to me, "Because in the past, when warriors would come, they would pile up livers of people. ¹¹Who-
ever was passing by, from whatever place they were coming, this
is where they were killed with arrows and finished by cutting.
¹²Here they [killers] would pile them up; people saw all sorts of
them, human livers."

¹³I said to her, "Mother, who were they?" ¹⁴She said, "They
were natives of the grasslands from Gran Pajonal who were kidnapping women. ¹⁵When they [families] defended women, this
happened. ¹⁶There were travelers from the area of the Salt River
and from downriver who would come here. ¹⁷When Pajonalinos

saw them, they would shoot them with arrows. ¹⁸They would shoot many soldiers, we say, warriors who would be dying. ¹⁹It stunk terribly when we smelled it. ²⁰Vultures would eat them."

²¹I said to my mother, "That's why it is called the Brook of Livers Parts." ²²We knew nothing about it when we are little children. ²³She said, "Yes, that's right, my son, that's why it's called the Brook of Liver Parts. ²⁴This is where our fellow men piled up livers, lungs, and intestines [of the killed people]. ²⁵That's why it is called the Brook of Liver Parts."

²⁶Now, I say, we are forgetting it, we are not handling it well. ²⁷In the area a little bit downriver, it is joined together with what is called the Brook of Tapir. ²⁸It is located near the village of Esperanza. ²⁹In this place, the Brook of Liver Parts is located. ³⁰This is all.

ELEVEN

Ovayeri inoshikantarori kooya
(When Warriors Kidnapped a Woman)

Paulina García Ñate

[1]Ampantsakoteri, arika ivayeritakia ovayeri, inoshikanakerika kooya, kooyanikipatsaini. [2]Yaanakero yampantsakotzimaita-nakiaro.

[3]Noshikachai chanaini,
noshikachai chanaini,
noshikachai chanaini.
[4]Nonoshikimate chanaini,
noshika chanaini,
noshika chanaini,
noshika chanaini.
[5]Chanaina, chanaina, chanaina, chanaina.
[6]Nosatekimatero chanaini,
nosatekimatero chanaini.
[7]Chanaina, chanaina, chanaina, chanaina.
[8]Nonoshikimate chanaini,
nonoshikimate chanaini,
nonoshikimate chanaini.
[9]Chanaina, chanaina, chanaina, chanaina.

[1]We will sing about it, when warriors were at war, they kidnapped women, young girls. [2]They will capture her and sing.

> [3]We are kidnapping a young girl,
> we are kidnapping a young girl,
> we are kidnapping a young girl.
> [4]I will kidnap a young girl,
> I am kidnapping a young girl,
> I am kidnapping a young girl,
> I am kidnapping a young girl.
> [5]Young girl, young girl, young girl, young girl.
> [6]I will place her in the middle of the circle,
> I will place her in the middle of the circle.
> [7]Young girl, young girl, young girl, young girl.
> [8]I will kidnap a young girl,
> I will kidnap a young girl,
> I will kidnap a young girl.
> [9]Young girl, young girl, young girl, young girl.

TWELVE

Ovayeri inoshikantzi eentsi
(The Warriors Kidnapped Children)

Ines Pérez de Santos

[1]Iyoka . . . pairani irojatzi neentsiyetapake ijatzi apa ikaye
Pampa Silvakinta, iroñaaka iyoka, iritaki nokantapintzimiri-
ranki. [2]Iyoka Mankori, te apantyari. [3]Ichekopite inkiake
itapikive. [4]Omaperotatya, nokantzimiriranki, okiyake
Mairikini, okiyake kipatsi, onariakero shitamenkotsi, ari
ankirotajeetya otapinaki. [5]Iritaki iroñaaka iyoka mava
ikantaiyani: iyoka, iroñaaka Mankori, ipoñaashitaka tsika
ipaitaranki Kochevari, ipoña yora tsipaitaranki . . . [6]Apaata
nokinkishiravakeri, oshe nokinkishiriavetapintari, akanterota,
Elena. [7]Mankoite, mava ikaratzi iriperori ovayeri ikoshitzi.
[8]Arika iñaapakai averayetya eentsipaye avankari, itsonka
inoshikanakeri, impimanteri, inkampiyateri irora vaaraki,
tonkamentotsi. [9]Aritaki ikanta yañaantari yoka, iritaki
jevatatsiri pairani.

[10]Ipoña ipokaki aka, yookanakai apani, apirovaitzi
ashikoirate, ikoshechatzi anta, Pampa Silvakinta, iroñaaka
anta osantanatzinta, ikosechatzi. [11]Okanta pokaki niyankiteni Mairikini, omairintakai, omanakai otapinakira amaa-
mentoporokinira, okitatakaira naari, nirento, opoña pashini
Shirora, opoña Tsirapa, opoña irento, *cinco* akaraiyini
otsinakakotakai. [12]Ikantaveta, "Chooki, piyove, nonintzi
pimpena." [13]"Tekatsi eentsi saikatsini. [14]Naaka saikatsi notsi-

patari noimi." [15]Iri kisakoventakairi iroñaaka, Oopani, iri kisakoventakairi. [16]Te ishintsitaje, inkantamatsitajero inchakii aka, "Aritaki novakemi." [17]Iritaki kisakoventaini, Oopani. [18]Tsika iveraka ooriatsiri, "Pisaiki, airo panivaitzi," nariamatsitajai ara irojatzi yareetantajia apa. [19]Ari yareetajia apa irojatzi yantanajana anta kosechapaiteki. [20]"Tsame aatai ankosechateta, inoshikimikari ovayeri, ipimantaitzimikari anta, arima noñaajemi." [21]Irotakitya oshekini ichakopite, ichokoripaye. [22]Maperove, chokori, ichokorite irora ivantanakiariri. [23]Apaata arika iñaakeri, airorika ishineta apa yaamachetai, ari inkintanakeri.

[24]Omaperotatsiri yoka tyarokinika, ikantapintzija, "Ikantaitaka?" [25]Iyoka iyanini atziri, ñaaperokive, iritaki nokantapintzimiranki. [26]Noñiiri, oñaakanari Mairikini, opoña nirentoni Hortensiani. [27]Iro kantatsi, "Tsame ashiyapitsateri, kooya, ivaikari Marinkaite." [28]Te apantyari, osheki ivi atziri, irotaki atsarovakantakariri.

[29]Ipoña Santoshi, iritaki nijantakairi, "Ari osaikajeetziri anta irishinto Sharishi, tsame anoshikeniri." [30]Naari, noyaririnta, inintzi inoshikaitenami, te onkantzimaintya inoshikaitena. [31]Omaperotatziro yoka otsirikakotantari. [32]Irojatzi pashini Santoshi irirori, aitaki isankinatakota iroñaaka irirori ovayeripaye Santoshini. [33]Te apantyarinive! [34]Maperorive! [35]Iñaapakeririka eentsi, "Pimpenari!" [36]Imishitovayetakero ivarakaitepaye, "Nompinantanakemita!"

[37]Osheki niraapintaka. [38]Nokantzi, "Ina, airo pookana, iroñaaka yaanakenari ovayeri." [39]Te apantyari ovayeri. [40]Nosaikimotziro entyo inoshikanakinakari. [41]"Pisaiki pintsipatyaro pirento, pamitakotero." [42]"Te, ivanakari ovayeri."

[43]Arima amaaje okimitara inkaranki amaanaki, airo. [44]Onkaimajena Mairikini, "Pimpoketa." [45]Tetamatsitanajana, kitatamatsitanajana otapinaki, maajeetatsi irori omenkoporo-

kini. ⁴⁶Oimaamachetena osavikira, okiyarontakenara. ⁴⁷Okimitaranki kaniri akitavaiteroranki, ari ikantamachetanari. ⁴⁸Osheki noñaashitakaro naari pairani. ⁴⁹Nokantapintzirori inaja, "Ina, naaka maperoteronimi noñaaperovaitya, okimiyeta asaropaye, airotaima nosaikataitzimi."

⁵⁰Noñaakoventakero Shirorani inoshikanakero, tema aajaitanaki inchapanki. ⁵¹Apanironira inoshikanakero, pashinipaye avisanaki, ijate yaye itzivini. ⁵²Inintzi yaanakeromi. ⁵³Oijatanakeri. ⁵⁴Nokinkishiriantariri, noposakiri aka iroñaaka tyarokinira Mayonkamara, iri noposakeri irakoki, yaapakantakarori Shirorani. ⁵⁵Aajeetavairo, otsonka omerianaka akoki inoshikavaitanakerora. ⁵⁶"Pamajenaro novarakite!" ⁵⁷Ikisakotaro ivarakite. ⁵⁸"Pamajenaro novarakitera, nopinakoventavaishitaro. ⁵⁹Pitsañatyaro." ⁶⁰Te impaitavajeri ivarakite. ⁶¹Yookanakiro inoshikavaitanaketzirora. ⁶²Akaraiyeni asaikamatsitzi pankotsiki. ⁶³Irotaki nokantavakeri.

¹This one (pointing to the drawing), long ago when I was a girl, and my father went to harvest coffee in Pampa Silva, this one is the one about whom I told you many times. ²This one is Mankori, he is worthless. ³He carried his arrows on his shoulders. ⁴This is true, I told you previously that [my fellow woman] the late Mairiki would dig a hole in the ground, put a wooden platform there, and we would cuddle below the platform. ⁵There were three of them: this one, Mankori, then Kochevari, then . . . whatchamacallit . . . ⁶Wait, I will remember, I will remember him forever, to tell you, Elena. ⁷Mankoite, [all] three of them, the warriors who kidnapped [children]. ⁸When they saw us, children of this size, they would kidnap us to sell, to exchange us for cartridges and rifles. ⁹That was their lifestyle, and he (pointing to the drawing in the textbook) was a chief long ago.

¹⁰When we came here [to Bajo Marankiari], my father left us; we were going to school, while my father was harvesting coffee over there in Pampa Silva and in Santa Ana. ¹¹Then the late Mairiki came in the middle of the night, made us keep silent and hide under the wooden platform; she made us bury ourselves: me, my sister, then Shiro, Tsirapa, and her sister, five of us, she made us lie flat under the platform. ¹²A warrior talked to her in vain, "Sister, come out, I want you to give [a child] to me." ¹³"There are no children here. ¹⁴Only me and my husband." ¹⁵The late Oopa [Mairiki's husband] defended us out of compassion. ¹⁶He didn't have much physical strength, but he would grab a wooden club with which he defended us, saying, "Truly, I will kill you." ¹⁷The late Oopa protected us. ¹⁸When the sun goes down, [he would say to us], "Stay here, don't walk around, lie down there," until my father arrived.

¹⁹Then my father arrived and took me to the coffee-harvesting area. ²⁰"Let's go and harvest coffee, otherwise warriors will kidnap you and sell you, and I will never see you again." ²¹They had a lot of arrows and spears. ²²This is true, many spears to kill [people]. ²³Later, when they saw my father and he wouldn't allow them, against their will, to take me away, they shot arrows at him.

²⁴This was a bad person, the small one, he would always say, "Why is it so?" ²⁵This small person is bad, he is the one about whom I told you before. ²⁶I knew him, the late Mairiki made me aware of him, and then my late sister Hortensia. ²⁷She would say to me, "Let's run away from him, woman, Marinkaite will kill us." ²⁸He is worthless; he killed a lot of people, that's why we were afraid of him.

²⁹Then Santoshi, he was the one who revealed to others, "They are there, Sharishi's daughters, let's kidnap them." ³⁰I was with my little brother, and he wanted to kidnap me but was

not able to do it. [31]He was dangerous, the one whose image is placed here [in the book]. [32]This one, Santoshi, it is written here about him, the deceased warrior Santoshi. [33]This is absolutely not good! [34]This is absolutely bad! [35]When he saw a child [he would say], "Give it to me!" [36]He would pull out his cartridges [and say], "I will pay you!"

[37]I cried a lot. [38]I would say, "Mother, don't leave me, the warriors will snatch me." [39]The warriors are worthless! [40]I stayed with my sister so that the warriors would not kidnap me. [41]"Stay with your sister, help her." [42]"No, the warriors will kill me."

[43]It was not possible for us to sleep like it was before. [44]The late Mairiki will call us, "Come." [45]She would put us in the hole, bury us under the platform, and we all would sleep there under her bed. [46]She made us sleep on the ground, against our will, where she had dug out [a hole] for us. [47]Like yuca, when we bury it in the ground, it happened to me [too], against my will. [48]I suffered a lot in the past. [49]I would always say to my mother, "Had I been a more active child, like my granddaughters, I would not possibly have been here."

[50]I witnessed the late Shiro's kidnapping, but we had wood planks at that time. [51]The kidnapper was alone; others passed on, carrying their salt. [52]He wanted to snatch her but failed. [53]We followed him. [54]What I remember of this is that I hit him here, that small person, Mayonkama, [with a wood plank], I hit him on the arm, and he let her go. [55]We rescued her, but all her hands were scraped because he had dragged her on the ground. [56]"Bring me my cartridges!" [57]He was angry because of the cartridges. [58]"Bring me my cartridges; I paid for her with them in vain! [59]You refused to give her to me." [60]He didn't get them back. [61]He left her where he was dragging her. [62]We lived with her together, out of compassion, in the house [of the late Mairiki]. [63]This is what I am telling you.

THIRTEEN

Nonkinkitsatakotero nayironi

(I Will Tell about My Deceased Mother-in-Law)

Victorina Roşas de Castro

[1]Kitaiteri maaroni, nonkinkitsatakotero nayironi. [2]Opoñaa-
naka pairani, inoshikiro ikantaitziri ovayeri. [3]Ari opoñaanaka
pairani aka ikantaitziro "kisaari nijaa." [4]Iroka iroñaaka avotsi
onatzi, ari okeni, okinapaki. [5]Osaikantari tonkariki antaroite
otzishi, oshiyarotaima Alto Marankiari. [6]Ijatzi iroñaaka iri
ikamotziri, ari ikamotziri aka nijaakika. [7]Ikanta ari ipokakeri
ovayeripaye. [8]Pairani intanakarori ovantzinkaripaye, ipokaki,
iñaapaintziro, yaapaintziro. [9]Ookanakiro otsipataro oyariripa-
tsaini. [10]Osaiki, okantzi, onikakotziri oyariri. [11]Ikantziro,
"Tsame aataje amenatero piniro. [12]Okantzi, pamajenaro
neentsitepaye."

[13]Itsaiyavaishita, yamatavitziro. [14]Ari yaanakerori iroñaaka,
ikenakakerori aka iroñaaka, itonkakapaintziro otzishikinta
tonkarikinta. [15]Ishonkakajaro aka iroñaaka, ovakota shontyo-
kika, ishonkakajaro, aajatzi ishitovakavetapanantaro. [16]Teka-
tsira yotatsini ikoshitatziro tsika ikinakaitakero aka iroka
Chinchivani, ikantaitziro añaaniki Shintsivani osaikira. [17]Oyo-
tavetapajaro, okantzi, imaakakero *siete días*. [18]Okinkishiriakero,
oyotanakero kitaiteripaye, onkantya ompiyajeta. [19]Oshiritajaro
oshiyapitsatajari, te ishinitero. [20]Ikaratzi amakerori *cinco*
itsikatziro, yoimaakiro niyanki. [21]Okantzija, ikintakavetanakaro

3. The kidnapped native woman Dominga Manuela Koñaari. Courtesy of the family of Dominga Manuela Koñaari, previoulsy published by Clark Graphics, 2010, ethnolinguistica.org

kentsori otzishitapakinta, te oyari. ²²Te onkove oya, te otashaje, otsarovakinta antaroite.

²³Ikenakapakero ikantaitziri nijaa Porokayari, irokamaja Anakayari. ²⁴Okantzi, okantapakaro iroñaaka imaakanajiro, imaakanajiro. ²⁵Yaniitakashitakaro aka, osamani imaakakero. ²⁶Yareetakakaro, imontyakapakaro, areetantapakari aka iroñaaka Koviriaki. ²⁷Ari isaiki aka atziri, irotaima *paujil*tatsiri, avajiro aka Paujil. ²⁸Ari iñaavakerori ashaninka, okantavetavakaro, "Kooya, inoshikaitatzimira, impimantaitatyemi. ²⁹Eero pipiyaja. ³⁰Yaatzimi iyoka, ovayeripaye inatzi." ³¹Okantzija, "Niraka, niraka, tekatsi nonkinaje, noshiyaje."

³²Okantapajero yamakero irojatzi yareetakantakaro Azupizu. ³³Okantzi pairanija irojatzi itzimavetani akantashityari *movilizable*paye, *soldados*, iyoshita *gringos*. ³⁴Saikatsi aka Azupizu. ³⁵Ikinakapakiro iroka, ipampitsatziro nijaa, aka nijaa irojatzi Meriteriani, Meritariki. ³⁶Jeroka, ikinakaitapakero irojatzi Shimaki. ³⁷Okantzi, ovakerani ari ishoshonkatakarori. ³⁸Iroma aka imaakanajiro iroñaaka, Shimaki.

³⁹Ari ikinakapakiro irojatzita aka ikantaitziro tonkarikika, otzishi onatzi. ⁴⁰Ikantaitziro Pamoroitoni, Cerro Paloma. ⁴¹Ikinakaitziro shonkaka intakerokika, ikantaitziro Sotziki, oyapiki Sotzini, irojatzi areetantajia Chorinkaveniki. ⁴²Ikinakaitapakero, aniitzi, omaanaji avotsiki. ⁴³Okinapaji irojatzi Mapiniki. ⁴⁴Ari okantzi, ari oshaikapake Mapiniki. ⁴⁵Ipoña ivakakaro ikinakapajiro iroñaaka Kishitariki, poña ikantaitziri *numero tres*, areetantyari iroñaaka ikantaitziro Pampa Whaley. ⁴⁶Arive. ⁴⁷Ari okantapakaro, ari okinapakiri. ⁴⁸Areetaka Pampa Whaley, yaaitanajiro, aisatzita ikiakotakaitanakaro mooraki irojatzita La Merced ikantaitziro pairani Tsiirishi.

⁴⁹Yaaitanakero, okantzi, aritaima yoyakotzirori ipimantai-

takerora. [50]Ipaitavakeri ooyapaye aanakerorira, yaanake ooya. [51]Okantzi, "Noñaakoventaka" vaarakipaye ipayetakiri inoshikayetakeniri saviri, kitsarentsipaye. [52]Yaanajiri. [53]"Ari nosaiki niravaita, te noya. [54]Yookaitanakena. [55]Opavetavakana shiñora ovarite, te noya. [56]Yookaitanakena, yashitakoitanakena, apite kitaiteri, okantzi, Tsiirishiki."

[57]Okitaitamanai yaaitanakero, yaaitanakero irojatzita Taromaki. [58]Ari osaikapakeri tsikataima okaratzi osarentsitakotake. [59]Te ayotero pairani osarentsite, iro osarentsitakotake. [60]Ivavisaitakero Taromaki irojatzitakia Irimashiki. [61]Pairani Irimashi tekira ontzimanaketa *pista* irojatzi maaroni okipatsitzi, intainapaye pankotsipaye. [62]Okantzi, ojatantapanantari, okantzi, "Te noyotajero, intaani noyotziro isaikakaitana ikantaitziro 'Lima Callao,' isaikakaitana pairani." [63]Okantzi, ari osaikiri, ipiyakaitajaro iroñaaka osaikantapajari ikantaitziri Chunchuyakoki.

[64]Ari osaikapajiri amenapajiri vaaka. [65]Jatayetatzi poñiinkaripaye Marankiaro, yantavaijeetzi iroñaaka Chunchuyakoki. [66]Ipoñanaka isaikayetatziri i*sirve*tayetatziri *su patria*, ikantaitziri pairani *movilizable*, isoraroyetzi. [67]Ari isaiki, opipiyatantari irorikia oñaajeetziri anta. [68]Okantzi, oyotakero okitsatakara monkiñaki, oshiyanakaro ashitarori oitsari chora. [69]Okantzija, "Aviroka ashaninka?" [70]Okantzi, "Je, naakataki." [71]Okantzi, "Tsame, aataje."

[72]Okantzi, antavaitzi *tres de la mañana*, ivasakiriaitziro antavaitzi. [73]Onkotsivaitanake, ompanakeri *pavo, pato, chancho*, otsitzipaye. [74]Ontsonka ontsiyanakeri ivaritepaye, jaitetzi om*paste*yateri vaakapaye. [75]Onkantakotya areetajia *a las diez de la anoche*. [76]Okantzi, ompokajerika arika ameniri ontsonka ampatotanajeri maaroni vaaka, *becerro*, oiminkianajeri, ontsonkia ontsiparianajeri. [77]Arika impia-

kia aparoni, iritaki opiaventapintari. [78]Areetajiarika, inkisaitavakero aajatzita, "Paita osamanitantakari?" [79]Okantzi, ari okantapintatya.

[80]Oñaakoventziro iroñaaka Isaverani, ikisavaitaitziro, okantzirokia, "Tsame aataje, ashaninka, tsame! [81]Okisavaitzimi osheki. [82]Tzimatsi nonampi okaakini, ari ajataje, ashiye. [83]Pipianitatyara pameni vaaka *hasta las diez u once,* ametakaro, eero okovityami. [84]Ajataje, ashiyaperopitsaterota." [85]Okantzi, ari okantakero. [86]Iroñaaka opoñaakanajaro, osamanitaki osaikake osarentsi. [87]Okantzikia, "Tetya nosamavetya, inaveta nantavaitzi, amivetakana nantavaitzi okantajeetanara, okinkishiriakakana, nojatetataima. [88]Noshiyakantzi, ari nareetajia nonampiki. [89]Nojatanaje iroñaaka Marankiaroki, nosaikapaje, nojataita nonampiki."

[90]Okantzi, "Nomanaka, nomanaka," opokavetatanakaro kaaro, aritaima okovanakerora. [91]Okantzi, omananakakaro. [92]Opoñaakakaro Chunchuyako, La Merced, "Iroñaaka arika nonkimiro kaaro, otamakoshitatzira, tzirianajana otamakoshiki." [93]Amenanavetyaro, te añeero. [94]Areetakajaro iroñaaka *numero tres.* [95]Okinakapajiro, omontyakapajaro ikantaitziri Pampa Silva, irojatzi osaikantakari Marankiaroki. [96]Okanta okokovavetaro, te iyoitajero tsika osaiki, te añaajero tsika osaiki.

[97]Okantzi, "Nosaikapaje apite osarentsi," okantzi, oyotakero osaikimotapajiri iroñaaka iririka *tío* Abdias. [98]Ikantakero iroñaaka, "Payeri Jurio Castro. [99]Tzimatsi ivani, tekatsi kovachani, iritaki pintsipatapajiari avirori." [100]Okantzi, "Ari nomairitzi, nokinkishiria. [101]Nojatzi namitakotantzi notsipatapajaro ishani Manonka." [102]Irotaki nosaikimotapajero. [103]Okantzi, "Nopokajira, ari nosaikiri Kemariaki. [104]Opoña omontyakajana nosaikantapajari Marankiaroki." [105]Osaikapaji Marankiaroki, ipaitakero Jurio Castro. [106]Aakeri

Jurio, yookanakero, ijatzi i*movilizable*tzi irirori San Ramonki *cinco* osarentsite. [107]Ipokaji, aajatzi yaapajiro. [108]Osaiki Marankiaroki irojatzi intzimantanakia eentsitepaye, irojatzita otsonkantapaja, okamantapakari. [109]Ari okantari irorija añaantari Dominga. [110]Yamaitziro, ikoshitziro, ikoshitakero. [111]Opoñaanaka jaka nijaa *negro*tatsirika Shintsivaki, ari opoñaanakari irojatzi okamantaja. [112]Te oñaajiro onampi, te ompiyaje areetajiaro, oshirivetapintari oshaninkapaye. [113]Ari okitatari iroñaaka aka Marankiaroki. [114]Ari overapakari.

[1]Good day, everyone, I will tell about my deceased mother-in-law. [2]She came [here] long ago, [when] she was kidnapped by those called warriors. [3]She came from here, from the area called Río Negro. [4]This is the trail, she walked [on this trail] here. [5]She had lived on a big hill, like the one of Alto Marankiari. [6]Her parents went fishing; they were fishing here in the river. [7]In the meantime, warriors came. [8]In the past, there were killers: they would come, see a woman, and snatch her. [9]Her mother had left my mother-in-law with her little brothers. [10]She says, she was inside rocking the hammock with her little brother. [11]They said to her, "Let's go see your mother. [12]She says, bring her the baby."

[13]They were lying, they deceived her. [14]They grabbed her and made her walk uphill to the highest point. [15]They made a circle here, around this point (pointing to the map), made another circle, and left one more time from the same place. [16]Nobody knew that she was taken from Chinchivani; in our language it is called Shintsivani, the place where she lived. [17]She recognized the place where they stayed overnight for seven days. [18]She remembered it; she knew how to count days, so that she could come back. [19]She was thinking about fleeing from them, but they didn't give her an opportunity. [20]Those who brought her [there] were five in number, and they held her tight, they made her

sleep between them. ²¹She says, they killed birds for her in the hills, but she didn't eat them. ²²She didn't want to eat, she wasn't hungry, [because] she was very frightened.

²³They made her walk to the river Apurucayali, then Anaca-yali. ²⁴She says, they stayed overnight in this area for a long time. ²⁵They stayed for many days. ²⁶Then they crossed the river to arrive in Puerto Bermúdez [Koviriaki]. ²⁷People lived in this vil-lage, called Paujil, we'll call it Paujil. ²⁸There my fellow men saw her, and a woman told her, "Woman, you are being kidnapped, they will sell you. ²⁹You will not come back. ³⁰These people are taking you away, they are raiders." ³¹She says, "I cried and cried; I didn't know how to get away."

³²They brought her to the settlement of Azupizu. ³³She said that long ago there were what we call "the mobilized," soldiers, pure whites. ³⁴They lived in Azupizu. ³⁵The raiders made her walk there, they followed the trail, walking along the river to the village of Meriteriani. ³⁶Here they made her walk to the village of Shimaki. ³⁷She says, at first they made circles. ³⁸Nonetheless, they stayed overnight in Shimaki.

³⁹From there, they walked up to the crest of the hill. ⁴⁰It is called the Hill of Doves. ⁴¹They made her walk, making circles on the other side of the area, called Sotziki, where the river So-tzini begins, before they arrived in the village of Churingaveni. ⁴²They walked and slept on the trail. ⁴³They walked to the area of the village of San Jeronimo de Yurinaki. ⁴⁴In this place, she said, they stayed overnight. ⁴⁵Then they walked to the village of Mariscal Cáceres, then to the privately owned plantation called "number 3," in order to arrive in Pampa Whaley. ⁴⁶Very well. ⁴⁷So she kept walking. ⁴⁸Then they grabbed her and made her ride on a mule all the way to La Merced, which was called in the past Tsiirishi.

⁴⁹There they held her, she said, perhaps waiting for someone,

in this place where they sold her. [50]Those who brought her were given pots, and they took pots. [51]She said, "I saw it," cartridges with bullets, axes, clothes were given to those who kidnapped her. [52]They took it. [53]"I stayed there and cried; I didn't eat. [54]The raiders left me there. [55]The owner gave me food, but I didn't eat [her food]. [56]They left me, they locked me up for two days in La Merced," she says.

[57]Early in the morning they took her to Tarma. [58]There she stayed for some years. [59]We didn't count years in the past, years would pass by. [60]From Tarma she was passed on to Lima. [61]In the past, there were no roads in Lima, only open land, and houses were at a distance. [62]When she went to Lima another time [many years later], she said that she didn't recognize it, only the area where they forced her to stay, called Lima Callao, "They made me stay [in this place] long ago." [63]She says, she lived there, and then they made her go back to live in the place that is now called Chanchamayo [San Ramon].

[64]There she lived and took care of cows. [65]Visitors from Marankiari would come, they worked in San Ramon. [66]There also were those who served the country, they were called in the past "the mobilized," "soldiers." [67]They lived there, that's why many women would come to visit them. [68]She said, a woman recognized her, although she was dressed in an Andean skirt, like the Andean female owner's. [69]She said to her, "Are you Ashaninka?" [70]She said, "Yes, I am." [71]She said, "Let's go."

[72]She says, she worked from three in the morning, [when] she was called to work. [73]She will cook food and give it to peacocks, ducks, pigs, and dogs. [74]After she has finished feeding the animals, she will herd the cows to the pasture. [75]She would come back at ten in the evening. [76]She says, she would go back after she gathers all cows and calves together and places them in their corrals, after she separates them all. [77]If an animal is lost, she has

to go and search for it, which takes a lot of time. [78]When she comes back, they will distress her with questions, "Why are you late?" [79]She says, it was always this way that she would come late.

[80]Isabel saw this, that they pestered her, and said to her, "Let's go, my fellow woman, let's go! [81]The mistress aggravates you a lot. [82]My village is nearby, let's go, we will escape. [83]Because you always disappear, herding cows until ten or eleven at night, she is accustomed to it, she won't look for you. [84]We will go and get away from her." [85]She says, this is what Isabel would tell her. [86]Many years had passed [since she began working in San Ramon]. [87]She says, "It didn't tire me, I didn't mind working, I was accustomed to doing what they told me, but she made me think, maybe, I should go. [88]I imagined that I would come to my village. [89]I will go to Marankiari, I will stay there, and then I will go to my village."

[90]She says, "I kept hiding," because a car passed that was probably looking for her. [91]She says, it forced her to hide. [92]She walked from San Ramon to La Merced, "When I heard a car, since there were steep drops alongside the road, I would slip down and hide in the precipice." [93]They were looking for her but she was never found. [94]She arrived at the plantation "number 3." [95]She came there, crossed to the other side, to the place called Pampa Silva; since then she [has] lived in Marankiari. [96]They kept looking for her, but they didn't know where she was, they didn't find out where she was.

[97]She says, she lived for two years in the house of Uncle Abdias's father. [98]He said to her, "Marry Julio Castro. [99]He has a piece of land, you won't lack food, and he'll be your companion." [100]She says, "I got quiet and thought about it. [101]I went to help the now-deceased grandmother Manonka. [102]I lived together with her." [103]She said, "When I came [to live with her], I stayed

in Kimariaki." [104]Then she crossed the river, "That's why I live in Bajo Marankiari." [105]She stayed in Bajo Marankiari, and they gave her to Julio Castro. [106]She married Julio, but he left her because he went to serve in San Ramon's garrison for five years. [107]He came back and took her as his wife again. [108]She lived in Bajo Marankiari until her children were born, until she died. [109]Such was Dominga's life. [110]She was brought [here], she was kidnapped. [111]She came here from the Río Negro, from Shintsivani, she came here from that place [and stayed here] until she died. [112]She never saw her village again, she never returned there, but she always longed to see her family. [113]She was buried here in Marankiari. [114]This is all.

FOURTEEN

Tsika okanta nosaikantakari Marankiaroki

(How We Settled Down in Bajo Marankiari)

Bertha Rodríguez de Caleb

[1]Naaka nonkinkitsatemi nokanta ovakera nosaikantapaka. [2]Ovakerani asaikantajari noshaninkapaye te iyote iñaanate, te iyote isankinate. [3]Tzimatsi aparoni yoimoshirinkaitziri, irotaki te iyoteri pava. [4]Tzimatsi irora paitachari mapi, iritaki ivavanitari. [5]Iritaki yamaniri ipaita Yompiri. [6]Tzimatsi iyotziri ivavani yoimoshirinkiri. [7]Yamaniri ikimoshirivintziri, iritaki ovavisakojeetziriri, iritaki opairi avari. [8]Yantzi antaroite pankotsi, ari impiyovintyari yoimoshirinkiri, yamanajeetziri ivavani ishinkitavintyari. [9]Pokatsi osheki evankaripaye, evankaropaye, ari okantari ovakerani aka.

[10]Aajatzi ivavanitari paamari. [11]Yaakerorika paamanto tsitsi, yshiyakakoventakerorika samampo, onkisotanakerika ovira, osaikaki onkisotanakerika, irotaki ivavanitari yamaniri. [12]Ari ikanta pairani noshaninkapaye ivavanitari irojatzita ovirapaka, irojatzi ipokantaka aparoni amakirori ñaantsi, poñaachari *los Estados Unidos* pishaninkapaye kimisantzinkari. [13]Yamakiro aka iñaani pava. [14]Ikimakovintakiro, areetapaka kinkitsarentsi irirori, ikantajeetziri, "Pava inatzi, areetaka, iritaki amanapintziri. [15]Koñaataki Pava, yamakiro tasorinkantsi, yamakiro iritaki

4. Fernando Stahl, an Adventist missionary, preaches the Christian Gospel to locals. By Daniel Bernales Quillatupa (Aroshi).

ovavisakotajaini." [16]Ikaimanakiri maaroni ishaninkapaye, kirinka pokayetaintsiri, irotaki ishekitantari atziri pairani aka.

[17]Iritaki amakirori [ñaantsi] aparoni kitamarantzi pishaninkapaye ipaita *pastor* Fernando Estar. [18]Amakirori ñaantsi, aka osaikantakari, okanta ayotantajari kapicheeni añaanavaitzi.

[19]Imapokapakiri. [20]Ipokakira oshekini ashaninka, "Iroñaaka ipokapaki, ikinkitsakapakiri." [21]Yaminapakiri oshekini ashaninka. [22]"Iroñaaka ontzimi aparoni *escuela*," iyotantajiari noshaninkapaye. [23]Isaikakira aka, yookakantakiri ivavani. [24]Te yamanajiro imapini, te yamanajiro ivaamarite, yookanakiro. [25]Iroñaaka tzimatsi ikantziri pava Pachaka, Pachakama, ivavanitari noshaninkapaye intanankarori.

[26]Iñaavakeri, ikantzi, "Iritaki Pava iripirori, yoka, areetaka." [27]Pokajeetaki, okaratzi ashaninka pokaintsiri, yaminakero, isaikajeetapaki Metararoki. [28]Ari osaikakeri *misión* yantakantakiri pastor. [29]Noshaninkapaye ipoñaashitanaka yaminakiro, tekatsi nijaa, "Tsame ajataje aka, ankaavaitapajiata pareniki."

[30]Oirinkajeetaka, ari osaikapakiri *misión* intatzikeronta, ikantaitziro Kemariani. [31]Ari ipoñaanakari iyotantajari noshaninkapaye kapicheeni. [32]Ari okantari ovakerani intanakarori aka, ipokakira pishaninka amakirori ñaantsi.

[33]Amakirori ñaantsi, ikanta iyotantajari, noshaninkapaye ovakerani te iyote iñaanate, te iriyotero isankinate.

[34]Okanta osaikatzika *compañía*, te ishinitero ante avanipaye intatzikero. [35]Te ishinitero ante avani ampankite parentzi, machaki, kaniri avantyari, itsañaakaro. [36]Arika iñaakiro apankite kaniri, machaki, yamakeri ivaakate, itsonkiro ivaro maaroni machaki, avakayaririmi eentsitepatsaini.

[37]Ovirantapakarori ikantzi, "Tsame ajate kirinka iroñaaka. [38]Ankenanake kirinka, tsame aminerota. [39]Pimpoketave kirinka, antaroite kipatsi. [40]Tekatsi ñaashirinkajaini, ampankitapaita apankite, ampimante, ayari, avakayari eentsitepaye." [41]Ari ikenajeetakiri.

[42]Ishekivita aka saikatsiri. [43]Itsipariantanakari, jatayetaji kirinka, tsika ikenayetzi yaayetaje iipatsite. [44]Kaari amitapaintya kirinka, piyayetaja isaikantapajari Marankiaroki.

[45]Maatsi intakantarori isaikita aka ikantaitziri Irasaro. [46]"Tsame ajataje, ajavitapainta kirinka, tsame ampiyaje." [47]Te iramitya saikapaje, imontyantakari, isaikantanakari, otzimantakari nampitsi Marankiaro.

[48]Tzimatsi intarori isaikita noshaninka aka, iyotziro ivitsikiro, ikantziri añaaniki poñiinkari. [49]Iritaki vitsikakiro apaniroini saviri, shecha, ipesantari itovantari ivani. [50]Noshaninkapaye ipoki kirinka yamayetziri vitzitsipaye, ivitzi tsimeri, vaneenkantzi, ipoki ikampiatziri.

[51]Añaavetyari virakochapaye noshaninkapaye, ikantzi noshaninka, "Eero paitziniri irooyate, eero paitziniri oka okaratzi iitsari, aritaki ankamake, yamatziro imantsiyarentsite. [52]Aitsari aroka akirikajeetatziro, antajeetzi noshaninka-

paye. [53]Nosaro ovametakero eentsipaye okirikairo, antzi kitsarentsi. [54]Irotaki okitsajeetari, te oninte okitsatyariri irashi virakochapaye kitamarantzi."

[55]Ari ipiyotari yantavaijeetzi aka, ikantziri noñaaniki poñiinkari. [56]Poñiinkaripaye evankaripaye yantavajeetzi, te iñeero kooya, te iyotero imayempitero kooya. [57]Evankaropaye te oñeeri shiramparipaye. [58]Irotaki antavaijeetatzi, opoña aka ikantaitziro Ashiropanko. [59]Ari ivetsikirori pairani poñiinkaripaye, ari isaikiri aka. [60]Ari okantari ovakerani aka, osaikantakari irojatzi impokantakia *pastor*.

[61]Ari yookanakiro yantavairi, iñaavakerira virakochapaye. [62]Iyotanakiro yantavaijeetzi opankitapakira *compañía*, okiapakira *compañía*. [63]Opankitakantaki kajai osheki, aritaki ijatzi yantavaijeetzi noshaninkapaye *como esclavos*. [64]Ari ikantari irojatzi okiantapakia *compañía*. [65]Ari otsonkapakari, tekatsi antavaitanatsini apaniroini evankiripaye irirori.

[66]Tekatsi atziri aka, inampi maranki, inampi kamari, inampi manitzi, tekatsite saikatsini. [67]Tzimatsi aparoni sheripiari. [68]Ikantzi paitaranki, imaaki, imishitakiri, iñaakiri aka, ari isaikiri tzimatsi iriniro maranki, iriniro manitzi, iriniro kamari. [69]"Tsame averi!" [70]Ipokajeetaki sheripiari, yapotojeetaka, irakiro isherini, imaajeetaki.

[71]Opariaki antaroite inkani, ookatsatanaka, opoña otarankanaki. [72]Antarotaki nijaa. [73]Otzimanaki omoro tonkariki, ari isaikiri ivanko kamari tonkariki. [74]Ookatsatakara, otonkanakera ookatsarontsi, ookantapakaro inchatora. [75]Otsonka okotariapakiro, otaapakiro. [76]Otsonkatanaka okotariakiro okaratzi iriniro kamari, maranki, manitzi. [77]Itsonkakiri yashitakotakiri sheripiaripaye. [78]Irotaki añaantajarori okameetsataji, ipokaki sheripiari, ivamakiri marankipaye. [79]Iroñaaka te añaajiro, kameetsayetaji.

[80]Ari okantari asaiki apaniroini, te osaikanite osheki pan-

kotsi, aparoni *o* mava pankotsi. [81]Pairani te ayotero ante anampitsite antaroite. [82]Intaina, intaina isaikajeetzi. [83]Nokantakiri inkaranki, opokakira amakirori ñaantsi, añaantajarori apototaja, tzimanaki anampitsite, saikajeetakai aka. [84]Ovakerani tekatsi, intaina isaiki, isaiki pashini, te intsipatavakaiya. [85]Ari okaratzi.

[1]I will tell you how we came to live here. [2]When my fellow men came to live here, they knew neither how to write nor to read. [3]They had one [god] who was celebrated, but they didn't know God. [4]There was one called Stone, this is what they worshipped. [5]What they praised was called Yompiri. [6]They acknowledged their god who cheered them up. [7]They worshipped him, they rejoiced on his account because he helped them and gave them food. [8]They made a big house in which they congregated, cheered and praised their god, and drank on his account. [9]A lot of my fellow men were coming, young men and women, so it was in the past.

[10]Also, what they worshipped was fire. [11]When they gathered wood, when it turned into ashes, when it hardened like this and sat like a solid structure, this was what they worshipped and praised. [12]So it was in the past that my fellow men worshipped it, until it ended, until came the one who brought the word from the United States, from your religious fellow men. [13]He brought here the word of God. [14]They heard that his book arrived and said, "This is God, he arrived, this is what we worship now. [15]God appeared and brought blessings, brought what will save us." [16]They called out all fellow men who came from downriver, and a lot of people gathered here.

[17]The one who brought [the Word], a white person, one of your fellow men, was called Pastor Fernando Stahl. [18]He brought

5. Locals harvest coffee on the orders of the Peruvian Corporation's foreman. By Daniel Bernales Quillatupa (Aroshi).

the Word here; that's why it [religion] exists here and we know how to read.

[19]He surprised them. [20]When he arrived, many fellow men [said], "He came and he has preached it." [21]He saw many of my fellow men. [22][He said], "Now we will have a school," to teach my fellow men. [23]When he lived here, the [old] god was abandoned. [24]They didn't worship the stone, the fire, they abandoned them. [25]There was another whom they called god Pachaka, Pachakama, which was [also] worshipped by my ancestral fellow men in the past.

[26]They saw him and said, "This is true God, this, he arrived." [27]They came, they all came, saw him, and settled in Metraro. [28]There was a mission that the pastor made them construct [in Metraro]. [29]Afterward my fellow men realized that there was no water source: "Let's go here, so that we could bathe in the river." [30]They went down the hill and established a mission on

the other side of the river, in Kimariani. [31]There my fellow men learned a little bit. [32]So the founders were this way in the past, when your fellow man came, who brought the Word.

[33]He brought the Word, that's why they learned [literacy], because my fellow men hadn't known how to write, they hadn't known how to read.

[34]Because the company [Peruvian Corporation] was here, they didn't allow us to clear land on the other side. [35]They didn't allow us to clear land to plant plantains, beans, and manioc for eating, they resisted it. [36]When they saw us plant manioc and beans, they would bring cows, and they will eat all beans that could have been fed to our children.

[37]The youngest said, "Let's go downriver. [38]We'll go downriver to look around. [39]Come downriver, there is a lot of land there. [40]Nobody will pester us, we'll plant our seedlings, we'll sell, eat, and feed our children." [41]So they went.

[42]There were a lot of them who stayed here. [43]They split, [one group stayed and others] went downriver where each took a plot of land. [44]They weren't accustomed to [living] downriver, and they returned, that's why they settled down in Bajo Marankiari.

[45]There was a founder who came to live here before others, called Lazaro. [46]"Let's go, you've gone in vain downriver, let's return!" [47]They weren't accustomed to living downriver, they crossed the river, that's why they live here, that's why there is the village Bajo Marankiari.

[48]There was a founder who had lived here before others did, and he knew how to fabricate things, [he was] what is called in our language "visitor." [49]He made by himself axes and machetes to clear grass and cut trees. [50]My fellow men would come from downriver, bring bird feathers of different colors, they would come to barter.

[51]My fellow men would see white people and say, "Don't take

their pots, their clothes, you'll die, they bring illnesses. ⁵²Our fellow men make our own robes with the loom, by weaving them. ⁵³Our grandmothers have taught little girls to weave, and they make clothes. ⁵⁴This they wear, they don't want to wear the clothing of white people."

⁵⁵So they congregated and worked here, [those] whom they call in our language "visitors." ⁵⁶Young male visitors were working, but they weren't seeing women, they weren't seeing women. ⁵⁷Young girls weren't seeing males. ⁵⁸They worked here, and they would come from the place called Ashiropanko (the Iron House). ⁵⁹The visitors fabricated things [from iron], and they lived here. ⁶⁰This was how they had lived here in the past before the pastor arrived.

⁶¹They abandoned their work when they encountered white people. ⁶²They learned to work, when the company [Peruvian Corporation] planted [its cultigens], when the company entered the area. ⁶³They planted a lot of coffee, and my fellow men worked like slaves. ⁶⁴This had been the way before the company made an entrance. ⁶⁵Then it ended, there was nobody to work [in Ashiropanko (the Iron House)], and young men were alone.

⁶⁶There were no people here, because of great quantities of snakes, evil spirits, and jaguars—there was no one living here. ⁶⁷There was one shaman. ⁶⁸They say, he fell asleep and saw it in his dream that there were the Master of snakes, the Master of jaguars, and the Master of evil spirits in this place. ⁶⁹[He said,] "We'll kill them." ⁷⁰Many shamans came, they all gathered together, drank tobacco syrup, and fell asleep.

⁷¹There was heavy rain, lightning, and then a landslide. ⁷²The river swelled. ⁷³There was a hole on the top of the hill—there lived the evil spirit, in his abode on the top of the hill. ⁷⁴When the lightning flashed and struck, it struck a tree. ⁷⁵It split the tree and burned it. ⁷⁶It split in two the Master of evil spirits, the Master of snakes, and the Master of jaguars. ⁷⁷It ended the shamanic

vigil. [78]That's why we live in peace, because shamans came and killed the snakes. [79]Now we don't see them, all is well.

[80]We each lived alone, and there weren't many houses, one or three. [81]We didn't know the custom of living in big villages. [82]They all were far, far away. [83]As I said before, because the one who brought the Word came, we live together, there is a village, and we are all here. [84]Before, no, we lived far away, in different places, and didn't gather together. [85]That's all.

FIFTEEN

Tsika okanta noñaakoventakiri matsipaye

(How I Witnessed Events
Involving Witches)

Bertha Rodríguez de Caleb

[1]Akinkitsatero nosaikantapaintari aka, ikantaitziro Nasarai-teki. [2]Ari noñaakoventakiriri matsipaye.

[3]Yamaitakiro. [4]Ipoki pashini ashaninka, ipoki aka, ikantaitziro Tziviarini. [5]Ari osaikiri tzivi, yaajeetzi itzivini. [6]Ipokaji, yamaji itzivini. [7]Iñaanajiro aparoni kooya. [8]Osaiki avotsiki, aparoni kooya iitamatsitziri. [9]Iñaapakiro osaiki, itsonka ichekaitakiro, oitoki maaroni, ovatsaki, oitziki, ovoroki, itsonka ichekaitakiro. [10]Iñaapakiro osaiki. [11]"Paita antakimiri?" [12]"Ichekaitatyana." [13]"Paita ichekaitantamiri?" [14]"Ikantaitatyana, matsi nonatzi."

[15]Iroka kooyaka ochekaka. [16]Tzimatsi mava okaratzi okanta ocharonenta. [17]Ikanta imantsiyatanaki eentsite, okantzi, "Irotaki matsikakiri. [18]Aviroka matsikakiniri neentsite." [19]Akakiro okantzi, "Naakataki ovakari." [20]Aakero otsipataro apiteroiteni ocharonentavakara, oposakiro. [21]Okanta oposavaitziro, aashitakiro kotsiro, otsonka ochekakiro maaroni. [22]Oitoki, otsonka ochekayetakiro. [23]Ovamakiro. [24]Onoshikanakiro osaiki antaroite inchamenta, ari onariakirori. [25]Otarovashitakiro kami-

6. The woman accused of sorcery is forced to dig for her charms.
By Daniel Bernales Quillatupa (Aroshi).

shi, opashikantakarori. [26]Opiyotakero, piyotaka okamishi,
otyakotakiro, opokapitsatajiro.

[27]Okantataima irori, okantakota okamakira tsika oviraka,
otzinaja, tzinaja. [28]Okimita kaarashira opashikantakaro,
otzinaja, jataji. [29]Okeni onoshikaja, onoshikaja. [30]Osaika-
vaitzi, omayi, okimitanta oparaimashiki, ari osaiki omayi.

[31]Korakitaji atziri amatsiri itzivini, iñaantapajarori osaiki.
[32]Yamenapakiro itsonka ichekaitakero, yamajiro iroñaaka
anampikika asaikira ikantaitziro, opaita nampitsi San Pablo.
[33]Ipokaji ivira yareetakajaro kimitaka mava, yareetakajaro
ashaninkapaye. [34]Ikantzi, "Tzimatsi yamaitakiro ashaninka,
ichekaitakiro." [35]Nojataki, namenapakiro. [36]Oh, noñaapakiro
ochekaka. [37]"Paita ichekantaitarori?" [38]Okantzi, "Ikantaitatziro,
matsi onatzi."

³⁹Ari amenakiro pashini ashaninka, amashitakiro tsikarika opaita aavintantarori. ⁴⁰Aavintakiro, aavintakiro.
⁴¹Okanta añiiro avisakotaji ichekayetakirora, avisakotaji.
⁴²Pashini ashaninka okantzi, "Irotaki noshaninka nirento,
novatziro nirentotsoripaye onatzi." ⁴³Avisakotanajira, jataji.
⁴⁴Oyotapajiro oshaninka, jaitetaji anta, ari osaikajiri. ⁴⁵Avisa-
kotajira, ari osaikimotapajiro irento.
    ⁴⁶Okanta osaikaki, osamanitaki. ⁴⁷Opoñaashitaka omapo-
kanaka irento omantsiyatanaki. ⁴⁸Nokemashitakari tsiteni,
ipokashitapaintana, "Omantsiyatatzi, onkamatye. ⁴⁹Opaita
Martha mantsiyataintsiri."
    ⁵⁰Okantzi, "Omishitavakiro saikimotzirori ovankokira."
⁵¹Okantzi, "Osaikapakiro otapiki." ⁵²Okantziro paitaranki,
"entyo, nosaikimi pitapiki, nonkarayemi, noshiyakantemi
shimpi." ⁵³Osakitanaki, okemataitziro oyatsinka ara.
    ⁵⁴Okanta iroñaaka kitaitetanaki, okantzi, "Maperotanaka,
onkamatye." ⁵⁵Ajatashijeetakiro ameniro, añaapakiro onariaka.
    ⁵⁶"Paita antakimiri?" ⁵⁷Okantzi, "Nokatsitatzi notapiki,
nomapokashitanaka. ⁵⁸Sheeteni tekatsi, nonkantya naapaintzi
sanko. ⁵⁹Nashiyajeetziri sanko, irotaki nokemantavakari.
⁶⁰Maatsi yotatsiri ochonkantzi?" ⁶¹Ochonkapakiro. ⁶²Irotaki
pariapaintziri osankoni ashiyajeetakiri otakipaye. ⁶³Irotaki
totanakirori otapiki otsakiki.
    ⁶⁴Iroñaaka pokaki, tzimatsi iritsoripaye. ⁶⁵Ikantzi, "Irotaki
matsikapakirori, iroka saikimotakirorira." ⁶⁶Iroñaaka, uh, ari
noñaakoventakirori iposaitakiro matsira. ⁶⁷Yaashitaitakiro
inchapanki atsinkantarori *arroz*, iposaitakiro iroñaaka. ⁶⁸Koo-
yara te onkemero katsiri. ⁶⁹Aritaima omatsiperotzira, te onkemero katsiri. ⁷⁰Noñaajantzi ari onkaimanake, te. ⁷¹Ikantziro,
"Aviroka matsikakiro pirento?" ⁷²Je, naakataki."⁷³"Paakotajero."
⁷⁴Okiyaki iroñaaka, okiyaki. ⁷⁵Onoshikayetaji, irotaki aajiri
sankotakipaye. ⁷⁶Ikanta ipokapaji pashini. ⁷⁷Ikantzi, "Tsame

avero." [78]Ikantzi pashini, "Airo piviro, tsame asampitero, asampitero. [79]Asaiki anampikika, tzimatsi matsi aajatzita."

[80]Isampitanakiro iroñaaka, "Aka tzimatsi matsi nonampikika?" [81]Okantzi, "Je, tzimatsi oshekini, noñaayetapakiri. [82]Naaka iroñaaka te nonkovavetya nomatsikeromi nirento. [83]Ipokajeetapakira pashini, ikantzi, 'Tsame ayaro, tsame amatsikero.' [84]Irotaki nomatsikantakarori."

[85]Isampitanakero iroñaaka, "Tsika iroñaaka? [86]Pinkaimenari!" [87]Ookotanakeri. [88]Ikantavetakari inkaranki, ikinkitsatzi ookotavakanaka, ari okantzirika, "Jiroka, jirika shirampari, jiroka kooya." [89]"Nokarajeetzika."

[90]Ikaimaitakiro iroñaaka pashini, pashini, pashini. [91]Oh, piyojeetapakave! [92]Ari noñaakoventakeriri ikantaitziri matsi, ari nokatziya nameni. [93]Opokapaji, tzimatsi aparoni isha, okatziya. [94]Okantana, "Nosaro, paita pipokantari pameniri matsi? [95]Tzimatsi peentsite, ari imatsitake. [96]Eero pameniri. [97]Te yamenaiteri matsitatsiri, pijataje." [98]Ari nopiyanaka, jaitetakina. [99]Te noñaakoventajero tsika ikantakiro osamanitanaki.

[100]Tsitenitanaki aikero yookotatziro, yookotatziro, "Jiro." [101]Ani-aniijeetanaki ashaninkapaye yamenayetziri matsi pankotsikipaye, "Jironta, jironta." [102]Tzimatsi pashini, nonatoto. [103]Yookotanakiro, "Irotaki matsitatsiri." [104]Pashini yaaitapaintziro. [105]Okantzi, "Te." [106]Iposaitakiro. [107]Okantzi, "Je, naakataki," tsavetayetanaki. [108]Piyotaka. [109]Tzimatsi aparoni pankotsi asaikajeetapintzi, apiyojeetapinta arika ampotoitajeetya. [110]Ari ipiyoitakirori yamaitakiro, pashini, pashini. [111]Ikiyakajeetakiro, ikiyakanakiro.

[112]Tzimatsi pashini ishataki, oshiyakaro Ines, antaro vatsanto onatzi. [113]Yamaitakiro irori. [114]Okantzi, "Te nomatsite." [115]Ikantziro, "Avirotaki matsi, pintsavete!" [116]"Te nomatsite, tsika añiiro yantaroitzi amatsite?" [117]Ikantziro, "Avi-

rotaki." [118]Iro opokapaki matsira intakarori iposaitakiro, okantzi, "Je, irotaki matsi onatzi. [119]Irotaki imantsiyatantari otomitsori, irotaki ameniri irinirotsori."
[120]Iposavaitaitakero. [121]Oh, otsonka okaatanakiro iraanive! [122]Tsarovanakina iroñaaka noñaakoventakiro. [123]Okantzi ovirantapakarori, okantzi, "Naakataki, matsi nonatzi. [124]Irotaki imantsiyatantari notomitsori, naakataki ameniri." [125]Ikantziro, "Paakotajeri." [126]"Je, ari naakotajeri, aritaki yavisakotaji."
[127]Pashini, pashini piyojeetakave! 1[28]Iroña ipiyotajeetakiro. [129]Tsiteni yaamaitakironta, itsonka ikiyakakiro. [130]Yaanakiro iroñaaka akantavetakari inkaranki. [131]Jevaripaye yaanakiro nijaaki, "Pinkivajantero iroñaaka, paayetakeri." [132]Okivavakero, ari yavisakotaje mantsiyayetatsiri, ari avisakotaje. [133]Okivajeetakiro.
[134]Okitaitamanaji jatzi pashini, okonkiri nonatoto. [135]Okonkiri jaitetzi, yaashitaitziro kavana, itotaki kavana. [136]Irotaki ipayetakirori matsitatsiririka, yoitakiro. [137]Ipoña yaashitakiro tsikana iyanirikitatsiri. [138]Imichovakiro ooyaki, ikaatantakaro maaroni ikaratzi matsipaye. [139]Ikaatakiro.
[140]Nojataki namenapaintziro nonatoto. [141]Maperotaka, kisotaki maaroni oitziki. [142]Kapicheeni añaaki asankaniki. [143]Akontsitakeniro kaniri, asaavatakeniro, apakiro aitakirori. [144]Kapicheeni iravaki.[145]Pashinipaye te omaperotya, maperotainchari nonatoto. [146]Opoña pashini, opoña iroñaaka nokantaitzi ishatatsiri, irotaki maperotainchari katsini. [147]Ipoñaanaka pashini shirampari. [148]Ikantzi irirori, "Iroñaaka noñaavakeri ishitovanake kamari saikantanari aka. [149]Kantanarika, 'Tsame ameneri amatsikeri ashaninkapaye, tsame ayari.' [150]Noñaavakiri ishitovantanaka kamari, pikaatantanarora tsikana. [151]Poitakina kavana, shitovanake kamari."
[152]Okantakota onaria kapichikitaite, onariajajeetaka nijaaki. [153]Otzinavetapananta, okimitaka tsivana otsonka

otaakiro maaroni ovatsaki. [154]Oshitovavetapananta, piyanaja. [155]Sheetyakotaji, onariajajeeta.

[156]Ontzimi opokimotakena. [157]Nameniro nonatoto, niravaita apaniroini novankoki. [158]Nokantziri oyaririra, "Paitaka pitsiro omatsitantakari irori?" [159]"Okantzi, 'Iro pakinaro,' otsavetakotavakanaka. [160]Okantzi, *estudia*jeetzira, oñaanajeetzira. [161]Okantzi, 'Tsame ajatapainte antsote mapocha.' [162]Jaitetzi oirinkajeetanaka, ari opakotakirori.[163]Tzimatsi matsiyetatsiri intarori, omatsiyetzi. [164]Opakero."

[165]Pashini okantzi, "Nomatsitantakari aanakina ovankoki. [166]Okantzi, 'Tsame irakite shinkia.' [167]Ari opakotakinari. [168]Nomaavetanaka, noñaavakiri kamari, irotaki nokaimantari tsiteni. [169]Arika nomaavetanakia, noñaatziri kamari ipokashitakena. [170]Nokaimantari tsiteni."

[171]Akemavetaro okarayetapaki eentsiyetzi okaikaimatzi, akantapintzi, "Arika otsavirivaitatya, oñaatziri kamari." [172]Kapichee osamanitanaki ametanakari kamari. [173]Iroñaaka ametanakari yatziritzimotanakiro, oñaanakiri atziri inatzi. [174]Te ontsarovakanajiari. [175]Ari okinkitsaki, ari okantari.

[176]Itsonkakira, yamajiro iroñaaka tsitenitanaki, yamaitajiro pankotsiki. [177]Ipiyojeetapaka. [178]Ari ipokakiri yora *anciano*tatsiri, jevatakantzirori ivanko pava. [179]Yampatsakairo irojatzita apapakoroni kitaiteri. [180]Ikitaitakakiro. [181]Te ishinitajero omaaje. [182]"Arika nomaanaje, aajatzi impiyapaje kamari, inkiantapajiana. [183]Irotaki airo poimaana." [184]Ikanta yampatsakajeetziro, ikantakota, ikantakota irojatzita aparoni *semana* yampantsakakiro. [185]Yamanakairo ampantsai. [186]Ivashitakiri poronkito. [187]Arika omaakiajeetapainte kapicheeni, imporonkakero, sakitanaji. [188]Ari okantajeetari apapakoroni kitaiteri, amanakojeetziro, yampantsakairo.

[189]Ari ikantari noñaakoventakiri matsi ovakerani nojataki kirinka. [190]Ari noñaakoventakirori, tekatsi irovaite. [191]Maa-

roni avisakotaji. [192]Okimitatya nonatoto, okantzi irori, "Ari iroñaaka te noñaajeri kamari." [193]Pashini okantzi irori, "Te noñaajeri kamari." [194]Iroma iroka nonkantakiri inkaranki ishataitsirira, yaaitapanantziro. [195]Ikantaitziro, "Apitanaja, pitomitsori imantsiyatanaji. [196]Pijate, paakotaiteri." [197]Jaitetaki, yaaitanakiro, okantakota ikiyakaitapajiro anta. [198]Opiyakotaja sheetyakotanaki, pokaji iroñaaka. [199]Tzimatsi ivanko otomitsori, okimitanta nijaa otapiki. [200]Apaniroini kirinka, ari osaiki omaapaji. [201]Okantzi irori tashaki, okanta opokajinta antamiki, oñaanaji shitovi. [202]Aayetanaji, akipatakiro shitovi, oisapakiro paamari. [203]Otsokaki kaniri, otashitakiro.

[204]Korakitaintsitaima overonirakia. [205]Yoijatakiro. [206]Iñaapajiro osaiki akishivaitzi. [207]Ishitsikakiro.

[208]Okitaitamanaji pashini kitaiteri ipokaji otomitsori yamenajantziro. [209]Iñaapajatziro ivankoki otapikinta, kamaki osaiki. [210]Añaashitakari ipokaki, ikantzi, "Kamaki nonirotsori." [211]"Paita ovakirori?" [212]"Ishitsikaitakiro ovira oponaataki okentsiki, irojatzi osaiki." [213]Yoimisaikanakiro osaikira oisapakirora ovaamarite. [214]Osaiki tsitsipaye, ari osaiki otzintaka. [215]Te onaree, irojatzi otzintaka. [216]Okantaka aka osaiki otashitakotziro oshitovite, otaashitzi oyaniri. [217]Kantzimaitacha kamaki.

[218]Ari okaratzi noñaakoventakiri nosaikantaitari kirinka pairani. [219]Aritaki noñaakoventakirori ikantaitziri matsi.

[220]Noñaakoventziro iposavaitaitakiro, pashini ivaitakiro. [221]Irotaki nokinkitsatziri iroñaaka naari okaratzi noñaakiri naari. [222]Ari ovirapaka.

[1]We will say that we once lived here, in the place called Nasaraiteki. [2]This is where I witnessed events involving witches.

[3]They brought one [to the village]. [4]Our fellow men were

coming by, they were coming here, to the place called the Salt River. ⁵This is where salt was, and men mined it. ⁶Men were coming, they were bringing their salt. ⁷They saw a woman. ⁸She was sitting on the trail, the woman who was identified as a witch. ⁹They saw her sitting, and she was cut all over: her head, her body, her feet, her face—she was cut all over. ¹⁰They saw her sitting. ¹¹"What happened to you?" ¹²"They have cut me." ¹³"Why did they cut you?" ¹⁴"They told me that I am a witch."

¹⁵That woman did the cutting. ¹⁶There were three women who were the wives of the same man. ¹⁷When a child got sick, the mother said, "She is the one who did the witchcraft. ¹⁸You cast a spell on my child." ¹⁹She responded to the mother, she said, "I was the one who has eaten him [the child]." ²⁰They grabbed her together, the two of them who lived with the man, and beat the witch. ²¹When they were hitting her, the mother grabbed the knife and cut her all over. ²²Her head, the mother cut her all over. ²³She killed her. ²⁴She dragged her to a big tree with hanging branches; this is where she lay her down. ²⁵She piled up dry leaves with which she covered her. ²⁶She gathered a lot of leaves, dumped them on her, and left her.

²⁷In the meantime, whatever time she was dead, she gradually got up. ²⁸As she was covered with leaves, she got up [to shake them off] and went. ²⁹She walked slowly—slowly. ³⁰She stayed for a while [in the forest] and slept there, then she slept on the riverbank.

³¹Men carrying salt came by, who saw her. ³²They saw her, that she was cut all over and brought her to our village where we were living, called San Pablo. ³³Our fellow men approximately arrived here at three o'clock [in the afternoon]. ³⁴They said, "There are some people, they brought a woman, she is cut." ³⁵I went and looked at her. ³⁶Oh, I saw that she was cut. ³⁷"Why did they cut her?" ³⁸"She said that they called her a witch."

³⁹Other fellow men came to see her and brought some stuff to treat her. ⁴⁰They kept treating her [wounds]. ⁴¹Later on, her wounds, where she was cut, healed, and she recovered. ⁴²A woman said, "She is my family, my cousin, we are cousins." ⁴³When the woman recovered, she left. ⁴⁴She knew her kinfolk, she went there, and this is where she stayed. ⁴⁵When she recovered, she began living with her cousin.

⁴⁶A lot of time passed when she was living there. ⁴⁷Then, suddenly her cousin got sick. ⁴⁸I heard one night when they came to me, "She is sick, she will die. ⁴⁹Her name is Martha, the one who is sick."

⁵⁰She said, "She [Martha] had a dream about someone who was living in her house. ⁵¹She said that it is in her back. ⁵²She [the person in her dream] said, 'Cousin, I am sitting on your back, I will break you, I will imagine you [to be] a *carachama* (fish species).' ⁵³She woke up and felt pain there [in her back]."

⁵⁴At dawn, she said, "She [Martha] is worse, she will die." ⁵⁵Many women came to look at her [Martha], they saw her lying prostrate.

⁵⁶"What happened to you?" ⁵⁷She [Martha] said, "I feel pain in my back, out of the blue. ⁵⁸Last night, nothing, I will say, I went to gather reed. ⁵⁹I was sucking on the reed, and this is when I got sick. ⁶⁰Is there anyone who knows how to do steam baths with herbs?" ⁶¹They did a steam bath for her. ⁶²The reed parts that she had sucked on fell out, a lot of reed stem parts. ⁶³The reed parts in the waistline of her back were those that she had cut [for eating].

⁶⁴Now they came, her uncles. ⁶⁵They said, "She is the one who cast [a] spell, who is living here." ⁶⁶Oh, I saw them beat up that witch. ⁶⁷They took a thick wood plank with which rice is pounded, and they beat her up. ⁶⁸That woman didn't feel pain. ⁶⁹Maybe, because she was a true witch, she didn't feel

pain. ⁷⁰I thought that she would scream, no. ⁷¹They asked her, "You are the one who cast [a] spell on your sister?" ⁷²"Yes, I am the one." ⁷³"Dig it out." ⁷⁴She was digging and digging. ⁷⁵She got each of them out, she dug out the stem parts of reed. ⁷⁶In the meantime, another man came. ⁷⁷He said, "Let's kill her." ⁷⁸Another man responded, "Don't kill her, let's interrogate her. ⁷⁹In the village where we live there are other witches."

⁸⁰The men interrogated her, "Are there witches here in our village?" ⁸¹She said, "Yes, there are many, I met each of them. ⁸²I didn't want to cast a spell on my sister. ⁸³When other witches came, they said, 'Let's eat her, let's cast a spell on her.' ⁸⁴That's why I cast a spell on her."

⁸⁵The men said then, "Where are they now? ⁸⁶Call them out." ⁸⁷She pointed at them [identified as witches]. ⁸⁸They said this in the past, they say that she identified the witches, that she said, "This woman . . . this man . . . this woman . . ." ⁸⁹"We are here."

⁹⁰They [the uncles] call out one after another. ⁹¹Oh, so many witches gathered! ⁹²This is how I witnessed events involving those whom they call witches: I was standing and watching. ⁹³An old woman came, she was standing [there too]. ⁹⁴She said to me, "Granddaughter, why did you come to see witches? ⁹⁵You have children, they will become witches. ⁹⁶Don't look at them! ⁹⁷They didn't see witches, go." ⁹⁸I returned home, I went quickly. ⁹⁹I didn't see what happened to them later on.

¹⁰⁰During the night the men kept locating witches, "Here she is." ¹⁰¹My fellow men were walking in search of witches into every house, "Here she is . . . here she is." ¹⁰²There was one witch, my sister-in-law. ¹⁰³They had identified her as a witch, "She is the one who is a witch." ¹⁰⁴Another woman was captured. ¹⁰⁵She said, "No!" ¹⁰⁶They beat her. ¹⁰⁷She said, "Yes, I am the one," she confessed in front of all. ¹⁰⁸A lot of witches gathered. ¹⁰⁹There was a house where we usually spend time together, we usually

gather there when we have meetings. ¹¹⁰The men who would bring witches gathered them there, one after another. ¹¹¹They made them all dig it out.

¹¹²There was an old woman, she looked like Ines, but she was fat. ¹¹³They brought her [to the communal house]. ¹¹⁴She said, "I am not a witch." ¹¹⁵They said to her, "You are a witch, confess!" ¹¹⁶"I am not a witch, where did you see old witches?" ¹¹⁷They said, "You are the one." ¹¹⁸But the witch who was first [brought in and] beaten up came and said, "Yes, she is a witch. ¹¹⁹It is because of her that her nephew got sick, she is the one who tended to him, his aunt."

¹²⁰They beat her for some time. ¹²¹Oh, blood, she was swimming in her blood! ¹²²I got scared when I looked at her. ¹²³She said, the one who was last [beaten], she said, "I am the one, I am a witch. ¹²⁴The reason why he got sick is because I had tended to him." ¹²⁵The men said to her, "Get it out!" ¹²⁶"Yes, I will get it out, he will recover."

¹²⁷More, more witches were brought in! ¹²⁸The men amassed many women.

¹²⁹During the night the men brought them, and they were all forced to dig. ¹³⁰They captured them [like] we said before. ¹³¹The leaders took the women to the river, "Wash it with water, all that you dug out." ¹³²They [the witches] will wash the charms, then the sick will recover, they will recover. ¹³³The women washed it.

¹³⁴The next day early another man came, my cousin's uncle. ¹³⁵He came quickly, he got the [poisonous] sap of the sandbox tree (*Hura crepitans*), he had cut the sandbox tree. ¹³⁶This is what they fed to all these witches. ¹³⁷Later on they brought small hot peppers. 1³⁸The men squeezed them in the pot and bathed each witch with it. ¹³⁹The men bathed the witches [with it].

¹⁴⁰I went to look at my cousin. ¹⁴¹She was in bad shape, she didn't move her feet. ¹⁴²Her heart was barely beating. ¹⁴³We pre-

pared manioc, we made it boil for her, and we gave it to her to drink. ¹⁴⁴She drank it a little bit. ¹⁴⁵Others didn't get worse, my cousin did. ¹⁴⁶Then another, the old woman about whom I talked, she was the one who was very sick. ¹⁴⁷Then another—a man. ¹⁴⁸He said, "Now I saw the demon, who was in me, leave. ¹⁴⁹He told me, 'Let's watch and make sick our fellow men, let's eat them.' ¹⁵⁰I saw the demon leave me when you bathed me in hot peppers. ¹⁵¹You fed the sap of the sandbox tree to me, and the demon left."

¹⁵²In the meantime, the women were lying, they all were lying in the river. ¹⁵³They would get up, but hot peppers were burning their bodies. ¹⁵⁴They would leave and go back [to the river] again. ¹⁵⁵It got dark, but all women lay [in the river].

¹⁵⁶Sometimes I felt sad. ¹⁵⁷I saw my cousin and cried when I was in the house alone. ¹⁵⁸I said to her brother, "Why did your sister turn out a witch? ¹⁵⁹She said, 'They [girls] gave it to me,' she confessed it. ¹⁶⁰She said that when she was at school, she met them [the witches]. ¹⁶¹She [one of the child witches at school] said, 'Let's go and eat papaya.' ¹⁶²They went downriver, and there they gave it to her. ¹⁶³There are various original witches, each of them casts spell. ¹⁶⁴They gave it to her."

¹⁶⁵Another witch said, "I turned into a witch, when a woman took me to her house. ¹⁶⁶She said, 'Let's have a corn drink.' ¹⁶⁷There she gave it to me. ¹⁶⁸I sleep and see a demon [in my dream], that's why I scream at night. ¹⁶⁹When I fall asleep, I see the demon come with the intent to enter me. ¹⁷⁰That's why I scream at night."

¹⁷¹We hear little girls talk in their sleep a lot, and we say, "They are talking in their dreams, they see a demon." ¹⁷²Little time later, the girls get accustomed to the demon. ¹⁷³Now she sees the demon in human form, she sees him as a person. ¹⁷⁴She

is not afraid of him any longer. [175]The girls told [about it], they are truly this way.

[176]When they finished [soaking in the river], the men took them to the communal house, when it was dark. [177]All women returned [back to the communal house]. [178]Then the elder came, the church leader. [179]He made them sing for a week. [180]The dawn broke. [181]He didn't allow them to sleep. [182]"If I fall asleep, again the demon will return to enter me. [183]That's why [I ask you, God], don't leave me." [184]They made all witches sing for a long time, for a week they made them sing. [185]They made them sing praise [to God]. [186]They applied a stinging nettle. [187]When a woman gets a little bit sleepy, they will use the stinging nettle, and she will wake up. [188]It continued this way for a week, when they made them all sing praise, they made them sing.

[189]This is what I witnessed on the account of witches when I went downriver. [190]I witnessed on their account that nobody was killed. [191]Everyone recovered. [192]For example, my cousin, she said, "Now I don't see the demon anymore." [193]Another woman said, "I don't see the demon anymore." [194]In contrast, the woman that I talked about, the old one, they captured her again. [195]They said to her, "It repeated, your nephew got sick again. [196]Go, dig it out."

[197]She went quickly, when they took her and made her dig for a long time over there. [198]She came back home when it was almost dark, she came back. [199]Her nephew's house was down by the river. [200]She was down there alone, there she slept. [201]They say, she was hungry, went to the woods and searched for mushrooms. [202]She picked [the mushrooms], wrapped them in leaves, and started the fire. [203]Then pulled out some manioc, roasted it on the fire.

[204]The one who was going to kill her approached. [205]He fol-

lowed her. [206]He saw her sitting and roasting [the food]. [207]He strangled her.

[208]The next morning her nephew came, because he was looking for her. [209]He saw her in his house downriver, she was seated — dead. [210]We saw him come to the village, and he said, "My aunt has died." [211]"What killed her?" [212]"A man strangled her until her neck became blue when she was sitting." [213]He [the killer] seated the corpse where she was sitting, when she started the fire. [214]She was sitting in the firewood, she was propped against it. [215]She didn't lie prostrate, she was seated up. [216]She was sitting in this position roasting her mushrooms, roasting her manioc. [217]Nevertheless, she was dead.

[218]This is all that I witnessed on the account of witches when I lived downriver long ago. [219]I truly was a witness to the events involving those called witches.

[220]I witnessed them beaten and some killed. [221]This is what I am telling now, all that I saw. [222]It [my story] has come to an end.

2

Landscape

History is argued to be "inscribed" into landscape through its presence in people's memories, in personal, mythical, and historical accounts, in people's intimate relationships with specific landscape features and landmarks, and through structural changes to the original landscape enacted in the process of people's appropriation of territory that they claim to be theirs (Connerton 1989; Schama 1995; Vansina 1985; Hill 1989; Rappaport 1989; Santos-Granero 1998).

According to Connerton, to remember their past, societies use "inscribing practices" "to do something that traps and holds information" (1989:73). In literate societies the inscribing is primarily done via writing books and digital materials. These are kept in libraries, electronic databases, and archives to serve as permanent repositories of human knowledge. In nonliterate societies, capturing and transmitting knowledge is done with the help of personal memories, oral tradition, mythical accounts, bodily practices, and "sacred geography" (Santos-Granero 1998:141), in which certain landmarks become the community's "mnemonic devices," being inextricably linked to its particular myths and ritual activities (Rappaport 1989:88).

In scholarly discussions of indigenous mythic and historical knowledge, the term "topographic writing" is commonly used to describe the process of "writing" into landscape, resulting in landscape transformation due to human or superhuman activities (Santos-Granero 1998:140). The created landmarks, called "topograms," are grouped into two classes: those produced by humans, such as vegetable gardens, bridges, buildings, roads, monuments, and graves, and those performed by "fantastic"

nonhuman agents, namely rocks, hills, or any other geomor-
phic feature that stands out in terms of its shape, size, or color
(Santos-Granero 1998:140). Adult community members, presumed to be familiar with the topograms, can "read" them like
a book while traveling across the territory appropriated by the
community (Santos-Granero 1998).

Ethnographic studies of Piro (Yine) Arawaks from the Bajo
Urubamba River of the Peruvian Amazon; the Yanesha (or Amuesha), the Upper Perené Ashaninkas' closest Arawak-speaking
neighbors; and some other nonliterate Amazonian societies,
notably the Wakuénai (Baniwa/Kurripako, Arawak) of Venezuela and the Páez (language isolate) of Colombia, are reported to reveal the topographic principle of history writing
(Gow 1991:78, 1995:54; Hill 1989, 1993; Rappaport 1989; Zucchi
2002). Rather than organizing historical events chronologically,
for example, through a sequence of narratives, the indigenous
historical thought of these societies has employed topograms
to anchor historical events in space. For example, the Yaneshas'
permanent migration and "transformation of the occupied
land" (Zucchi 2002) into land of their own are "inscribed" into
mythic narratives about the peregrinations of the solar divinity
Yompor Ror (Santos-Granero 1998:144). Past Yanesha ritual
performances, conducted at temples dedicated to the solar or
fire divinities, were another means of landscape construction
and appropriation. For example, the Palmaso temple, a historical landmark, used to be a place for the worship of three stone
divinities: Yompor Yompere, Yachor Mamas, and Yemo'nasheñ
Senyac. The temple priest conducted regular worship services,
which included offerings of coca, *chamairo*, and lime to the stone
divinities (Santos-Garnero 1998:141–42). From the topographic
writing perspective, Yanesha history is recalled through sacred
landmarks and the myths and rituals associated with them.

In the Upper Perené documentary corpus, landscape constitutes an essential part of the recorded narratives. Upper Perené
Arawaks have various topograms inscribed into their oral tradition, myth, and ritual, as seen on map 3. The topograms are
imbued with "sacredness," which, in accordance with the native
views of divinity, is perceived to be omnipresent in the experi-
ential world (Varese 2002). Elick states that "the 'real' world, for
the Campa, comprises in one space-time continuum those phe-
nomena we designate as natural and supernatural. The 'other'
world is not 'other', then, but merely outside man's present-day
diminished perception" (1969:xv). The sacred landscape is perceived to be "an animated entity," saturated with "extraordinary
spiritual subjectivities" (Santos-Granero 2004a:103). "Notions
of immanent divinity," being "part of everyday life" (Veber
2003:191), constitute Ashaninka habitus, that is, their "sedi-
mented" values, dispositions, and ways of living, accounting for
their social practices.

Landscape is argued to be "a cultural process" (Hirsch 1995:3).
From the Upper Perené animistic perspective, landscape is not
a mere static setting for people's daily lives, it is part of a dynamic process of their perennial engagement with the outside
world, inseparably tied to a complex web of relationships with
its omnipresent spiritual beings. The animated universe of the
forest, rivers, streams, caves, rocks, and hills, with their sacred
"owners" and other spiritual inhabitants, constitute an invisible
world, familiar only to those who have been part of this environment since birth and have been "actively moving around in
the landscape and leaving traces in it" (Gow 1995:51). The sacred
landscape is certainly accessible to those in possession of mystical powers, like shamans and healers.

As landscape-transforming agents, indigenous living humans
generate *pankotsi* (house), *ovaantsi* (garden, *chacra*), *ovaan-*

tsiposhi (regenerated garden, *purma*), *nampitsi* (village), and *oparai* (the communally used stretch of the riverbank). Dead humans leave behind *pankotsiranki* (abandoned house), which is the house deserted after an adult person died in it and was buried inside in a shallow grave. (Now corpses are buried in a nearby cemetery.) The agentive, powerful beings of the outside world are given credit for even more extraordinary landscape transformations; for example, the solar divinity Pava created the entire Ashaninka land, as the narrators Cristobal Jumanga Lopez and Raul Martin Bernata, respectively, note in *Pava vitsikirori kipatsi* (Pava, Who Made the Earth; part 1) and *Otzinantakari otzishi omontero Samamparini* (How the Hill Appeared across from the Village of Villa Progreso; part 2).

There are at least four topograms associated with idolatrous rituals, most of which are poorly known to the younger generations of Upper Perené Arawaks. This lacuna is perhaps explained by the short time span of people's memories and recollections, which failed to crystallize into the mythic oral tradition of much longevity. The pagan topograms are not embedded in Upper Perené mythic narratives; neither do they remain the sites of ritual ceremonies. The influential Seventh-Day Adventist Church condemns the rituals as shameful heathenry, which is another reason why the memories of these sites and related rituals have been fading so quickly.

The most familiar landmark is Ashiropanko (the Iron House), an abandoned temple-forge located to the north of Bajo Marankiari, on the right side of the Perené River. The forge functioned as the fire-veneration center and was visited by pilgrims. Originally, iron forges were established by Franciscan friars as a way of supplying metal tools to the mission workers in the Chanchamayo and Upper Perené valleys (Amich 1854). Native converts were initially trained by the missionaries and imported mestizo blacksmiths in the art of repairing metal tools, but later on indigenous laborers evidently mastered the metallurgic skills and were able to produce metal tools independently, using local iron deposits (Veber 2003:195–96; Santos-Granero 1988:4–5). Santos-Granero (1988:10, 20) states that there were a dozen well-functioning local forges at the time of the mid-nineteenth-century military conquest of the Upper Perené area; some forges continued to function even in the early twentieth century.

The Gerardo Castro Manuela text *Ashiropanko* (The Iron House) provides a detailed description of the Upper Perené landmark. The Ashiropanko forge served as a training center for those males who desired to make metal tools to satisfy their own needs and for trade. The narrator states that only males who practiced sexual abstinence, or *shantyoshi* (the pure), were allowed to stay on the premises of the forge and receive training; "fornicators" were forbidden to enter, lest they die in the inferno of the sacred fire. The text was recorded in 2011, at the narrator's sister-in-law's house in Bajo Marankiari. Ashiropanko is also mentioned in two other texts, *Tsika okanta nosaikantari Marankiaroki* (How We Settled Down in Bajo Marankiari," by Bertha Rodríguez de Caleb, and *Apinka*, by Bertha Rodríguez de Caleb and Abdias Caleb Quinchori (both in part 1).

Two other topograms are located in the uplands of Metraro. One is a veneration site for the stone divinity Paatsiri (Father), also known as Mapinini (Little Rock), located to the south of the current village of San Jeronimo de Yurinaki, on the old trail to Metraro. Now only a few remnants of the sacred stone are found in this place. The other site, in Tsonkishiroki, not far from Kishitariki, present-day Mariscal Cáceres, was a temple dedicated to the fire divinity. There was a communal house for worshippers, called *parahua*, and a headman who acted as the temple's priest. Both sites are described by Elías Meza Pedro in an interview with his son-in-law, Gregorio Santos Pérez, titled *Atziri yama-niri mapi poña paamari* (People Were Worshipping Fire and Stone). The interview was recorded in 2010 at the narrator's home in Kishitariki, present-day Mariscal Cáceres. The narrator witnessed the worship of the fire divinity when he was a boy.[1]

Another pilgrimage site's location is not clear. It is described as being located *katonko pareniki* (upstream Perené River) by the now-deceased Cristobal Jumanga Lopez, from Pucha-rini. The term *katonko parenini* covers the headwaters area of the Perené River, including the Chanchamayo and Paucar-tambo Rivers. Cristobal Jumanga's text, *Atziri yamaniri paa-mari* (People Were Worshipping Fire), recorded in 2010 in Villa Perené, at the narrator's nephew's house, reproduces his grand-father's account of the trip upstream to a temple dedicated to the fire divinity, called Pava by the narrator. The temple was visited daily by many pilgrims, who participated in vigils and worship under the guidance of the Yanesha priest named Santiago (Shan-tyako). The jointly venerated Yanesha-Ashaninka temples were in the "ethnic patchwork" tradition (Renard-Casevitz 1992:205–6) of interethnic political alliances and commercial exchange of goods (Santos-Granero 1998:142, 2002a:30–31, 2004a:107–8).

The open salt mines, located along the left bank of Tziviarini (the Salt River; Río Paucartambo in Spanish), were the pilgrim-age site par excellence. This place is also known as the Cerro de la Sal (the Salt Hill) (Varese 2002). Found at the intersection of the major intertribal trade routes, the salt mines attracted heavy Indian traffic during the months of June–August in the *osaren-tsi* (dry season), reaching as many as five hundred (or even one thousand) visitors per harvest season (Tibesar 1950:104). In the 1960s the salt mines lost their commercial value and their stra-tegic role as the pan-Campa sociopolitical hub.

The documentary corpus contains multiple versions of the

mythic origin of this topogram. Nonetheless, all of these texts re-volve around the travels of a feckless fellow woman called Tzivi (Salt), who was spontaneously transformed into salt deposits in this area. The woman's transformation was preceded by her dra-matic death. At her own request, the Tzivi person was clubbed in the head by her brother. Two narratives, both titled *Tzivi* (Salt), by Ruth Quillatupa Lopez, from Bajo Marankiari, and by Abra-ham Jumanga Lopez, from Pucharini, are included in this collec-tion. They elaborate on Tzivi's restless travels and blood-chilling death. Note that both texts, recorded in 2011, remain mute with regard to any ritual activities associated with the landmark.[2]

Another place of pan-Campa ritual gathering is reported to have existed in the area not far from present-day Pichanaki, at the intersection of the trails leading to the Pichis, Gran Pajo-nal, and Tambo-Ene valleys (Rojas Zolezzi 1994:147). The festi-val took place at the onset of *kiarontsi* (wet season), in January, when *savoro* (wild cane) blossoms. The headman in charge of the festival was adorned with *savoro* blossoms, called *chakopi-shi*, and led dances. The festival theme was to defy death: no one was to sleep during the celebratory night, lest he or she die in the new year (Rojas Zolezzi 1994:147). The tradition was dis-continued in the 1960s (Rojas Zolezzi 1994:150), and collective memories of the celebration are presumed to be gone.

The Upper Perené documentary corpus does not contain any mention of this landmark. On a much smaller scale, similar end-of-the-year festival events, known as *mavira*, were reported to have taken place in the communities of Pampa Michi and San Miguel Centro Marankiari (see texts 42–44, *Okoñaatantakari mavira* (How *Mavira* Appeared), by Luis Mauricio Rosa, with Raul Martin Bernata and Victoria Manchi de Martin; and two texts titled *Mavira*, by Elena Nestor de Capurro and by Ines Pérez de Santos and Moises Santos Rojas).

Among the notable topograms whose creation the oral tradition attributes to humans are Manitzipanko (the Jaguar House) and Imoro Naviriri (the Naviriri Hole). They stand out due to the fame they are accorded by the local population and the consistency of the "myths-cum-history" (Santos-Granero 1998:144) accounts of their origin. According to the narrator Ruth Quillatupa Lopez (*Manitzipanko* [The Jaguar House]), the cave called Manitzipanko is the murder scene and gravesite of a "marauding" jaguar-shaman (Elick 1969:210) who relocated to the Upper Perené area to become a nocturnal predator-killer of local people. The cave can be seen not far from the village of Chivanari, on the left bank of the Perené River.

The large oval-shaped indentation found in the uplands of Mariscal Cáceres (now it is filled with water) is believed to be the place where the cultural hero and trickster Naviriri was entrapped by his fellow men and found his end. Elías Meza Pedro, in the text *Imoro Naviriri* (The Naviriri Hole), elucidates the existence of the hole, which was so deep that it was impossible to hear the sound of a discharged arrow hitting the hole's bottom. The myth claims that the hole was dug by Naviriri's brother-in-law Ashoshi (Armadillo).

Many contemporary features of the Upper Perené landscape are attributed to the transformative powers of Naviriri, exemplified by the large landmass in the middle of the Perené River across from the village of Villa Progreso (the settlement's native name is Samamparini). The history behind the appearance of the landmass is detailed in the text *Otzinantakari otzishi omontero Samamparini* (How the Hill Appeared across from the Village of Villa Progreso), recorded by Raul Martin Bernata in 2009 in Pampa Michi. According to the narrator, the landmass in the main channel of the river is one of Naviriri's most fateful pranks, for which he was punished by Pava.

Upper Perené texts also mention outsiders, *chori* (Andean settlers) and *virakocha* (non-Indian outsiders, white people), among the agentive powers transforming the human-controlled sphere of the Ashaninka landscape, imposing alien "viewpoints" and marginalizing the native "viewpoint" (Bender 1993:3). The "contested" and "tensioned landscape-in-movement" (Bender 1993:4) was generated by the British-owned Peruvian Corporation, which turned Upper Perené tribal lands into *cafetales* (coffee plantations), and by Andean and European settlers who created cattle-raising haciendas, *naranjales* (orange orchards), and *pastizales* (grazing pastures). To claim indigenous land as their own, outsiders stuck Hispanic names to those places they inhabited. The deceased Augusto Capurro Mayor, former chief of Pampa Michi, pointed out that Pampa Whaley, the headquarters of the Peruvian Corporation, located on the left bank of the Upper Perené, was named after a colonist who had cultivated coffee in that area. In the same manner, Michel and Silva, the names of the mestizo colonists who leased tribal lands for a short period in the nineteenth century, have been adopted as the names of the villages of Pampa Michi and Pampa Silva (Veber 2009:176–77). Map 3 is an illustration of the "tensioned landscape-in-movement."

Old-generation speakers deeply lament this subtractive naming practice, which gives legitimacy to the outsiders' annexation of Ashéninka Perené ancestral lands. In the text *Anashironi* (The Anashirona Stream), Julio Castro Shinkaki, the founder of Bajo Marankiari, comments on the ceased practice of indigenous place-naming and the spread of outsiders' place-names. The interview with Julio Castro Shinkaki was conducted by Delia Rosas Rodríguez, his distant relative, in his house in Bajo Marankiari. The recoding was made in 2011.

The native principles of place-naming can be explained in

terms of "affordances" the place offers to humans (Gibson 1979: 127), that is, its contribution to the subsistence economy and daily existence of hunter-gatherers and horticulturists. Rivers, streams, lakes, cliffs, and hills were given names because of their value as a material resource in the exploitation of the environment.[3] Typically, the toponym's ontology emphasizes an abundance of a particular species or substance encountered in a given place, for example, the name of the river Tziviarini is derived from *tzivi* (salt); the rock outcrop Shamorokiarini received its name because of its deposits of lime, called *ishiko*, which, in powdered form, is chewed together with coca leaves; and Totzironi was named after the aquatic snail *totziroki*, known to inhabit the stream in great quantities. Human settlements were given names on the basis of their proximity to an already named natural resource, for example, the native community of Pomporiani (in Spanish, Pumpuriani) was given the name of the adjacent stream Pomporiani, whose banks are teeming with *pomporo* (land-snail species).

Some landscape features were named to reflect their unusual physical properties (e.g., shape, color) or due to speakers' spiritual concerns, steeped in the native animistic cosmologies. For example, Pakitsapanko (the Hawk House) is a towering cliff, reportedly inhabited in the old times by an enormous cannibalistic bird that would prey on humans paddling down the Perené River in their canoes and rafts. The place name's ontology is probably rooted in the Upper Perené Ashaninka history of frequent ambushes by warriors from the Gran Pajonal, Piro (Arawak), and Panoan tribes, the latter called *ovantzinkari* (killers). The enemy would lie in wait in the forested areas of the narrow river canyons and then pounce on passersby.

Many indigenous names were replaced with those of Spanish origin. For example, La Merced is the former Tsiirishi, San

Ramon is the former Shimashironi (some say its original name is Potooki), Kishitari is the ancestral name of present-day Mariscal Cáceres, Santa Ana used to be called Kovatsiroki, and the Chanchamayo River's original name is Tsantsa or Santsa, to name a few.

Landscape has its secret spiritual names revealed to shamans during their hallucinogen-induced spiritual flights to the remotest corners of the Upper Perené landscape, otherwise off-limits to ordinary folks (see Weiss 1975:245; Santos-Granero 2004a:102).[4] In their dream travels, shamans assume a jaguar body and acquire the predator's supremely dangerous powers. In the text *Pichanaki*, Otoniel Ramos Rodríguez describes a meeting of a traveling shaman, in a jaguar disguise, with a fellow jaguar-shaman who was native to the area. The visitor receives the following explanation of the Pichanaki place-name: *naaka pichaantatzi* means "I crush with a stone."[5] The text was recorded by Daniel Bernales Quillatupa in the narrator's home in Churingaveni in 2012. A different version of the place-name's origin is put forward by Almacia Benavidez Fernandez, who attributes it to the exodus of spiritual beings inhabiting the surrounding hills. The ensuing earthquake and flooding obliterated the whole area. This recording of the text *Pichanaki* was made in the narrator's home in La Merced in 2013.

The animated spiritual landscape is hostile toward humans (Narby 1989:263–73; Reichel-Dolmatoff 1975:70–73; Gow 1991: 78–81). As Weiss observes, considering infinite threats emanating from the spiritual world, "How unmanageable is the universe in which the Campas live, where mortals are weak and must exercise great care and circumscription to prevent being crushed by the greater forces of cosmos[?]" (1975:266). The spaces of the river, the forest and the hills, and the high and low elevations are controlled by unsympathetic spiritual beings in possession

of superlative powers. Danger comes from the elevations surrounding the headwaters of the Perené River, the realm of the
cannibal creature *janaite*. The landscape of dead humans, *pankotsiranki* (abandoned house), is patronized by the dead person's
shiretsi (dead person's spirit), which is said to be hanging out at
the vacated sites, taken over by vegetation, pleading with the
survivors to accompany it in its lonely existence.

Certain areas of the deep forest, called *niyankimashi* (the
middle of the forest), are especially perilous since they are inhabited by all sorts of *kamari* (demonic beings). There are particular places contaminated by demonic spiritual beings whose
breath is so toxic to humans that, after inhaling it, they choke
and could die unless swiftly treated by herbal remedies. Some
believe that it is possible to have an encounter with toxic air
even within the perimeter of a home compound. In Spanish, the
disease caused by poisonous air is called *mal aire*. In Ashéninka
Perené, the condition is described by the phrase *aajenkakina
tampia* aa-jenka-ak-i-na tampia [take-stench-PERV-REAL-1O
wind] (I've breathed in bad air).

The depths of the forest are a grave threat to men, where
the sexually deviant bone spirit *peyari* (ghost) lurches, looking
for a male human to satisfy his sexual desire. The copulative act
brings death to the victim. The bone spirit is also known under
the name of *manironari* (deer-like), due to its physical likeness to
male deer. Gregorio Santos Pérez's text *Peyari* (The Bone Spirit)
is a recollection of the account he heard from a fellow woman
when he was a child. The story is about the woman's and her
husband's encounter with *peyari*. The text was recorded in 2011
in Villa Perené.

Even stretches of forest not far from human settlements are
not safe because they hide demons that kill by "breaking" bones,
described as *ikitoriakai kamari* i-kitori-ak-ai kamari [3M.A-

break.off-PERV-1PL.O demon] (the demon will break our bones). Bone-breaking demons "break" the human's neck, then put the body parts back, blow onto the body, and resuscitate it. The person regains consciousness and comes back home but eventually dies after an illness. A mere glimpse of a demonic creature may prove to be lethal, resulting in sickness and death, as illustrated by the text *Iñaaventa kamari Kovatsironi* (Speaking with Regard to the Demon from Kovatsironi), recorded by Ines Pérez de Santos in 2011 in Bajo Marankiari.

The nonhuman landscape spaces are also inhabited and controlled by the spiritual beings *ashitarori* ashi-t-a-ro-ri [own-EP-REAL-3NMASC.O-REL] (master-owner), alternatively called *iriniro* (his mother) or *iriri* (his father) of their respective domains (Rojas Zolezzi 2002). If the protected species is *maniro* (deer) or *shintori* (peccary) or *tsamiri* (curassow), all of masculine gender, the object slot is filled with the third-person masculine suffix *-ri*, *ashitariri*. Mountain heights are a dwelling place of *maninkaro* man-ink-a-ro [hide-NMZ-EP-NMZ.NMASC] (invisible woman) and *maninkari* man-ink-a-ri [hide-NMZ-EP-NMZ.MASC] (invisible man). Other "autonomous spaces" (Gow 1995:55)—rock formations, salt mines, caves, and lakes—have their owners as well.

Water space is the permanent abode of the creatures of dubious morphology that resemble anaconda-like snakes, called *kiatsi*. The generic term is *nijaaveri* nijaa-veri [water-STAT.NMZ] (male water inhabitant), or *nijaavero* (female water inhabitant). The distinction is made between a *tsomiri*, which lives in self-contained water reservoirs like deep stream pools and lakes, and a *kiatsi*, which can inhabit more turbulent river waters. The regularly observed whirlpools in the water are regarded as warning signs of the master-owner's presence. The *tsomiri type* has long, flexible whiskers designed to wrap tightly around a person's leg and drag him or her into the water. Many consultants contend that *tsomiri* are akin to sirens. To entrap a person, they can take the form of a beautiful blonde *gringa* (white woman) and lure the victim into the river, so that they can take him as their lover. The drowned are believed to have been seduced by a water demon. Some consultants associate *tsomiri* with *oye(chari)* (malevolent rainbow spirit), which strikes by burning human skin to the bone.

The *kiatsi*, enormous anaconda-like creatures (some say it has an armadillo-like physique), are also reported to be of either sex. At midday, one could hear the snake's signature sound, *kin kin*. Male *kiatsi* are sexual predators who stealthily impregnate young girls when they are bathing in the river. The mad circular movements of a *kiatsi* once caused an earthquake and a flood, subsequently destroying the villages of Pichanaki and Pucharini. The *kiatsi*'s sinister exploits are described by Carmen Pachiri Quinchori in *Kiatsi* (The Owner of the River), recorded in her home in Ciudadela in 2013.

The owners' task is to protect the territory and their "pets" or "children," so they are, in a sense, their territory's "keepers" or stewards. For example, masters-owners of game animals keep them in caves in the hills and regularly release a limited number of prey into the forest for hunters (Elick 1969:chap. 3). The masters-owners are not indestructible and can be physically removed if they show a pattern of aggression toward humans. Upper Perené accounts show that when masters-owners show tolerance of intruders and let hunters go unharmed, humans leave them alone, as illustrated by the text *Maninkaroite* (The Invisible Women) (narrator Moises Santos Rojas). But when masters-owners turn violent toward locals, as seen in *Tsamirimenta* (The Curassow Crest Stone; narrated by Moises Santos Rojas) and *Ashitarori otzishipaye* (Masters of the Hills; narrated by Elena Nestor de Capurro, with Victoria Manchi de Martin), they are swiftly dealt with. The owner of the rock outcrops, Iriri Tsamiri (the Father of curassows) was shut away in a cave by the local shaman and his helpers; Atsityopi (male *kiatsi*) had to be clubbed to stop his aggression against locals. The texts were recorded in 2011 in Bajo Marankiari and Pampa Michi.

The masters-owners of places can be human, but their bodies are not cosubstantive with Upper Perené Arawaks. Two texts about Churingaveni Lake attribute the ownership of the lake either to *virakocha* (non-Indian outsiders, white people) (*Inkaari Churingaveni* [Lake Churingaveni], narrated by Moises Santos Rojas, recorded in 2011) or to *chori* (Andean settlers) (*Chorinkaveni* [Churingaveni], narrated by Daniel Bernales Quillatupa, recorded in 2012). Although seemingly human, non-Ashaninka people are nonetheless endowed with supernatural powers. As the texts reveal, non-Ashaninka people walk on the lake as if it were a hard surface, they dive into the lake without drowning, and most miraculously, they permanently inhabit the lake's space.

The collected narratives about landscape transformations and the resultant landmarks do not construct a coherent panorama of Upper Perené history. The landmarks are dispersed in Upper Perené space-time and are not interwoven into a chronologically linear sequence of events. Nonetheless, they serve as faithful reminders of the pivotal episodes from Upper Perené history. The transformed landscape bears witness to the process of indigenous "appropriation" of the land (Santos-Granero 1998), transparently marking its boundaries and signaling the land's belonging to its rightful "owners" (Bender 1993). Each topogram carries unique significance by highlighting specific spiritual aspects of the Upper Perené landscape mosaic.

SIXTEEN

Ashiropanko

(The Iron House)

Gerardo Castro Manuela

[1]Kitatiterika nonkinkitsakoteri tsika okanta pairani acharinite ivetsikantakarori ashiropaye yantavaitantyari, aajatzita shacha, maaroni yantavaitantyari, iroñaaka ipaitantakarori ashiropanko ashaninka. [2]Ipoña kirinka, te ayotero tsika isaiki. [3]Ikantzi acharinitepaye ipoki kirinkasatzi, ipokanake yameniro, ankante, tzivi. [4]Ipoki avotsiki, pashinipaye ipokantari ivito, itziyaata iroñaaka parenini ishintzipariki. [5]Eero yareetzita, ontzimatye imaye akante itziyaatakotanta. [6]Te oshiye ishintzipari, te onkimitya ankante inkaari. [7]Okimita pitotsi arinironka oshiye.

[8]Ipokinta, yami iyaniri, yamake ivarentzite, itzivini pityokini, yami ichekopite inkintantyari shima. [9]Aajatzita yami poshiniri impoñiyarika kirinkanta irojatzita yareetantyari Tziviariniki. [10]Iroñaaka atzirika ashaninka yaake akante tzivi inkatyonkatyari iroñaaka poshiniripaye.

[11]Iroñaaka ashaninka saikapaki, yantapaki ivani jaka ashiropankoki. [12]Ari opaitari ashiropanko, ari yantavaitapaki ivintzi iyaniri, yantapaki ivanko. [13]Iroñaaka yoka atzirika antatsiri saviri, shacha, pashini ashitzikantyari akoki kitsapi, yoka atzirika mainari inatzi. [14]Kaari ñeeroni kooya, ankante, iñaaniki virakocha *virgen*. [15]Iroñaaka iritaki anteroni apaniroini, pashini eero ikiashita. [16]Arika inkiaki pashini atziri, aritaki ovamakeri

paamari, ari ontaakeri. [17]Eerorika ari ontonkashitanakia okaratzi ikotsitziri. [18]Yoishiro mapi, opiantyari ankante kotsiro.

[19]Iyoka mainaripaye imaashitya apaniroini, eero itsipatari iriri, iriniro, aajatzita irirentzipaye, isaikashitya apaniroini yaviantyarori, yantero maaroni ipokashitzirinta. [20]Te ayotero pairani tsika okaratzi kashiri osamanitzi yantantyarori okaratzi saviri, shacha, kitsapi, kovitzinaki, okaratzi ikovayetziri yanteri, ankantashitavakia apite kashiri yantero oka okaratzi yantziri.

[21]Avisakerika osamani, osamanitanakerika, yaviakerorika maaroni okaratzi inintakeri, yookanakero iroñaaka. [22]Yaanakero maaroni, itetanakero ivitoki, ishintzipariki, amaatakotanake, jatanaje kirinka. [23]Iroñaaka ijatanakerika kirinka, okaratzi yantakeri iyomparitya, impakeri pashini inintakotapakeri. [24]Pashini ashaninka ikantziri, "Tsika paakeroka? [25]Nonintakotakemi kovitzi, shacha, saviri, nokovi." [26]"Pinintakotakenarorika, pimpena kitsarentsi, pimpena tonkamentotsi," paitarika inintakotziriri iyomparitavaka. [27]Ikantzi, "Nomperi nashi naaka okimitatya naaka nomperi pashini paitarika tzimatsiri pashini." [28]Ari okantari pairani, tekatzi kireki, intaani ampavakaiya okaratzi tzimimotatsiri.

[29]Itsonkatakerorika okaratzi yantakiri, poñaashitaka ikanteri evankaripaye, "Tsame iroñaaka, tekatsitanaki atzivini, tekatsi antavaitantyari. [30]Tsame ajate, ajatapainte antavaite." [31]Ovakera ipiyaje yantavaite. [32]Iroñaaka tziyaatajeetaja irojatzita Tziviariki, irotaki ishiretari Tziviari. [33]Isaikapainte, iviriatakero tzivi, okarate iponatakero ikaraiyeninta. [34]Aririka ivetsikakero maaroni tzivi, pokaji irojatzi iroñaaka ashiropankoki. [35]Irotaki ikantantaitarori ashiropanko. [36]Ari osaiki omorona. [37]Irotaki ipaitantaitarori ashiropanko, ari ivetsikaitzirori shachapaye, kotsiro, okaratzi yantavaitantari. [38]Ari okaratzi iroñaaka, overapaka.

¹Today I will tell about how our ancestors made iron tools in the past with which to work, they made axes and all things with which to work, that's why our ancestors called it the Iron House. ²They were coming from the area downstream and didn't know where to stay. ³Our ancestors say that they came from the area downstream, they came to look for, so to speak, salt. ⁴They were coming on foot [by the trail]; others came by canoe or pushed their rafts upriver with the poles. ⁵They wouldn't arrive at their destination [the same day] and had to sleep in the area where they were traveling as passengers. ⁶The rafts didn't advance much upriver, it was not like, so to speak, moving it on a lake. ⁷For example, a canoe advances more or less faster.

⁸When they would come, they would bring their manioc, their plantains, a piece of salt, and arrows to fish. ⁹When they were coming from the area downstream, they also brought meat, [which lasted] until their arrival at the salt-mining area. ¹⁰These people, our fellow men, would mine salt to salt their food.

¹¹Our fellow men would settle down and clear a *chacra* here at the Iron House. ¹²So it was called the Iron House, there they worked, planted manioc, and constructed their homes. ¹³These people who made machetes, axes, and other things for sewing with a needle, these people were bachelors. ¹⁴They didn't see women; so to speak, in the non-native language, they were virgins. ¹⁵The ones who make things live alone because others should not enter [the area]. ¹⁶When a person enters the area, the fire can kill him, it can burn him. ¹⁷If not, all that is melting [being cooked] in the fire can explode. ¹⁸They would light a stone, and it would transform into a knife.

¹⁹These bachelors slept alone, their father and mother did not accompany them, nor their brothers—they lived alone to gain the power to make iron things, since they came with this objective in mind. ²⁰We didn't know in the past how many months

they stayed to make machetes, axes, needles, pots, all that they wanted to make; we will guess, two months to make them.

[21]When a lot of time passes, a great deal of time later, when they have mastered all that they wanted, they abandon it [the place]. [22]Now they pick all up, load it into a canoe or raft, and go downriver. [23]When they go downriver, they make exchanges, they give a person what he wants. [24]This other person says, "Where did you get it? [25]I would like a pot, an axe, a machete, I want [this]." [26]"If you want all this, give me a traditional robe, and give me a rifle," whatever he wants in exchange. [27]He says, "I will give him mine, like I give him other things, whatever I have."' [28]This is how it was in the past, there was no money, only we would exchange all that we had.

[29]When they finish all that they were making [in the forge], then they would say to [other] young people, "Let's go, we have no salt, let's bring our salt, there is nothing to work with [in the forge]. [30]Let's go, let's work [in the salt mine]." [31]They will return to their work [in the forge] quickly. [32]They all push their fleet upriver with the poles up to the salt-mining area, they aim to get there. [33]They will stay there for a while, dry their salt, and wrap all [that they have mined]. [34]After they process the salt, they will come back to the Iron House. [35]That's why it is called the Iron House. [36]There is a cave there. [37]That's why it's called the Iron House, because there they made axes, machetes, all tools to work with. [38]This is all, it ends here.

SEVENTEEN

Atziri yamaniri mapi poña paamari

(People Were Worshipping Fire and Stone)

Elías Meza Pedro, with Gregorio Santos Pérez

[1]–Ipokayetzi irorave, ashaninkapaye poñaachari ikantziro kishiiki, kishiisatzi, maaroni ipokayetzi, ari imakoriapakiri ara, ikantziro "paatsiri." [2]Imakoriapakirika paatsirikira, je, impoñaakia, arika yamonkoyetzirika. [3]Yamonkotaki, impoñaaki iyokani, impiri ivantekira, iparankatzitya. [4]Impirikia, ishenakiri. [5]Ari yamanirikia, yamaniri paatsiri.

[6]–Ityerovashitatyari? [7]O tsika ikantzirika?

[8]–Intaani ikatziyakara antave. [9]Yamaniri ikantziri, "Aviroka paatsiri pinatzi. [10]Pimpina tsika paita nokoviri."

[11]Iroña orave paatsirira iñaatziri, ikantziri, "Ari, nompakimi tsika paita pikoviri." [12]Iroñaaka ikovakotakirira, iroñaaka ikantzi, yaaki iirikite, iyora, ikantaitziri *oro*, iyora ashaninkara yaaki kiriki, ipakiri, ikantziri anta ikovintsakiri ipakiri. [13]Ipakiri iroñaaka itsipariakayetakari ikaraiyenira isheninkara, itsipariayetakiri. [14]Ikantzi, "Arive, kameetsataki ipakairi iyora paatsiri iirikite. [15]Iroñaaka ontzimatye amaniri." [16]Arika impoki, intyerovapaki, yamaniri. [17]Je, ikantziri anta iñaapinkatsatziri paatsirira, iñaapinkatsatziri.

[18]Arika yamanakirika, onkaratapakirika, inkantzimaintatyari, "Tsika paita pikovakotanari aviroka iroñaaka?" [19]Yankamaintyari inkanteri, "Nokovi pimpina piyokani, chamairo, ishiko." [20]Yaanakiro ichamairote, ivanakiro irishikote, ivana-

7. The ceremony of the adoration of fire is conducted by "the pure."
By Daniel Bernales Quillatupa (Aroshi).

kiro iyokani. ²¹Ari imisaikanakiro, impiyotanakiro okantata-
pita mapi, ari okantaka, ari impiyotanakiro irishikote, chamairo, iyokani.

²²Avisaki iroñaaka jaka, irayi itzivini janta, yaapintaitzinta
Tziviariki.

²³–Ari okaratzi pikimakovintziri?

²⁴–Arika impiyaji, impiyajirika aajatzi ari okinanaji avotsi
pairani, aritaki ikinayetzi maaroni intayetarori, kinkivaripaye
ashaninka. ²⁵Aririka iroñaaka impiyajirika, iñaapinkatsatairira,
yamanapairi. ²⁶Inkanterikia iroñaaka, "Aritaki okantaka, pipakinaro okaratzi nokovakatakimiri, pipakinaro. ²⁷Iroñaaka
piyajana, irotaki nojatai." ²⁸Impasonkitanajirikia iyorakia
paatsirira. ²⁹Ishiyari atziri, mapi onamaintatya.

³⁰–Oshiyaro ivante atziri?

³¹–Je, ari oshiyaro ivante atziri, iroka *isomperi*rote maaroni.
³²Iporokakitziri, iyora, tsikataima ipaita iporokaitakitziri, je,

iporokaitakitziri. [33]Iporokaitakirira, te añaajiri, intaani kapicheeni iroma ovakeraini.

[34]–Oh, *padre*, iritaki paatsiri.

[35]–Ikantziri, "Paatsiri inatzi." [36]Osheki aka itsipanampitari, pashini aka, pashini, isatekaitziri niyanki.

[37]–Irokama, apa, pikantzirika Josekika?

[38]–Jose janto, ariitantyarori San Jeronimoki. [39]*Es padre*, ikantaitziro paatsiri, ari ikantaitziro *padre*, paatsiri. [40]Ari okini pairani avotsi kinkivaro, avotsi, paitakamakia. [41]Ashaninkapaye arika impoki, ari imakoriapakirika, aitaki intyerovashiteri, yamaniri. [42]Inkantekia, "Pimpina iroka nokoviri." [43]Ikantzityakia ovakeraini ipakiri kiriki, *oro*, irotaki yamitantanakariri, irotaki yamitantanakariri. [44]Pashinipaye ashaninkara ikantzi, "Kameetsarini."

[45]Aka pairani isaiki aani ikantaitziro Tsonkitsiroshiki. [46]Isaikayetzi pairani Shariva. [47]Ari pairani otzimi antaroite pankotsi. [48]Ivitsikaitziro, ikantziro "parahua." [49]Aritaki ipiyoyetari maaroni ashaninkapaye. [50]Irokia intatzikiroinikia tzimatsi pankotsi,tekatsi ariitatya, tekatsi ariitatyani. [51]Iyotashita yareeta, kaari anteroni ochaa. [52]Ikantzi kaari mayempitatsiri, ochaa, iyotashitakari. [53]Antaro pankotsi, aitaki isaikiri iyorave ikantaitzirika jevatakantzirorira, te noyoteri tsikarika ipaita, aritaki isaikirikia. [54]Ari isaikaiyeni okimitanaka intyatzikiroini, ari otzimiri antaro pankotsi.

[55]Aritaki yoisaitziro paamari. [56]Ikantzi irorave yamanirirakia iyora maaroni ashaninkapayera, je. [57]Kaatsite aparoni jatatsini, akantakiri ayirorira ochaa, akantziro arori. [58]Kaari mayempitatsini, iyotashita ijate, kaari mayempitatsini. [59]Inkimavanteteri irora ivavanika, tsikarika ikantzi, iñaavaitzi. [60]Ishiyakavintziro iroñaaka okanta *maatsiri*paye, oshiyaro *maatsiri*paye, ari ikantaitziro. [61]Ari okantari pairani. [62]Te

añaajiro, te ankimakovintairo. ⁶³Noñaashirivitakaro pairani
naarikia anta isaikakantanari aaniyeni, inayeni ikantaitziroka
Tsonkitsiroshiki, ari noñaakirori. ⁶⁴Maatsikia pankotsi nokantakiri ikantziri "parahua." ⁶⁵Iyoshiyetziro imisaikaitziro. ⁶⁶Kaa-
tsi jatatsini ikantzirirakia antzirori ochaa. ⁶⁷Kaatsi jatatsini,
eero ijatzi. ⁶⁸Ikantziro mayempiro kooya airo ojatzi anta. ⁶⁹Ari
yoisaitzirori ivaamarite. ⁷⁰Aritaki ara yamaniririkia ivavanira.
⁷¹Ikantziro iroñaaka jevatzirorira, "Te noninte ompoke aka
antzirori ochaa, akantziri piyatsatachari. ⁷²Iyotatyeya kaari
anteroninta, iritaki jatatsini inkimavanteteri ivavanira
paamari."

¹–Our fellow men from Gran Pajonal, those who are called Pajonalinos (dwellers of grassy uplands), would come, they all would
come and rest here, by the stone called Father. ²When they were
resting near this Father, they chewed their coca leaves. ³They
chewed them, they would take out their coca leaves and place
them in the stone's mouth, because [it seemed that] the stone
had an open mouth. ⁴They would give coca to the stone, and it
would stick there. ⁵This way they worshipped the Father.

⁶–Did they kneel in front of it? ⁷Or what did they do?

⁸–They only stood there. ⁹They would worship and say, "You
are the Father. ¹⁰Give me what I ask for."

¹¹Then the Father would look at him and say, "All right, I
will give you what you want." ¹²Now, because he had asked the
Father, they say, he got the Father's money, this, what is called
"gold," and this fellow man takes the money that the stone gave
him, they say, and gets lucky. ¹³What the Father gave him, he
would share with all his fellow men [present there]. ¹⁴He [that
man] says, "Very well, this is good that the Father gave us money.
¹⁵Now we have to worship him."¹⁶When they come, they kneel

in front of him and worship. ¹⁷Yes, they say, they showed deference to the Father, they showed deference to him.

¹⁸When they worship, when they finish their worship, they
will ask him, "What is it that you want?" ¹⁹The Father will respond, "I want you to give me your coca, *chamairo*, and powdered lime." ²⁰They will take their *chamairo* and place it, and
lime, and coca [in the stone's mouth]. ²¹They will put it there, pile
it up under the stone, like this, there they will put large quantities of lime, *chamairo*, and coca leaves.

²²They pass this area on the way to the salt mines, where they
mine salt by the river Paucartambo.

²³–Is this all you heard about it?

²⁴–When they return, they return by this trail that existed in
the remote past; the founders, our ancient fellow men walked on
it. ²⁵When they return, when they pay respects to the stone, they
worship it. ²⁶They will say, "So it was, you gave me what I asked
for, you gave it to me. ²⁷I am back, and will be going." ²⁸They will
give thanks to the Father. ²⁹It resembles a person, but it's a stone.

³⁰–Does its mouth resemble a person's mouth?

³¹–Yes, it's like a person's mouth, and the hat, everything. ³²It
was destroyed, whoever destroyed it, but it was destroyed, yes,
it was destroyed. ³³Because it was destroyed, we can't see it anymore, only a little bit of it [is seen].

³⁴–Ah, padre, that's why Paatsiri [in the native language].

³⁵–They said, "It is a true Father." ³⁶They [worshippers] will
stand on one side [of the stone], others on the other side, others
in the middle.

³⁷–Father, is this [stone], which you are talking about, is [it]
in the vicinity of Jose's? [The residence of a man who lives not
far from Kishitariki, present-day Mariscal Cáceres, is alluded to
here.]

³⁸–It's farther away from Jose's, toward the village of San Jeronimo de Yurinaki. ³⁹It's padre, it was called *paatsiri*, [that's why] they called it Paatsiri. ⁴⁰An old trail passed through that area long ago, whatever its name was. ⁴¹When our fellow men would come and rest there, they would kneel and worship the stone. ⁴²They would say, "Give me what I want." ⁴³They say, the Father would give them money, gold, that's why it became a custom for them. ⁴⁴Other fellow men would say, "This is good."

⁴⁵Here long ago lived my deceased grandfather, in this place called Tsonkitsiroshi. ⁴⁶Here lived the Shariva family. ⁴⁷There was a big house there. ⁴⁸When it was constructed, it was called *parahua* (communal house). ⁴⁹There many of my fellow men gathered together. ⁵⁰Across [from] it, there was another house, and nobody would enter it but virgins who do not commit fornication. ⁵¹They say that those who are not promiscuous, who do not commit fornication, are pure. ⁵²It was a big house, and there was this . . . called "the one who leads," I don't know what it [his position] was called, but he was there. ⁵³They were all aggregating in this big house, on one side. ⁵⁴There they would start a fire.

⁵⁵They say, my fellow men worshipped it. ⁵⁶A person who commits fornication, we call them fornicators, will not walk in, they say. ⁵⁷Those who are not promiscuous, the pure ones, they walk in. ⁵⁸They will hear the voice of God, whatever he says and talks. ⁵⁹They are similar to religious sisters, *madres*, this way they are called. ⁶⁰This was in the past. ⁶¹Now we don't see it, we don't hear on its account. ⁶²I saw it long ago when my deceased grandfather and mother made me live there, in the place called Tsonkitsiroshi. ⁶³There I saw it. ⁶⁴There was a house called *parahua*. ⁶⁵The pure would stay separated. ⁶⁶Those who commit fornication will not enter it. ⁶⁷They will not go, they will not go. ⁶⁸They say, adulterous women won't go there. ⁶⁹There they will start a

fire. ⁷⁰They truly worshipped their god there. ⁷¹The leader will say, "I don't want a woman who commits fornication to come, we say this to them, the disobedient ones. ⁷²The pure ones who don't commit fornication, they will come to hear the voice of the god of fire."

EIGHTEEN

Atziri yamaniri paamari
(People Were Worshipping Fire)

Cristobal Jumanga Lopez

[1]Okanta ikinkitsavaitzi pairani, ikantzi nocharinini irora, ikantzi paitari, ikantzi ipoki katonko pareniki. [2]Maatsi aparoni amaisha, yamaniri irora paamari. [3]Ikarajeetzi ipokaki, ipokakija osheki pokaintsi. [4]Ikarajeetaiyenira, osheki ipokaki.

[5]Iro yariitzimotyari mapininiranki. [6]Iñaapaki, yareetapaka ivankoki, iñaapaki isaiki antarite amaniriri. [7]Ipaita Santiago, Shantyako antarive, antari sheripiari inatzi. [8]Ikantavakai, "Ari, pipoki?" [9]"Je." [10]"Ari," ikantzi.

[11]Yantaipitsatapakiri jenoki, iñaapakiri ipiyojeeta osheki, piyotacha amaniriri, tyerovajeetaka, yamanajeetziri ivaamarite, paamari. [12]Piyotaka tsitsi, tsitsi iropirorive, kameetsa. [13]Oisapaki, oisapakiro, *pok pok*. [14]Saikaki Santiago ikimisantziro paamari, ikantzi, *pok pok*. [15]"Kameetsa pipoki aviroka? [16]Te pinkishimateri pava ara, te pitsainkiri, te pinkishimateri ivaamarite, te pintsainkiri, pipokatzi kameetsa."

[17]Ikanta osamanitaki, ikantzi, yamanakairi, yamanakairi, yamani, ityerovakairi, ipantsakavaitziri. [18]"Arive, ari osaitekira ampitamanairi." [19]Osaitekira pashiniki kitaiteri, jatzi iroñaaka. [20]"Tsame aakite tsitsi. [21]Pashini impiyoteniri." [22]Ipantsakavaitziri, ikanta ipantsakairi, ipantsai yamanakairi. [23]Ikantzi, "Je, kameetsaki iroñaaka, kameetsataki, monkarapaka iroñaaka, monkaraka." [24]Ikantzi, "Iro nompiyaje iroñaaka kirinka."

²⁵"Arive, iro pimpiyaje, pijataje, kameetsataki iroñaaka. ²⁶Oka-
ratzi amanakiri, aritaki intasonkaventakimi, aritaki pariitajia
kameetsa."

²⁷Osaitekira pashiniki oshekira pokatsi. ²⁸Okanta ijatajee-
taji, ariitajeetapaja kameetsa. ²⁹Ari okanta otsonkatapaka
ñaantsi.

¹My deceased grandfather told [me] long ago, he said this, he
said that he [and his companions] went upstream along the river
Perené. ²There was one Yanesha there, and he worshipped fire.
³There were a lot of people who would come [to that place]. ⁴A
lot [of pilgrims] would come there.

⁵They [grandfather and his companions] would be arriving
in the area of sacred rocks. ⁶When they arrived at his house,
they saw a big person seated who was worshipping. ⁷He was
called Santiago, and he was really big, he was a big shaman. ⁸[My
grandfather said], he asked the visitors, "Have you come?" ⁹"Yes."
¹⁰"All right," he said.

¹¹They climbed uphill, and they saw a lot of people, those
who were worshippers gathered there, they were kneeling and
worshipping fire, there was a fire there. ¹²There was a lot of wood
piled up, good-quality wood. ¹³They lit the fire, then they stirred
it, *pok pok* (sound of a fire). ¹⁴The shaman was sitting listening
to the fire, which said, *pok pok* (sound of a fire). ¹⁵[The shaman
transferred the message,] "Have you arrived with good intentions? ¹⁶You are not speaking badly of our god here, you are not
making fun of him, you are not speaking badly of the fire, you
are not making fun of him, you came with good intentions [to
hear the voice of the fire divinity]."

¹⁷Awhile later, my grandfather said, the shaman made them
worship the fire for a long time, he made them kneel and sing
songs to it. ¹⁸Then the shaman said, "All right, tomorrow we'll

continue." ¹⁹The next morning they went [to gather firewood]. ²⁰"Let's gather firewood. ²¹Then, they [other visitors] will pile it up." ²²The shaman made them sing songs for a long time, my grandfather said, he made them worship, singing songs to the fire. ²³The shaman said, "Very well, this is good, this is fine now, it [the worship] is fully accomplished, it is accomplished now." ²⁴They [my grandfather's companions] said, "Now we will return to our place downstream." ²⁵The shaman said, "Very well, now you will return, you'll go back. ²⁶After all this time that we've worshipped, it [the fire divinity] will magically blow on you, and you'll arrive at your destination safe and sound."

²⁷On other days, a lot of people were coming. ²⁸My grandfather and his companions left and arrived home safely. ²⁹Here my story ends.

NINETEEN

Tzivi

(Salt)

Ruth Quillatupa Lopez

[1]Iro pinintziri nokinkitsatakaimi. [2]Pairani ashaninkapaye poña-yetachari anta akantziro añaaniki Saatzipoki, ari ipoñaayetari pairani aayetatsiri tzivi. [3]Intziyaatakotakia ivitoki, intziyaata-kia irojatzita ari imaapintziri pairani aka iroñaaka akantajee-tziri Intsipashiki, ari imaajeetziri. [4]Onkitaitamanai intziyaata-kia irojatzi imaantapakia aka anampiki Marankiaroki. [5]Impoña ivavisakiro irojatzi oponkityatapaka Tziviarini, ari ijajeetziri iroñaaka iitziki. [6]Ikantya irojatzi yareetantakia anta, ari imaa-jeetapakeri. [7]Okitaitamanai inchekaki itzivini, irojatzita aririka yaajeetaki maaroni, amaatakojeetaji irojatzita imaapaje Maran-kiaroki. [8]Onkitaitamanai irojatzi yavisantajia tsikataima imaa-paje Pichanaki. [9]Onkitaitamanaji sheeteni ariitajeetaja inam-piki irirori aatsiri itzivini. [10]Maaroni iinapaye, itomirikipatsaini, maaroni yaajeete itzivini.

[11]Te ivinkiro. [12]Iyotatzi, tzimatsi pokanaintsini. [13]Impaika-jero shintzipaki, amaatakojeetaje itzivini irojatzita inampiki. [14]Yaaronta osheki tzivi, kaatsite intsote, kaatsi ikatyokan-tyari ishimate. [15]Irojatzita arika yariitajeetajia anta, intonon-kajeetapajero. [16]Ivayetakiro voteyakipaye, tekatsi iñaashitya-rokia ishemiavaite, pachakakipatsaini, iyovitziteki ivayetakiro. [17]Yamponatayetakiro otakiki parentzi, yoisotayetakiro. [18]Imen-kotashitakiro, yoisashitakero paamari, tekatsi ontsaatya.

8. Locals mine salt in the vicinity of the river Tziviarini (Salt River). By Daniel Bernales Quillatupa (Aroshi).

[19]Iroma airorika yoisashitziro, ivayeterotya jeñokini onkisotantyari, kaatsi iraaya irori. [20]Kisoki onkantya, airo iraaja. [21]Itononkayetakiri, irotaki intsoteri.

[22]Tzimatsi avotsi osamanitatsiri tsika osaiki irinini. [23]Aririka yaanaje iroñaaka avotsiki, tsika inkinakairoka? [24]Tema tenarini itzivini. [25]Impoñaakia kirinka, intziyaatatyeya pitotsiki. [26]Arika impokayetaki evankaripaye, iritaki vitsikanatsini iroñaaka ishintzipari, iro yamaatakotantajiari. [27]Maatsi pashini kinatsiri irojatzi Ashivantziniki, irojatzi Metararoki, oirinkajeetaja. [28]Tzimatsi aisatzita iñaajaitziri tzivi, ovaaki intaani okotsitziro, opaita "katsori." [29]Aka irora Metararoki, Kishitarikira iñiiro, tzimatsi nijaateni, intaani nijaa, irora nijaara, irotaki ikotsitziri itzivini. [30]Irotaki inkotsitziri kitamarovanitaki. [31]Pairani niri, apa naari ikamitantziro, opaita "katsori."

[32]Ninkarika jatatsini iitziki, ari imaajeetapajeri iroñaaka. [33]Yamayetaki erotzitepaye poñaachari Saatzipoki, yamayetaki erotzitepaye, itsamirite ipimantanairi ijatantajiarira. [34]Pashini

amanaintsini iyaniri, yakishitanaki ivariantzite. [35]Airo ipoki
apaniroini, osheki inkarajeeteni. [36]Poñanainchani Pichanaki,
aka ikantaitziroka irora nijaa ... paitaranki ... nijaateni irorave
Kivinaki, ari ipoñaayetakari, ikantaitziri ivairo Chekopiari.
[37]Iritaki amantanaintsini, iritaki ivinkatsarite, arika inkante,
"Tsame ajajeete aye tzivi."

[38]Iroñaaka arika ontyakitanaje piyoro, ari inintajeetzirori
yaye tzivi, ari okitamarotziri irori. [39]Maatsi ikantaitziri irora
Iniro, maatsi ikantaitziri Choritovaro, tzimatsi ikantaitziri
Imatsa. [40]Tzimatsi tzivi ovairopaye. [41]Choritovaro kisaapom-
poinaro tzivi, iro Inirora irotaki kitamarori onatzi.

[42]Airomi osaikimi Tzivi, airorikami opokakimi pairani Tzivira. [43]Nokantzimiranki atziri onatzi pairani, osaikantakari aka
opoña kirinka. [44]Pairani te añiiro tzivi, ivavaishijeeta okanta
omasankatzira. [45]Irotaki okamapakira, okanta omantsiyatakira
okantzi, "Aririka iroñaaka nonkamakirika, airo patsinakantana
mapi, notenatzikari. [46]Nonintzi patsinakantyanaro shintzipa
nompiyonkateta." [47]Añaashitari atziripaye, ñaaperoshirivai-
tachari irirori. [48]Okanta, okanta. [49]"Otzinakamarotajakari,
tsame atsinakantyaro mapi." [50]Arika yatsinakantakiaromi
shintzipaki, airo otenatzimi iroñaaka, ompiyonkatatyemi
tzivira.

[51]Tema aririka aye tzivi, tema tenarini. [52]Nonintzirika
naakite tonkariki, tenarini. [53]Naantari naaka ovira, noniveta-
karo kitamarori, naavetara tenave! [54]Noposantakaro mapiki,
tyak, tyak, tyak, nokaviriajerokia. [55]Nookatzi tonkariki,
nopiyanaka, aparoni tsantsaki namavitaka. [56]Otenatatzira,
te naaviro. [57]Ontzimatye atonkakajero *karretera*kika. [58]Ari
okantari. [59]Otarankakotakerakia, *eeeeh,* kitamaro merontanaki, kimivaitaka ikantaitziri *"tiisa"* mapi, kitamarorive!

[60]Choritovarora kisaapanitaki. [61]Aririka inchekaitakiro,
yamashitatziro shecha ichekantaityarori. [62]Pairani iro nokantzi

atziritzira, oñaapaki ikotsitajitzi shima. ⁶³Okantzi, "Tekatsikia oposhinitantyari," ovinkakero ako iroñaaka. ⁶⁴Añaashitaroma atziripaye okantzi, *ejeee*, antavaitakero. ⁶⁵Irotaki iratakiro, "Kameetsa oposhinitanaki." ⁶⁶Irotaki ikantaitziro okamaki tzivi. ⁶⁷Irotaki Iniro irori tzivi, maatsi merontanaki ikantaitziro Choritovaro, apite okanta. ⁶⁸Ari okaratzi.

¹This you want me to tell you. ²In the past, our fellow men, who come from the place which we call in our language Saatzipoki, would come in the past those who mined salt. ³They would push their canoes upriver with poles and sleep on what we call avocado branches, there they slept. ⁴The next day, they will push their canoes upriver and sleep here, in the village of Marankiari. ⁵Then they advance up to the mouth of the Salt River; from there they walk on foot. ⁶They keep moving until they arrive there, then they sleep. ⁷The next day, they cut salt for everyone and go downriver in their canoes to the village of Marankiari to stay there overnight. ⁸The next day, they reach a place to sleep, perhaps the village of Pichanaki. ⁹The next day, those who mined salt arrive in their village in the late afternoon. ¹⁰Everybody— wives, little children, all of them—come to get the salt [ashore].

¹¹They didn't submerge their salt [i.e., they protected it from water]. ¹²They knew that there would be those coming to get the salt. ¹³They will nail together the rafts and go downriver with their salt until they reach their village. ¹⁴They cut a lot of salt for others, because they have no salt to add to food and to salt fish. ¹⁵When they arrive, they will grind it. ¹⁶They will store it in bottles, so that its granules don't scatter, in gourds, and pots. ¹⁷They will gather the peel of plantains and wrap the peel around the salt. ¹⁸They will make an elevated platform and make a fire [to dry it], so it doesn't dissolve. ¹⁹If no fire is made, they will put it on the upper level of the house, so that it stays hard

and doesn't "cry" [melt]. [20]It will be hard and won't "cry" [melt]. [21]They will grind it and consume it with food.

[22]There was a path from where their mothers lived. [23]If they carry salt via the path, how will they carry it? [24]It's heavy. [25]They would come from downriver and push their canoes with poles upriver. [26]When young people would come on foot, they would make rafts and use them to go down. [27]There were others who would go to Ashivantziniki, Metraro, would go downriver. [28]They also discovered salty water, which would turn into liquid after being boiled, called *katsori*. [29]They found it here, in Metraro and also in Mariscal Cáceres, where there is a creek, simply water; this was boiled to get salt. [30]They boiled it, and it was white salt. [31]My father would buy it, it's called *katsori*.

[32]Those who will come on foot, will sleep there. [33]They will bring their guacamayos and curassows to sell when they go back home. [34]Others will bring their yuca, grilled plantains. [35]They won't come alone, but in large groups. [36]The one who would come from Pichanaki, from the stream . . . whatchamacallit . . . called Kivinaki—from this area they all came—was called Arrow-shooter. [37]He will bring them (he was their chief), when he says to them, "Let's go and mine salt."

[38]When *tucnay* (Lamiaceae sp.) blossoms, they all want to mine salt; during this time the salt gets white. [39]There is salt called Iriniro, there is Choritovaro, and also Imatsa. [40]Salt has names. [41]Choritovaro was a black-headed Salt person, and Iriniro was white.

[42]The Salt person wouldn't have lived here, hadn't she come [here] long ago. [43]As I told you before, she was a person who came from the downriver area to live here. [44]In the past, there was no salt, food was eaten bland. [45]When she died, when she got sick, she said, "When I die, don't crush me with a stone, lest I be heavy. [46]I want to be crushed with balsa (light wood used

to make rafts), so that I will be light." [47]There are people who are miscreants. [48]Some time passed. [49][The miscreants said,] "To prevent the demonic creature from getting up, let's crush her with a stone." [50]Had they crushed her with balsa wood, she wouldn't be heavy today, she would have been light.

[51]When we want to mine salt, it weighs a lot. [52]When I wanted to carry it uphill, it was heavy! [53]I cut out this much, and I liked it because it was white, but when I carried it, it weighed a lot. [54]Then I struck it with a stone, *tyak, tyak, tyak* (hitting action), and split it into parts. [55]I left one on the hill's top and returned and brought another big chunk. [56]Because it's heavy, I didn't bring it [all]. [57]I had to go uphill, toward the highway. [58]So it was. [59]When the mining area collapsed, *eeeh* (sound of a collapsing hill), the flat white wall was exposed; it was like, what is called chalk, pure white!

[60]Choritovaro was pulverized black salt. [61]To cut it, they would bring an ax. [62]In the past, I say, when Salt was a person, she saw someone cook fish. [63]She said, "There is nothing to make it taste good," and put her hand in the cooking food. [64]People saw her do that, said, *aha* (interjection expressing understanding), and touched the food. [65]They drank it, "It tastes good." [66]The one who was called Salt died. [67]There was the Salt person called Iriniro, and there was another flat, wall-like deposit of the Salt person called Choritovaro, two of them. [68]This is all.

TWENTY

Tzivi

(Salt)

Abraham Jumanga Lopez

[1]Tzimatsi aparoni ashaninka antarokona, iñaashirinkakiro nirontoki, sanii, itsonkavaitakiro ikintakiro maaroni. [2]Poña okantakiri oimi, oimintari ikantaitziri Pantyo, "Paanakina aka imperetaki." [3]Irotaki iroñaaka paitanakiro, Tsaavarini, Mavonarini, oka iroñaaka opaitanakiro iroka nijaatatsiri anta Kovirikini, Shintoriatoki, jero, okinakotaki aka.

[4]Ariitapaka jaka, iroñaaka aka Potyarini. [5]Jero, okinanaki aka Morinakishi, opoña Mapinini. [6]Poña aminanakiro, opaitanakiro Kisotenkari, Manitzipanko. [7]Ojataki irojatzi irorave ikantaitziroka Pampa Michiki. [8]Avisanakiro, opaitanakiro Tziviarini, okiantanakaro anta. [9]Osaikapaki, ikantaitziri kooya osaikantapakaro, ikantaitziri nijaa. [10]Osaikinta Tzivira iroñaaka anta, opiapaka tzivi imperetani, ari osaikapakiri.

[11]Okantziri oimi, "Paashitena paroto, pishimiantyana." [12]Ikantavita ishimiavitakaro, piriintanaja, piriintanaja, piriintanaja, te. [13]Sheetyaki. [14]Ikisaka Pantyo, ikantzi, "Paitakakia?"

[15]Yaaitaro iyora oyariri Chamanto, yaashitakiro mapi, ipichakiro. [16]Irotaki añaantarori iroñaaka tzivi otenatzi. [17]Poña yaminakiro iroñaaka oimi, intakotajaro, ishevatantajaro paroto. [18]Paroto, ikantzi, iraani ishetakiro irori. [19]Iraniri Chamanto piyanaka, amaatakotanaki. [20]Iri intakotavitaro iritsiro, ari

9. The Tzivi person is crushed by her brother. By Daniel Bernales Quillatupa (Aroshi).

opiapakari iroñaaka imperetaki, osaikira iroñaaka tzivi. [21]Irotaki añaantarori okaratzi atsojeetziri maaroni, aisatzi iponaashitaro asheninkapaye. [22]Nocharinipaye ijatzi yaye iroñaaka, jiro ikinashitziroka avotsi. [23]Jatzi yaye tzivi anta, ikiye.

²⁴Irotaki te ompaivaishitya nijaatenipaye, maatsitaki ovanakirori, opaitantankari. ²⁵Pashini opaitanaka Tziriari. ²⁶Maatsi ovanakirori ovairo anta, ñaakiro. ²⁷Okimitaka aka, nampitavakiro Tsaavarini.

²⁸Aritapaki okaratzi ikinkitsatakotziri acharini. ²⁹Osamani arika añaavintero, osamani ankinkitsate. ³⁰Kantzimaintacha te antsonkiro, ankantero ayoperotero añaanatakotero. ³¹Te onkantzimotai asampiteri acharinitepaye. ³²Iroñaaka tzimanatsiri ikimiyeta pashinipaye, tekatsi sampiterini. ³³Aisatzita te onkantzimotena nosampiteri, nonkanteri, "Tsika okantavaitaka?" ³⁴Iro okantatya pochokitapaki tsiteni, te inkinkitsate kitaite, tsiteni ikinkitsatzi. ³⁵Ari okaratzi, kapicheeni nokantakiri, kinkitsarentsitatsiri nonampiki.

¹There was an adult female person long ago who was hassled by gnats and wasps, which would sting her incessantly. ²Then she said to her husband, called Pantyo, "Take me to those little rocks." ³That's why she named these places—the Waterfall, the Wild Potato Hill, the river of Corvina Fish, the White-Lipped Peccary Hill, look, she passed by them here.

⁴She arrived here, what is now the Somewhat Salty settlement. ⁵Look, she passed by the Hill of Morinashi Herb [unidentified], then by the Little Rocks Hill. ⁶Then she looked around and named [a steep-sided valley] "the Ravine" and [a cave]"the Jaguar House." ⁷She went toward the Pampa Michi area. ⁸She passed it and named the river "Salt River," because she entered the area. ⁹She settled down there, and the river was called after this woman, because she lived there. ¹⁰When the Salt person lived there, she turned into salt, tiny stones, and there she stayed put.

¹¹She said to her husband, "Bring me balsa wood and crush me with it." ¹²He repeatedly pounded her head with the wood,

but she would get up, and he couldn't kill her. [13]It was getting late. [14]Pantyo got angry and said, "What the hell?"

[15]He took along his brother-in-law Woodpecker, who picked a stone and crushed his sister's head with it. [16]That's why salt is heavy. [17]Then her husband looked at her and pitied her, so he cleaned her with the bark of the balsa tree. [18]Balsa tree, they say, has the woman's blood that was shed when she was killed. [19]His brother-in-law Woodpecker returned in his canoe down-river. [20]He pitied his sister, because she disappeared among the tiny stones where salt is found. [21]That's why we have salt now to suck on, as my fellow men do who come from other places. [22]Our grandparents were mining salt, look, over there passes the [salt] trail. [23]They were going over there to mine salt, to dig it.

[24]The streams were named for a reason, there was a person who named them, that's why they're called this way. [25]Another stream is named the Split Open One. [26]There was someone who gave a name to these places, you've seen it. [27]For example, I will repeat, the Waterfall.

[28]Here it ends, the story of my grandfather. [29]It takes time to tell stories. [30]Nevertheless, we don't stop narrating stories because we can't read. [31]We didn't ask our grandfathers questions. [32]Now those who were newly born, like others, don't ask questions. [33]I didn't ask questions either, like, "Why are things this way?" [34]Dreams always come at night, but one doesn't tell them in the morning, only in the evening. [35]Here it ends what I briefly talked about, the story of my settlement.

TWENTY-ONE

Manitzipanko

(The Jaguar House)

Ruth Quillatupa Lopez

[1]Iritaki ashitakoyetantatsri maperotzirori isheripiaritzi, ikimitatziri Manitzipankokiranki. [2]Tema maperotzirori isheripiarita yashitakotantakariri, ñaakero, ikantaitziri Manitzipanko. [3]Atziri inatzi irirori, ipokaki anta, ivantaka, ivayetari atziri.

[4]Ikantzirija, "Te noninte iroñaaka piñaashirinkina," pashinira sheripiari saikatsiri ashi arori aka. [5]"Pinintzirika, pijate pavishi katonko. [6]Iroma aka nosaikaiyeka, te ishikite atziri." [7]Ikantzi, "Pinintzirika, katonko inampini."

[8]Ikantakiri pashinira, "Te noninte nojate katonko. [9]Te onkameentsate ajate aya katonko shintori." [10]Ikantai aroka shintori. [11]"Iriririja katonko shitzirini inatzi, ishiki ivaro *cebolla*." [12]Iroma akaja te ashitzite aroka.

[13]Ikantziri pashinirakia, iyoka anampisatzika arori ikantzirija, "Airo piñaashirinkiri iyoka akarajeetzini."

[14]Ikantzi, "Te, iyoka shintori saikatsira jaka poshinikirini." [15]Shintori anatzi, piratsi.

[16]Ikantziro iritsiroka, iritsirotari irirori yorave tsika ikantaitziroka, manitzika, ikantakeri iyorave Ovaatzira, "Ñaamisa, pishinkitya, tsame ashinkijeetya." [17]Atziri pairani iroñaaka, akantzirika "shinkiatyonki," pitsitatsiri. [18]Iroñaaka otononkaki oshinkini, pashini tsinkanaintsini oyaniri. [19]Iroñaaka ishinkitakiri, imisaikaitzirira iroñaaka manitzipankokinta.

10. Naviriri, with his grandson, Poiyotzi, and onlookers, gaze at the cave where the jaguar-shaman was shut away. By Daniel Bernales Quillatupa (Aroshi).

²⁰Ishinkitakiri iroñaaka ashoshi, iritaki iraniri, ikantziri iroñaakakia, "Pinkiye, tsame aminkiirita iyoka, itsonkajeetaikari,"
sheripiarika pashini. ²¹Ishinkitakakari.

²²Iroñaaka manitzira iyovetaka. ²³Ikantziri, "Airo, te noninte nomaye, ari nomayeri aka." ²⁴Ikantziri, "Tsame ajate
anta amaye novankoki. ²⁵Pinariita kameetsa menkotsiki."
²⁶Ikantziri, ikantziri, yavitsanotziri, yavitsanotziri, iminkiakeri
iroñaaka. ²⁷Tsañatsañavetaka paitama ikantatari iroñaaka,
intaani yatsinakakeri ikintsiki irojatzi ikoñaatzi itziyamorokira.
²⁸Ari yamenakakeri katonko, otzimiranki iroñaaka iminkii-
tzirinta anta okantapakaranki aka, ari okoñaatziri iito. ²⁹Ari
okaratzi.

¹An expert shaman is the one who has the power to shut away
[the evil], like it was done in the Jaguar House. ²It was the expert
shaman who locked him up [the Jaguar man], you've seen it, it
is called the Jaguar House. ³He was a person who came from the
downstream area, and he ate people.

⁴The other shaman, who was living here with us, said to him,
"We don't want you to bother us. ⁵If you wish, go upriver. ⁶Here,
there are few of us, not too many people." ⁷He said, "If you wish
to go, there are more people upriver."

⁸The other shaman said, "I don't want to go upriver. ⁹It's not
good for anyone to go upriver to eat white-lipped peccaries."
¹⁰He called us "peccaries." ¹¹"Those upriver stink, they eat a lot
of onion." ¹²In contrast, we don't stink.

¹³The other shaman said, the one from our village said, "Don't
bother our people here."

¹⁴He said, "Yes, I will, the white-lipped peccaries here are
tasty." ¹⁵We are peccaries for him, animals.

¹⁶The Jaguar man's sister, Tayra, said to him, "What a pity,
you haven't had a drink, let's drink." ¹⁷There was a bee, we call

her Little Honeybee, who was a person in the past. [18]She ground corn kernels, and others pounded manioc. [19]They got him drunk, the one who is now shut down in [the cave of] the Jaguar House. [20]When they got him drunk, the Armadillo man, who was Jaguar man's brother-in-law, was told by the local shaman, "Dig, let's place him in a hole in the rock, or he will finish us." [21]They made the Jaguar man drunk.

[22]The Jaguar man at that point knew. [23]He said, "No, I don't want to sleep here, I will sleep over there." [24]The shaman said to him, "Let's go sleep in my house. [25]You'll lie down nicely on a sleeping platform." [26]He kept saying it, and they took him by the arms and pushed him through the hole. [27]But he forcefully resisted, that's why only the area of his neck was crushed, and his anus is visible. [28]He is seen downstream, where they squeezed him [into the hole in the rock], there his head appears. [29]This is all.

TWENTY-TWO

Imoro Naviriri

(The Naviriri Hole)

Elías Meza Pedro

[1]Noñaavintero okanta pairani ikantziri Naviriri. [2]Aparoni ashaninka paitachari Naviriri, ashaninka inatzi, osheki ipiantzi, ninkarika iñaakiri. [3]Impiakiri maaroni inchatoshipaye, osheki ipiayetziro. [4]Iroñaaka osamakari iritsiro, maatsi iritsiro, opaita Piyoro, okantzi, "Tsika ankanterika? [5]Osheki ipiantaki aari. [6]Tsika ankanterika onkantyanta ontsonkantyarikia? [7]Tsame avitsikakero piarentsi." [8]Ivitsikaitakero iroñaaka piarentsi, ontzimatye inkantyero inkarajeetaiyenira yante piarentsi. [9]Iroñaaka okantaki iritsiro ikarajeetaiyenira, "Tsame ante piarentsi onkantya antetantyariri aarika, aarika osheki ipiantzi." [10]Aritaki okantzirokia.

[11]Iroñaaka antakiro antaroite omorona, opakiri irora piarentsi, poña ishinkiperotakara irora inkantaitziri Naviriri. [12]Ikiyashitakiri antaroite omorona, ontzimatye yashitero. [13]Yashitakero, ontzimatye ovishiriakairi iritsiro. [14]Ivishiriaka, ishonkashonkatakakari ontetantyariri. [15]Ikanta, ikanta, ishinkiperotaka Naviriri, yakatsaitzirira. [16]Ivishiriakakari, ivishiriakakari, ivishiriajeetaka. [17]Ishonkashonkatakakari, ivishiriaka, ivishiriaka. [18]Ipantsajeetzi iñaanikira, ipantsajeetaki. [19]Ikanta ishinkiperotaka shirampari, te iyotaje, te inkinkishiriajia. [20]Iroñaaka ashitakotakiro omorona.

[21]Poña okantziri, "Aka aari, pinkinanaki." [22]Yaatzikakiri

omorora, soronkanaka, itetaitakiri omorokira, jaitetzi intsompointa. [23]Ikantzi iñaavaitzi Naviririka, "Onkantyatama ovasankitakina chooki, otetakina omoroki, iroñaaka ompiya piyoro." [24]Jaitetaki intsompointa Naviririra, jaitetaki. [25]Okantakira, pianaka piyoro, iritsirora Naviriri. [26]Ashaninka onavitatya, pianaka inchashi. [27]Ipiakiro iritsiro, piyoro onatzi. [28]Ikantzi, "Ovasankitakina chooki, iroñaaka ompiya, ompaitya piyoro." [29]Aparoni inchashi, kantzimaitacha tzimatsi inchatyaki.
[30]Arika omonkaratya, ontyate, kameetsa okitamarotzi inchashira, kitamarori onatzi. [31]Vaniinka okanta, iro kantacha osheki okasankatzi.

[32]Irotaki ipiiri pairani ikantaitziri Naviriri. [33]Ari ovirapaka, ari ovira, otsonkapaka jaitetaki iroñaaka Naviriri anta kirinka. [34]Iroñaaka yookanakiro omoro irojatzi okanta iroñaaka, otzimi omoroka anta kishiikika, te ompiya. [35]Ari okantakari pairani.

[1]I will speak with regard to the one called Naviriri. [2]He was our fellow man, called Naviriri, he was our fellow indeed, but he transformed anyone whom he would see. [3]He transformed many people into trees, he did it a lot. [4]Now, his sister got fed up with him, he had a sister, called Piyoro, and she said, "What shall we do to my brother? [5]He converts [people] a lot. [6]What shall we do so that it could stop? [7]Let's prepare manioc beer." [8]They made the beer, and [in order to accomplish the goal] they had to work together, to make manioc beer. [9]His sister said, when they were all together, "Let's make manioc beer, so that we could confine my brother, because he transforms [people] a lot." [10]Truly she said it.

[11]They made a big hole, and she gave him manioc beer, and he got drunk, the one called Naviriri. [12]They dug a big hole for him, which they had to cover up. [13]They masked it, and the sister needed to make him dance and sing. [14]Naviriri danced and

sang, they made him make circles for a long time, so that she could confine him to the hole. ¹⁵It went on and on, and he got so drunk that they dragged him. ¹⁶They made him dance and sing for a long time, they all danced and sang. ¹⁷They made him walk around this hole, they made him sing and dance again and again. ¹⁸They were singing in their language, they all sang. ¹⁹It went on and on, the man really got drunk, and he had no clue or misgivings [that it was intentional]. ²⁰Now, the hole was masked.

²¹Then she said, "Brother, you will walk here." ²²He stepped into the hole, and he slid down, he was confined to the hole, he went down there. ²³Naviriri said, "It won't matter that my sister made me suffer, and that she confined me to the hole, because she will transform into the *piyoro* tree." ²⁴And he went down, Naviriri went down. ²⁵Naviriri's sister turned into the *piyoro* tree. ²⁶She was our fellow woman, but she got transformed into a tree. ²⁷He transformed his sister, and she is a tree [now]. ²⁸He said, "My sister made me suffer, now she will transform into a tree called *piyoro*." ²⁹It is a tree but it has flowers. ³⁰When the flowers blossom, it is a nice-looking white tree, it is white. ³¹It is beautiful, but it has a strong aroma.

³²It is what the one called Naviriri transformed people into in the old times. ³³So it ended, it ended, it stopped when Naviriri went down there. ³⁴The hole has been in existence until today, it exists in the grasslands over there; it didn't disappear. ³⁵This is how it happened long ago.

TWENTY-THREE

Otzinantakari otzishi omontero Samamparini

(How the Hill Appeared across
from the Village of Villa Progreso)

Raul Martin Bernata

[1]Iroñaaka tsame kapicheeni ayotavakero okaratzi pikovakotanari. [2]Pisankinatakotero okaratzi. [3]Nosaikajeetzi aka, tzimatsi parenini akantziri shentajairi okaakini. [4]Opoñaanaka otzi-
mantanakari aatatapakara nijaa Tziviarini, aajatzi Santsa. [5]Ari
antarotanaki parenini paitanajachari Pirinini.

[6]Pairani ovakera ivitsikanakiro Pava kipatsi. [7]Aparoni atziri
ipaita Naviriri osheki ipiantzi tsikapaita inintakari, airorika
ikimisantaitziri.

[8]Opoñaaka aparoni kitaiteri aminakotero nampitsi opaita
Samamparini. [9]Ari otzimi otzishi.

[10]Iroñaaka tzimatsi aparoni atziri ipaita Naviriri. [11]Irotaki
intetzimatya kashiri, ikantakiri Naviriri iraniri [Tsiyarato],
"Tsame aipitsokatero parenini, okinanajeta Chuchurashiki."

[12]Yaajeetaki antaro mapi. [13]Tsiyarato yaaki osheki tsipana-
shi, karashi. [14]Iñaakiri itetzimataka kashiri, ikantziri, "Tsamera
iroñaaka aavakero mapipaye, añeero otzishi." [15]Ivavitapakaro
Tsiyarato iyamini. [16]Oonkatapaka irojatzi katonkonta.

[17]Irotaki intetzimatya kashiri, opiyapaka, oshonkatapakara
intatzikironta otzishi. [18]Osonkarianaka, oshevatanakara mapi.
[19]"Añaakero iroñaaka." [20]Ookanakiro otzishi.

²¹Iroñaaka Pava ikisanaka osheki. ²²Ipianakiri maniro Naviriri, ipianakiri Tsiyarato tsimiri. ²³Iroñaaka yaminavaitzi paita iviari.

²⁴Aririka pinintzi piñeero, ari pishiyakantapaintero, piñaantyarori otzishi omontero nampitsi opaita Samamparini.

¹Now, we'll learn a little bit of what you asked me [to tell you]. ²Write it all down. ³[Where] we live here, there is a river, we say, it is located close to us. ⁴There are other rivers that flow into it, the Salt River and the river Chanchamayo. ⁵Here the river that is called Perené gets big.

⁶Long ago the solar divinity Pava created our land. ⁷The person called Naviriri was transforming people into whatever he wanted, when people didn't pay attention to him.

⁸One day we'll see the village of Villa Progreso. ⁹There is a hill there.

¹⁰There was a person called Naviriri. ¹¹When the moon was about to disappear behind the mountains, he said to his brother-in-law Tsiyarato, "Let's change the course of the river Perené, so that it flows into the river Chuchurras."

¹²They gathered huge stones. ¹³Tsiyarato brought a lot of big and small leaves. ¹⁴When the moon began to disappear into the mountains, Naviriri said to Tsiyarato, "Now, let's pile up the rocks, then we'll have a hill." ¹⁵Tsiyarato [also] placed rotten leaves. ¹⁶They built a tall dam.

¹⁷When the moon was in its resting place in the mountains, the water was completely dammed and began flowing around the hill. ¹⁸The dam burst and the rocks moved. ¹⁹Naviriri said, "Now we have a hill." ²⁰He left the hill.

²¹The solar divinity Pava got angry. ²²He transformed Naviriri into a deer and Tsiyarato into a bird. ²³Now they look for something to eat.

²⁴If you want to see the hill and take a picture of it, it is located across from the village called Villa Progreso.

TWENTY-FOUR

Anashironi

(The Anashirona Stream)

Julio Castro Shinkaki,
with Delia Rosas Rodríguez

[1]–Paita ikantantaitarori Anashirona?
   [2]–Ipaitaitziro Anashirona, irorave ashaninka Anashironi ari isaikiri pairani, ikantaitziri, asheninka paitachari Anashironi. [3]Apaata ipaitzirokia, ipaitajeetziro pairani Anashironi. [4]Iro Vachiroki kinanaitziri nijaa aka, Vachiroki. [5]Ari isaikiri pashini asheninka, paitachari Vachironi. [6]Ari ipaitavaijeetari pairani. [7]Iroñaakamakia, eero añaajiro, iroñaaka impaitavaishitajiaro pashinisatzi nijaapatsaini, te ampaitavaitajiro. [8]Ari otsonkata, iroñaaka pashinijeetajai. [9]Eentsitepaye, te, eero añaajiri impaitayetajiaro nijaatenipatsaini.
   [10]Ari otsonka, ari overapakari Anashironi. [11]Iroka Tsipishiroki, tema iro ikantaitziri intatzikironta.
   [12]–Irotakitaima?
   [13]–Irovetaka. [14]Tsipishironi intatzikeronta. [15]Ankantakotero Tsipishironi, ari isaikiri asheninka. [16]Ari isaikiri manitzi pairani, aajatzi kamari isaiki, ikaimi Tsipishiroki. [17]Arika ajate, aritaki ikantzirikia iratsikakai manitzi Tsipishiroki. [18]Ari isaikiri manitzi antarite, iroñaakama kitaiterikika te añaajeri manitzi, jatayetaji antapaye. [19]Ikaratzi yokapayeka atziritepaye ikiapaki yantaki ivani, imishiyayetakeri. [20]Iro kantzimaitacha kamari saikatsitaima, te ijate, intaani anta kimitachari imperetaki isaiki

kamari Tsipishiroki. ²¹Ikaratzi jatayetatsiri ipatsimatziri ikovi inkitoreri, ivamairi. ²²Iroñaaka okaratzi okovirika *señorita*, ari isaiki kamari Tsipishiroki, antaritepaye manitzi. ²³Kamari ikaimi anta. ²⁴Ari ovirapaka.

¹–Why do they say Anashirona?

²–They call it Anashirona because our fellow man Anashironi lived there in the past, it is said, our fellow man called Anashironi. ³That's why the stream is called, they called it Anashirona. ⁴Vachiroki is the one that divides the river over there, Vachiroki. ⁵There was another fellow man, called Vachironi. ⁶So it was called in the past. ⁷In contrast, nowadays we won't see it [this practice], because other people will give names to streams, and we don't name places ourselves. ⁸It ended, we are different now. ⁹Our sons, no way, they won't name waterstreams.

¹⁰Here the Anashirona stream ends. ¹¹This is the Tsipishironi stream, and it's the tributary of the river Perené on the other [left] side.

¹²–Really?

¹³–Sure. ¹⁴Tsipishironi is on the other side of the river Perené. ¹⁵Speaking of Tsipishironi, our fellow men lived there [too]. ¹⁶There were jaguars, and also the demon lives there, he calls out in Tsipishiroki. ¹⁷If we go there, they say, jaguars will bite us in Tsipishiroki. ¹⁸There were big jaguars there, but these days we don't see them, they went away in various directions. ¹⁹After all these people entered [the area] and cleared land for crops, they made jaguars escape. ²⁰But the demon is there, he didn't go away, he lives in the big rocks in Tsipishiroki. ²¹The demon wants to break bones and kill those who go in pursuit of him. ²²This is all whatever the young woman wants to know; there is a demon in Tsipishiroki and big jaguars. ²³The demon calls out over there. ²⁴Here it ends.

TWENTY-FIVE

Pichanaki

Otoniel Ramos Rodríguez,
with Daniel Bernales Quillatupa

[1]–Iroñaaka aikiro ajate amaatakote kirinka, amaatakote, amaatakote irojatzi areetantapakiaro tzimatsi nijaa opaita Pichanani.
[2]Ikantzi pairani ashaninka, okaratzi nampitsi, nijaateni koñaayetatsiri ipaitziri ashaninka. [3]Te impaitashiyetyaro, tzimatsi shiyakaventarori. [4]Pichanani, ikantzi, iñiiri aparoni ashaninka, ikantzi, yora sheripiari. [5]Ikantzi, imanitzijeetzi, iñaavakaka. [6]"Tsika pipoñaaka?" [7]"Nopoña pichaanaki."
[8]–Paita ikantantaitarori "pichaanaki"?
[9]–Tzimatsi aparoni antaro impereta, irotaki ari ankante ovayeri pairani, ari ipichapintziri akante iyorave ashaninka. [10]Eero ikoñaatantaja, ipichaperotatyeri anta. [11]"Naaka pichaantatzi, osheki nopichaantzi." [12]Irotaki opaitantari nijaa Pichanani.
[13]–Tsika opoñaaka?
[14]–Ijate tonkariki sheripiari, yoijatziro nijaa.
[15]Iñaavaka, irotaki okoñaatantari opaita nijaa Pichanani. [16]Iroñaaka antaroite nampitsi, isaikaji osheki chori. [17]Pairani tekatsi, intaani ashaninka saikavetachari. [18]Yareetapaka ankante chori, ishonkapakaro inampitsitapakero iroñaaka. [19]"Ari akenajeetajiri," maaroni ashaninka poñaayetachari

11. The jaguar-shaman from Pichanaki crushes the body of his victim with a rock. By Daniel Bernales Quillatupa (Aroshi).

pairani. [20]Pairani, yora paitari, ashaninkapaye iyotziro tsika inkeni iraniite. [21]Tsaronkantsini pairani, eero yaniivaitzi apaniroini. [22]Tzimatsi antarite manitzi ovantachari.

[23]–Arika irovakai, tsika inkantaika?

[24]–Intaani iraanakai imperitaki antaroite, ari ipichaapintziri. [25]Irotaki ikantantari, "Nopoña Pichanaki." [26]Irotaki kinkitsarentsi ikantakota nijaa Pichanani.

[1]–If we keep going downriver, we arrive at the area where the Pichanaki River flows.

[2]They say that in the past my fellow men, the entire community, gave this brook a name. [3]It does not have a random name, it is a snapshot of something. [4]This is a place where my fellow man

shaman had a vision. [5]He came across a fellow man, when [both of them] converted into jaguars. [6]"Where do you come from?" [7]"I come from Pichanaki."

[8]–Why did he call it Pichanaki?

[9]–There is a big rock with which warriors of the old times would grind my fellow men. [10]So in order for them to disappear, their bodies were pulverized there. [11]"I am the one who crushes with a stone, I do it a lot." [12]That's why it was called Pichanaki River.

[13]–Where does the river come from?

[14]–The shaman came from upstream, he followed the river.

[15]He "saw" it in his vision, that's why the name Pichanaki River came into being. [16]Now it is a big town, many Andean settlers live there. [17]In the past, there were none, only our fellows lived there. [18]When Andean settlers arrived, they turned it into their town. [19]"Let's go there [to visit]," many Ashaninka were born in this place in the past. [20]In the past, our fellow men knew where they could travel to. [21]It was dangerous in the past, so people wouldn't travel alone. [22]There was a big jaguar-shaman who ate people there.

[23]–When he would kill us, what did he do?

[24]–He would take [a victim] to a big stone and crush him with this stone. [25]That's why [people would say], "I am from a place where people are pulverized with a stone." [26]This is a story of the Pichanaki River.

TWENTY-SIX

Pichanaki

Almacia Benavidez Fernandez

[1]Nonkinkitsatakotero okinkitsatakonari ina pairani okantakota Pichanaki. [2]Pichanaki opaita nampitsi, ikantaitzi iroñaaka.
[3]Otarankaki antaroite. [4]Tzimatsi aparoni onijaate Pichanani,
okajanikitzini otenkana. [5]Ari ojaikitapakari pairani antaroite
mapipaye, otarankantanakari, otzimaki antaro onika. [6]Opoñaa-
shitaka tzimatsi tasorentsipaye saikatsiri otzishikinta, itsonka
ishitovanake. [7]Okinkitsavaitakana ina aajatzita iroñaaka, "Oon-
kanaka antaroite, oonkaka antaroite, irojatzi osokantakia."
[8]Iroñaaka nampitsikira Pichanaki, irotaki opaitantari "pichaa,"
irotaki "oonkaronaki" irotaki nampitsi, irotaki opaitantana-
kari, aakakotantanakari "picha-naki." [9]Ari opaita. [10]Okantako-
takenaro ina iroñaaka, "Antaroite oonkaro, antaroite, aajatzita
onika." [11]Airikaka irori inchatoki antaroite, airo ookantaro
onika. [12]Ari opoña opaitantajari Pichanaki. [13]Okaratzi
noyotakeri.

[1]Long ago my mother told me about Pichanaki. [2]Pichanaki is
the name of a village, as they call it now. [3]There had been enormous landslides. [4]A stream flows into the river Pichanani, and
its waterbed is small. [5]The stream became filled with boulders,
when the hills collapsed during a big earthquake. [6]The masters-
owners of the hills left. [7]My mother told me that in the aftermath
of the earthquake there was a big depression in the ground filled

with water, a very big one; later on the water seeped through the ground. [8]The village Pichanaki is called [on the basis of] *pichaa* (demolish, grind, pulverize) and *oonkaro-naki* [water. pool-CL:round.hollow] (depression filled with water), that's why the village is called this way, when we put the two together, *pichaa-naki.* [9]So it is called. [10]My mother told me that there was a big depression filled with water there, and also an earthquake. [11]She clung to a big tree, so that the earthquake would not hurl her away. [12]Since then has existed the name "Pichanaki." [13]This is all I know.

TWENTY-SEVEN

Kiatsi

(The Owner of the River)

Carmen Pachiri Quinchori

[1]Opaitantari Pichanani, ipichanakeri atziripaye. [2]Ivaitakeri iyora antarite maranki, ikentaitakeri. [3]Ikamanatanakira parenikira, oonkanakero antaro, antaro, maaroni oonkanakero, aayetanakeri atziripaye saikayetatsiri Potyarini, saikayetatsiri Pichanaki. [4]Maaroni, maaroni opichanakeri. [5]Aajatzita kipatsi tarankanaki, maaroni atziripaye saikayetatsiri otyanakeri, maaroni ivanko, maaroni. [6]Irotaki opaitantari Pichanaki, irotaki opaitantari. [7]Airo ikentaitzirimi yora maranki antari, airo opichanakerimi atziripaye, airomi opaita Pichanaki.

[8]Sheripiari ikisajeetaka. [9]Tsinanipayera, evankaropaye, ari ojamatsite nijaaki, arika ompiyamachevetajia, opoñaaka omotyatanake. [10]Imotyatakakero iyora kamariperori maranki. [11]Yasamajeetapakari, ikentajeetakeri. [12]Irotaki opaitantakari Pichanaki, maaroni atziritepaye saikajeetatsi opichanakeri. [13]Iyora maranki, iritaki kiatsi, iroñaaka ijatake Tampoki, ikantaitziri Ene, Tampo ipiyojeetapajari. [14]Jataji anta, Amazonaski, tekatsitaji aka, iroñaaka akaavaita. [15]Tzimavetacha iro kapicheeni. [16]Akemajeetapintziri atziripaye, choripaye piinkaki, piinkaki, irotaki ari yasamapaita. [17]Te ikantaperotaita, ikimita pairani, airo aniivaitzi kameetsa tsinanipaye. [18]Okantya airo añaajiro omotyatakiri yora maranki. [19]Arika itzimapaki, tzimatsi ikimitari jetari, shankoro.

[20]Añiiri itampatzikatapake kimotatanake, arika iraanakia *kin kin.* [21]Pokapaki irira yora kiatsira, ari ipokapaki kiatsira, maranki antarite, ari itsonkapakari atziritepaye saikajeetatsirira, ari yamanakero inijaate yora maranki. [22]Ari ipokashitapakai iroñaaka ikimitaranki iyanipayeranki. [23]Añeeri porenchaki, porenchaki, yamapakero maaroni inijaate, oonkapaka antaroite nijaa. [24]Ari otzimapakeri nijaa Parenini. [25]Arika impiyanaji, piriatanaji, ari okantari pairani. [26]Okantana isha, "Paamaventya, ari impiyaje." [27]Tsika okantapaintya? [28]Ari impiyaje, te ayote.

[29]Airo aniivaishita, arika añaavaitya, arika amairintya, asaiki avankoki, airo aniivaitzi, ari ikiantakai kiatsi. [30]Tekirata ipoke kiatsi, arika akimapairi chorito iraaya, kamari inatzi, ari yaakai kamarira, ari impianakia chorito. [31]Yoka savaro, ankimapajatyeri imperitaki *aaaa*, iraaya savaro, ameni, ameni, ari añaakeri, aakeri. [32]Ompiashitajia iroñaaka kooyara aakerira. [33]Motyatanake, airo okantaji aniitaje. [34]Jaka otziyamoroki yovatziitaki, arika osaikapaje paamarikira, jaikitataika aka akooyatantarika. [35]Okantya, okantya, ari ontzimavetakia, ari intzimanake osheki shitsanentzipaye. [36]Ari okantari pairani. [37]Iroñaaka te, te okantaje, kameetsa asaikavataji, ajate pareniki, apiyaje, tekatsi avisaini.

[1]For the name Pichanaki to come into existence, people were annihilated. [2]They had killed that enormous snake, they had shot arrows at it. [3]When the snake died, the river began growing bigger and bigger [from the snake's blood], sweeping away all people living in Pucharini and Pichanaki. [4]Everything was annihilated. [5]And the earth collapsed, and all people and their houses were swept by the landslides. [6]That's why it was called Pichanaki, that's why it is called this way. [7]Hadn't they shot at

this big snake, hadn't people been annihilated, it would not have been called Pichanaki.

[8]The shamans were angry. [9]Poor young girls, single women would go to the river and would come back pregnant, against their will. [10]That demonic snake would impregnate them. [11]The males got fed up with it and shot arrows at the snake. [12]That's why it was called Pichanaki, because all people in the area of Pichanaki had been annihilated. [13]That snake was *kiatsi*, the owner of the river, and it went down to the river Tambo, where the rivers Tambo and Ene meet. [14]It went there, to the Amazon river, it is not here anymore, and now we bathe [safely] in the river. [15]Still, there is some danger, but not much. [16]We always hear about our fellow men and Andean settlers getting drowned, this is troubling. [17]But it is not as bad as it was in the past, when the girls wouldn't go to the river safely. [18]Time has passed, and we don't see girls getting pregnant by that snake. [19]When a baby would be born, it would be like a *carachama* (fish species) or a lizard.

[20]We have seen them at midday, when the river grows big, and we hear someone cry, *kin kin* (sound made by a crying baby snake). [21]That Father of *kiatsi* has come, he has come, that big *kiatsi*, and he will finish all people residing by the river, he will bring his water. [22]Small snakes have come. [23]We [also] have seen many medium-size snakes bring their water, and the river floods. [24]This is where the river Perené begins. [25]When the *kiatsi* returns, the river will dry out, as this was the way in the past [the snake is able to lower the water level and snatch those who foolishly walk on the exposed riverbed].[26]My grandmother would say to me, "Be careful, he may come back." [27]Who knows? [28]He may come back, we don't know.

[29]When we had our menses, we couldn't walk to the river,

lest the *kiatsi* enter us. ³⁰Also, before the *kiatsi* comes, we hear a blue-headed parrot cry; it is a demon, it will snatch us, it is disguised as a blue-headed parrot. ³¹We hear a macaw parrot in rock outcrops calling *aaaa* (a macaw parrot's call); it is crying, and we look and look at him, and we grab him. ³²The girl who grabs him will perish. ³³She will get pregnant and won't be able to walk. ³⁴Here, in her anus, there will be something ready to come out, and when she sits on the cold ashes from the fire, her vagina will be filled [with water]. ³⁵Later on, she will give birth; she will give birth to intestinal worms. ³⁶So it was in the past. ³⁷Now, no, it does not happen; we live well, we go to the river and come back, and nothing happens.

TWENTY-EIGHT

Peyari

(The Bone Spirit)

Gregorio Santos Pérez

¹Iroñaaka nonkinkitsatakotavakiri ikanta peyari pairani ovakera isaikajeetapaki atziri aka nampitsikika. ²Onampini ikinkitsatakotakiri anakotakinari. ³Nokimiri aparojatzini isha okantzi, "Nojatzi notsipatari noimi antamiki naminavaite shitovipatsaini. ⁴Noimi yaanaki ichakopite inkinte shirintzi. ⁵Arika iñaaki maniro, aritaki inkintakiri, sharo, tsika opaita inkinteri, yaminavaite. ⁶Yoka iroñaaka maatsi peyari kaimatsiri intaina." ⁷Arika isaiki intaina, arika ankimakiri, airo okantzi ashiyanaji. ⁸Kantzimaintacha kooya ari oshiyanaki. ⁹Osheki inintzi yairikai aroka, isantavaitai atziyamoroki.

¹⁰Okantzi iroñaaka ishaka ojataki otsipatari oimi, okinavaitzi otenkanaki, otsipatari otsitzite. ¹¹Okaimakotziri isha okantzi, *jooo joo*, arika intsarote. ¹²Ojatzi, ojatzi, niyankimashiki ojataki. ¹³Iro oshavityaki, okimatziri ikaimi, *joom joom* intaina, *joom*. ¹⁴Osaikajeetakira niyankimashi, okantziri oimi, "Paita kaimatsiri?" ¹⁵Ikantzi iyoshiriaka, "Ah, iyoka peyari inatzi, ari ikitoriakai. ¹⁶Tsame ampiye."

¹⁷Ipiyajeevita inavita, ishiyavita, ishiyavita, tema kamari inatzi iyoka peyarika, yoijatakeri, ikiminkatakiri. ¹⁸Ishiyavita inavita, ishiyavita, ari imakotaki, ikimiri okaakitaki.

¹⁹Poña iroñaaka ikimaperotakiri okaakiperotaki. ²⁰Iyoka shiramparika kamanaki. ²¹Tsomikitanaka, ikantanaka aka.

²²Ari ikantanaka ikamanaki, kamaki. ²³Aminakiri oimi ikama-
kira, okantzi iroñaaka, "Tsika nonkantyaka iroñaaka? ²⁴Non-
kanterika noimi novavisakotantyariri?" ²⁵Okinkishiriaka apaniroini. ²⁶Otsarovavitapainta okimakirira. ²⁷Okantzi, "Intsi,
noyavakeri."

²⁸Oñaatziri antari, okantzi, ishiyari koshiri. ²⁹Aparoni iitzi
atziri, aparoni iitzi, ankanteri, maniro, antaro itzinko, antaro
ichee, antaro ishivive ovira aka. ³⁰Iñaapakiri itsomikitzitaka,
iro ijatashitakiri, ankante, isantavaiterita ishivi. ³¹Oñaatziri
iroñaaka, irotaki yairikantyaririmi oimi. ³²Okaimakotziri irori,
"Tsika paita pantziri? ³³Tzimatsira noshivi naari." ³⁴Aanakiro
otsomi, okantanakiro jaka, *petak petak petak*, otsomi. ³⁵Iñaa-
vakiro peyarira, te iñaavakiro iravo, pianaka, shiyanaka.
³⁶Okimiri ikaimanaji, okimiri ikaimanaji intainataki.

³⁷Poñaashitaka opokapaji, oñaakiri oimi itsomikitzitaka.
³⁸Aapajiro iroka tsika paitaranki otsomi, oposantakiri itapiki,
tek tek. ³⁹Ari ipiriintanaja oimi, ari yaminavaitzi, ikantzi,
"Oh, tsikama paita antakairi?" ⁴⁰Ari ikantziro, "Tsikama paita
antakairi?" ⁴¹Okantzi, "Tekatsite. ⁴²Itsitavitakami peyari,
nookajiri."

⁴³Piyajitaja iroñaaka ivankoki. ⁴⁴Ari isaikajeetapaji kameetsa, tekatsi avishimoterini. ⁴⁵Ari okaratzi akimakoventziri
pairani. ⁴⁶Nokimakovintziri naaka aparoni isha okinkitsatzi.

¹I will tell about the bone spirit of the old times who existed
when people lived here in this village. ²They told a lot of stories
about the bone spirit that I picked up. ³I heard one old woman
say, "I went to the forest with my husband to look for small
mushrooms. ⁴My husband took his arrows to hunt partridge.
⁵When we see a deer, he'll shoot it, or an agouti, or some other
animal that he is able to find. ⁶There was this bone spirit who

made calls far away." ⁷When he is far away, when we [males] hear him, we can't escape. ⁸In contrast, a woman, she can. ⁹The bone spirit looks for men, to copulate with us through our anus.

¹⁰The old woman said that she walked on the ravine floor with her husband, along with her dog. ¹¹She heard her dog bark, and she would call her dog back, *hoo hoo* (sound made by a human calling a dog), when it barked. ¹²They reached the center of the forest. ¹³When the sun was going down, she heard someone call out *hoom hoom* far away, *hoom* (sound made by the bone spirit). ¹⁴Because they were in the middle of the forest, she asked her husband, "Who is calling out?" ¹⁵Her husband had a premonition and said, "Hmmm, this is the bone spirit, he will break our necks. ¹⁶Let's return."

¹⁷They were on the way back, they were running and running, but the bone spirit is a demon, so he picked up their scent. ¹⁸They were running for a long time and were exhausted, when they heard him nearby.

¹⁹Then they heard him really close. ²⁰The man died. ²¹He was bent over at the waist, like this. ²²He was positioned this way, and he was dead. ²³The woman watched her husband die and said, "What am I going to do now? ²⁴What am I going to do to save my husband?" ²⁵She had to do her own thinking. ²⁶At first, she was afraid when she heard the bone spirit call out. ²⁷Then she said, "Well, I will wait for him [to come]."

²⁸She saw something big, she said, he resembled a monkey. ²⁹He had one human foot, another foot was like a deer hoof, a big tail, big horns, and a big penis, of this size. ³⁰The bone spirit saw the man who was bent over and headed toward him, we say, to insert his penis [in the man's anus]. ³¹She saw that the bone spirit was about to seize her husband. ³²She yelled, "What are you doing? ³³I have a penis too." ³⁴She grabbed her breast and

moved it up and down, *petak petak* (flapping action). ³⁵When the bone spirit saw her, he lost his bearings, he disappeared, he ran away. ³⁶She heard his calls, she heard him call out far away.

³⁷Then she returned to her husband and saw him standing crouched. ³⁸She hit him on his back with her breast, *tek tek* (action of hitting). ³⁹He straightened up, looked around, and said, "What happened to us?" ⁴⁰This is what he said, "What happened to us?" ⁴¹She responded, "Nothing. ⁴²The bone spirit nearly had sex with you, but I got rid of him."

⁴³They returned to their home. ⁴⁴There they stayed and nothing happened to them. ⁴⁵Here the story [of the bone spirit] ends, which I heard long ago. ⁴⁶I heard it when an old woman told it.

TWENTY-NINE

Iñaaventa kamari Kovatsironi

(Speaking with Regard to the Demon from Kovatsironi)

Ines Pérez de Santos

[1]Ikantantaitarori iroñaaka Kovatsironi, arika inkonaataitero. [2]Pairani osheki nosheninkapaye ishemiaki iyoñapite. [3]Aparoni kitaiteri yaake iyoñapite, ishemiakero, aitaki ivetsikakero maaroni, ishempitakerorika inkante iroñaaka. [4]Niyankite ankonaate, ajatai anta, asaiki shimperiki. [5]Inkonaatakerorika anta, airo okantzi impokanake yamenero, airo apiyantaro. [6]Arika ampiyantakiaro, ari ikitoriakai kamari. [7]Ontzimatye oijatero, oijatero irojatzi shimperikira, aritaki ayeri osheki shima. [8]Arika ijatanaki, ikimitatya otsitzi, arika iroyatanakai, intsarotanakeririka, inkitoriavakeri.

[9]Apokaiyaji pankotsikika, "Tsame ookaiteri ashimate!" [10]Pokaiyajai, añaapajatyeri otsitzi avotsiki, ikatziyaka isantakeri itziyamorokira inchakii, yamenakaimaitari.

[11]"Paita antakeriri otsitzi?" [12]Avisaiyanakai, airo amenanakeri. [13]Pairani te añeero ootamentotsipaye, intaani sampityonkini. [14]Amenavetanakari ishenakashita otsitzi. [15]Ookapaintziri ashimate avankoki, apiyaiyanaja maaroiteni. [16]Yamenaperotapairi pashini, amayetapatziri sampi, yotapakeri, iñaatziri isantakeri itziyamoroki.

[17]"Paita antakeriri?" [18]"Isantakiri kamari." [19]"Tsameta, ikitoriaventairikari."

^{20}Piyaiyanakai shimperiki asaikaventeri, oisapai paamari.
^{21}Pashinipaye yotantakeriri, yaanake tsikana intaakero.
^{22}"Antaashiterita! ^{23}Ari ishiyanake, airo ipokapaintzi kamari, ari ikantakerorika." ^{24}Apiyoitakero osheki saimpiki, itaakero tsikana, kameetsa avaitajeete shivapatsaini irojatzi akitaitakotantaja. ^{25}Asaiki ara, okitaitanaki, añiiro okanta okitamaroityanaki.

^{26}Okantana inani, "Tsame aatai amenapajeri ashimate." ^{27}Akiakotanairi ashimate, jatajai, añaanajatziri, aitaki itziyamoroki otsitzi isantakeri. ^{28}Yamenakairi avotsiki, ikantayetakiniri irakopatsaini otsitzi aka.

^{29}Jatajai impoitatzirinta, iñaanajiri saikatsiri atziri ivera jaka, kamari inatzi, ipashikatya, antaro ikirimashi. ^{30}Yavisapitsaiyajiri yaakerira, ivapajiri ishimate. ^{31}Kamarankanake, irotaintsi inkamemi. ^{32}Ikanta isaavataitziri, ipayetziri ivenkipatsaini, yoitayetakiri, amataja ashaninka. ^{33}Ikantantari te onkameetsate apanironkavaitya, ajate ankaraiyeni, mava, apite ajatantyari, airo aniivaitzi apaniroini. ^{34}Ari okantatya.

^{35}Ipoñaashita ipokaki iroñaaka antyaviari, ikantzi, "Aka airo anintatzi asaiki, tzimatsi sonkavaitori, aritaki intsonkakai, ikaratzi ivamakeri *ocho* asheninka. ^{36}Iro kovachari iroñaaka, tsame ankaviriñatero." ^{37}Ijataki aayetatsiri kaviniri, itzikakero katonkonta, ikaviriñatakero. ^{38}Aparoni tsiteneri antarotaki, otsonkantanakarori iroñaaka anta opaitara Santana, otsonkatanakero maaroni.

^{39}Arive, te ankemairi aka, iroñaaka kirinkainika, ari iñaaitakiri antarite moora. ^{40}Tzimatsi apite, iito anta, iito ajatzi itziyamoroki. ^{41}Te ayoteri tsikarika ishita, aririka iipiyiro ivanteki itziya ivarira. ^{42}Antari moora, iro kantacha iitzikika mooprataki maaroni iitzikikaja, intaani irora apite okanta. ^{43}Te ishiyari oisha iitzikinta, aka tekatsi, aka ikantatsantsatapaka, te imoorate. ^{44}Kimitaitapaka atziri ivoro. ^{45}Ari ikantari itsonkantakari iroñaaka. ⁴⁶Katyonkoinira Kovatsirokira, Anashironaki itsonkantakari kamari. ⁴⁷Ikaviriñataitakitziro ipiantajariri iroñaakama kamari.

⁴⁸Ajavaivetya, tekatsi avishimotaiyeni, kameetsatanaki iroñaaka. ⁴⁹Isaikayetapakera pishaninkapaye, kameetsaini iroñaaka aniivaitaje. ⁵⁰Intaani itsañapakaro, te ininte ankonaavaitajero, itsañanakari shima. ⁵¹"Pinintzirika poya shima, pinkitsatatyeri, airove pikonaatajiri."⁵²Ari ikantziri iroñaaka ashiyetapakarori saikayetapaintziri nijaatsapiakipaye. ⁵³Irotaki nokantavakeri naari.

¹They speak of Kovatsironi when fishing with poison. ²Long ago many of my fellow men manually pounded the roots of the koñapi plant, which is used to stupefy fish. ³One day males will take their koñapi, pound it, get it all ready, and construct a fish fence [before introducing the prepared poison into the river upstream], so to speak. ⁴At midnight, we will throw the poison into the river, we'll go, and we'll sit down by the fish fence while males will be putting the poison into the river over there [upstream]. ⁵Males can't go back to look at the dead fish, we shouldn't retreat. ⁶If we retreat, then the demon will break our bones. ⁷We have to keep [wading in the water] following [the current] until we reach the dammed area with the fish fence; there we catch a lot of fish. ⁸If a male returns, his dog, when it follows his master and barks, will be killed by a demonic spirit [it will break its bones].

⁹[Once] we were coming home, "Let's leave the fish [at home]." ¹⁰We were coming back, and we saw a dog on the trail; it stood there with a long stick stuck in his anus, and the demon made it [the dead dog] look at us.

¹¹"What happened to the dog?" ¹²We passed, we didn't look at the dog. ¹³Long ago we didn't have flashlights, only [burning] wood sticks. ¹⁴We looked at the dog, propped against a tree, in

vain, we didn't see it. ¹⁵We left the fish at home and were all re-
turning [to the fishing site]. ¹⁶Others saw it [the dog] well, those
who had brought thicker wood sticks and who had known about
it, they saw what was embedded in his anus.

¹⁷"What happened to the dog?" ¹⁸"The demon stuck it in his
anus." ¹⁹"Let's go, for Pete's sake, lest the demon break our bones."

²⁰We returned to the fishing fence to sit down, and made a
fire. ²¹Others who knew [about the dog] brought hot peppers to
burn.

²²"Let's burn them [to shoo away the demon]! ²³He will run
away, the demon won't come, this is what he does [he comes
back, if we don't burn hot peppers]." ²⁴We piled up a lot of firewood, burned hot peppers, caught nicely many anchovetas
[small fish species] before dawn. ²⁵We were seated there, it became light, and we saw something whitish.

²⁶My late mother said to me, "Let's go and look for [stupe-
fied] fish." ²⁷We loaded our fish on the backs and went off, and
we saw it, exactly in the dog's anus he [the demon] stuck it. ²⁸He
[the demon] made the dead dog look at us on the trail, he did it
to his paws like this.

²⁹The one who walked behind us saw a seated person of this
height, it was the demon, his head was covered, and he had a
big nose. ³⁰The fisherman passed by him when he was carrying
his fish; he guarded it [the fish]. ³¹The fisherman began to vomit,
nearly died. ³²Later they gave him a steam bath, different people
gave him magic herbs *ivenki*, gave him a drink, and my fellow
man recovered. ³³That's why they say it is not good to be alone,
we go collectively, in threes or twos, to the forest, we shouldn't
walk solo. ³⁴This is what happened.

³⁵Later a powerful shaman came and said, "We don't want
to stay here, the demon calls out here, he will finish us, already
eight fellow men died. ³⁶What is needed is this: let's place leaves

of the *kaviniri* plant into the river."[6] [37]Those who obtained the leaves of *kaviniri* went and blocked the river in the upstream area with stones and threw the leaves in the water. [38]One night the river overflowed and decimated [the place] that is now called Santa Ana, it decimated everything.

[39]Very well, we didn't hear about it [the demon] here, [but] a little bit downstream, there they saw a big mule. [40]It had two heads, one head here, and another in its anus. [41]We don't know how it defecates, whether the feces come out of his mouth when he eats. [42]A big mule, looks like a mule, nevertheless his feet [hooves], there are only two [i.e., they are cloven hooves]. [43]It doesn't look like the sheep's hoof either, here, no, it is wide, nor is like the mule's [hoof]. [44]It seems to have a person's face. [45]What had happened, that ended now. [46]A little bit upstream, there are the rivers Kovatsironi and Anashirona, [where] the demon was finished. [47]They cleansed the area with *kaviniri*, that's why the demon disappeared.

[48]We walk around and nothing will happen, it is fine now. [49]Your fellow men live here, it is fine to walk around. [50]Only they [colonists] resist it, they don't want us to fish with poison, they are stingy with the fish. [51]"If you want to eat fish, you should fish with a net, you shouldn't fish with poison." [52]This is what they say, those who own it [the land], those who live on the river-banks. [53]This is what I say.

THIRTY

Tsamirimenta

(The Curassow Crest Stone)

Moises Santos Rojas

[1]Pairani tzimatsi iroka kirinkanta, Potyarinikinta, ari osaikiri ikantaitziri Tsamirimenta. [2]Ikantantaitarori Tsamirimenta, osheki nijaa katyojari, ari ipokiri osheki tsamiri. [3]Ikaratzi tziyaatachari, amaatakotatsiri, iñiiri tsamiri. [4]Ikantzi atziripaye, "Paitakama itzimantari osheki tsamiri?" [5]Ijatashitakiri okaakini, iñaakiro irotaki itsimini tsamiri, irotaki isaikavintzi. [6]Ari okantari, iroñaaka, ari isaikiri iriri tsamiri.

[7]Ijatzi asheninka isaikashitziro tsimi, iñaakiri antarite tsamiri. [8]Ikitoriavaitakiri asheninkara, ivamakiri. [9]Kamaki iroñaaka asheninkara. [10]Poñaaka ikantzi aajatzi sheripiari, "Tsame amairenteri, antziyaavaityata kameetsaitenikia." [11]Ari okantzimaintakari. [12]Iroñaaka imairintaitakiri iririka tsamiri, imairintakiri iyoka sheripiarika. [13]Pairani arika antziyaatya, ari inkoñaatzimotakai iriri tsamiri.

[14]Iroñaaka tekatsitaji, kameetsa avisayete pitotsi, amaata-yettsiri aisatzi tziyaatachari. [15]Ari okantari intanakarori pairani. [16]Pomirintsitaka, arika antziyaavaitya, irotaki akamantavakari.

[1]In the past, in the area of Pocharini downriver, there was a stone called Curassow Crest. [2]It was called Curassow Crest because there was a lot of salt in the river, and many curassows would flock there. [3]All those who would go upriver, or go downriver in

12. Iriri Tsamiri, the Father of curassows and master of a rock outcrop, watches passersby. By Daniel Bernales Quillatupa (Aroshi).

their canoes, saw curassows. [4]People would say, "Why are there so many curassows?" [5]One walked close to them and saw that there was a water trough there; it was the water that attracted the birds to this place. [6]So it was that there was the Master of curassows in this place.

[7]When my fellow man went there with the purpose of killing a bird, he saw a big curassow. [8]The curassow broke the man's neck and killed him. [9]My fellow man died. [10]Then a shaman said, "Let's calm him down [i.e., block the entrance to the cave with stones], so that we could push our canoes upriver safely." [11]So it happened. [12]The Master of curassows was calmed down, this shaman did it. [13]In the past, when we went upriver, the Master of curassows would always appear in our presence.

[14]Now this is not the case, canoes pass safely, piloted by those who go downriver or upriver. [15]So it was during the times of the founders. [16]It was difficult to go upriver in a canoe, this is what we are advising [you] about.

THIRTY-ONE

Maninkaroite

(The Invisible Women)

Moises Santos Rojas

[1]Nonkantavakeri iroñaaka okantakota otzishipaye otzishikinta. [2]Tzimatsi saikatsiri, ikantzi nocharini pairani, ikantaitziro maninkaroite. [3]Aitaki okimitajeetaka akoñaatzi, aitaki saikatsiri irori, saikatsiri otzishikinta. [4]Ari okantari, aitaki saikatsiri irori otsipatari shirampari.

[5]Kantzimaitacha, eero añiirotsi, okovirika oñaakajai, aritaki oñaakajai koñaaroini. [6]Aitaki ompakai tsikarika paita akoviri arori, oyotakotakairi anintzirira aka. [7]Eero akamitsi, ampiashitaka antamishiki tsikarika ajate akomintsate. [8]Ari okantari iroñaaka maninkaroite.

[9]Aparojatzini ikamantana sheripiari, ikantzi, "Nojatzi nokenavaitzi yametapintari, arika areetya *veinte ocho de julio*, yantajeetzi yoimoshirinkajeetaiyeni nampitsiki. [10]Iroñaaka ityankaitakeri ikenapaki ikaraiyeni *seis* irirori."

[11]Ikenapaki ikaraiyeni apite ikantaiyani. [12]"Pashini ikeni tonkariki, pashini ikenanaki otapiki, pashini, nokenanaki niyanki. [13]Noirinkanaka, nojataki tonkariki, nantapaki novankoshita. [14]Sheetyaimatanaki, nokantziro notsipatari, 'Nakishivaitake kaniri, noisakera paamari, posayetake nakishiri. [15]Nokimisantapainte sankatzi terika yonkiri.'" [16]Ikenanake irirori otapiki, pashini ikenanake tonkariki. [17]Ari okantakari.

[18]Opoñaashitaka ikemakiri, imanataka *took*, ikantzi, "Iro-

ñaaka noya tsimeri irirori." [19]Ikenapaki otapiki, yoirinkanaka, yoirinka, yoirinka. [20]Ikantzi, iñaapakitziri yatsamankivaita osheto, imanatakeri, yaaitari, *tooo*. [21]Iroñaaka iparianakimi, yampitzitanakero itzinkoki ochevo inchatokinta, ari itsatzinkotaka. [22]Ikanta, ikanta, pariaki. [23]Yaanakiri, ikianakiri, itonkanaji, itonkanaji.

[24]Ikantzi, iñaakero mapitapi. [25]Osheki ari iitsoki kentsori. [26]Ikantzi, ari ikemiri shiyakotariri kentsori ikonkavaitzi. [27]Yakakeri kentsori otapiki. [28]Ikantzi, "Nojatapainteta tyonkarikini, ompoña nompiyapaje naanake iitsoki." [29]Ikantarika, ijatapaintzinta tonkarikinta.

[30]Ipiyapaja, ikiiri iyoshirite itonkakeri inkaranki, yamenavetapajaro inkaranki ikinanaka. [31]Te añaajero iitsoki kentsori iñaanakeri inkaranki, tekatsitanaki, pianaka. [32]Ikantzi, "Oh, tsika ikenanaki? [33]Ari isaikavetari inkaranki." [34]Yamenavaitzi, tekatsite, yoirinkanaka, yoirinkanaka. [35]Itonkaji, iñaapaki sankatzi, imanatakeri, parianaki. [36]Yoirinkashitanakari, yaapanantziri.

[37]Itonkanaji iroñaaka, *tonka tonka tonka*, yareetajaro iroñaaka anta yantanake ivankoshita. [38]Ari isaikapaji. [39]Osamani ikemajatziri imanataja, aajatzita pashini. [40]Apitetanakaki imanatzi, imanatziri isankatzite. [41]Osamani oyakotziri, iñaatziri iyovapaji irirori.

[42]Yapotojeetakero paamari, ikantzi, "Ashinkoteri avavakiata tsimeri." [43]Ishinkotakeri iroñaaka isankatzite, ishinkotakeri. [44]Ipoñaashitaka tzimatsi inkaranki yakishitakeri kaniri, ovajeetaka. [45]Ikantzi, pashini ipokapake, ivavaitaka, ivavaitaka. [46]Ikantzi, "Makotakinave, nopochokitatzi." [47]Ivetsikantaka, ari inariaka. [48]Ivetsikantaka, ari inariaka pashinira.

[49]Te ompoke ivochokini. [50]Isaiki yapotovaitzi paamari, yapototziro paamari omorikanaketa. [51]Ari okantakari, omorikanakintaja. [52]Ari isaiki yamonkovaitzi, yamonkovaitzi. [53]Ikema-

tziro aparoni shirontachari otapiki, *jojo jojo.* ⁵⁴Ikantzi, "Tsika opaitaka?"

⁵⁵Ashitarori ikantaitziro onampi otzishinta, okantapaka anta ikenapaji inkaranki itonkaji. ⁵⁶Ari okenapakiri irori, oijatakeri.

⁵⁷Ikemiro oshirontajeeta, ikantzi, "Irotaintsi okaakitake."
⁵⁸Opoña itzinkakeri itsipatarira, ikantziri, "Pimpiriinte, korakitaintsi ashitarori onampi aka, aanakaikari. ⁵⁹Aritaima aakerimi, apaniroini isaikimi."

⁶⁰Ipiriintanakara, ikantzi, "Koñaaro nokemakiro, osaiki okaakitapake." ⁶¹Oñaavaitzi, okantzi, "Tsika akanterika iroñaaka? ⁶²Apite ikantaiyani. ⁶³Eerotaima antamintsatziri."
⁶⁴Piyanaja. ⁶⁵Ikishokavakero isherinira, ikishokantakaro.
⁶⁶Ikemavairo jataji, piyanaka oshirontanaja otapikinta, ikantavakajeetani iroñaaka.

⁶⁷Aka ari osaikiri ikantaitziri maninkaroite. ⁶⁸Ari okantakinari, aritaki nosaikiri ikinkitsavaitzi sheripiari. ⁶⁹Okanta nokemantakariri noyotantakari naari tzimatsi asheninka maninkaroite. ⁷⁰Ikantzi, tekatsi onkantavaitya kooya, tekatsite onkantya. ⁷¹Okimitaka kooya, ari okimitari kooya, aajatzi shirampari akimitaka ashiramparitzi. ⁷²Tekatsite pashinitatsini, irotaki ikantaitziro maninkaroiteni.

⁷³Irotaki nokamantavakimiri okaratzi nokemiri naari. ⁷⁴Nokamantzimiri iroñaaka avirori okaratzi piyotantyari. ⁷⁵Tzimatsi ashitarori otzishipaye saikantayetarori. ⁷⁶Ari okaratziri.

¹I will tell about the hills located over there. ²They are inhabited, our grandfathers told [us] in the past, by *maninkaroite* (invisible women). ³There they would appear, there they live, in those hills. ⁴They are this way, the invisible woman and her male companion.

⁵Nevertheless, we can't see them, [but] when she wants us to see her, we can see a vision of her. ⁶She can give us what we

want, because she knows that we want it. [7]We won't die, but we will disappear in the forest when we go hunting. [8]Such are the invisible women.

[9]Once a shaman informed me by saying, "I went on a hunting trip, due to the custom: when July 28 arrives, they organize an all-village celebration. [10]Six hunters are sent in total [to bring meat for the communal meal]."

[11]They went in twos. [12]"Two walked across the upper section of the hillside, two walked at the bottom of the hill, and we walked along the middle section of the hill. [13]We went down, then up, then built our hunter's shack. [14]When it was about to get dark, I told my companion, 'Because we made the fire, the manioc is being cooked, we are roasting the manioc. [15]I will listen to the calls of Spix's guans or mountain hens.'" [16]So the shaman went down the hill, then he went up the hill. [17]So it was.

[18]Then the shaman heard the call of a partridge, shot it, *took* (sound of a discharged gun), and said, "Now I will eat this bird." [19]Then he went down, he kept going down. [20]He says, he saw a monkey hanging on a tree, took aim, and pulled the trigger, *too* (sound of a discharged gun.) [21]It nearly fell down, but it gripped the tree branch with its tail and was hanging by the tail. [22]Then, after a while, the monkey fell down. [23]He picked it up, loaded it on his back, and went up the hill.

[24]He says, he saw an opening under a rock. [25]The gray tinamou quail had laid its eggs there. [26]He says, he heard what seemed like a gray tinamou quail call. [27]Another gray tinamou quail down the hill responded. [28]He said, "I'll go up the hill, afterward I will return to pick up the eggs." [29]He climbed the hill for a while.

[30]The shaman returned, carrying the monkey that he had shot recently and looking for a trail that he had walked on before. [31]There were no eggs that he had seen before, no eggs, they

disappeared. ³²He said, "Hmm, where did they go? ³³They were here before." ³⁴He searched for a while, nothing, so he went down the hill. ³⁵Then he went up and saw a Spix's guan, he shot it, and it fell down. ³⁶He went down to pick it up and grabbed it.

³⁷Then the shaman went up the hill, *tonka tonka tonka* (action of going up, and arrived where the hunter's shack was. ³⁸There he stayed. ³⁹Later on, he heard a shot, then another. ⁴⁰There were two guans, and the hunter killed them both. ⁴¹After a long while of waiting, he saw the other hunter come out of the woods.

⁴²They piled up firewood, and the shaman said, "Let's roast and eat the birds." ⁴³They roasted the birds. ⁴⁴Then they had the manioc roasted before, and he ate [the whole meal]. ⁴⁵He says, the other hunter came and ate [the meal]. ⁴⁶Then the shaman said, "I am tired and sleepy." ⁴⁷He fixed his bed and lay down. ⁴⁸The other hunter fixed his bed and lay down.

⁴⁹But the dreams didn't come to the shaman. ⁵⁰He was sitting and piling up wood, so that the fire would remain ablaze. ⁵¹So it was, the fire was burning strongly. ⁵²The shaman was sitting and chewing [tobacco]. ⁵³He heard someone laugh down the hill, *jojo jojo* (sound of female laughter). ⁵⁴He said, "What is this?"

⁵⁵They are called masters of the hills that he had walked recently. ⁵⁶There she [an invisible woman] had walked and followed him!

⁵⁷He heard a few women laugh and said, "They are coming, they are close." ⁵⁸Then he woke up his companion, saying, "Get up, the masters of this place are coming, lest they seize us. ⁵⁹They may seize us, if one stays here alone."

⁶⁰When the other hunter got up, the shaman said to him, "I heard her in a vision, she is close." ⁶¹The invisible woman said to another, "What shall we do to them? ⁶²There are two of them. ⁶³Perhaps we shouldn't accost them." ⁶⁴And they returned [to the lower area of the hills]. ⁶⁵The shaman spit out his tobacco.

⁶⁶The men heard the invisible women go away, they returned, laughing, to the lower part of the hill, and they were talking to each other.

⁶⁷There reside those who are called "invisible women." ⁶⁸So it was, there I was sitting when the shaman told the story. ⁶⁹Because I heard it, that's why I know that there are invisible women. ⁷⁰They say, the woman does nothing [to us], she doesn't have [an unusual shape]. ⁷¹She is like other women; likewise, the invisible man is like our fellow men. ⁷²They don't have anything [strange about them], but they are what is called "the invisible ones."

⁷³This is what I informed you about that I heard. ⁷⁴I informed you, so that you know it. ⁷⁵There are masters of the hills, those who live there. ⁷⁶Here it ends.

THIRTY-TWO

Ashitarori otzishipaye

(Masters of the Hills)

Elena Nestor de Capurro,
with Victoria Manchi de Martin

[1]–Tzimatsi pairani Pamoroitoni. [2]Poñaaka maatsi pashini, Kiniritoni, Kiniritoni anta, poñaaka iroñaaka Manankaniro. [3]Poñaaka iroñaaka intatzikironta Avitaroni, Teroritoni anta. [4]Mitzicharini anta, ari opaitari. [5]Opoña aka Sharokitsini, Samoterintsini jaka, ari okantari pairani. [6]Ikantziro irirori orave, Mitzicharini anta, anta amenarini pairani otzishinta.

[7]–Paita opaitantaitarori Samoterintsi?

[8]–Okantzi opaitantari Samoterintsi, iyora isamoteta, nokantzi, iroñaaka ashoshiranki. [9]Poñaaka ajaterika ankatziyavaite, añaapakeri irirorika otsitzi intsarote, *jau jau.* [10]Irora nokantajeetziri naaka kiatsi, arivitaka ashoshi. [11]Inkantanakiarika impiinkapaki, oh, antaro omotonkanive, *te te te.* [12]Ari aanakai, ashiyavitanakia, aanakai, okantakanakai. [13]Irojatzi opaitantanakai Atsityopini. [14]Iritaki samotetachari iroñaaka Atsityopini, kiatsi antarite. [15]Iroñaakaja aajatzi oshiyajarove, ikimitaja pairani ikantaitziro. [16]"Ari otsonkajai, ovajai. [17]Aka nijaaka iroñaaka antaro."

[18]Poñaaka Ponironani iroñaaka ikantaitziro, *shoi, shoi, ta,* orave *shoi ta.* [19]Shoinkakateri, *apishoi shoi ta,* kiatsi aajatzi irirori. [20]Apishoinkakave, intaporiromi aajatzi, ari okantari.

[21]–Atsityopira, paita ikantantaitarori Atsityopira?

²²–Atsityopi, kiatsi inatzi, *jem*. ²³Yatsamankita, osheki ishitsa, kitsa inavita. ²⁴Ipiinkanaki, *motok*, irotaki yaanakai, ari impitamonkakotavakai aajatzi irirori. ²⁵Pairani sheripiari yatsinakatziri, yatsinakakiri kipayeki antaroite. ²⁶Maatsi iyarinate, aajatzi ikarinatakotakiri, ikarinatakoitziri kiatsi. ²⁷Airo itsonkantajai, osheki ipitamonkakotziro pitotsipaye. ²⁸Iroñaaka te, aritaima inkantajia.

²⁹Arika iroñaaka impitamonkariakotajia, ipampitsatzi iroñaaka ikantakiri nijaara ikantakiri Tziviarini. ³⁰Aririka inkimakai, yaake. ³¹Maatsi pairani yoisotziri atziri, yoisotakiri aka. ³²Poña ikantzi, "Paita oka oisotanarika?" ³³Maatsi ivosorote, yaaki tsiyaroshi, ichenkitaki, *chenki*. ³⁴Kimitaka ashitsatantapintariranki nairotsa. ³⁵Iñaatziro, yaakiro, *shoi shoi*, shiyanakave, *terempiri terempiri*. ³⁶Jaitetzi *joo*, saikapaki kirinkanta. ³⁷Ninkarika pokatsiri, ari ikantatya. ³⁸Yaantzi irirori, osheki yaantzi Atsityopi, *eh, eh*, Atsityopi, *eh eh*, antari tsomontetatsiri pairani, kiatsi inatzi.

³⁹Iroma akantzirika Pamoroitoni, manitzi inatzi, manitzi pairani antarite. ⁴⁰Ooh, ikantatzi, *joom joom*. ⁴¹Iñaavakerika, ijiniki inatzi antarive, kimitaka pamoro. ⁴²Aajatzi iroñaaka kiniri, aajatzi irirori manitzi inatzi. ⁴³Iñaavavitya irirori ikimitari kiniriranki, *hoo ooh oooh*, iritaki.

⁴⁴Iroma aka Manankaniro, omaniri atziri pairani. ⁴⁵Mainari ijatzi irirori, ikinavaitzi, yaminavitari. ⁴⁶Ikantajeetzi, "Tsika ikinakika?" ⁴⁷Piaka, ari imanakai jara, omanakiri kooya maninkaro. ⁴⁸Onintavakeri shiramparira, aavakeri. ⁴⁹Irotaki ikantaitarori Maninkaroiteni. ⁵⁰Ari ikoñaatzi ara, arika oshirontajeetya, *jo jo joo*. ⁵¹Okantapontsotapaka.

⁵²–Mavonari, paita ikantantaitarori?

⁵³–Mavonarini, iñiitziri kimitaka mavona, pontsotzi, ñaakiro, kaari mavona. ⁵⁴Anintzi airikiromi, *shepi*, ari yankovitanakai irojatzi pareniki.

⁵⁵–Kiatsi?

⁵⁶–Je, kiatsi. ⁵⁷Osheki atziri inavita pairani okantapatsata-
pakanta. ⁵⁸Ari ivariantzi iroñaaka, okanta okovenkatzinta,
aritaki ivariri osheki, je, je, aritaki okantavaita.

⁵⁹–Irora Avitaroni . . . paita ikantantaitarori?

⁶⁰–Avitata, avitata, ari ajate, okaratenkatzini jaka. ⁶¹Osheki
oshintsinkani mapi, okanta impiakiarika aka, irotaki ovakiri.

⁶²–Pairani?

⁶³–Je, pairani, iroñaakama te. ⁶⁴Intaani ookanaki omani-
tzitepaye. ⁶⁵Arika ankinavaite avotsi, ankimiri, *jam, jam, jam*.
⁶⁶Ookanaki, yashitakoitakiri. ⁶⁷Pairani irojatzi añaavitani
kipatsikaja, ari okantari. ⁶⁸Jiro, okinira avotsi, nirora, noshi-
rinkantajari ora mapira, *chee*. ⁶⁹Iro aviravitanakia anta, ishirinkanakia, *shiri*. ⁷⁰Ashonkantyarimi intakironta, ari okiniri
pairani avotsi irojatzi intakironta. ⁷¹Iroñaaka te onkinaji,
pairani, ari okiniri avotsi.

⁷²–Sharokishi, paita ikantantaitarori?

⁷³–Inampi pairani [sharo]. ⁷⁴Isaikavitani [aparoni atziri]
Akotovani, iritaki orave osheki iñiiri sharopatsaini, osheki
sharo pairani. ⁷⁵Ikantaitzi, aajatzi yamintajaro. ⁷⁶Ari ikamaji
arika itonkaiteri. ⁷⁷Ari ikantari Sharo, Sharopishi, irotaki
okantanaja Sharopishi irojatzi janto, ari okantana.

⁷⁸Iroñaaka okantanaka Teroritani anto. ⁷⁹Teroritoni
ikantaitarori, osheki terori, ikantantaitarori Terori. ⁸⁰Aajatzi
ankimapakiri manitzi. ⁸¹Ankimapaki, *teroo teroo teroo*, nirika,
yoka otyapinakinika. ⁸²Iyorave aminaintsini okaakini, ari
impiakakai, je. ⁸³Ari okantari pairani ovitsikantanakari pairani
irirori ashitarori inampini aka. ⁸⁴Iro iyenkitsarini noimi,
iyora tsika ikantaitziroranki kokoni, iyorave Manueri Mayor
Kinchori, inampitsite pairani irirori aka, *capitan, capitan*
Kinchori. ⁸⁵Kamaji irirori. ⁸⁶Ari okaratzi noyenkitsari, ari
okaratzi.

[1]–In the past, there was the Dove Hill. [2]Over there is the Howler Monkey Hill, then the Hill That Hides. [3]On the other side, there is the Hill That Embraces, and the Macaw Hill is over there. [4]The Hillock with Water is over there, this is what it is called. [5]Then there is the Agouti Hill and the Hill That Hides Something in Its Interior. [6]They say, the Hillock with Water is over there, we saw it [the hill's owner] in the remote past on that hill.

[7]–Why is it called the Hill That Hides Something in Its Interior?

[8]–They say, it's called this way because it has inside, I say, an armadillo. [9]When we go there and stand still, we will see a barking dog, *hau hau* (sound of a barking dog). [10]We say, this is a *kiatsi*. [11]When she dives into the water, she forms an enormous whirlpool, *te te te* (sound of whirlpool). [12]She seizes us, we fail to escape, she seizes us and drags us [to the river]. [13]That's why she is called Atsityopini. [14]The hill has Atsityopini inside, a monstrous armadillo-like creature. [15]In the past it was called this way. [16][They would say,] "It will eat us all. [17]This river is big."

[18]Then there is a hill called the Hill That Entangles, *shoi shoi ta* (action of quickly coiling around en entity). [19]A person is entangled, *apishoi shoi ta* (action of rapidly coiling around an entity), by [a male] *kiatsi*. [20]The *kiatsi* coiled himself around the prey, because he wanted to envelop the victim, he was this way.

[21]–Why is he called Atsityopi?

[22]–Atsityopi is a *kiatsi*, [who makes this sound] *hemm*. [23]He hangs on trees and has a lot of veins, looks like a bunch of threads from woven fabric. [24]When he dives in the water, *motok* (quick entry [into the water] and disappearance), he seizes us, [when] he turns a canoe with its passengers upside down. [25]Long ago, shamans crushed him with a big piece of thick wood. [26]The *kiatsi* has colors, colors of different kinds. [27]He won't kill us but

he turned over many canoes. ²⁸Now it doesn't happen, but perhaps it will.

²⁹When the canoe returns to its upright position, its passengers walk along the river called the Salt River. ³⁰When the *kiatsi* hears us, he will seize us. ³¹There was a person who was tied up, like this [at night]. ³²The person said, "What is this that tied me up?" ³³He had matches, so he took palm leaves and struck a match, *chenki* (action of striking a match). ³⁴It looked like a nylon cord with which we weave. ³⁵The *kiatsi* saw the light, released the man, *shoi shoi* (action of making circular movements), and fled, *terempiri terempiri* (movement in a curved trajectory). ³⁶He was gone, *hooo* (sound of big splash), and stayed downriver. ³⁷When someone would come along, he did it to them. ³⁸Atsityopi snatched a lot of people in the past, *eh eh* (swallowing action) he had a big stomach, because he was a *kiatsi*.

³⁹In contrast, what we call the Dove Hill is inhabited by a jaguar, a big jaguar. ⁴⁰Oh, he would roar, *hoom, hoom* (sound of a roaring jaguar). ⁴¹When they saw the jaguar, he had monstrous lice, like doves. ⁴²The Howler Monkey Hill is also inhabited by a jaguar. ⁴³When they saw the jaguar, he made a sound like a howler monkey, *hoooh, oooh* (sound of a howler monkey).

⁴⁴But the Hill That Hides is here, it hid a person long ago. ⁴⁵He was single and went to the forest to look for game. ⁴⁶They said, "Where did he go?" ⁴⁷He disappeared there; there we are hidden from others, the invisible *maninkaro* woman hid him. ⁴⁸She fell in love with the man and married him. ⁴⁹That's why the hill is called the Hill That Hides. ⁵⁰It appears over there, when the *maninkaro* women laugh, *ho ho ho*. ⁵¹It does not have a summit.

⁵²–Why is that hill called Wild Potato?

⁵³–Because when they looked at him [the hill's master, *kiatsi*],

his shape resembled a wild potato, you've seen it, without sharp angles. [54]We want to grab him, *shepi* (action of snatching something in the air), and he [*kiatsi*] drags us to the river.

[55]–*Kiatsi?*

[56]–Yes, it was a *kiatsi*. [57]Many people lived where there was a swampy area. [58]This was a dangerous area where people were pushed to fall down, a lot of people were eaten there, yes, yes, so it was.

[59]–The Hill That Embraces, why is the hill called this way?

[60]–It "embraces" [crushes those who walk through a narrow passage between its two rocks], it "embraces" us when we draw near it, and it is of this size. [61]The hill's rock has a lot of strength; when someone disappears, it is the rock that has killed him.

[62]–Long ago?

[63]–Yes, it was long ago, nowadays, no. [64]There are only jaguars left in the hill's cave. [65]When we walk on the trail, we'll hear *hmm hmm* (sound made by jaguars). [66]They were locked up in the cave under the rock. [67]In the past, when the hills were alive, it was this way. [68]Look, when the trail was over there, I came close to this rock, *chee* (action of jumping away). [69]When we draw near this rock, it moves closer, *shiri* (slow-motion action). [70]When we went around behind the hill, there was a trail there, on the other side of the hill. [71]Now there is no trail, but it existed in the past.

[72]–The Agouti Hill, why is it called this way?

[73]–There were a lot of them there. [74]There was a person, Akotovani, who lived there, and he saw many agoutis, a lot of agoutis. [75]They were saying that people were accustomed to them. [76]He died there, killed by a gunshot. [77]So it was the Agouti Hill; it's located over there.

[78]The Macaw Hill is over there. [79]They called it the Macaw Hill because there are many macaws there. [80]We'll also hear

jaguars. [81]We'll hear, *teroo teroo teroo* (the call of macaws); here it is, in the opening under the rock. [82]The one who is watching down there will make us disappear. [83]So it was in the past, when the masters of this place were created. [84]This is a story of my deceased husband, and my father-in-law, called Manuel Mayor Kinchori, from this pueblo, who was Chieftain Kinchori. [85]He is dead already. [86]Here my story ends.

THIRTY-THREE

Inkaari Chorinkaveni

(Lake Churingaveni)

Moises Santos Rojas

[1]Yoka nokimakovintziro inkaari saikatsiri Chorinkaveniki.
[2]Ikantzi aparoni nosheninka, amaajeetzini oparaiki, ari
ikinkitsavaitzi. [3]Ikantzi, "Novamaatziri aparoni ishipañori.
[4]Ipoñaaka iroñaaka Pampa Voiriki. [5]Irojatzi areetantaka
Chorinkaveniki, ari asheetyakotakiri. [6]Ishipañorika ikantziri,
'Ari amayeri aka oparaikika, sheetyaki.'
[7]"Poña ikantziri, 'Pimontyavakina katyonkoininta, otsata-
pintanta pitotsipaye katyonkoininta.' [8]Ari osaikiri okimita
antaitaminto. [9]Ari itonkanaki, atzirira ishipañorira itonkanaki, itonkanaki, itonkanaki irojatzi inkaarikinta. [10]Inkaari-
kinta ivanaka pashini, ikitsatanaka pashini imatsara, pashini
ichenko, ichenkotari ishipañoripaye, ivootashite, maaroni."
[11]Ikantzi, yaniitanaki kimitaka ontzimatyerika aniitamento.
[12]Jaitetzi.
[13]Iñaavakiri, iñaavakiri tsitziyanaki, ikimatziri inkaarikinta
intsompaikinta. [14]Iñaavatzi, ikinkitsavaitakari saikatsi intsom-
poikinta. [15]Ipiaka, okimita osamanitaki apite oora, ipiaka.
[16]Osamani, iñaajatziri iyovataji. [17]Iyovatajira ipaitavakiri
tanta, ipaitavakiri pariantzi iyari. [18]Iroñaaka yamakiro
tsika isaikajeetapaki noshaninkapaye intatzikironta tsika
imaajeetapakini.
[19]Iroñaaka ikinkitsavaitapaji, ikantzi, "Ari isaiki nosha-

ninka inkaarikinta. ²⁰Niroka, tanta ayari, niroka pariantzi
ayari, intaani novakaro pariantzi." ²¹Ari okantakari iroñaaka,
ikinkitsavaitzi iyoka ishipañorika.

²²Ikantzi ashaninkaka, "Noñaajantzima, iroka inkaarika
osaikashivaishita, ñaakiroma tzimatsi saikantarori. ²³Arika
asaiki okaakini, ari ankimakiri paato intsompaikinta. ²⁴Ari
ankimakiri iñiiri varipa."

²⁵Te ayote saikatsirika iroñaaka, o terika vaajarika. ²⁶Irotaki
akamantavakari.

¹I heard this concerning the lake, located in Churingaveni. ²One
of my fellow men said, when we slept on the beach, he told us
[this]. ³He said, "I paddled downriver with a Spaniard. ⁴He came
from Pampa Whaley. ⁵When we reached Churingaveni, it was
late. ⁶Then he said, 'We'll sleep here, it's late.'

⁷"Then the Spaniard said, 'Take me a little bit upstream, where
canoes are beached.' ⁸There was what looked like a ladder. ⁹The
Spaniard person climbed this ladder, he climbed it for a while
until he reached the lake. ¹⁰By the lake, he changed his clothes,
he put on different clothes, different pants, the pants worn by
Spaniards, boots, everything." ¹¹He said, the Spaniard walked [on
the lake] as if there were a walk there. ¹²He was gone.

¹³They saw him submerge in the lake. ¹⁴Then they heard
people talk at the bottom of the lake. ¹⁵He was gone for what
seemed like two hours, he was gone. ¹⁶Later on, they saw him
come out. ¹⁷When he left, he was given bread and plantains to
eat. ¹⁸He brought it to my fellow men who were on the other side
of the river, where they slept overnight.

¹⁹He informed them, saying, "In this lake, my fellow man
lives. ²⁰Here you are, bread for us to eat, here you are, plantains
for us to eat, I only eat plantains." ²¹So it was, what that Spaniard told.

²²My fellow man said, "I imagine, this lake is inhabited, I've seen it that there is someone residing permanently there. ²³When we are in the vicinity of the lake, we hear the sound of ducks from the inside of the lake. ²⁴We hear roosters."

²⁵We don't know if they live there now, or they moved. ²⁶This is what we are advising [you] about.

THIRTY-FOUR

Chorinkaveni

(Churingaveni)

Daniel Bernales Quillatupa

[1]Nonkinkitsate pashini kinkitsarentsi okanta opaitayetantari nampitsipaye, okanta otzimantari ovairo nampitsipaye. [2]Nonkinkitsate okaratzi ikamantanari aani Kasanto opaitantari aparoni nampitsi paitachari Chorinkaveni. [3]Aani Kasanto ari isaikanampitziro iroka nampitsi paitachari Chorinkaveni. [4]Ikantzi, pairani temakia iyora aani kovintsari, ikantziri pairani te ajate irora amanante otzimayetzira okaratzi ivaitari akantavakero asoka, mosaki, tanta, ipimantayetziri chori, tekatsi pairani. [5]Ikoverika ontzime paitarika iyari ashaninka ontzimatye ijate antamiki, ari yayiri irora paitarika ikoveri iyari. [6]Irotaki ikantziri ani, ijatzi antamiki yamine paitarika ivakaiyarori isha aisatzi itomipaye.

[7]Ikantzi iroñaaka iyora ijatzi antamiki, yaniitzi yamine poshiniri, yariitakaro aparoni inkaari. [8]Aririka ariitzimatakiaro, ikantzi aani, osaikera inkaari, ari opiyotapakari irora chorinashi. [9]Tzimatsi irora tsiyaro, shiyarori tsiyaro, paitachari chorina. [10]Te akinkishiriaperotajero. [11]Inchato, tzimatsiri oitsoki ipokoriantaitaro, te nokinkishiriaperotajiaro.

[12]Asampitatyerika pashinipaye asheninka yotakoperotzirira. [13]Ikantzi iroñaaka ari oshookiri chorinashi, ari opiyotari oshookimotziro okaakini irora inkaarira. [14]Ikantziri aani,

13. A native man reels in alien people from Churingaveni Lake. By Daniel Bernales Quillatupa (Aroshi).

aririka ariitzimotapakiaro, ari aaityapakia. [15]Ari irora ontsitenitanake, ari ominkoritanake. [16]Aririka ajatatyerika okaakini osaikira inkaari, okatsatanaka iroñaaka. [17]Tampiatapaki osheki. [18]Aririka antsarovanaki, piyanaje iroñaaka. [19]Ikantzirira aani Kasanto, tzimatsi ashitarori irora inkaarira. [20]Iritaki tsikakoventarori, irotaki iroñaaka añaantayetavakarori, iroñaaka otsiteninkatapaki, ominkorityapaki, ookatsatanakia, irotaki kantakantziro ampiantanajiari iroñaaka. [21]Ari okantapintatya, ikantzi aani, ari opiyota chorinashi, oshookimotzirora inkaarira.

[22]Ikanta, ikanta avisaki osheki osarentsipaye. [23]Ariitapaka pashini atziripaye poñaayetachari pashiniki nampitsipaye. [24]Iñaapakirora osheki chorina, ari iroñaaka ompoñaari ompaitya nampitsika chorina, Chorinkaveni. [25]Okanta, okanta,

okanta, iñaaniyetanakaro iroñaaka. ²⁶Pashinipaye atziri arii-
yetapainchari okantziri, "Tsika pipoñaaka?" ²⁷"Nopoña anta,
oshookinta osheki chorinashi."

²⁸Iroñaaka, ikantziri aani, inkaarikira anta saikantayetana-
kirorira, iñaayetanakero akachaarontsi, ari ijatzi yakachaate.
²⁹Tzimatsi aajatzi shimapaye saikatsiri inkaarikira. ³⁰Ikantzi,
aririka ijate inkachaavaite, aririka osheetyanaje, intsompaikinta
inkaarikira ari ikimaitzirikia yañaanaje varipa (ikantziri tyapa)
oo-ri-oo. ³¹Tzimatsi otsitzipaye tsarotanatsiri osheetyanajera,
jao, jao, jao. ³²Aisatzi tzimatsi iyora ikimaitziri vaaka, *muu,
muu.* ³³Aijatzi ikimiri eentsi iñaatsavaitanajia, ikaimavaijeeta-
naje, ishirontavakajeetya.

³⁴Ikantzirikia iroñaaka iyoka akachaariantzika ijatanaji
nampitsikira, ovakera otzimayetanaki kapicheeni pankotsi,
ikantzi, "Ari okantavaita iroñaaka inkaarika: aririka osheetyanaje, ari ankimayetakiri kantashiyetachari piratsipaye. ³⁵Aisa-
tzita eentsipaye kimitaka intsompaikinta tzimatsi atziri
saikatsiri." ³⁶"Arima." ³⁷Pashini iroñaaka ikantziri, "Intsityami."

³⁸Iyotakira tzimatsi varipa, ikoveri iyari, ivaki iroñaaka
iyachaarokira apakichokiroini shinki. ³⁹Yookakiro, iñaatziri
inoshikanakiro kachaarontsi, *shiririri.* ⁴⁰Inoshikashitaro, *tzinik.*
⁴¹Inoshikiro, inoshikiro iyachaaro, iñaatziri tyapa, *tsapok, tsapok,* intaani tyapa. ⁴²Yaavakeri iroñaaka, ivamakeri. ⁴³Ikantzi
iroñaaka, "Otsitzi osheki ivari vatsatsi." ⁴⁴Yaaki iroñaaka kapicheeni vatsatsi. ⁴⁵Isatekakeri iroñaaka akachaarontsiki, yookakero iroñaaka, *tsapok.* ⁴⁶Iñaavakitziri oshirinkanaka iyachaaro,
shiririri, inoshikiro, *tzinik.* ⁴⁷Inoshikiro, inoshikiro, iñaatziri
otsitzi, yairikavakeri. ⁴⁸Ishiyanaka, piinkapaki, *tsapok.*
⁴⁹Ikantzi, "Tzimatsi otsitzive."

⁵⁰Ari okanta avisaki osheki osarentsi. ⁵¹Ikantzi iroñaaka
intakantarori, ikantzi, "Aitaki tzimaki iroñaaka atziri intsompaikinta." ⁵²Yaaki iroñaaka aparoni ikantziri *cebolla,* ipi-

mantaitziri janta, irora ipimantatayetziri choripaye. [53]Yaake iroñaaka *cebolla*, itsatakero iyachaaro, yookakero, *tsapok.* [54]Iñaavakitziro oshirinkanaka iroñaaka iyachaaroka, *shiririri, tzinik.* [55]Inoshikiro, inoshikiro, inoshikiro. [56]Iñaavakitziri kantavaishitachari shipatonantzi, te kaari ashaninka. [57]*Shiririri*, shitovapaki. [58]Iñaavakiri ishitovapaki pashini, yoijatavakaka iroñaaka. [59]Piyotajeetapaka, avisanaki iroñaaka ikinaiyanaki janta. [60]Iritaki akantziri iroñaaka "chori."

[61]Ari ompoñaanakia iroñaaka pashini kinkitsarentsi opaitantyari iroñaaka iroka nampitsika Chorinkaveni. [62]Tema jara inkaarikira ari ishitovakeri iroñaaka choripayeka, shekitatsiri iroñaaka pareniki. [63]Paitanaka iroñaaka irora inkaarira Chorinkaveni, tema ari ishitovatziri, ishitovatakakeri pairani ashaninka, inoshikakeri iyachaaroki choripaye. [64]Ari okaratzi nokimiri ikinkitsatzi, kinkitsatakana aani Kasantoni.

[1]I will tell another story about how villages were named, how the village name came into being. [2]I will tell exactly what my grandfather Kasanto informed me about why a village is named Churingaveni. [3]My grandfather Kasanto lived next to this village called Churingaveni. [4]He said that long ago he was a hunter, and he said that long ago we didn't go to a vending place to buy food, say, sugar, potatoes, bread, which Andean colonists sell — it didn't exist in the past. [5]If my fellow man wanted something to eat, he will have to go to the forest and there he will obtain whatever he wanted to eat. [6]This is what my grandfather said, that he would go to the forest to look for something in order to feed his old woman and his sons.

[7]He said that he would go to the forest to look for game and would come to a lake. [8]When he would get there, he said, in this place where the lake was, there were many plants called *cho-*

rina. ⁹They were palm trees, they looked like palm trees, called *chorina* (*Oenocarpus mapora*). ¹⁰I don't recall it very well. ¹¹The tree might have fruit with which body painting was done, but I don't remember it well.

¹²It might be better to ask others because they know more about it. ¹³He said, that a lot of *chorina* plants grew there; they grew in abundance, close to the lake. ¹⁴My grandfather said that when he would reach the lake area, something would happen. ¹⁵It would get dark, clouds would gather. ¹⁶When one would get close to the area where the lake was, lightning would strike. ¹⁷The wind would begin blowing. ¹⁸When one gets afraid, he should return. ¹⁹As my grandfather said, this lake has its master. ²⁰He is the one who takes care of this place, that's why we see this: it gets dark, clouds gather, lightning strikes, that's why we have to back off. ²¹It was this way, my grandfather said, that there *chorina* plants were abundant, in this place where they grew by the lake.

²²Many years passed. ²³Other people from different villages arrived. ²⁴They saw a lot of *chorina* plants, that's how it got to be named "the village of *chorina* plants," Chorinkaveni. ²⁵Later on, it got entrenched in the language. ²⁶People would ask those from the village, "Where are you from?" ²⁷"I am from over there, where many *chorina* plants grow."

²⁸My grandpa said that those who lived there, in the lake area, were familiar with the fishing hook and would go fishing [in the lake]. ²⁹There was fish in that lake. ³⁰He said that when they would go fishing, when it got dark, they heard a chicken (they call it "rooster") from the depths of the lake, *cock-a-doodle-doo.* ³¹There were dogs that barked, *baw-waw,* when it got dark. ³²There were also cows, they heard their sound, *muuh.* ³³They also heard children play, call out, and laugh.

³⁴He said, that a fisherman went to the village—at that moment there were a few houses there—and said, "Such is the lake: when it gets dark, then we hear various animals. ³⁵Also, we hear children, it seemed like people live in the lake." ³⁶[The listeners would respond], "Maybe." ³⁷Others would say, "Let's see."

³⁸Because he knew what a chicken wants to eat, he put a tiny corn kernel on his hook. ³⁹He cast the line and saw that the line was being taken out, *shiriri* (slow-motion action). ⁴⁰The fisherman slowly took in the line, [but it stopped moving], *tzinik* (frozen, static state, lack of movement). ⁴¹He kept taking in the line and saw a chicken, *tsapok, tsapok* (shallow splash), it was only a chicken. ⁴²He grabbed it and killed it. ⁴³He said, "The dog likes meat a lot." ⁴⁴He took a little bit of meat. ⁴⁵He put it on the hook and cast the line, *tsapok* (shallow splash). ⁴⁶He saw the line being taken out, *shiriri* (slow-motion action), and he began taking it in, then, *tzinik* (frozen, static state, lack of movement). ⁴⁷He kept taking it in, saw a dog, and grabbed it. ⁴⁸The dog ran away and dove into the water, *tsapok* (shallow splash). ⁴⁹The fisherman said, "There are dogs [in the lake]!"

⁵⁰Many years passed. ⁵¹The founder of the village said, "Truly, there are people in the lake." ⁵²He took what they call "onion," which is sold over there, Andean settlers sell it. ⁵³He took an onion, tied it to the hook, and cast the line, *tsapok* (shallow splash). ⁵⁴He saw the line being taken out, *shiriri* (slow-motion action), then *tzinik*, (frozen, static state, lack of movement). ⁵⁵The fisherman kept taking it in for a while. ⁵⁶He saw a strange thing with a beard, it wasn't a fellow man. ⁵⁷[When he slowly took the line in], *shiriri* (slow-motion action), he came out of the water. ⁵⁸He saw another come out, another followed. ⁵⁹A lot of them amassed and walked over there. ⁶⁰They were those whom we call *chori*.

⁶¹So the name comes from a different story about why the vil-

lage is called Chorinkaveni. [62]Because the *chori* came out from this lake and multiplied in the Perené area. [63]The lake is called Chorinkaveni because our fellow man made them come out in the past, when he brought in the line with the *chori* people. [64]This is what I heard, what my deceased grandfather told me.

3

Ritual

When the past is relived and reexperienced in the habitual ritual behavior of indigenous performers, the oral society's memories of its history are continuously reinforced. In Connerton's words, "For images of the past and recollected knowledge of the past . . . are conveyed and sustained by (more or less ritual) performances" (1989:3–4). Performed by the "committed actors" (Demmer and Gaenzle 2007:12), rituals are activities that invoke mystical powers and "form part of a tradition or canon of rites" (Bell [1997] 2009:91,93). Rituals are often accompanied by verbal acts or "performative utterances," in Austin's (1962) sense, whose illocutionary force expresses the speaker's intention to accomplish a particular goal, "sufficient to create or change social reality" (Demmer and Gaenzle 2007:8). For example, an act of human bodily transformation, from the native perspective, could be achieved by the physical action of blowing of breath through pursed lips, accompanied by the verbally articulated ritual formula *afuu* (be it), which explicitly "performs" the act of transformation.

The Ashéninka Perené language describes any form of habitual cultural behavior with the term *ametapintari* ame-t-apint-a-ri [be.accustomed.to-EP-HAB-REAL-REL] (what we are accustomed to). There are also specific terms referring to particular rituals, exemplified by *imairentaitziro ovankoshiki* i-mairi-nt-ai-tz-i-ro o-vanko-shi-ki [3MASC.A-be.quiet-EP-IMP-EP-REAL-3NMASC.O 3NMASC.POSS-house-leaf-LOC] (she is placed to rest in the menarche hut). Along with the native terms, for the sake of convenience, I will use the designations found in scholarly literature on rituals. Following the contemporary typologies of ritual (e.g., Turner 1967:7–15; Grimes 1985:68–116; Bell [1997] 2009:chap. 4; Santos-Granero 2004a:102–6), this brief presentation of Upper Perené ritual behavior draws on the distinctions made between place rituals; exchange rituals (or offering rituals); calendrical rites; feasting and festival rites; rites of passage (or life-crisis rituals) such as initiation, marriage, and funerary rites; and rites of affliction, which serve either to prevent a potential threat or to redress the damage done to a fellow man by an evil entity. In addition, ritual blowing, ritual spitting, and prayer are distinguished here as separate ritual categories.

It should be borne in mind that these terms are limited in their utility inasmuch as they merely capture the most salient substantive characteristic of a ritual, while disregarding its other dimensions. For example, the boys' initiation rite involves complexes of ritual activities, incorporating the ritual of exchange, such as offerings to divinities and masters-owners of plants, animals, and fish; ritual blowing and spitting; and other rituals that include vomiting, abstinence, administering eyedrops or/and rubbing magic plant-based substances into the hunting and fishing gear (Anderson 2000:186–88).

Saturated in culture-specific mythic and historical contexts, ritual practices of indigenous Amazonian societies invariably highlight the central role of ritual specialists as power brokers between the native community and the spiritual powers of the cosmic universe. Ritual interventions conducted by ritual specialists of Amazonian indigenous groups are described in ethnographic studies of Wakuénai, Arawak (Hill 1989, 1993); Yanesha, Arawak (Daignealt 2009; Santos-Granero 1998, 2002a, 2004a, 2009a; Smith 1977); Ashaninka Tambo-Ene, Arawak (Weiss 1973, 1975); Machiguenga, Arawak (Johnson 2003, Baer 1992; Shepard 2002), Cashinahua, Panoan (Lagrou 2007); Shipibo-Conibo, Panoan (Illius 1992); Desana, Tucanoan (Buchillet 1992; Reichel-

Dolmatoff 1975); and Canelos Quichua (Lowland Quichua, Que-
chuan, Quechua B II) (Whitten 1985). The ethnographies underscore the profound significance of ritual specialists in shaping
the community's social behavior. For example, during the boys'
and girls' Cashinahua initiation rite Nixpupima, chant singers
are understood to model the initiates' spirits through the ritual
ceremony of child naming, interwoven into the naming of all influential creatures of the Cashinahua cosmic universe; the chant
leader and other chanters are seen as ultimate "fabricators" of
a new society's member, who is ritually transformed into the
Cashinahua with the necessary "productive skills" and "social
values" (Lagrou 2007:190).

Among the Upper Perené Ashaninka, the extant ritual interventions are basically restricted to affliction rituals that seek to
restore an afflicted person's health by identifying and removing the disease-causing agent. They are performed either by an
aavintantzinkaro (healer) or by an individual him- or herself.
Notwithstanding the shamans' total withdrawal from the highly
missionized area, Upper Perené Arawaks continue to recognize
the curative and social power vested with the ritual specialist
sheripiari (shaman; a very powerful shaman is called *antyaviari*)
in the treatment of the afflicted human condition. In contradistinction to shamans, who end their interventions with a call to
action by explicitly identifying the disease-causing aggressor
and spelling out the countermeasures, the healers make only
tenuous suggestions on this subject. For the most part, lay folks
perform affliction rituals on their own, resorting to the mystical powers of the family-owned *ivenki* (magic plant; in Spanish, *piripiri* [*Cyperus piripiri*]), *pinitsi* (medical plant with magic
properties; in Spanish, *tilo* [*Justicia pectoralis*]), local medicinal
herbs, or manipulations with Christian paraphernalia such as a
candle or a cross.

The Upper Perené calendrical thanksgiving festivals and ceremonies, ritual cannibalistic feasts, initiation ceremonies, offering rites, and shamanistic performances are consigned to oblivion, recalled by a handful of surviving old-generation speakers. Nonetheless, Ashéninka Perené–speaking individuals continue to privately practice a variety of low-key symbolic activities, "inscribed" into the group's "environmental" history, which is constituted by the people's interactions with nature (Hill 1989). On the individual level, ritual blowing, spitting, abstinence, place rituals, and affliction rituals remain relatively uncompromised, being inexorably entrenched in the people's "animistic" ontology.

Like histories of other small-scale Amazonian societies, Upper Perené "environmental" history is approached in terms of the hunter-gatherers' direct and indirect interaction with the surrounding universe (see Hill 1989; Whitten 1978, 1985). Upper Perené ecological cosmology, understood as a set of ideas about the totality of reality, is rooted in "animism," defined as indigenous "thought which extends human agency to beings of other species" (Viveiros de Castro 1998:469). The universe is seen as totally animated, that is, saturated with various divinities, forces, spirits, and beings, all of which are being interconnected and interdependent in a complex way (Torre López 1966; Rojas Zolezzi 1994; Weiss 1973, 1975; Santos-Granero 2004a; Mario Brown 1974; Lenaerts 2006b, 2006c). This indigenous ontology encompasses cultural beliefs and assumptions that "the universe is populated by extra-human intentionalities," mostly animals, who "have lost the qualities inherited or retained by humans" (Viveiros de Castro 1998:472).

In line with an integrative worldview that animates the whole universe as a sociocultural dynamic construction, Upper Perené Arawaks have to continuously negotiate with a legion of powerful spiritual beings inhabiting their environs, by any available means. Santos-Granero (2004a) observes that the negotiation strategies of Peruvian Arawaks vary from worshipping, cajoling, and coaxing to simply physically removing the evil entity when the appeasement doesn't work. In other words, the basic functions of the ritual are to ensure the spiritual beings' cooperation in everyday human endeavors and to fix any glitches in the system of spiritual interrelations that might take place.

The documented Upper Perené rituals are often tied to a certain geographical location in the recognized environs. The so-called place rituals are conducted in a particular spot in the familiar landscape known to serve as a divinity worship site or presumed to be the abode of a spiritual master-owner or a place inhabited by a hostile human entity (Santos-Granero 2004a:103–4).

Place rituals involve an exchange ritual, in which people make offerings to spiritual beings with an expectation of it being reciprocated (Bell [1997] 2009:108). Among Upper Perené Arawaks, offerings take the form of first fruits or other traditional food. For example, the stone and fire divinities were placated with the traditional offering of coca leaves; *chamairo* (*Mussatia hyacinthina*), which is a bitter vine; and powdered limestone, the stimulant regularly consumed by male Ashaninkas to quench hunger and maintain an adequate energy level. Accompanied by a simply phrased entreaty, a sort of unpretentious prayer, the offering would be placed next to the divinity, as it was the case with the stone divinity Paatsiri (Padre/Father) described by Elías Meza Pedro in *Atziri yamaniri mapi poña paamari* (People Were Worshipping Stone and Fire, part 2).

Offerings to the solar deity Pava and masters-owners of cultivated plants, especially those of the staple cultigens of sweet manioc and plantains, were proffered in the form of either manioc beer or the manioc itself, as evidenced in the text *Am-pinateri Pava* (What We Will Offer to Pava), by Clelia Mishari, recorded by Gregorio Santos Pérez in 2011, in Mariscal Cáceres. The manioc beer was placed in a new *pachaka* (gourd made of squash; *calabaza* in Spanish) and left on the household prem-ises or on the cultivated land for the divinity to have its fill. As part of the exchange ritual, thanks were verbally articulated to acknowledge the critical interference of the solar deity Pava or the spiritual master-owner of the plant in Ashaninka well-being.

The texts *Kamenantsi* (Traditional Advice), by Daniel Ber-nales Quillatupa, recorded in 2009 in Bajo Marankiari, and *Tsika okantya ashimaapakotantyari* (How to Be a Good Fisher-man), by Gregorio Santos Pérez, recorded in 2010 in Villa Perené, give accounts of the boys' initiation rite. As the texts reveal, the boys' initiation ritual was intertwined with an offering to the masters-owners of animals and fish, made in a particular loca-tion. The offerings were made in the form of the species them-selves, which were left untouched by the neophyte hunter or fisherman after he was either killed or caught, respectively, by a boy. In addition to food prohibition, the offering ritual was aimed to initiate the novice hunter or fisherman by honoring the master-owner of the species, so that the young man was magi-cally "blown on," that is, transformed into an expert hunter or fisherman.

During a young boy's initiation rite, the fish was let back to the river in exactly the same spot where it was caught, while the game was offered to the fierce *kanaiki* (tangarana ants) teeming in the *kanai* (tangarana) tree (*Triplaris americana*). The peculiar choice of the offering site was due to the human origin of the *kanaiki* ants. As it was explained to me by the narrator, in the old mythic times the *kanaiki* ants used to be people who had a reputation of being outstanding hunters.

In native ritual behaviors, the use of *ivenki* or *ovenki* (magical herb; *Cyperus articulatis*, or piripiri) is conspicuously pervasive (Anderson 2000:chap. 6; Rojas Zolezzi 1994:106–18; Veber 2009:135). Small gardens of *ivenki* plants are always planted next to the house. Every plant is believed to serve a particular function, ranging from assistance in birth to protection from the enemy (Anderson 1991, 1996, 2000:183–85).[1]

The magic plant *ivenki* was commonly used in place rituals, when a new *chacra* (plot of land) was mouth-sprayed with *ovaantsivenki* (the magic plant of *chacra*) to make the clearing job less difficult, or during the weeding season, when the *chacra* was mouth-sprayed with *kanirivenki* (the magic plant of sweet manioc) to make sure that the sweet manioc plants grow big (Rojas Zolezzi 1994:107–8). In the old times, before leaving on a hunting expedition, hunters would mouth-spray the trail with *ivenki* to have better luck (Rojas Zolezzi 1994:113). The *ovayeri* (warriors) would make fires and burn a combination of *pochokiroshi* pochoki-ro-shi [dream-NMZ-leaf] (herb causing drowsiness) and *masontovenki* masonto-venki [dumb-magic.plant] (magic plant causing a mental state of confusion) to generate toxic smoke and stupefy the Spaniards.

As a form of protection or counteraction, each *ivenki* plant is administered in a particular way, depending on its function. It can be burned, chewed, chewed and then mouth-sprayed on the hands or on an object, rubbed onto the entire body, its leaves eaten, its brew drunk, a person bathed in it, or the plant's liquid squeezed into the eyes (Anderson 1991:107–10; Shepard 2002:218–19).

At present, *ivenki* is widely used in the place ritual in the context of a visitor's arrival. Upper Perené natives chew and mouth-spray the trail with *masontovenki* masonto-venki [dumb-magic. plant] (herb causing a mental state of confusion) before arriving

at a native community, to prevent a potential psychophysiologi-
cal attack launched by an evil fellow man. The common suspicion is that a *matsi* (witch) might reside in the village and be
capable of inflicting bodily and psychological harm on the visitor. *Ivenki* also serve as a cure in the affliction rituals. Language
speakers mention the treatments by *matsivenki* (herb against
witchcraft) of their infant children, who were bathed in water
boiled with the herb when the child was suspected of having
been "contaminated" by a witch.

Among modern Upper Perené Arawaks, *ivenki* seem to have
assumed the social function of behavior modification and control. To alter the target's behavior in a desired manner, the plants
are used to counteract aggression by a *matsi* or police; to help
keep peace in the family, that is, to prevent physical abuse and
violence by one of the partners; and to assist with bringing up
healthy and obedient children.

Old-generation speakers continue to use *ivenki*, perhaps as
a cleansing agent, in their labors and commerce, exemplified by
the Gregorio Santos Pérez narrative *Tsika okantya ashimaapakotantyari* (How to Be a Good Fisherman). The narrator points
out that to be able to catch *mamori* (*sábalo*), the fisherman needs
to apply *mamorivenki* (the magic plant of *sábalo*) by rubbing it
onto the fishing rod and the nylon fishing cord.[2]

The performative act of prayer or incantation was a significant part of the habitual ritual behavior of Upper Perené Arawaks. There is no special native term for a prayer as a ritual
category. The verb roots *kant* (say) and *aman* (exalt, petition,
worship) often co-occur to describe the act of an invocation of
a divinity. The prayer serves two basic functions, reflected in
its ordering structure: it gives thanks, encoded by the verb root
pasonki (thank), and it petitions, expressed by *aman* (exalt, peti-

tion, worship). Simple prayers were known to be recited, usually by headmen, on the ritual scene.

Due to the fleeting nature of this sort of ritual knowledge, it was possible to write down only a stylized version of the prayer directed to the stone divinity. The Delia Rosas Rodríguez text *Yamaniri pava impereta* (They Were Worshipping the Stone Divinity) is a product of a collaborative effort. The narrator asked her mother, Bertha Rodríguez de Caleb, and her stepfather, Abdias Caleb Quinchori, both in their seventies, to "reconstruct" the prayer from memory. The text was recorded and written down by Delia Rosas Rodríguez in 2010, in Bajo Marankiari. It should be borne in mind that all three collaborators are members of the local Adventist church. The narrator's language choices are significantly influenced by the Christian supplication canons. For example, the lines in the prayer that make allusions to the god's eternal existence (sentence 3) and the offering of sweet-scented wood (sentence 4) are calques from the Spanish-language prayer books.

Being part of the exchange rituals, prayers often accompanied an offering of the traditional beverage, manioc beer, or first fruits to a divinity that was thought to be responsible for keeping food supplies plentiful. The Clelia Mishari text *Ampinateri Pava* (What We Will Offer to Pava) cites unpretentious petitions like this (sentence 22):

Pava, jiroka, pinatachari pipakinaro aviroka.
Pava, here it is, my offering [payment to you],
you have given it to me.

The offering-plus-prayer's purpose was to confirm the reciprocal nature of the relationship and negotiate a mutually satisfactory transaction between the parties involved to ensure the sustained abundance of crops in the future.

While prayers exhibited fluidity in terms of language choice and structure, incantations addressed to the spiritual masters-owners were more rigidly constrained due to their peculiar function of casting a spell by using certain words, idioms, and bodily actions. When an incantation is recited, the ritual activity is described by the verb root *kant* (say). The texts *Arika ashimaatya* (When We Fish) and *Ookantyarori inkani* (How to Chase Away Rain) by Daniel Bernales Quillatupa illustrate the invariant focal point, expressed by the ritual ideophone-based formula *kisho kisho*, evoking a spitting action, coarticulated with the act of spitting. The ideophone is derived from the verb *kisho* (spit). What is spewed out is either saliva or a mixture of saliva and masticated plant leaves. Ritual spitting is incorporated into a variety of affliction rituals; I will elaborate on this below.

In both texts, whether the goal is having fish stupefied by poison or driving away unwanted rain, the illocutionary force of the *kisho* formula, coupled with the magical act of spitting, is used to neutralize the resistance of the targeted entity.

In the context of fishing, the *kisho* formula is embedded in the insistent plea "to drink" (expressed by the verb root *ir*) the poison, which is likened to manioc beer, the traditional Ashaninka beverage. The plea, addressed to river inhabitants, is recited collectively by male fishermen: *kisho, kisho, pirero, pirero* (*kisho, kisho*, drink it, drink it). In addition, language speakers point out that the name of a toad species, *mashero* (*Bufo marinus*), can be used repetitively with the *kisho* formula as well. The toad *mashero* is known for its venom-secreting glands (Rojas Zolezzi 1994:196), so its invocation is believed to strengthen the vegetable poison.

The *kisho*-based ritual act of driving away the rain is framed as a forceful command, directly addressed to the black-haired suitor. The rain entity is portrayed as an unwelcome, impudent visitor who is seeking a spouse and even brought along *kompiro* (*humiro* palm tree; *Phytelephas macrocarpa*) planks to build a house. Both texts were recorded and transcribed by the narrator Daniel Bernales Quillatupa in 2010, in his home in La Merced.

Ritual spitting is distinct from ritual blowing. The two have different cospeech affiliates and illocutionary forces in the construction of a transformative act. As mentioned previously, the ritual blowing of breath through pursed lips is accompanied by the formula *afuu* (be it). The act of blowing is referred to as *tasonk* (blow) in the language. When native speakers comment on the semantics of the ritual formula *afuu*, they underscore the word's narrowly defined transformative sense. The ritual blowing-plus-*afuu* act can be employed in combination with the application of magic plants *ivenki* or *pinitsi* or accompanied by a food offering, or a small prayer-petition to the manioc plant (which has white flesh) can be recited before drinking manioc beer, for example, *afuu, airo pikantanaro noishi kitamarori* (be it, let my hair never turn gray).

In contrast to the intimate, low-key place rituals, calendrical rites bear a conspicuously public, festive character, recalled by older speakers as collective events celebrated with abandon. The rites mark the passage of time, occurring at well-delineated points of "seasonal changes in light, weather, agricultural work, and other activities" (Bell [1997] 2009:101–2). They involve the whole community, acknowledging "the passage from scarcity to plenty . . . and from plenty to scarcity" (Turner 1969:171). Among Upper Perené Ashaninkas, calendrical rites essentially overlap with feasting and festival rituals, since they follow the same schematic template for a festive communal event. The ritual event's basic structural elements are singing, dancing, panpipe music, and ebullient consumption of manioc beer.

The calendrical rituals are straightforwardly related to the changes in two seasons. The Upper Perené "season of scarcity" is *kiarontsi*, the wet season, which lasts from December through March, whereas the "season of plenty" is *osarentsi* (or *aarontsi*), the dry season, from April to November, the beginning of each being marked by the flowering period of a particular plant. In December *savoro* (wild cane; *Gynerium sagittatum*) produce aromatic white blossoms called *chakopishi* (arrow-cane plumes); in June, yellow blossoms appear on the *shimashiri* tree (Pino chuncho; *Schizolobium amazonicum*).

In addition to their attention to the cyclical changes in the availability of food supplies and the precipitation level, Ashéninka Perené natives also rely on the lunar phases in their agricultural activities. They distinguish between *tetaja* or *porataji kashiri* (the moon is about to disappear/fall down the mountains, or full moon), and *iyovachekitapaji kashiri* (the horn-like moon has come out, or new moon). The full moon is associated with fertility and abundance, whereas the new moon is linked to emptiness and scarcity. The importance of the seasonal and lunar calendars is demonstrated in manioc cultivation: the staple crop of sweet manioc is not planted during the *kiarontsi* (wet season), or when the moon is new.

The seasonal pattern of Upper Perené calendrical rituals is illustrated by a few texts presented in part 3. In particular, the transition from scarcity to plenty was celebrated during the endo-cannibalistic event described by Abdias Caleb de Quinchori in *Shinavaite ovariri atziri* (*Shinavaite* Who Ate People). The text was recorded in 2010 in Bajo Marankiari, at the narrator's stepdaughter's home. Based on the narrator's grand-

mother's testimony (her name was Mananka), the text presents
the minute details of the ritual scene, its actors, the ceremony's
formalized scenario, specifics of the preparation of a communal
meal, and its consumption. The context of the ritual is also pains-
takingly explained. According to the narrator, his grandparents'
generation conducted an annual ceremonial celebration of *osarentsi* (dry season) in June, when the *shimashiri* tree begins to
blossom. In advance of the ceremonial event, children, typically
girls, were captured and fed well to ensure the celebrants' gas-
tronomic satisfaction.

The cannibalistic ritual was conducted in three stages. First
the celebrants would dance and sing a ritual song, together with
the victim. The song contains a refrain, *vaya-veya*, glossed by
language consultants as an expression of grief. This word belies
the narrator's dispassionate rendition of the whole ceremony by
exposing the celebrants' gripping angst. Then the child would
be carried to the pot and boiled until her death, followed by
the corpse's disrobing, cleaning, and removal of the head, hands,
and intestines. After a prolonged period of cooking in boiled
water, the corpse would be cut up in small pieces and the meat
consumed communally. The exact geographical location of *shinavaite* is not possible to ascertain. The narrator believes that
shinavaite resided in the uplands area, not far from present-day
Puente Herreiria, to the west of Bajo Marankiari.

To mark the transition from "plenty to scarcity," the collective end-of-year *mavira* ceremony was performed in the area of
present-day Pampa Michi and San Miguel Centro Marankiari,
in December, at the beginning of the wet season, when *shinki*
"maize" is harvested and the plant *savoro* "wild cane" produces
blossoms called *chakopishi*. According to the Pampa Michi narrators Luis Mauricio Rosa (*Okoñaatantakari mavira* [How
Mavira Appeared]) and Elena Nestor de Capurro (*Mavira*),

the ritual was borrowed in the old times from non-Ashaninka natives who came from Cuzco and stayed for a short while in the headwaters of the Upper Perené, in the Cerro de la Sal area. *Mavira* is an assimilated loan from the Spanish Navidad (Christmas). Until recently, Upper Perené Arawaks annually celebrated *mavira* by wearing headdresses of *chakopishi* (some say only the leader was adorned with a headdress), aromatic grayish-white plumes of wild cane, while dancing in a circle, playing panpipe music, singing *mavira* songs, and drinking large quantities of manioc beer. Both texts were recorded in 2011 in Pampa Michi.[3] The annual *mavira* festivities conducted in San Miguel Centro Marankiari are described by Ines Pérez de Santos and Moises Santos Rojas in the text *Mavira*, recorded in 2013 in the narrators' residence in Bajo Marankiari.

The calendrical rituals draw on the "symbolic grammar" of "human-divine interactions" in an attempt to "organize the human world most effectively" (Bell [1997] 2009:111). The Upper Perené calendrical rituals are transparently "instrumental" (Bell [1997] 2009:93) in that they aim to influence the forces of nature in order to enlist their help in improving the people's overall well-being.

The Upper Perené calendrical rituals, as well as thanksgiving festivals and other sorts of publicly celebrated events, are conspicuous in that they lack a staged enactment of the group's mythic and historical events. For other Arawak-speaking populations, reenacting the group's past migrations is part of their ritual repertoire. For example, during male and female initiation ceremonies among the Wakuénai of Venezuela, ritual specialists name rivers, forests, and savannahs located in a large area of Amazonia between the rivers Negro and Orinoco, which broadly covers the territory occupied by northern Arawak-speaking peoples at the time of the colonial conquest (Hill 2011:263).

Ritual feasting, festival rites, and exchange rites coalesce during the sun and moon thanksgiving festivals in that during the event, the celebrants would make offerings of song, dance, and music to Pava (solar deity; also called Ooriatsiri), the highest-ranking divinity. Kashiri, the lunar deity, was also acknowledged, but with much less pomp. Bell observes that native societies "use distinct cultural conventions to ritualize human-divine interaction and exchange" ([1997] 2009:111). The festivals were the projections of the Upper Perené cultural schema of a festive celebration, with the main components of singing, dancing, tambor and panpipe music, and manioc beer drinking.

The genre of festive celebration is designated in Ashéninka Perené by the verb stems *oimoshirink* (celebrate; literally, make happy) and *shinkitavint* (drink manioc beer on account of somebody or something). Another verb root, which is also used by Ashéninka Perené speakers in the context of Adventist Christian discourses describing worship, is *aman* (petition, exalt). Native speakers translate the verb into Spanish as *rezar* (pray) or *adorar* (praise). The object of veneration is called *ivavani* i-pavani [3MASC.POSS-deity-POSS] (their god).

The Upper Perené feasting and festival rituals incorporate music accompanied by dancing and singing. The collective singing activity of repetitively articulating short choruses while dancing, known in scholarly literature as "chanting" (Beier 2002), is called in Ashéninka Perené *vishiriantsi*. On the basis of studies of festive behavior among Nantis, Southern Kampan–language speakers of Arawak, Beier notes that chanting often involves "vocables," "sound sequences that are procodically, phonologically, and even morphologically Nanti 'words', but that carry no referential meaning in terms of daily discourse" (2002:4). Ashéninka Perené chants and songs exhibit the same tendency of employing native-sounding monosyllabic or dysyllabic units like *(o) ya* and *ma*, which are found attached to the preceding word. For example, the nonce word *ma* appears many times in *Iyovapaji-rika ooriatsiri* (When the Sun Comes Out), by Paulina García Ñate.

Among Upper Perené Arawaks, panpipe and tambor music is recognized as both sacred and aesthetically pleasing. On many occasions, when I saw practicing musicians in Pampa Michi or witnessed communal festive dancing accompanied by music and singing, it was evident that the performers immensely enjoyed the act. Most dances are energetic and vigorous, featuring a lot of turns, circles, and quick upper-body movements.

Two kinds of native flutes are distinguished, *shoviri(ntsi)* (single-pipe flute; *quena* in Spanish) and *sonkari* (panpipe; *antara* in Spanish). The Upper Perené collection contains recordings of music produced on the six-to-ten-pipe *sonkari*, which seems to be more common than the *shoviri* flute. The percussion musical instrument *tamporo* (tambor) is used either on its own or together with the flute during festive activities. Some scholars attribute the existence of flutes to the local Andean influence (Weiss 1975:536), while others consider "intensive regional and interregional exchanges" (Hornborg and Hill 2011:16–17) to be instrumental in the widely spread ritual use of wind-music instruments among Amazonian Arawak-speaking peoples, including groups residing on the eastern slopes of the Andes.[4]

Panpipe and tambor music, festive dancing, singing, and manioc beer drinking at the Perené-based sun festivals involved an emphatic evocation of Pava, the divine solar being (e.g., Weiss 1975:469–70; Torre López 1966:71–72; Mario Brown 1974:58). A detailed description of the sun-honoring ritual ceremony is provided by Father Manuel Navarro (*La tribu Campa*, 1924), cited in Torre López: "When the disk of the sun sinks in an ocean of greenery, facing the sun, they celebrate, formed in a semicircle,

with the witch [shaman] in the middle, they worship the afore-
mentioned deity, and offer it *masato* and coca, recite for it certain prayers; these ceremonies are finished to the sound of the
flute and the drum" (1966:72). Weiss notes that in the Perené
area panpipe dances were "specifically intended to be acts of
homage to Pava" (1975:470), that is, to the solar divinity.

This collection contains ritual sun- and moon-honoring songs
recorded by Bertha Rodríguez de Caleb in 2009 (*Pavankiri ooria*
[Solar Deity]) and by Paulina García Ñate in 2011 (*Iyovapaji-
rika ooriatsiri* [When the Sun Comes Out] and *Ipantsakoitziri
kashiri* [They Sing about the Moon]). All three texts were recorded in Bajo Marankiari at the singers' residences. According
to Paulina García Ñate, the ritual songs were performed either at
sunset or at sunrise. The offering of the solemn songs to the solar
deity was meant to express the performers' eager anticipation of
seeing the sun disk return the next day. With great earnestness,
the celebrants sought assurance of the solar deity's cyclical jour-
neys in the hope that it would return. The supremacy of Pava
or Ooriatsiri (male solar divinity) is ascertained on the basis of
the sun's intense splendor, exceeding that of the nocturnal deity
Kashiri (male lunar divinity). Nonetheless, the brilliance of the
moon and his service to Ashaninka as a source of light is grate-
fully acknowledged. Panpipe music, dancing, and manioc beer
drinking invariably followed the singing performances.

The widely spread ritual practice of worshipping "sacred
fires," perceived to be manifestations of Pava, is described by
Elías Meza Pedro in a recorded conversation with his son-in-
law, Gregorio Santos Pérez, titled *Atziri yamaniri mapi poña
paamari* (People Were Worshipping Stone and Fire), in part 2.[5]
In the vicinity of his native settlement of Kishitariki, the narrator witnessed an orderly ceremony of worship in a big house,
attended and conducted exclusively by sexual ascetics, *shan-*

tyoshi (the pure). To those who were sexually active, called *an-tzirori ochaa* ant-tz-i-ro-ri ochaa [do-EP-3NMASC.O-REL lack. of.sexual.restraint] (those who engage in fornication), access to the (sacred fire) was denied. The nonascetic pilgrims would stand on the other side of the house. The ascetics, comprising males and females, kept vigil in front of the fire in order to hear "the voice" of the divinity, *inkimavanteteri* i-n-kim-a-vante-t-e-ri [3MASC.A-IRR-hear-EP-mouth-EP-IRR-3MASC.O], literally "they will hear his mouth." According to the narrator, the head-man in charge of the house of worship, called *jevatzirori* (the one who leads), preached on the subject of fornication. As indicated in the text, the headman lived on the temple's premises.[6] The recording was made in 2011, in Kishitariki (Mariscal Cáceres), at the residence of Elías Meza Pedro.

Ashéninka Perené "life-crisis" initiatory rituals for boys and girls, marked by physical suffering, served "as a means of entry into superior ritual and social status" (Turner 1968:16). Neo-phytes of both sexes were initiated individually, with the rites emphasizing the value of endurance of hardship.

For boys, the rite of passage was conducted "in informal ways," as they were gradually "toughened to the demands of the adult life" (Weiss 1974:393), as seen in Daniel Bernales Qui-llatupa's *Kamenantsi* (Traditional Advice), recorded in 2009, and Gregorio Santos Pérez's *Tsika okantya ashimaapakotantyari* (How to Be a Good Fisherman), recorded in 2010. Both texts are based on the narrators' personal experiences and were recorded and transcribed by the narrators themselves in their home resi-dences.

During the essentially unstructured transition period, boys were neither separated from their kinfolk nor subjected to the numerous restrictions and prohibitions imposed on a pubescent girl. A boy's new social status as a mature community member was achieved through a prolonged period of training in hunting and fishing skills under the supervision of the boy's father and other male relatives. A neophyte had to undergo a cleansing ritual of vomiting, when he was forced to drink vomit-inducing herb concoctions (e.g., Rojas Zolezzi 1994:114–15), and dieting (the boy was prohibited from eating before hunting or fishing expeditions). As a general rule, the body-cleansing ritual is strictly practiced by any expert in Upper Perené society, be it a shaman, a healer, a hunter, or a fisherman, since it is believed that food abstinence, or at least dieting restrictions, is helpful in accumulating the spiritual energy needed to be finely attuned to the wills of spiritual beings in the cosmic network.

Apart from dieting, according to both narrators, at the end of a particularly successful outing (typically, after the voice change has occurred), the boy was fed pieces of *tsikana* (chili pepper; *Capsicum* sp.). The peppers were cut into tiny strips and placed on the inside of the boy's right forearm, making them difficult to pick up with the mouth. Other consultants report the pepper being rubbed into small pieces of the fish caught by the neophyte. The rule was to keep the excruciatingly hot pepper (or the peppered meat) in the open mouth as long as saliva runs down the chin, without swallowing the food or showing any sign of physical pain.

The incidence of blood running from the boy's nose was a putative sign of the neophyte's physical transformation. Gregorio Santos Pérez reports that when a teenage boy would have a nosebleed, adults would jokingly comment, *antaritaki* antarit-ak-i [big.MASC-EP-PERV-REAL] (he had his menses).

The girl's first menstrual blood was described by the same clause-like verb, inflected for nonmasculine gender, *antarotaki* antaro-t-ak-i [big.NMASC-EP-PERV-REAL] (she had her menses). The girls' puberty ceremony is detailed by Daniel Ber-

nales Quillatupa in *Arika antarote kooya* (When a Girl Had Her
First Menses), on the basis of his memories of his sister's initiation rite. The narrator recorded and transcribed the text himself,
in 2010, in his residence in La Merced. The girls' puberty rite was
a rule-governed affair with regard to its time span (it begins at
the onset of a girl's puberty and ends in three months — although
the number of months varies, according to other narrators) and
behavior code (the secluded girl spends days spinning cotton
and has to show complete obedience to her female caretakers).
The ritual's objective was to prepare the girl for marriage (Turner
1967:7), that is, "to fatten the girl and to force her to learn to
work and not to be lazy, to learn to spin, and to learn to obey
her husband" (Weiss 1974:393). Nonetheless, being confirmed as
a newly acknowledged adult member of a society didn't mean an
immediate entry into a union with a man and the formation of a
family unit. Bodley comments on the period of "early marriage
instability" among Campas, that is, before settling down, it was
common for young people to experience consecutive hookups
with various partners (1970:69).

The initiated girl has to undergo "certain ordeals" associated
with the transitional state of her social existence before she
was "reborn" into a new life as a mature woman (Eliade [1959]
1987:185,192). The girl's hair was cut (some narrators insist that
this was done at the beginning of the seclusion period, some
say that it happened at the end) to signal the onset of the transitional period. Language speakers consider hair cutting to be a
prophylactic measure taken to avoid the girl's early death.[7]

In addition, to prevent premature aging and contamination
by evil spiritual beings, the girl's head and face were to be covered
at all times when she would leave the hut to attend to her natural needs, and she had to avoid seeing males, wasps (which were

known to be demonic), and certain kinds of demonic birds. She stayed all day in the darkness of the menarche hut, with no sunlight. Her diet was limited to sweet manioc; other foods were prohibited. When she would emerge at the end of the seclusion period, her kinfolk would paint her with the black juice of huito (*Genipa americana*) as a form of disguise, to avoid her being recognized by evil spirits who might have known her in the past.[8]

Ritual songs prominently contributed to the puberty ceremony. Victorina Rosas de Castro and Elena Nestor de Capurro mentioned to me the significance of the sacred songs performed by the women on the day of the girl's emergence from the menarche hut. I wasn't able to record these songs, however, since Victorina contends that the songs are secret and, once captured on film, the mystic power attributed to them would be greatly diminished, thus causing harm to the souls of the previously initiated girls. Among the Yanesha neighbors, the ritual women's songs are especially critical in the molding of the pubescent girl's spirit and in her gaining of spiritual strength for her future life (Daignealt 2009).

Marriage and burial rituals were conducted in a most efficient manner and without much ado, according to the narrators. Gregorio Santos Perez's *Aavakantsi* (Taking a Spouse) gives the specifics of two types of marital arrangements. One is a forced marriage, when the girl was simply given to a man without her consent; another concerns a girl-initiated arrangement, when she would communicate to a visiting male that she was interested in becoming his marital partner. The girl's proposition was signaled by approaching the male from behind and touching him with a freshly roasted piece of manioc root. The consenting male was expected to show his readiness for a marital union by demonstrating his hunting prowess. After a great deal of game was procured by the suitor and delivered to the bride's family, the union was sealed at a festive party. At the party, a headman could give his word of wisdom to the couple. The text *Aavakantsi* was recorded and transcribed by the narrator in 2010, in his home residence in Pampa Silva (Villa Perené).

In the numerous marriage stories told by female language consultants, kinship relations did not seem to matter, in that there was no preoccupation with marrying someone from the rigidly delineated pool of cross-cousins, that is, the offspring of the parents' siblings. The only story of a marriage between cross-cousins was that of the maternal uncle of Bertha Rodríguez de Caleb, Santos, who had married Bertha's father's sister, Susana, in the early twentieth century, before Bertha was born. Some of the recorded stories indicate that within families, prohibitions against marrying close kin were quite strict. For example, in my exchanges with Carmen Pachiri Quinchori, she cited her grandmother's warnings not to fall for closely related male kin but to look for a marital partner far away from the native community.

The burial rite was marked by the same simplicity and pragmatism (Weiss 1975:432–33). Old-generation Upper Perené language speakers remember burials in a shallow grave inside the dead person's house, in which case the settlement was abandoned. The Delia Rosas Rodríguez text *Kamaki aparoni atziri* (When a Person Died) describes the aftermath of the home burial. The text is a narrator's rendition of the chief's speech made on the occasion of a female's death from an unknown disease. The narrator was a member of the grieving native community of Miraflores in 1970s and witnessed the burial and the relocation. The corpse, called *kaminkari* kam-ink-a-ri [die-NMZ-REAL-REL], was wrapped in a mat, trussed up, and laid in the ground face down, to make sure that its spirit will get disoriented if it decides to get out. The recording was made in 2010, at the narrator's home in Bajo Marankiari.

Other narrators' commentary referred to river burials, in which the corpse was dumped into the river or tied to a raft or canoe, which was then let go. Or the body was burned in a big fire on a riverbank, if its spirit was suspected to be demonic (Mihas 2011:117–18). Currently corpses are buried in wood coffins above the ground, with a thick layer of cement placed on the grave to insulate the grave site from the elements and prowling animals. The burial site, called *ikitaitatzirinta* i-kit-ai-t-atz-i-ri=nta [3MASC.A-bury-IMP-PROG-REAL-3MASC.O=ADV] (where they bury them) is typically located not far from the community, within walking distance.

Affliction rites are perhaps the most deeply entrenched in the ritual behavior of Upper Perené Arawaks. The term "affliction rites" refers to those rituals that seek to neutralize the harm done by dead people's spirits and that are "devised to propitiate and to get rid of the spirit that is thought to be causing the trouble" (Turner 1967:9). Among Upper Perené Ashaninka, the cultural notion of "trouble" refers to illness and death, understood to be caused by "being caught in the sight of the other" who is "feeding" on the victim's body, causing the corporeal "disintegration" or "disembodiment" of the afflicted person (Lenaerts 2006c:14).

The ontology of affliction can be fully grasped only in the context of the indigenous perspectivist theory of interrelational networks and bodily shifting, in which people see themselves as people and animals as prey, while animals, plants, divinities, dead people, and evil spirits see people as prey (Viveiros de Castro 1998). Human bodies' boundaries are believed to be extremely vulnerable, unstable, and fragile. While having a dream or being absentminded and alone in the forest or recounting the tension-filled moments of life crises, a human being can be easily caught in the crosshairs of a stronger-willed spiritual predator and shift to the predator's perspective, thus losing his or her human body (Vilaça 2005; Lenaerts 2006c).

Based on the native ontogenetic theory of disease, the generic term is *(y)aanakina* (I have been taken), with the verb root *aa* (take, seize) indicating the violent onset of the aggressor-caused disease. To be contaminated with bad air, or *mal aire* in Spanish, is expressed by the verb *amontsajenkavaitzi* (one is choking from bad air). The verbs *montsa* (encounter, cross, intersect) and *ant* (make, do) in the affliction context have a sense of "damage," "do harm," for example, *yantatziri shiretsi* (the harm is done to the soul), meaning a person is choking from contamination by bad air. When the sickness is explicitly attributed to sorcery, the verb *matsik* (bewitch, cast a spell) is used. The generic verb *mantsiy* (be sick) is used to characterize an infirmity in all contexts.

Among Upper Perené Ashaninkas, the illness-causing predators involve a legion of spiritual beings, ranging from all sorts of human and nonhuman *kamari* (demons) to *shiretsi* (dead people's spirits). Affliction rituals in the Upper Perené context refer to herbal and shamanistic interventions, with the shamanic cure being especially effective. In addition, individually employed prophylactic methods, or "body nurturing" (Lenaerts 2006c:16), are believed to fortify the body against a potential predatory attack. These include a combination of ritual blowing, spitting, abstinence, vomiting, use of ritual formulas, and application of magic herbs.

To be successful, the healing ritual has to be performed by a thoroughly trained expert. The Daniel Bernales Quillatupa text *Ikantakota sheripiari pairani* (About Shamans Who Existed in the Past) provides specifics of the shaman training in the Upper

Perené area, on the basis of an account by Daniel's deceased grandfather Kasanto, who had a brief exposure to the shaman career at a young age and practiced as a shaman and healer. The text was recorded and transcribed by the narrator in 2012, in his home residence in La Merced. As the text shows, in the past the neophyte was to undergo a long period of apprenticeship under the guidance of an old shaman and to lead the life of an ascetic.

The Daniel Bernales Quillatupa text emphasizes the link between the shaman's physical handling of the sick patient's material body and his drug-induced visits and negotiations with *nijaaveri* nijaa-veri [water-NMZ], the master of the river and aquatic life who is identified as the predator in possession of the sick patient's body. The patient's corporeal infirmity is connected to the wills of two predatory spiritual beings, those of a rogue shaman and of the master of the river. As the text makes clear, there were corrupt Upper Perené shamans who could offer their fellow man's soul to a malevolent *nijaaveri* as an act of revenge.

Shamans were credited with the power of self-transformation, with the most widely practiced disguise being that of a jaguar, the ultimate jungle predator, capable of confronting any antagonistic entity. The shaman's bodily transformations were achieved in drug-induced trances. The drugs *sheri* (tobacco leaves; *Nicotiana tabacum*) or *pochari* (tobacco syrup) and *kamarampi* (ayahuasca; *Banisteriopsis caapi*) were taken either separately or in combination by Upper Perené shamans (see Lenaerts 2006b, 2006c; Weiss 1973:43). Weiss notes that tobacco, when taken in large doses, intoxicates the shaman and enables him to see and communicate with the spirits, while ayahuasca, a hallucinogenic drug, "puts him directly in communication with the spiritual world" during his soul flights (1973:43). The Daniel Bernales Quillatupa text *Ikantakota sheripiari pairani* (About Shamans Who Existed in the Past) depicts the neophyte's major challenge of gradually gaining tolerance to ingested tobacco and other drugs, while the narrative *Sheripiari Julio Quintsori* (Shaman Julio Quintsori), by Frida Thomas Huamán, describes the process of tobacco preparation and treatment. The shaman's wife was responsible for making the tobacco syrup for Frida Thomas Huamán's grandfather, according to the narrator. The text was recorded in 2012, in the narrator's home in Pumpuriani.

Ritual singing was an essential component of the affliction rite. In a trance, shamans performed songs, understood to be the visiting spirits' songs, which have "an eerie, distant quality of voice" (Weiss 1973:44). A song praising the power of tobacco and ayahuasca called *Impantsakoteri isherini* (He Will Sing about His Tobacco), by Paulina García Ñate, was recorded in 2011 in the singer's residence in Bajo Marankiari. The singer's grandfather was a shaman who used to sing this song while treating his patients. The singer points out that an intoxicated shaman is transformed into an equal of the Master of jaguars, allowing him to be the jaguar's spouse. The female tobacco spirit is also thought of as the shaman's spouse (Elick 1969:221; Rojas Zolezzi 1994:238).

The collective nature of a shamanistic ritual intervention is underscored by Lévi-Strauss, who identified three parties involved in the "shamanistic complex": the shaman, the patient, and "the public who also participate in the cure, experiencing the enthusiasm and an intellectual and emotional satisfaction which produce collective support" (1963:179).

The observers' involvement in the ritual act of psychosomatic therapy is also stressed in Weiss's (1973) analysis of the Ashaninka shamanistic rituals. Weiss observes that "the shaman not only engages in individual curing, but also in a particular form of group ceremony or ritual which we recognize as a shamanistic performance or séance . . . . [His] behavior combines frenzy and

trance, while the assembled laymen remain passive observers"
(1973:42). The social power exercised by the shaman during the
collective ritual ceremonies is illustrated in three selected texts
that describe a curative ritual intervention ending with the
identification of a *matsi* (sorcerer) as the aggressor. The punishment of the discovered *matsi* is detailed in *Yantavairi sheripiari*
(Shaman's Work), by Moises Santos Rojas, *Sheripiari* (Shaman),
by Ines Pérez de Santos, and *Okantakota matsitantsi* (About
Witchcraft,) by Ruth Quillatupa Lopez, with Daniel Bernales
Quillatupa. The texts were recorded in Bajo Marankiari, at the
narrators' residences, in 2012.

Conducted by the shaman and other headmen, the intervention consisted of the identification of a *matsi*, encoded by
the verb root *ita* (suspect) combined with the noun incorporate
matsi (witch), *ita-matsi* [suspect-witch] (identify as a witch). The
next stages were questioning and beating, described by the verbs
sampi (ask questions) and *posa* (beat brutally). Then the *matsi*'s
confession followed (*tsave* [confess, divulge]), and the *matsi* was
made to dig out the offensive items from the ground (*kiy* [dig]).
The intervention concluded either with the killing of the *matsi*
or, if she was allowed to live, with the exorcism of a *kamari*
(demon), who is regarded to be the *matsi*'s demonic teacher.

As shown in the selected texts, the shaman's ritual performance begins with the diagnosis: spitting tobacco mass on the
ailing part of the patient's body, sucking the mass with the
mouth, and then spewing a mouthful of the collected substance
into his hand. After the items are examined and the diagnosis is
made, the shaman "sees" in a vision who is responsible, and this
person will be brought in for questioning. The accused (usually
a young girl or a single or widowed woman) is asked about her
instructor, and if she denies the charges, she is beaten until she
confesses to the crime. Eventually the accused will name some-

body as her human teacher (although nonhuman teachers are reported to be invoked too), and that person will be taken and killed without being questioned, according to the testimony of Ruth Quillatupa Lopez in *Okantakota matsitantsi* (About Witchcraft). The methods of the *matsi* execution, as the narrator states, were either by hanging, drowning in the river, beating to death, burning in a big fire, or by immolation with kerosene. For the specifics of child sorcery among Ashéninka and Ashaninka, see Anderson (2000:171–80), Santos-Granero (2002b, 2004b), and Weiss (1975:292–94).

Digging out the sorcerer's charms was the next step in the intervention. The sorcerer has to show where the evil charms are buried and remove them from the ground. The buried refuse is "something belonging to or used intimately by the victim" (Elick 1969:213). From the native perspective, only after all disease-causing items are dug out does the afflicted person recover. If the sick person gets better, the accused is spared and is forced to undergo a cleansing procedure, for example, she is bathed in chili peppers or fed the poisonous milky sap of the *cavana* tree (Sandbox tree; *Hura crepitans*), as described in the text *Tsika okanta noñaakoventziri matsipaye* (How I Witnessed Events Involving Witches), by Bertha Rodríguez de Caleb (part 1). The narrator's sister-in-law, along with the other accused, was bathed with hot peppers; to endure the severe skin burn, the accused were laid in the shallow waters of the river for an entire day. Then the local Adventist Church leaders exorcized *kamari* from the suspected *matsi* by making them sing praise to God for a week without sleep.

After the diagnosis was made, shamans also treated the patient with herbs, addressing the disease's symptoms. The text *Sheripiari* (Shaman) by Ines Pérez de Santos spells out how the narrator's mother was cured by the local shaman Eusebio's herbs, although shamans are generally not good botanists, as Lenaerts (2006c:9–10) observes, and herbal medicine is not their forte.

In contrast, Upper Perené healers and older layfolks have an extensive knowledge of medicinal herbs, which Lenaerts calls "really outstanding" (2006c:6). They employ a variety of healing techniques, such as steam baths, "baths of leaves, plant compresses, plant juices used as eye drops" (Lenaerts 2006c:2). Healers undergo a period of training and apprenticeship before they learn to make objects fall out of the patient's body during steam-bathing (Luziatelli et al. 2010). Typically, training of Upper Perené healers is conducted in Puerto Bermúdez, located on the Pichis River. Upper Perené healers earn their living primarily as steam bath specialists charging for the treatment in the range of fifteen to fifty Peruvian soles.

During the steam bath, vapor is produced by stones that have been heated in the fire and placed into a pot that contains a thick bunch of herbs barely covered with water. The patient stands next to the steamy pot wearing a robe that prevents the rising vapor from escaping. The verb roots *chonk* and *shipok* (steam with herbs or heal with vapor) refer respectively to the process. The examination of the pot concludes the therapy: the foreign objects found in the pot with the herbs are believed to have fallen out from the body during the treatment, and their extraction is understood to begin the recovery. The body is considered to be purified after the disease-causing items are purged from it. The texts *Ochonkiri Abdias* (She Steam-Bathed Abdias) by María Virginia Lopez, Abdias Caleb Quinchori, Bertha Rodríguez de Caleb, and Victorina Rosas de Castro, recorded in 2010 in Bajo Marankiari, and *Antavairi aavintantzinkaro* (Healer's work), by Luzmila Machari Quinchori, recorded in 2012 in Pumpuriani, disclose the specifics of the native perspective on ritual cleansing during a steam bath treatment.

In both shamanistic and herbal ritual interventions, restoration of psychosomatic health is achieved through the purification of the afflicted body, namely through "the symbolic removal of the disturbing agent from the patient's body" (Elick 1969:215). In shamanistic ritual interventions, however, the sociopsychological aspect of purification comes to the fore, when the malevolent spiritual entity is identified and neutralized. As a result, the wrong is redressed and social order is reinstated.

Ritual behavior of Peruvian Arawaks is often discounted as "impoverished," and the group is described as having "hardly any ritual worthy of the name" (Weiss 1975:513). While it is certainly true that Ashéninka Perené indeed lack "grandiose community rituals" and "showy forms of prayer" (Varese 2002:36), the documentary corpus and my own observations suggest that the picture is much more complex and nuanced, providing evidence of a deeply entrenched, coherent, and sophisticated system of ritual behavior.

THIRTY-FIVE

Ampinateri Pava

(What We Will Offer to Pava)

Clelia Mishari, with Gregorio Santos Pérez

[1]–Iroñaaka arika impankite parentzi, kaniri, aririka, tekirata ayarota, iyotakiro tsika okaratzi avantyarori. [2]Intavakiaro atsokavakiro, poñaashitaka atsinkaki, antaki piarentsi, poña ampiantaki pachakaki ovakerari, poña avakotakiro, okantzi, ampasonkiteri pava, opajairori.

[3]–Ampinateri?

[4]–Je, ikantziri ampinateri, eero yaapitsatajairo avari ayaniri, avarentzite, eero yaapitsatajairo, oshekitantyari avankiri. [5]Eerorika iroñaaka aakiro, atsokakiro, avakiaro, eerokia otzimanaji, ikisaka ashitarori irirori. [6]Tekatsi apiri, opakairora pava, akantziri iritaki opakairori Apinka, iroñaaka pava Apinka. [7]Maatsirika avarentzite, ontzimatye intavakiari.

[8]Aisatzi ikimitziro choripaye. [9]Aparojatzini nojatatzi sharakamashiki, ari noñaakirori aisatzi chori, yaakirika imosakite, ipinatziri ashitarori mosaki. [10]Te apaniroini arokaite ampasonkiteri, irirorite itsokiro imosakite yamaniri ivavani. [11]Intsitavakiari yaavakiniri akimitaka asheninkatzi. [12]Noñiiri pashinipaye acharinipaye, intarori kaniri, parentzi intarori oshitovanaki, eero avitaro. [13]Iroñaaka apavakirita akantzirikia ashitarori, arika aaji iroñaakakia, ovakera ayarokia. [14]Noñiiri pashinipaye iroñaakakia, arika yaaki kanirikia, intavakiaro inkotsitakiro aparoni kovitzi, ovakirari kovitzi. [15]Akantziri

14. A prayer is offered to the master of *kaniri* (sweet manioc).
By Daniel Bernales Quillatupa (Aroshi).

pairani antzi ayovite kipatsinaki, te ayotero kovitzika ashiro-
naki, antziri arori ashi sampovatsa, sampovatsa onatzi.

¹⁶Ari ikantaitzi pairani, nonirotsori irojatzi otzimi iroñaaka
oyovite paisato, nonirotsori Sabina okotsitantaro. ¹⁷Okantziri
okotsitaki iroñaaka, omposataki, oyetaki, ivakoitakiniri, "Afuu,
Pava, arika iroñaaka oshekitantyari, eero paapitsatanaro iroñaaka novankiri, nonintziri iroñaaka osarentsikika, aviroka
intavakiarori ashitanari." ¹⁸Ivaitakinirija.

¹⁹Iroñaakakia pashiniki kitaiteri aajate pashini kaniri iroñaakakia, "Pivajeetya," akantziri, "asheninkatzi maaroni, avajeetya." ²⁰Ari akantari asheninkatzika, ari ikantajeetziri. ²¹Okimita
osheeteji nokinkitsatakavaitziri notomi aajatzita, "Ari akantari
pairani irojatzi nokimiri aapini." ²²Iroñaakaja otzimanaji avarentzite, achekachekatatzi, apimantatziro, te ankante iroñaaka,

"Pava, jiroka, pinatachari pipakinaro aviroka." [23]Iroñaaka paitari patsaini aroka intavakiaroni avavakiaro.

[24]Pairanikia te onkantya, intakarori te ari inkantya, tekatsi iyote, te iyote isankinate, kantzimaintacha ishiritari pava. [25]Te ayiro iroñaaka, te ashiritajiari pava. [26]Pairanikia nokantziri noñiiri apayeni irirori, ikantzi, "Apaatara, kooya, irorave intavakiarita ashitajairi apavakirita irorave ipajairo. [27]Iroñaaka onintantayetari pankirintsipaye, tera onintashitya, maatsi nintakarori, iroñaaka apavakirita."

[28]Otsokakiro, ari okantapinta ina. [29]Ikantziro, "Marakarita, pivitsiki piarentsi, irotaki pitsokiro iroñaaka evankaro kaniri, iroñaaka pintavakiaro pivitsiki piarentsi. [30]Ontzimatye ankimisanteri, airo apiyatsavaita. [31]Terika ari yaapitsatajairo ashitarori, airorika apiri, airo onintanaji kameetsaini pankirentsi. [32]Airorika onintanaji kaniri, tekatsi avajia, arika yaapitsatajairo ashitarori opajairori. [33]Ankimisantatye."

[34]Atsokaitziro intarori kaniri evankaro, poña pinchopitaki, poñaashitakia pimpiantakiniri pachakaki ovakirari, ovakotainirija. [35]Okantziri ashitarori, "Apa, jiroka iroka pinatachari, pipanaro." [36]Arive, ari ivakotakiro, ari ivakoitero. [37]Poña impiyapajie pashiniki kitaiteri ovakera iroñaakakia, "Tsamera ayarokia." [38]Ari ovakira itsokakiro ajeete avajeetya maaroiteni. [39]Ari ikantziro pairani. [40]Iroñaaka tekatsi ashiritajia, iroñaakakia te añaavitya, iñaanavaitaki. [41]Te, pairani nokantziri paisato, nokantziri, aapini paisatzipaye ishiritari pava, iñiiri pava. [42]Aroka te añaajiri pava.

[1]–When we planted plantains, manioc, we didn't eat them right away, there was time for us to eat them. [2]First, we will gather manioc, then we will pound it, will make manioc beer, then we will pour the mass into new gourds, then we will place it aside, they say, we will thank Pava, the one who gave it to us.

³–You will pay him?

⁴–Yes, they say, we will pay him so that he will not take away from us what we eat, our manioc, our plantains, he won't take it away from us, so that our harvest is bountiful. ⁵If we harvest it [manioc], if we pull it out and eat it, nothing will bear, [because] its master has been angry. ⁶We didn't give him, when he has given us, we say, it is Apinka who gives us [food], god Apinka. ⁷If we have our plantains, we have to [give some to him] first.

⁸Andean natives do the same. ⁹Once I went to the highlands and saw them, when they were harvesting their potatoes, and they made an offering to the potato plant's master. ¹⁰It is not just us who thank him, they too pull out their potatoes and worship their god. ¹¹Andean natives pull them out from the soil, like our fellow men. ¹²I saw others, our elders who would plant manioc, plantains, they planted, it grows, and we wouldn't eat it. ¹³We will give it, they say, to the master, when we harvest it; afterward we will eat it. ¹⁴I saw others, when we harvest manioc, we will first cook it in a clay pot, a new clay pot. ¹⁵We say, long ago we made pots of clay, we didn't know metal pots, we made them of our clay, it was clay.

¹⁶It was said in the past, my aunt Sabina had her ancient pot of clay in which my aunt cooked. ¹⁷She said, she boiled [manioc], it would be ready to eat, she would serve it, and they would put it aside for him, "*Afuu* (be it), Pava, when it [the offering] is bountiful, you will not take away from me my harvest that I grow this year, you will be the first to eat it." ¹⁸They place it [the offering] aside for him.

¹⁹Some other day, when we harvest manioc, we say, "Eat, all of you, all our fellow men, we are going to eat." ²⁰They were this way, our fellow men, they all said it. ²¹Yesterday I talked to my son, "This is the way we were in the past, I heard it from my late grandfather." ²²Now, when our plantains bear fruit, we cut and

cut them and sell them, we won't say, "Pava, here it is, I offer [pay] you what you gave me." ²³Now, whatever [we harvest]— that we will begin to eat.

²⁴In the past, it wasn't this way, the founders weren't this way, they didn't know anything, they didn't know how to write, but they believed in Pava. ²⁵We didn't pick it up [faith from them], we don't believe in Pava. ²⁶In the past, I am saying, I saw my late father, he would say, "Wait, woman, first, we should give to our master what he gives us. ²⁷He makes our plants grow, and they did not grow much, but there is one who makes them grow; now we will give it to him."

²⁸She will pull out manioc—this was what my mother always did. ²⁹He would say to her, "Margarita, prepare manioc beer, you will gather unripe manioc and begin making manioc beer. ³⁰We have to pay attention to him, we shouldn't disobey. ³¹If we do, the master will take it away from us; when we don't give him [an offering], he will not make our plants grow. ³²When manioc does not grow, there is nothing for us to eat, when its master takes it away from us, the one who gives it to us. ³³We should pay attention."

³⁴We will pull out unripe manioc first, then you will pound it into a mass, then you will pour it into new gourds, and they will be put aside [for the divinity]. ³⁵She would say to the [plant's] master, "Father, here it is, the offering that you gave me." ³⁶Very well, it will be placed aside, and they will eat it at some point. ³⁷Then they will come back the next day, and only then [will they say], "Let's eat it." ³⁸Only then will they harvest manioc and everybody will eat. ³⁹This is what they did long ago. ⁴⁰Now no one believes in the master, we don't know him, [although] they know how to read. ⁴¹No, in the past, I am saying, the ancestors, I am saying, the deceased grandfathers, the ancestors believed in Pava, they knew Pava. ⁴²We don't know Pava.

THIRTY-SIX

Kamenantsi

(Traditional Advice)

Daniel Bernales Quillatupa

1. ASHI SHIMPIRINTSI

[1]Okantzi kamenantsi, aririka pintsonkakero pante pishimperi, paanakero nijaaki. [2]Tsikarika osoronkata, ari pantsinakakotakerori. [3]Iroñaaka itetakiarika jetari, shiva, kepavori, mereto, aririka paajero, airo paminero ovantekira. [4]Tzimatsirika tetainchari, intaani paakero iroñaaka, paanakero oparaiki. [5]Ari pisokerori maaroni tetainchari. [6]Aririka paminakero opante pishimperi, ari opashiventanakia. [7]Airo itetaja maaroni saikatsiri nijaaki. [8]Aririka amonkaratakero maaroni kamenantsika, airo apiyashita aririka ajate nijaaki aanakero ashimperi. [9]Ari okaratzi.

2. IROPEROTANTYARI AKOVINTSATE

[10]Okantzi kamenantsi, aririka pijate pankoshintsiki, pikintakirika aparoni tsimeri, shintsipayeni paanakeri, pamine ovaato kanai. [11]Pantakotapakeri, aririka ishitovanaki kanaiki, ari pivanakeri oponkitziki inchatoka. [12]Pimpiyapitsatajeri, iyarita kanaiki, intasonkaventemita, ikimitara ivari pitsimerite. [13]Ari pikantyari, apaata pivajiari, osheki tsimeri pinkintakeri.

[14]Omaperotatya kamenantsi. [15]Ari ikantakakinarori pairani apa, irotaki nokovintsatantari. [16]Ikantzi pairani apa, aririka

pinkintake aparoni tsimeri, aparoni poshiniri, airo pivari,
ikantai apa. [17]Paitanikia? [18]Itasonkanakaikari. [19]Ontzimatye
antsitavakia avantyariri. [20]Ontzimatye charini intsikanatai
okantyakia onkatsitantyari achakopite, aririka akintaje pashini
tsimeri. [21]Irotaki kaari ivakantairi charini, aririka intanakiaro
akintavaite. [22]Ari okaratzi.

3. OSHEKITANTYARI OVATSA KANIRI

[23]Okantzi kamenantsi, aririka pantake pivani, piviriakerika
kaniyatzi, pookanakero ovaantsiki, pimpiyotanakero, itsinte-
rota impookero. [24]Okantyakia okimitara itsine impookero,
oshekiteta ovatsa piyaniri. [25]Pivintamanairorika, airo pikain-
tziro pitavaato, okisotonkitanakikari, apaata kaniri okimitara
otonki pitavaato, okimitara pitonki. [26]Aririka amonkaratakero
maaroni kamenantsika, aririka omonkaratapakia antsokan-
tyarori, ari añaakero osheki ovatsa kaniri. [27]Ari okaratzi.

1. FISHING WITH A FISH TRAP

[1]The advice says, when you finish making your fish trap, take it
to the river. [2]In any shallow inlet of the river, this is where you'll
place your fish trap. [3]When the fish trap is filled with *carachama*,
anchoveta, *kepavori* [unidentified], and *palometa*, when you re-
trieve them, don't look at the opening of the fish trap. [4]If there is
fish inside the fish trap, take it to the shore. [5]This is where you'll
empty the contents of the trap. [6]If you look at the opening of
the fish trap, it will embarrass [you]. [7]There won't be more fish in
the trap [when it's placed] in the river. [8]If we follow this advice,
we won't return empty-handed when we go to the river and take
along our fish trap. [9]This is all.

2. HOW TO BE A GOOD HUNTER

[10]The advice says, when you go to your hunting blind and kill a bird, take it immediately to the tangarana tree. [11]Hit the tree; when ants come out, leave the bird on the ground by the trunk. [12]Go away immediately, they should eat the bird, itt will magically blow on you, when they eat your bird. [13]You'll be [like] them, later you'll eat many birds that you'll kill.

[14]This advice is true. [15]This is what my father made me do, that's why I am a hunter. [16]Our fathers told us long ago, "When you kill your first bird, [or] something tasty, don't eat it," our fathers told us. [17]Why? [18]So that it magically blows on you. [19]It is necessary for us to abstain from eating. [20]Our grandfather must feed us hot pepper in order for our arrows to be fatal when we shoot another bird. [21]That's why our grandfather won't make us eat game when we begin hunting birds. [22]This is it.

3. HOW TO GROW A LOT OF MANIOC

[23]The advice says, when you work on your land, if you cut manioc into pieces, leave them on your land, pile them up so that stars urinate on them [dew will appear]. [24]It will be similar to the urine of stars [dew]: there will be a lot of manioc. [25]When you plant manioc the next day, don't scratch your shinbone, otherwise the manioc will be hard later, like the bone of your shinbone, like your bone. [26]When we follow this advice, when we harvest manioc, we'll see a big quantity of manioc. [27]This is all.

THIRTY-SEVEN

Tsika okantya ashimaapakotantyari

(How to Be a Good Fisherman)

Gregorio Santos Pérez

[1]Pairani yamitari ashaninkaitepaye, arika inintzi iyotero ishimaatya, yaaki aparoni ivinki, ikantaitziri mamorivinki. [2]Inkamintantaki akachaarontsi, ompoña nairotsa, yaaki oishi inchashi, yamponatakotakiro akachaarontsira. [3]Ompoña intashitakotakiro. [4]Arika iñaakiro oitonkanakia, yakishirira, yaakomaintyaro ivakiro jeñokini aparoni kitaiteri. [5]Ompoñaashitakia yaakiro nairotsara, intzimpatakiro. [6]Poñaashitaka intzirimaintyaro ivinki yaponatakotantakarori yakachaaro. [7]Poñaashitaka yaanakiro parinikinta, yantsinakakoterori.

[8]Iroñaakakia yaaki kaniri, imposakiro, arika oshipitanaki. [9]Ivamaintyaro yakachaarokira, yookamaintyaro niyankiakira. [10]Airo yaminavaitzi tsika janta irojatzita inkimantakiari yantsiki mamorinta. [11]Arika yantsikaki intzimpatakiro yakachaaro, inkimavakiri, intsikotakia intzimpatakomaintyari irojatzita ivaatantakiari. [12]Iroñaakakia, airo imanintanairitsi, ari onkantatyeya yaapinte mamori. [13]Iro kantzimaintacha airorika ivaatziri, intsampiriashikiaririka. [14]Ari onkantapintatyeya intsampiriapinteri.

[15]Aisatzi arika yankachaataki, airo ivitari, intaani impaitakiri imorimashi. [16]Kapicheeni ivaitakiniri yakojanoriki, intsirinkaitakiniri tsikana. [17]Arika onkatsikanakiri, airo ikantatsi, *shi shi*. [18]Intaani intsariya irojatzi ontsonkatapajia itsari. [19]Ovakirakia

ivia iniyakiri. ²⁰Ari okaratzi akimakovintziri tsika ikantaitziri atziripaye inkovintsatantyari pairani. ²¹Iroñaakamaja iro apiakotajaro.

¹In the past, my fellow men had a custom, when they wanted to fish, they would take magic plants called "the plant of *sábalo*." ²A fisherman will buy a fishing rod, then a nylon cord, take the *ivenki* plant's leaves and rub with them the fishing rod. ³Then he will put the leaves in the fire. ⁴When he sees that the leaves are burning, when they are charred, he will take them out and put them aside for one day. ⁵Then he takes the nylon cord and unwinds it. ⁶Then he will rub the [charred leaves of the] *ivenki* plant onto the nylon cord. ⁷Then he takes the *ivenki* leaves to the river and places them in shallow water, anchored by a stone.

⁸Then he takes [a piece of] manioc and pounds it until it turns into a mushy mass. ⁹He will put it on the hook and throw it into the depth of the river. ¹⁰He shouldn't look over there until the moment he feels that *sábalo* bit the bait. ¹¹When it bites, then the fisherman pulls the nylon cord, he will sense that the fish is on the hook, and he will pull it until it gets out of the water. ¹²Now they [other males] will never ridicule him, he will always catch *sábalo*. ¹³When the fish is out of the water, he will yank the hook out. ¹⁴It will always be this way that he will tear it off.

¹⁵Also, when he catches fish [later], he won't eat it, although he will be given the best part. ¹⁶They will put little pieces of fish on his right arm and rub hot pepper in this meat. ¹⁷When the fisherman is in pain, he shouldn't do *shi shi* (making grimaces caused by pain). ¹⁸He has to keep holding the meat in his mouth until the saliva stops coming out of his mouth. ¹⁹Then he will eat and swallow the meat. ²⁰This is all, as we heard about what people did to be good fishermen. ²¹Now we have lost this custom.

THIRTY-EIGHT

Yamaniri pava impereta
(They Were Worshipping the Stone Divinity)

Delia Rosas Rodríguez

[1]Ikantzi pairani ashaninka ijatzi yamaniri ivavani.

[2]Pava imperita, aviroka kameetsari, pamitakotena. [3]Koñaatakemi irojatzita, pikantana avisavetaka osarentsipaye, añaatsimi pikantaitatya. [4]Naakaite nopokajeetzi, notyerovashitami, nokovakotzimi aviroka, itzimi kotariachari kasankatatsiri. [5]Pamenero avaamarite omoreki, avakiro piitziki akovakotantyamiri. [6]Airo pipiakojeetana, pamenena onkantaitatyeni. [7]Airo amantsiyatanta, pivavisakoyeteri amantsiyarite. [8]Pimperi ishintsinka onkantya ivayeritantyari, paamakoventyari ikaratzi kisanentairi. [9]Pintasonkaventai anampitsiteki, avaaniki, avankiripaye, onkantya oshookantyari, onkantya oshekitantyari avankiri, airo atashanentanta aajatzi evankaripaye. [10]Pintasonkaventeri inkantya ijevatantyariri antarikonapaye, airo ivantaitari arika ijate imanatya, impiyajeeta pankotsiki.

[11]Irotaki ivavani pairani, ari ikantaitzi yamaniri imperita.

[1]They say, long ago our fellow men would go to the forest and worship their god.

²Stone divinity, you are good, help us. ³You've existed since
your appearance up to now, you've existed many years, and
you live forever. ⁴We all came and are kneeling in front of
you, we are asking you for help, and we have sweet-scented
wood planks. ⁵Look, our fire is burning; we placed it at your
feet to ask you for help. ⁶Don't leave us. ⁷Look after us always
so that we won't get sick, and cure our sick. ⁸Give them their
strength to fight at war, and protect them from all enemies.
⁹Bless our villages, our land, our plants, so that they are bountiful, so that our harvests are bountiful and our youths don't
starve from hunger. ¹⁰Bless those, so that male adults could
lead others and they don't get killed when they go to war, but
all will return home.

¹¹This was their god long ago, so this was said, [when] they worshipped the stone divinity.

THIRTY-NINE

Arika ashimaatya
(When We Fish)

Daniel Bernales Quillatupa

[1]Aririka ajate ashimaatya, aanakirika vakoshi tononkainchari, tzimatsirika kooya motyanto, airo ashaatziro nijaa. [2]Ikantaitzi opochatzirokari nijaa, opiirokari oshintsinka vakoshi. [3]Ontzimatye omairentavakia oparaikira irojatzi ikamaperotantakia shivari, shima, chenkori, jetari, maaroni saikatsiri nijaaki. [4]Ovakerakia ashaatyaro nijaa, onkoye shivapaye kamaintsiri. [5]Irimakia shirampari aririka intetakero kantzirikipaye vakoshi, aajatzi irorika koñapi, intakiarorika osoronkatara nijaa, ari intanakiarori imitsitziyatero irorika koñapi, irorika vakoshi kantzirikira. [6]Yoirinkakairo irojatzi yariitantakiaro osampanakira. [7]Yashaamaitakia osaanatzira ikantzimaitya.

[8]*Kisho, kisho*, pishinkiteri, pishinkiteri,
nokimita noshinketa.
[9]*Kisho, kisho, kisho*, kepiyari, kepiyari, kepiyari,
[10]Pirero, pirero, kepiyari, *kisho, kisho*.

[11]Iro yampiyampite shiramparika irojatzita itsonkatantakia maaroni oshitovate ovaaki koñapi, aisatzi ovakira vakoshi. [12]Airo aitari shintsipayeni shima kamayetatsini, irojatzita ishitovayetantanakia maaroni, ivatantapakia otsapiakipaye.

¹³Ovakerakia yayeteri maaroni shimariantzipaye, ovakera
ashaatanakia irori motyantopaye.

   ¹⁴Ari okantakotari iyotani acharinitepaye, iro ampiakota-
jiaro iroñaaka. ¹⁵Temakia tekatsite iroñaaka shima nijaaki.
¹⁶Aisatzita itsañanakaro virakochapaye nijaa, te inintaje
ashimaatajia. ¹⁷Irotaki avantariri iroñaaka maaroni ipiman-
taitziri ovanarontsiki, akante yora: sarimonka, atoonka,
poroootora. ¹⁸Te ashimaatajia. ¹⁹Ari okaratzi.

¹When we go fishing, when we take the ground root of the fish
poison *vakoshi*, if there is a pregnant woman, she shouldn't go
into the water. ²They say, if she does, she will sweeten the water,
if she does, the fish poison will lose its strength. ³She has to stay
quiet on the beach right up to the moment when anchoveta,
huasaco, or *pez negro* [*Hoplias malabaricus*], all water beings die
completely. ⁴At that moment she will go into the water to gather
dead fish. ⁵In contrast, when a man puts the pulverized *vakoshi*
or *koñapi* in the basket, when he begins to wade through the
water downstream, he will begin to submerge the basket with
the *vakoshi* and *koñapi* into the water. ⁶He will walk downriver
until he reaches the shallow area. ⁷He will walk toward the deep-
est part in the water, saying,

   ⁸*Kisho, kisho,* get drunk,
   get drunk, like I would get drunk.
   ⁹*Kisho, kisho, kisho,* strong odor, strong odor, strong odor,
   ¹⁰Drink it, drink it, strong odor, strong odor.

¹¹He will keep saying it until all fish come up to the surface,
stupefied by *vakoshi* and *koñapi.* ¹²He should not immediately
gather dead fish, only after all fish come up to the surface and

lie on the riverbank. [13]At that moment all fishermen will pick it up, at that moment pregnant women will walk into the water.

[14]Such was my ancestors' knowledge, but we will lose it. [15]Anyway, there is no fish in the river. [16]In addition, settlers are miserly about the river, they don't want us to fish. [17]That's why we eat what is sold in a store, like salmon, tuna, and *portola*. [18]We don't fish anymore. [19]This is all.

FORTY

Ookantyarori inkani

(How to Chase Away Rain)

Daniel Bernales Quillatupa

¹Añaavakerorika onkisaatapaki menkori, terika ankove omparii inkani, onzimatye añaanaatavakero. ²Ikantziri ashaninka tzimatsi jevatzirori inkani. ³Ankantavake.

⁴Pimpiyanake inkani, pimpiyanaje.
⁵Tema pipashiventya.
⁶Kisaateroinatakemi,
⁷Pijate paanajero piyompiroshite pashinikinta piina.
⁸Te nonintajemi.
⁹Ankishokamaitavakiaro, *kisho, kisho.*
¹⁰Pimpiyanaje, te nonintajemi.
¹¹Tzimatsi pashini noina, tzimatsi pashini noime,
¹²Pimpiyanaje!

¹³Arika akantavakero, pokapake antaro tampia, ookajeroni maaroni menkori oipiyavajerori inkanira pariavetainchari.
¹⁴Omaperotatya iroperanto yotanitantsi irashi acharinite.
¹⁵Irojatzi iroñaaka yantziro ashaninkapaye. ¹⁶Iromakia ivanka-ripaye ipiakotakaro, ikantzi, "Te onkameetsate, pashinitajana, kaariperori iyotani ashaninka." ¹⁷Ari ikantziri evankari iroñaaka.

¹When we see that clouds are black, and we don't want rain, we have to say this. ²My fellow men say that rain has somebody who directs it. ³We will say,

⁴Go back, rain, go back.
⁵Perhaps you don't have shame.
⁶Your head is black,
⁷Go and take your *humiro* to your other woman.
⁸I don't want you.
⁹We will spit on this, *kisho, kisho.*
¹⁰Go back, I don't want you.
¹¹I have my wife, I have my husband,
¹²Go back!

¹³If we say this, there will be [a] strong wind that will dispose of all clouds that have amassed rain that failed to fall down.

¹⁴This is true that the knowledge of my ancestors is good. ¹⁵It has been used by my fellow men up to now. ¹⁶But young people have lost it, they say, "It is not good, I am different, the knowledge of my fellow men is bad." ¹⁷This is what young people say today.

FORTY-ONE

Shinavaite ovariri atziri

(*Shinavaite* Who Ate People)

Abdias Caleb Quinchori

[1]Nonkinkitsatakoteri nocharinite, ikanta nocharinipaye ovariri atziri, yovajeetari atziri. [2]Ijatzi, ishitovapakirika, yaapainte eentsipaye. [3]Yaanakiri ivankoki arika iñaapakero; ivakakiaro. [4]Yayetziniro tsimeri, yayeniro kemari, maniro, osheto. [5]Ivakakiaro irojatzi antarotantakia eentsipayera. [6]Arika antarotapake, yenkatayetapake evankaropayera, ikanta atziritatsirika nocharinitepaye, inapaye ovetsike antaroite ooya kipatsinaki ikotsitantari, imoyantari nijaa.

[7]Iro yamaitziri ikoshitantatziri atzirira, eentsipaye. [8]Antaroyetaki, ivakakarora. [9]Itsiyakero, ovatsitaka osheki.

[10]Impoñaaka areetapaka shimashiripaitetaki. [11]Okantzi, okinkitsatatzi isha kamayetatsiri, okantzi, areetapakia yoimoshirinkero, yakatsatakerorika, imoyake nijaa. [12]Yankatsatanakerorika kooyara evankaro, yamasheetakaiyero, yampantsakakero, "Shimashiripaite nishintayeraye, *vaya-veya, vaya-veya.*"

[13]Yaanakero, yantsomakero. [14]Intetakero evankaro ooyaki omoyakira nijaa. [15]Yairikajero oitsari, isapokakerorika. [16]Intotakero, yookakero amporetsa. [17]Yaakero ako, oito, intsatyakeniro, yookakero. [18]Intetzimaityaro kooyara evankarora ooyakira omoyakera. [19]Intotayetakiro, arika omposatake, ari ivajeetyari.

[20]Ari ikantzirori intanakarori nocharini tekirata yareetyata yoka kitamarantzipaye, akantziri "virakochapaye." [21]Tekirata

iñeerita, te iyoteri virakocha. ²²Isaiki tonkariki, te yareetaityari, te isaike parenitsapiaki, ari isaiki tonkariki. Te iyoteri atziripaye pokatsiri. ²³Arika impokake, aritaki ivakiari.

²⁴Tekatsite, te añaajeri nocharinitepaye, piaja. ²⁵Te noyotakotairi tsikarika isaikaji iyoka ovantacharika. ²⁶Naakataki icharini ikantaitziri "shinavaite." ²⁷Tzimatsi oshekini nokarajeetaiyeni: Virijinia, irotaki nonirotsori, opoñaaka pashini, koki Isayashi, pashini nokarajeetaiyeni aka saikatsiri Marankiaroki. ²⁸Kamayetaji irirori, iritaki nokarajeetaiyeni ashaninkatavaka ivaiyani "shinavaite."

¹I will tell you about my grandparents, how they ate people. ²When they leave their homes, they go and snatch children. ³When they encounter little girls, they will bring them to their homes and make them eat. ⁴They will hunt birds for them, will bring tapir, deer, and monkeys. ⁵They make the girls eat until they get big. ⁶When they get big, and have a lot of fat, these people—my grandparents, women—make a big clay pot for cooking and boiling water.

⁷What they would bring home was kidnapped humans, children. ⁸Because they made children eat, they grew big. ⁹They would put food into the children's mouths, so they ate a lot.

¹⁰Then would come the season of the *shimashiri* tree. ¹¹My deceased grandmother told me that when the feasting time would come, they would lead the child by the hand [to the ritual area] and boil water [in the big pot]. ¹²In this place, where they lead the girl to, they make her dance and sing, "During the time of the *shimashiri* tree, my daughters are wretched, *vaya-veya, vaya-veya*."

¹³Then they take her and carry her in their arms to the pot. ¹⁴They place her in the pot with boiling water. ¹⁵When they remove her clothes, they take them [they don't throw them away].

[16]They cut her corpse and throw away her intestines. [17]They cut off her hands and head and throw them away. [18]They put her again in the pot with boiling water. [19]When the corpse is cooked, they cut it into pieces and eat the meat together.

[20]This was what my ancestors had done before the whites arrived, we call them *virakocha*. [21]During those times they hadn't seen the whites because they lived in the uplands. [22]They wouldn't go down to the riverbanks, they lived in the uplands, so they didn't know the newcomers. [23]When someone comes by, they will eat him.

[24]My grandparents aren't living, they are gone. [25]Now I don't know where those who ate people live. [26]I'm a grandchild of those who were called *shinavaite*. [27]There are many of us: Virginia, my aunt, there is also another relative, my uncle called Isaya, and others, who live here in Bajo Marankiari. [28]Others are dead, but we are all descendants of the group called *shinavaite*.

FORTY-TWO

Okoñaatantakari mavira

(How *Mavira* Appeared)

Luis Mauricio Rosa, with Raul Martin Bernata and Victoria Manchi de Martin

¹–Akinkitsatakoteritaima ikantakiri iroñaaka mavira kapicheeni. ²Nonkinkitsatakoteri, Elena, irora amirori pantsantsi iyoka mavira. ³Tsika ikanta otzimantari ayotantarori arori mavirate? ⁴Ikanta ipokaki poñaachari Kusko. ⁵Ari isaikapakiri iroñaaka ikantaitziro parenikika, tsika ikantaitziroka iroka?

⁶–Ah, Meantari.

⁷–Te. ⁸Aka, aka. ⁹Poña yavisaki iroñaaka aka. ¹⁰Apototapaka parenini Samoterintsikinta, ñaakiro. ¹¹Tsika ikantaitziroka? ¹²Ari isaikapakiri.

¹³–Paukari Tampo.

¹⁴–Ja, ja, ari, ikimiriri ashaninka *tin, tin, tin*, ipantsairokia mavira. ¹⁵Ikantzi, "Intsi, naminajantaiteta paita antziriri." ¹⁶Ijatzi, ijatzi, ikimisantziri, *tin tin tin tin*. ¹⁷Yaminiri, iñaatziri itsirotzirojeetani, itsirotzirojeetani. ¹⁸Poña ari ivashaantziro. ¹⁹Osamaninintzi . . . ah, Tziviari ikantaitziro, aka, intyatzininta. ²⁰Poña ikantzi, "Intsitya, nonoshikashityari noñiiterita, otzimantarika itamporoteka." ²¹Poña ikantziri, "Ari pipokajeetzi?" ²²Iñaajantzima, ari ikisavakeri. ²³Ikantziri, "Nonintakotatzimiro pivantsanira." ²⁴Ikanta iñaakiri, ikantzi, "Pinintakotanarorika novantsani, otzimantarikia mavira."

²⁵Ari okantari, "Pinintzirika nompimiro novantsanika, nopantsavaiteta."

²⁶Poña ikantzi, "Pimpoke sheeteni." ²⁷Ipokaki sheeteni. ²⁸"Tsamera iroñaaka ampantsai." ²⁹Ipantsakakiri, ipantsakakiri. ³⁰Ikantzi, "Ari pikanterori avirori." ³¹Tzimatsi osheki ivantsani. ³²"Pinintzirika, ari pimatakiro avirori. ³³Kantzimaitacha, nantzirika, airo pimatziro aviroka. ³⁴Airo pitzimaventziro kitaiterikipaye, iyotatya. ³⁵Ari oshitovanaki, piyotantyarori opoki mavira, oshitovanakirika chakopishi. ³⁶Poña paakero, pisatetatyeyaro avirori. ³⁷Iroma airorika, ari intzimashitakimi maranki ikantaitziri Otsa, je, iritakitaima Otsa. ³⁸Ikanta ivamiñakiri, ivamintsakiri ivantsani."

³⁹Aritaki ikantakirira maaroni, "Airo pantziro kitaiterikipaye, avisanakirika, ari pivashaanterori. ⁴⁰Tera itzimashitzimikari maranki, ikintzimikari yora Otsara. ⁴¹Terika, ari piñaakeri maranki antarite, inkisakotyaro ivantsani. ⁴²Iritakitaima, ashitaro maranki ivantsani.

⁴³"Airo pisonkatzi, airo pipotsotavaka, airo pipokoriavaka." ⁴⁴Okanta, okanta, ikantzi, "Arima okanta." ⁴⁵Je, ari okaratzi, ivaashantziro. ⁴⁶Ari otsonkapaka.

¹–Perhaps we'll tell a little about *mavira*. ²I will tell, Elena, about the one who brought the song of *mavira*. ³How have we learned the song of *mavira*? ⁴What happened is that a man came from Cuzco. ⁵He stayed in the area, what is this river called?

⁶–Ah, [the river] Meantarini.

⁷–No. ⁸Here, here (pointing). ⁹Later he passed toward here (pointing).¹⁰[Two rivers] join [here] where the hill Samoterintsi is located, you've seen it. ¹¹What is it called? ¹²This is where he stayed.

¹³–Paucartambo [River].

[14]–Aha, aha, my fellow men heard *tin, tin, tin* (the sound of *tambor*), they were singing about *mavira*. [15]He [one man] said, "Well, I am going to look [at] what they are doing." [16]He walked and walked, he listened intently to the sound of their tambor, *tin, tin, tin* (the sound of *tambor*). [17]He looked, and he saw them dancing in a circle holding hands. [18]Then they [the dancers] took a break. [19]Sometime later . . . ah, it is called Tziviarini, the Salt River, here, farther away. [20]Then he said, "Well, I'll go [crawl around] slowly to look at them because they have a *tambor*." [21]Then he said to them, "Hello [have you come?]." [22]He thought that they [the newcomers] would bother them [the locals]. [23]He said to them, "I like your songs." [24]Then a newcomer looked at him and said, "If you like my music of how *mavira* came into being . . ." [25]So it was, "If you want it, I will give you this song, I will sing [it]."

[26]Afterward the newcomer said, "Come in the afternoon." [27]The Ashaninka man came in the afternoon. [28]The newcomer said, "Let's sing." [29]He made him sing again and again. [30]He said, "This is how you will do it." [31]There were a lot of songs. [32]"If you want it, you'll manage it. [33]Nevertheless, what I am doing, you won't be able to do [all the time]. [34]You won't do it every day, it has its time. [35]When the wild cane blossoms appear, you will know that *mavira* arrived. [36]Then you'll take the plant flowers and put them inside your *cushma* (traditional robe). [37]If not, the snake called Otsa [Otsa is the master of the *savoro* (wild cane) plant, whose flowers are used to make festive *mavira* head-dresses] will wait for you, yes, it's possible that Otsa [will wait for you]. [38]It will make you remember, it will make you remember his songs."

[39]This is all that he told the Ashaninka man, "You won't do it every day, and when it [*mavira* season] passes, you should take

a break. ⁴⁰If not, the snake will wait for you, and Otsa will bite you. ⁴¹If not, you'll see a huge snake, angry with your song. ⁴²He is the Master of the snake's song.

⁴³"We shouldn't play the panpipes, we shouldn't rub annatto onto our bodies, we shouldn't paint our faces like we do at a *mavira* festival." ⁴⁴Then he said, "This might be it. ⁴⁵Yes, this is all," and he took a break. ⁴⁶Here it ends.

FORTY-THREE

Mavira

Elena Nestor de Capurro

[1]Nompantsairo irora mavira.

[2]Jeya, jeya, areetaka mavira,
[3]jeya, jeya, areetaka mavira.
[4]Jeya, jeya, jeya, mavira,
[5]jeya, jeya, jeya, jeya, areetaka mavira.
[6]Jeya, jeya, jeya, areetaka mavira.
[7]Jeya, jeya, jeya, mavira, jeya, jeya, jeya.
[8]Kashipachorinka mavira, jeya, jeya, jeya, mavira.
[9]Kashipachorinka mavira, jeya, jeya, jeya,
[10]jeya, jeya, areetaka mavira.
[11]Shookakira, shokakira shinki,
[12]areetaka mavira, mavira.
[13]Jeya, areetaka mavira, mavira,
[14]jeya, areetaka mavira, mavira.
[15]Jeya, jeya, areetaka mavira.
[16]Jeya, jeya, areetaka mavira,
[17]jeya, jeya, areetaka mavira.
[18]Añaavitavajaro mavira, mavira,
[19]heya, jeya, jeya, areetaka mavira.
[20]Irotaki avisaitaki mavira,
[21]jeya avisaitaki onampiki.
[22]Koramani añaavairo mavira.

²³Jeya, jeya, areetaka mavira, ²⁴jeya, jeya, areetaka mavira.
²⁵Jeya, añaavairo mavira anampitsite.
²⁶Irojatzima okantaitya añee.
²⁷Jeya, jeya, jeya, mavira, areetaka mavira.
²⁸Kusko oivariaiyeni *ma,*
²⁹jeya, jeya, jeya, areetaka mavira.
³⁰Kusko oivariaiyeni *ma,* oivariaiyeni *ma,*
³¹jeya, jeya, areetaka mavira.
³²Pookiro piina, mavira,
³³Jeiriyakiya, mavira.
³⁴Jeya, jeya, jeya, jeya, jeya, ³⁵areetaka mavira.

¹I will sing a song of *mavira.*

²Heya, heya, *mavira* arrived,
³heya, heya, *mavira* arrived.
⁴Heya, heya, heya, *mavira,*
⁵heya, heya, heya, heya *mavira* arrived.
⁶Heya, heya, heya, *mavira* arrived.
⁷Heya, heya, heya, *mavira,* heya, heya, heya.
⁸*Chakopishi* flowers are hanging from *mavira* headdresses,
    heya, heya, heya, *mavira.*
⁹*Chakopishi* flowers are hanging from *mavira* headdresses,
    heya, heya, heya,
¹⁰heya, heya, *mavira* arrived.
¹¹When corn has grown big, when corn has grown big,
¹²*mavira, mavira* arrived.
¹³Heya, *mavira, mavira* arrived,
¹⁴heya, *mavira, mavira* arrived.
¹⁵Heya, heya, *mavira* arrived.
¹⁶Heya, heya, *mavira* arrived,

17heya, heya, *mavira* arrived.
18We celebrated *mavira, mavira* for a short time,

19heya, heya, heya, *mavira* arrived.

20Mavira passed on,

21heya, heya, it passed on to its pueblo.

22We'll see it soon, we'll see it soon.

23Heya, heya, *mavira* arrived, 24heya, heya, *mavira* arrived.

25Heya, we'll see it in our pueblo.

26If we stay alive.

27Heya, heya, heya, *mavira* arrived.

28They came from Cuzco in large groups,

29heya, heya, heya, *mavira* arrived.

30They came from Cuzco, they came from Cuzco,

31heya, heya, heya, *mavira, mavira* arrived.

32Leave your spouse, *mavira,*

33heriyakiya, *mavira.*

34Heya, heya, heya, heya, heya, 35*mavira* arrived.

FORTY-FOUR

Mavira

Ines Pérez de Santos and Moises Santos Rojas

[1]–Noñaapakitziri ikatziyaitakeri atzirira, yoisotakeri iroñaaka-kia oshi chakopishi. [2]Ikatziyaka, ishonkaventaiyarini.

[3]Okaakitapakera mavira, noshonkaventaro nochakopite. [4]Omaviratakera chakopinira, kitepotenkataki chakopi. [5]Mavira, mavira, mavira, irotaki mavira areetapaka. [6]Ovaneenkata mavira chakopini, chakopini.

[7]Ari okantari. [8]Yampantsakotziro irirorikia, sonkarikia shirampari isonkaventziro. [9]Iroñaaka okaratanakera, kooya shonkanaka, shirampari isonkatzi. [10]Isonkatzi iroñaaka shirampari, isonkaventziro ichakopitera. [11]Okaratapakerika isonkaventero, iroñaaka yaanake ivoronkitote, imporonkavakaiya irojatzi ontsonkantakia. [12]Iroñaaka imishitovanakeri iyora ivaritera, arika intonkake isamanite, isharoni, ikimoshirinkero chakopira. [13]Ari okantari.

[14]Pairani noñaakero naari tonkarikinta opaitara San Miguel, ari noñaakero naari. [15]Nokantzi, "Arima ikantaitzirori." [16]Nokimavetaro ina, okantana, "Piritsori yantziro. [17]Arika areetapajia mavira, irotaki ivishiriamento irirori, irotaki ikimoshiritantari iyora piritsoripaye pairani." [18]Te noñeerita naari, iro noñaakerokia nokinkishirianairo. [19]Arima ikantari.

15. The annual festival *mavira* is celebrated to mark the transition to the rainy season and the beginning of the new year. By Daniel Bernales Quillatupa (Aroshi).

[20]Inkantakotajia tsiteni, kitaitakotaji. [21]Iro onkitaitamane, ari onkarate mava tsiteniri, mava kitaiteri inkitaitakoventero ivishiriaventyaro chakopi. [22]Ari okantari. [23]Noñaakeri naari, je, irotaki noñaakeri naari.

[24]–Tekatsite pashini, irotaki apaniroini mavira. [25]Otsonkantapakiari, arika ontsonkapakia imasatote irajeetakirira. [26]Otsonkapakiarika, tsonkatanaka isonkajeetzi, itamporotaki irojatzi okitaitetanakerika, ari ontsonkatapakiari. [27]Jaitetzi imaajeeteni. [28]Ari okantari pairani. [29]Yantziri nosheninkapaye, kaarinta yoteroni kimisantantzi.

[30]Tzimatsi aparoni, yorave tsika ikantaitziroranki, savoro. [31]Arika ontzimanake, chakopitanake opena-openarianakerika, iroñaaka jevatatsiri inkante, "Tsame aimoshirinkero, aimoshi-

rinkero chakopi. ³²Ivetsikajeetaka, antero iroñaaka aimoshirinkero chakopinta, tema oyotatya." ³³Opoki aparopaye osarentsi,
opoki okimitatya *diciembre*ki, aitaki yantaitziriri mavira.
³⁴Onkantya ontsonkata, koraketaintsi ovakerari osarentsi,
irotaki yantantarori mavira.

³⁵Iroñaaka okimitaka tekatsi antajeroni mavira. ³⁶Kamaye-
taki intanakarori. ³⁷Iroñaaka te añaajero, tekatsite oijatakote-
rini. ³⁸Ikaratzi nosheninkapaye yotziriri mavira, tsonkataka,
ikamake iroñaaka. ³⁹Isaikavetanaka itomipaye, te iyotero, te
iyotero mavira, irotaki kaari ayotantajaro arorite. ⁴⁰Tsonkataka,
ikamake, irotaki akamantavakemiri okanta pairani mavira.
⁴¹Iyotakero tekira inkamajeeteta, iyotakero okaakitaje, ika-
mantavakajeeta, "Tsame aimoshirinkero, aimoshirinkavairo
chakopi, irojatzi ankiantapajia ovakerari osarentsi." ⁴²Ari
ikantajeetari pairani yoka.

¹–I saw a man who was standing [in the middle] and who was
adorned by the flowers of wild cane called "arrow leaves." ²They
were standing around the man [and singing].

³*Mavira* is coming, I am making a circle around my arrow.
⁴When my arrow stalk begins to grow in December, its
    flower turns white and yellow.
⁵*Mavira, mavira, mavira* has arrived.
⁶The time to be beautiful for the festive arrow, arrow.

⁷So it was. ⁸They would sing and play panpipes on account of
the arrow plant. ⁹When they were finished, the women would
go around, and men would play panpipes. ¹⁰The men would play
panpipes on account of the arrow plant. ¹¹After they finish playing panpipes, they take stinging nettles and hit each other with
them until there are no more nettles left. ¹²Then they take out

their food, when they had shot paca, agouti, to celebrate the arrow plant. ¹³So it was.

¹⁴Long ago I saw [the festival] in the uplands, the place is called San Miguel, there I saw it. ¹⁵I said, "This is how they do it." ¹⁶I had heard about it from my mother; she would say to me, "Your uncles do it. ¹⁷When *mavira* arrives, this is a festive time for them, that's why your uncles would celebrate this." ¹⁸I had not seen it before, but I saw it [later on], I remember it. ¹⁹So they did it.

²⁰They would celebrate it all night until daybreak. ²¹Until the next day, they would do it for three days and nights in a row celebrating the arrow. ²²So they did it. ²³I saw it, yes, I saw it.

²⁴–There was no other [festival], *mavira* was the only one. ²⁵They would finish [celebrating] when their *masato* (manioc beer drink) ended, which they drank. ²⁶To finish, they would stop playing panpipes and *tambor* at daybreak, then they would finish. ²⁷They [would] all go to sleep. ²⁸So it was this way in the past. ²⁹My fellow men did it when they didn't know religion.

³⁰There is one [plant,] whachamacallit, wild cane. ³¹When its new shoots appear, and its arrow-like stalks produce plumes, the chief says, "Let's celebrate, we'll celebrate the arrow plant. ³²They are all ready, we'll do a festival to celebrate the arrow plant, since it is its time." ³³Another year comes, it comes approximately in December, and they would do the *mavira* festival [again]. ³⁴When it ends, a new year comes, that's why they would do the *mavira* festival.

³⁵Now it seems that there is nobody [left] who will do the *mavira* festival. ³⁶All founders have died. ³⁷Now we don't see it anymore, there is nobody who will continue [the tradition]. ³⁸All my fellow men who knew about the festival have expired, they have died. ³⁹Their sons don't know it, they don't know *mavira*, that's why there is nobody who knows it among us. ⁴⁰All have

died, so we are advising you about it, how *mavira* was [cele-brated] in the past. [41]They had known it before all died, they had known that it would come and would advise everybody, "Let's celebrate; we'll be celebrating the arrow plant, when we enter the new year." [42]So they did this way in the past.

FORTY-FIVE

Pavankiri ooria

(Solar Deity)

Bertha Rodríguez de Caleb

[1]Pavankiri ooria, pavankiri ooria,
[2]Pavankiri ooria, pavankiri ooria,
[3]Jenokityapakira pava *ya,*
[4]Pavankiri ooria, pavankiri ooria, pavankiri ooria.
[5]Tampatzikaityapakira pava *ya,*
[6]Pavankiri ooria, pavankiri ooria, pavankiri ooria.
[7]Savinkaityanaki *ya* pava *ya,*
[8]Pavaninto *ya,* pavaninto *ya,* pavaninto *ya.*
[9]Kitaityakotapakira pava *ya,* pavankiri ooria,
[10]Pavaninto *ya,* pavankiri ooria, *ja-ii, je-jeee.*

[1]Solar deity, solar deity,
[2]Solar deity, solar deity,
[3]It is high up, the sun.
[4]Solar deity, solar deity, solar deity.
[5]It has reached its zenith, the sun,
[6]Solar deity, solar deity, solar deity.
[7]It has gone down, the sun,
[8]Solar deity, solar deity, solar deity.
[9]It has come out, the sun, solar deity,
[10]Solar deity, solar deity, *ha-hii, he-heeee.*

FORTY-SIX

Iyovapajirika ooriatsiri

(When the Sun Comes Out)

Paulina García Ñate

[1]Iroñaaka ikantaitziri, kimitatyari paitaranki, arika ishitovapaji ooriatsiri, ooriatsiri ishitovapajirika, ampantsai avishiriakotyari. [2]Aisatzi intetanajiarika, okantzi vishiriantsi, nokantajeetziro naaka avishiriajeetya.

[3]Arika iyovapajirika ooriatsiri, okantzi.

[4]Aayaaee, aayaaee, aayaaee,
[5]Namini *ma*, nirintyo, okirinkatanaki, yovayetapaji
   ooriatsiri.
[6]Aminakoyetapajiri irojenkatepaye.
[7]Irotakima intetajia *ma* ooriatsirika irirove.
[8]Irotaki *ma* irirori *ma* ooriatsiri *ma*.
[9]Ontsitenitanaji, antsitenitakotanajive,
[10]Irotaki *ma*, nirintyo, amaaji *ma*, ayarori *ma*, irotaki *ma*
   itziriavankoyetapaji ooriatsiri *ma*.
[11]Okitainkaityapaji iriromakiave, ooriatsirive, ooryatsirive.
[12]Pamini *ma* katonko, ooriatsiri *ma* oorintaityapaja,
   okatonkotanaki ooriatsirive.
[13]Ñaakiro, nirintyo, irotaki *ma* arori amairintantanajiari.
[14]Otsitenitanaki, amaantanajiari, nirintyokave.
[15]Okantayetziro irori ashitanakairi, oyotakotziri *ma*
   ooriatsirive.

¹⁶Yaminakoyetapajai okirinkatanaki irirori *ma* ooriatsirive.

¹⁷Oshavityapaji irokavee otsitenityatantanajiari, iro
imaajiave ooriatsirive.

¹It is said like it was said in the past, when the sun rises, when
the sun rises, we will sing and dance. ²Also, when it sets down,
the song says, we all say this and dance.

³When the sun rises, the song says.

⁴Ayae, ayae, ayae,

⁵I will look, my little sister, at the horizon.

⁶The sun will rise, we will see its whiff.

⁷It will go down, the sun.

⁸It's the sun.

⁹It will get dark, darkness will fall upon us,

¹⁰That's why we will go to sleep, my little sister, that's why
the sun is going home.

¹¹The sun will give off little light, the sun will.

¹²Look up at the sun's splendor, look up at the sun.

¹³You've seen it, my sister, that's why we will get rest.

¹⁴It gets dark, and we'll go to sleep, my little sister.

¹⁵It says to her about the one who is our master, she knows
about the sun.

¹⁶The sun looks at us from the horizon.

¹⁷It will go below the horizon, it will get dark, the sun is
going to sleep.

FORTY-SEVEN

Ipantsakoitziri kashiri
(They Sing about the Moon)

Paulina García Ñate

[1]Ampantsakotavakero. [2]Pairani okantzi intakantarori, iniro ina, naari, nosaropaye naari, avishiriakotari ooriatsiri, paitaranki ikantaitziri, kashiri, ovakira iyovachekitapaji. [3]Aririka intetajia, aajatzi okantakotziri pantsantsi, pantsantsi okantakotziri irori intakantarori.

[4]Pameninatyami, pamenina otapikinta.
[5]Irotaki *ma* ooriatsiri *ma* iyovapajiri irori okatonkotanaki.
[6]Pamini *ma* katonko, iyovapajinave pavave, pavave
    okatonkotanaki.
[7]Yamapajiri *ma*, yamapajiri *ma* kashirira,
kashirira iyovatyetapaji.
[8]Yamapajero *ma*, yamapajero *ma* iitaiterite, iitaiterite
ooriatsirika, ooriatsirika.
[9]Aajatzi *ma* irirori *ma*, aajatzi *ma* irirori *ma*,
Kashiri *ma* irirori *ma* iitainkatakairo.
[10]Ikitainkatakairo tsitenirika, tsitenerika.
[11]Okimitajantaka *ma*, okimitajantaka *ma* onkitaitatyerika
    ma, onkitaitatyerika *ma*.
[12]Iyotziro irirori *ma*, iyotziro irirori *ma* kashiri *ma* tyami,
    kashiri *ma* tyami.
[13]Irotaki irirori *ma*, kashiri irirori,

impiyaje irirori okatonkotanakinta,

katonko *ma* parini, katonko *ma* parini.

¹⁴Yamapaajiro irirori *ma*, yamapaajiro irirori *ma*,

ooriatsiri *ma* kitaiteri irirori *ma*, kitaiteri irirori *ma*.

¹⁵Ojenokityapaji okitaitamanai, ojenokityapaji
okitaitamanai.

¹⁶Irotaki *ma* ayarori *ma* aminavaitantyari iitaiterite
ooriatsirira, ooriatsirira.

¹⁷Tekarika ooriatsiri *ma*, eero *ma* ayarori *ma* okantzi *ma*
arori aminavaitantyari.

¹⁸Irotaki ooriatsiri *ma* intevankatajia *ma*

Amaantapajiarori *ma* otsiteniterave, tsitenirira *tyami*.

¹We will sing it. ²Long ago, they say, the ancestors, my mother's
mother, I also, and my grandchildren danced at the sight of the
sun and whatchamacallit, moon, when it was new. ³When it was
full, there was also a song about it sung by ancestral women.

⁴Look at me, look at me down below.

⁵The sun rises skyward.

⁶Look up, Pava, Pava rises skyward.

⁷He will bring him, he will bring him, the moon,
the new moon.

⁸He will bring, he will bring his light, his light,
the sun, the sun.

⁹And the moon makes his light shine intensely,

¹⁰He makes it shine intensely at night, at night.

¹¹It seems, it seems that it is dawn, it is dawn.

¹²The moon knows it [his time], he knows.

¹³He is the one who will return to the heights,
to the headwaters of the river.

¹⁴He will bring it, he will bring it,

the sun will bring his light.
¹⁵There is already morning in the mountain heights,
¹⁶only in this light we can see, in the light of the sun.
¹⁷If there is no sun, we won't be able to see.
¹⁸The sun is going to slip away,
so that we sleep at night, at night.

FORTY-EIGHT

Arika antarote kooya

(When a Girl Had Her First Menses)

Daniel Bernales Quillatupa

[1]Pinkimajeri Aroshi ikinkitsatakotero okantakota aririka inta-
nakia aparoni tsinani oñaavaitya. [2]Aririka intakia oñaavakia
aparoni tsinani oñaavaitya, akantaperotavaki, oshitovatana-
keririka iraani okooyatantarikira, okamanterota iniro. [3]Iro-
ñaaka iniroka tzimatsirika osaro, okantero, "Ina, pisaro
osokatziro iraani."

[4]Shintsipayeni iri ijatzi, yaakite kompiroshi. [5]Yantake
iroñaaka ivankoshi antaroite, ivankokira omaamentoki tsinani.
[6]Intsivitakatyero kameetsa, eiro ikiitzi kapicheeni ooriatsiri,
ari iminkiitero iroñaaka ivankarora. [7]Onkarate mava kashiri,
osaiki intsompaikira tsinanika, irotaki osaro, terika iniro,
irotaki aminironi.

[8]Impaitakero tsinanika kirikantotsi, ampee, pajo, kapicheeni samampo oviri pajokira okirikavaitantyari. [9]Ovarite
intaani ooya kaniri tavakorentsi. [10]Eiro ovaro katyori, pochari,
poshiniri, ontzimatye otziventya. [11]Aririka oninte ojate otsinte,
irotaki oimishitoveroni osaro.

[12]Ompashikainatatyeya tsinanika. [13]Tekatsirika ovaañote,
osatevoinatatyeya maaroni oitoki, intaani amenaki kapicheeni
oñaantyarori avotsi. [14]Ikantaitzi osatevoinatantari kooyaka,
iñeerokari achontzi, omashiriantotzikari, apaata aajatzi iñeero-

kari poiyotzi, aparoni tsimeri ipaviyerokari ipai, opaitzikari shintsipayeni. ¹⁵Irotaki osatevoinatantari kooya.

¹⁶Otsonkarika mava kashiri, iroñaaka maaroni oshaninkapaye shirampari ijate antamiki yamini poshiniri. ¹⁷Kooyapaye, maaroni oshaninkapaye ompokaiyaki aye kaniri, otakiriaki, onkotsitayetaki, otsinkakero, otsipatayetakero koritzi, onteyetakero pitotsikipaye irojatzi okachotantakia. ¹⁸Impiyaiyajerika maaroni shirampari jataintsiri ikomentsatya, iroñaakakia ovakera yoimishitovaitero ivankaroka.

¹⁹Kantzimaitacha ontzimatye intotaitero maaroni oishi. ²⁰Yaaitaki osheki anaa, irotaki impotsoitantyarori maaroni ovatsaki. ²¹Aririka oshitovaje, kisaatepokitaki maaroni ovatsa. ²²Ikantaitzi oñaavakirokari kamanitaantsi, okamanitzikari apaata kooya itzimakirika eentsite, añeeta osheki osarentsipaye.

²³Iroñaakakia imishitovaitero kooyaka. ²⁴Shinkitaiyakani iroñaaka ikimoshiriventziro irishinto, ikimoshiriventziro iritsiro, okimoshiriventziro irento, maaroni oshaninkapaye. ²⁵Ivayetya iyomentsanipaye. ²⁶Otsonkatantanakyari iroñaaka kimoshiritantsika okarate apapakoroni kitaiteri ishinkijeetya. ²⁷Otsonkaperotantanakiari, aake iroñaaka tsinanika poronkito, irotaki oporonkajeetantyariri maaroni saikatsiri pokaintsiri ishinkijeetara. ²⁸Irotaki overantarori kimoshiritantsi. ²⁹Ari okaratapaki.

¹You'll hear Aroshi again, he will tell about a girl who is [placed] in seclusion for the first time. ²When a girl is in seclusion, or to put it more clearly, when blood comes out of her vagina for the first time, she will advise her mother. ³The mother, if she has her mother, says, "Mother, your granddaughter, her menses came."

⁴Her father immediately goes to the forest to bring *humiro*

(palm species) [its stalks and leaves are used in building houses].
⁵He will make a big hut where the girl's bed is. ⁶There is a very
narrow entrance, hardly any sun will enter, and there they will
place her. ⁷The girl will stay inside for three months, and her
mother or her grandmother will take care of her.

⁸They will give her a spindle, cotton, a vessel, and ashes to put
in it, so that she could turn the tip of her spindle. ⁹Her food consists of only unskinned roasted manioc. ¹⁰She should eat neither
salted nor sweet food, nor meat, since she has to diet. ¹¹When
she goes outside to urinate, her grandmother will watch her.

¹²The girl's head should be covered at all times. ¹³If she does
not have a kerchief to cover it, she has to pull up her *cushma* (traditional robe), only enough for her eyes to see a trail. ¹⁴They say
that the head is covered, so that the wasps do not see her, so that
she does not become morally corrupted, so that *poiyotzi* (a gray-
headed bird species) does not contaminate her, and she does not
turn gray-haired quickly. ¹⁵That's why she had to cover her head.

¹⁶When three months pass, all her male relatives and other
men go hunting to look for animals. ¹⁷Women and all her female
relatives will come and harvest manioc, skin it, boil it, and crush
the manioc mass, together with sweet potato, and empty the
mass into the wood tubs to ferment. ¹⁸When the males come
back from the hunting trip, at that point they begin celebrating
on behalf of the girl.

¹⁹However, they have to cut off her entire hair. ²⁰They will
[also] bring a lot of *huito* fruit to paint the entire body of the girl.
²¹When she emerges after the period of seclusion, her body will
be black. ²²They say this is done so that she will not see death,
so that later on, when she has children, she does not die, so that
she has many years of life.

²³Now they will make her leave the hut. ²⁴They will get in-

toxicated and celebrate on her behalf: her parents, her brothers and sisters, all her family. [25]They will eat the animals killed in the forest. [26]The celebration will end after five days of drinking. [27]To finish the celebration, the girl will bring a stinging nettle and will whack with it those who came to the feast when they got intoxicated. [28]This is the last event of the celebration. [29]Here it ends.

FORTY-NINE

Aavakantsi

(Taking a Spouse)

Gregorio Santos Pérez

[1]Yañaantariki asheninkapaye pairani, maatsi okantavaishita aavakantsi, iro yamijeetari iriroite intajeetakarori. [2]Iroñaaka nonkinkitsatavaki aparoni ikantaitziri "tsiyantsi atsikonakiki." [3]Ari okanta.

[4]Arika isaikajeete ashitanitatyari intsipatyaro iina, irishinto-paye, maaroni ikarajeetaiyenira, kameetsa ikantajeeta, poñaashitaka imapokashitakiari. [5]Yariitakia aparoni atziri poñiinkari, tsikarika, te iyoteri. [6]Inkinapaki, tsikarika ijate. [7]Inkitsatanakia iitsari, ivanakia yamatsairi, intsatetanakiaro itsarate. [8]Intetanaki iyokani, pinitsipatsaini, yaanakiro ichakopite, imitsiyanaki iviamini. [9]Jatzi tsikarika inkinavaite, airo ayotzi.

[10]Ari ikimita iroñaaka atzirika ariitaincharika ishitovapaki pankotsiki, ivitsatapakari ashitarorira ivanko.

[11]Aisatzi yamitari asheninkapaye, irojatzi okantamainta iroñaaka, arika iñaavaki ninka ariitachani, piyojeetapakani, yaminavintsateri, inkimiri arika isampitavakiri ashitarorira ivanko. [12]Ari ikantakari: iyoka shiramparika isaikapakitzira inkinkitsavaitakairi ashitarorira ivanko, piyojeetapakani, irishintopaye otapiki iniro. [13]Aparoni irishinto katziyanaka oñaavakirira shirampari ikinkitsavaitakairi iri.

[14]Shinitsini akishitaki kaniri, oñaakiro omposataki, ampinaikonatanakiro omatsaraki. [15]Ompokamaintapakia, onoshikapa-

kia itapiki shiramparira, otsiyakonatapakiri. ¹⁶Inkantanakia, *varok*, okatsirinkatatzira kaniri. ¹⁷Ompaimantyari shirampari, ontzimatye yaavakotero. ¹⁸Airorika yaavakotziro, te inintero kooyara. ¹⁹Iroma arika yaavakotavakero, itashatzira, ivamaintyaro kanirira. ²⁰Irira kooya inkantakiri iroñaaka, "Paavakotakiro nishinto, payiro. ²¹Tema onintatzimi, irotaki otsiyakonakitantakamiri akishirira."

²²Iyoka shiramparika ontzimatye yayiro evankarora. ²³Jatajeetanaki tsikarika osaiki omaaminto imaavakaiya. ²⁴Poñaashitaka osaitekira ijate antamiki yamini poshiniri ivajeetyari. ²⁵Arika apaata ishinkijeetakia, kooyarama iro vitsikatsini piarentsi.

²⁶Aajatzi pairani yamitari ashaninkapaye, arika iñaavaki aparoni shirampari ariitapainchani pankotsiki ivitsatapakiari, inkantapakiri, "Sheeteni, koki." ²⁷Iñajeetapakiro osaikajeete kooyapaye. ²⁸Inkantavakeri, "Tsika pipoñaaka?" ²⁹"Naaka nopoña kirinka," terika katonko. ³⁰Arika inkinkitsavaitakakiri, inkanteri, "Paita pinintziri?" ³¹Shiramparira pokatsirira inkantaki, "Koki, nonintataitatziro pishintora."

³²Inkantanaki ashitanitachari, "Omapiro pinintatzi noshinto?" ³³Yankanakiri inkanteri, "Je, nonintatzi pishinto." ³⁴"Aja, kameetsataki, ari aitakitaima iroñaaka nompakimiro." ³⁵"Tsika otzimika pinintziri?" ³⁶Shiramparika yookotaki aparoni tsipashi kooya. ³⁷Ikantzi, "Irotaki nonintzi."

³⁸Irinta jaitetzi inkinkitsavaitakairo itsipataro iinara, inkantero, "Evankarinta pokatsiri inintatzi ashinto."

³⁹Irori onkantanakiri, "Avirokataima yotziro, aja."

⁴⁰Yankanaki irirori, "Kameetsataki, iroñaakataima, tsame ampiri." ⁴¹Opiyojeetatyara kooya, yookotakiro, "Ninka pininteri?"

⁴²Intzimpatanakiro, onkantavitatya, airo onintzi, ontekatekavitanakiarika, onkante, "Airo, airo."

⁴³Intzimpatanakiro irojatzi impantakiari shiramparira. ⁴⁴Iroñaaka impakiri shiramparira, inkantzimaityari iroñaaka irora, "Ontzimatye pijate antamiki, paminaite aavakotavakiarori. ⁴⁵Pamini piratsi antari, maniro, kemari, tsikapaita payiri aviroka."

⁴⁶Iroma kooyara irotaki jatatsini ayi oyaniri, ontsipatyaro irintopaye antantyari oviari. ⁴⁷Ari impokaji iroñaaka shiramparira, inkonkapajiro. ⁴⁸Intaina pokaji iriori. ⁴⁹Yamaji ishinkori, terika osheki tsimeripaye ovankoki. ⁵⁰Irori kooyara antake ontsinkake oyaniri, ontsikatake, oyakotakiri. ⁵¹Ipoña yampotoijeetakia iroñaaka iriroite ovakira impiro, ovakira ishinkijeetya, ovajeetaka iroñaakakia ivarite. ⁵²Opoña yamampajeetakia, yamasheejeetakia onkarataki ishinkijeetakia. ⁵³Imaajeetaki iroñaaka, shiramparira yaanakiro kooyara tsika anta ivankoki, yantavaite, tsika paita inintakarori imaantajeetyari. ⁵⁴Ari okaratzi nokimakovintziri pairani aavakantsi.

¹During the era of my ancient fellow men, there were various types of marriage "hookups," to which the founders were accustomed. ²I am going to tell about one called "a hot-food hookup." ³So it goes.

⁴When a family man resides, accompanied by his wife and daughters, all united together, and they are doing well, someone surprises them. ⁵A visitor arrives, from whatever place, they don't know. ⁶He walks to someplace. ⁷He is dressed in his traditional robe and has his headband on, and a cotton bag hangs over his side. ⁸He keeps in the bag coca leaves and his magic herbs, and he carries his arrows and a bow. ⁹He goes to wherever he goes, we don't know.

¹⁰So it happens this way, like, this person arrives, enters a house, and salutes the owner of the house.

¹¹A custom of my fellow men, which is kept unchanged until today, is when they see someone arrive, they all gather to watch him and listen, when the visitor begins asking questions of the owner of the house. ¹²So it happened this way: this person sat down to converse with the owner, and all family members gathered together, daughters sitting behind the mother's back. ¹³One daughter was up on her feet, watching the man talking to her father.

¹⁴She will quickly put manioc in the fire, cook it until it is ready, and wrap it in her robe. ¹⁵She will slowly approach the visitor from behind and press the hot manioc against his body. ¹⁶He will jump in surprise, *varok* (a startle reaction in response to sudden stimuli, e.g., noise or touch), because the manioc is hot. ¹⁷Then she will give the manioc to the man, and he will have to take it from her hands. ¹⁸If he doesn't do it, he doesn't want the girl. ¹⁹But if he takes the manioc, when he is hungry, he will eat it. ²⁰The girl's father will say, "Since you received the manioc from my daughter's hands, take her. ²¹She wants you, that's why she gave you the roasted manioc."

²²Now the man should marry the girl. ²³They will go to wherever her bed is located to sleep together. ²⁴Then he will go to the jungle to hunt animals for the collective meal, which they will have later on, when they all will get intoxicated. ²⁵The woman will prepare manioc beer.

²⁶There is another old custom of my fellow men, when they see a male who arrives at a house and says, "Good evening, father-in-law." ²⁷Then the visitor sees a group of women. ²⁸They ask him, "Where are you coming from?" ²⁹"I am from downriver (or upriver)." ³⁰When they talk, the father will ask, "What do you want?" ³¹The newcomer will say, "Father-in-law, I would like your daughter."

³²The father of the family will say, "Is this true that you want

my daughter?" [33]He will respond, "Yes, I want your daughter."
[34]"Aha, very well, I will perhaps give her to you. [35]Which of them
do you want?" [36]The man points to a girl. [37]He says, "This I want."

[38]The father goes to talk to his companion wife and will say
to her, "That young man who just came wants our daughter."

[39]She will say, "You, perhaps, know what you are doing."

[40]The father will respond, "Very well, perhaps, we'll give her
to him." [41]When all women are gathered together, the father will
point to them, "Whom do you want?"

[42]They will drag the girl, although she doesn't want to go, she
doesn't want him, she resists, she says, "No, no."

[43]They will drag her until they hand her to the man. [44]When
she is given to the man, he is told, "You have to go to the forest
and look for food for us to eat. [45]Look for big animals, deer, tapir
whatever you will get."

[46]The woman will go harvest manioc from the garden, together with her sisters, in order to make manioc beer. [47]When
the man comes back, he will blow with his two hands to call her.
[48]He will go hunting far away. [49]He will bring to the house big
prey to smoke in the fire or many birds to roast. [50]The woman
will prepare and pound cooked manioc, sift the mass through
the sieve, and wait for the man. [51]When all unite in the house,
they give him manioc beer, and everybody gets intoxicated
and eats his food. [52]Then they all dance at the end of the feast.
[53]When they all go to sleep, the man takes the woman to where
his house is or where he will work, to sleep together. [54]This is all
that I heard about marriage, the way it was in the past.

FIFTY

Kamaki aparoni atziri

(When a Person Died)

Delia Rosas Rodríguez

[1]Iyekitepaye anampitsitekika, okantaitakena novashirita, okamaki ashaninka Kitamaranto, irotaki antavairianto. [2]Irotaki amitakotapintatziri opankitzi kaniri, koricha, pitoka, mavona, shoñaki, osheki pashinipaye. [3]Avirokaite piyotakero tsika okantavaita ashaninka. [4]Pashini, irori komintsanto, ami tsamiri, sankatzi, varipa antamisatzi, kovacheri. [5]Irotaki kaari okovityanta piarentsi, aisatzi ovaritentsi ovankoki. [6]Maaroni oshaninka osaikajeetzi okimoshirijeetzi, irotaki antavairianto. [7]Amenakotziro oshaninka aisatzi ashi anampitsite oijatakotziro irojatzi areetantapaka mantsiyarentsi paitachari jojotantsi.

[8]Iroñaaka te ayotero tsika okanta areetantakari oka mantsiyarentsika, paitama aroka tera añaapintero oka kantavaitachari mantsiyarentsi ovamajirori ashaninka. [9]Iroñaaka tzimatsi ametapintari akantavaijeete. [10]Arika onkoñaatapake aparoni mantsiyarentsi, kaari añaapintzi, ovamantanaki aparoni anampitsitekika, ontzimatye amene pashini tsika asaikaje, aironta añaapajiro mantsiyarentsi.

[11]Te ayote tsika okanta areetantakari oka mantsiyarentsika. [12]Iroma amakiri kivantapaintairiranki saikapaintatsiriranki? [13]Tetya aparopaye avirokaite pishitove anta, kaarira saikatsini anampitsitekika? [14]Osaitekera ontzimatye oshitove maaroni shiramparipaye,

evankaripaye. ¹⁵Aanake saviri, shacha, chekopi, ovaritentsi, ajate avitsike tsika asaikajeetaje. ¹⁶Ontzimatye nijaateni onkine ashimaatya, okaakini itsimini piratsipaye, imaapintzi piratsi antamisatzi. ¹⁷Aparopaye avirokaite piyotataikeroma, aviroka pijate pijevate shintsipaiteni. ¹⁸Eero okanta asaikaje aka okian-tapakaro mantsiyarentsi. ¹⁹Aparoni avetsikapakero avankopaye ajatzimaitya añaajeri ashaninkapaye. ²⁰Paasonki, iyekitepaye, okaratzi pikimisantakena, ari onkantyari.

¹Brothers of this village, I feel sadness that our fellow woman Kitamaranto died, because she was very industrious. ²She helped to plant manioc, sweet potato, taro, wild potato, sweet corn-root, and many other plants. ³You have known her, the way our fellow woman was. ⁴Besides, she was a good hunter, bringing home curassow, Spix's guan, Andean cock-of-the-rock, and gray-necked woodrail. ⁵That's why her household never ran out of manioc beer and food. ⁶All her family was happy, because she was very industrious. ⁷All her family and members of our village observed her behavior and imitated her, until this illness arrived, called "coughing disease."

⁸We don't know how this illness arrived here, this we haven't seen here, this type of illness that killed our fellow woman. ⁹But we have a custom. ¹⁰When a disease occurs that we haven't seen and kills someone in our village, we have to look for another place to live, where there is no illness.

¹¹We don't know how this illness arrived in our village. ¹²Maybe it was brought by those who visited and stayed here for a short time in the past? ¹³Didn't some of you leave to stay outside of this village?

¹⁴Tomorrow morning we have to leave, all adult males and youths. ¹⁵We'll take machetes, pick-axes, arrows, and food, and we'll go to prepare for us all a place to live. ¹⁶It has to be near

a stream, so that we are able to fish, and close to animal water troughs and dens. [17]Some of you may know this custom, so you'll be moving forward quickly. [18]We can't stay here, because of the illness's invasion. [19]One more time we'll construct our houses, together with our families. [20]Thank you, brothers, for listening to me, so be it.

FIFTY-ONE

Ikantakota sheripiari pairani

(About Shamans Who Existed in the Past)

Daniel Bernales Quillatupa

[1]Arive, iroñaaka nintyaro nokinkitsavaite ashi Elena, okovakotzinari okantyakia okamantajeri oshaninkapaye, anta onampikiopoñaanta. [2]Nokinkitsakoteri ikantakota sheripiari pairani. [3]Ikantzina aani Kasanto, ikamantana pairani irojatzi yañaavetani. [4]Aririka inkove aparoni ashaninka isheripiarite, osheki opomirentsita. [5]Okovatya ashaninkaka kovatsiri ishiripiarite, osheki okova itziventya, okantyakia yantyarori maaroni, yaviantyarori isheripiarite.

[6]Ikantzina aani yoka ashaninka opaviyerini okantya isheripiaritantyari iritaki opaviakeri antarikona sheripiari iroperantzi, kaari kaariperovaitatsini. [7]Ikantziri aani, sheripiari kaariperori iritaki pimantziriri ashaninkapaye nijaaki, pimantziriri ashaninka inchatopaye, akantakotavakero irora shina, irotaki inchato kaariperori ovamairiri atziripaye. [8]Iritaki sheripiari kaari aavironi maaroni ikovakaitziriri aparoni sheripiari iriperori, ovavisakotantatsini, aririka imantsiyavaite atziri.

[9]Ikantzikia aani, vamitairika isheripiarite, ontzimatye iriperote evankari, kaari antamintsateroni kooya. [10]Irotaki kovaperotachari maaroni kovatsiri isheripiarite, ontzimatye ishantyoshite. [11]Ikantziri aani, airo yantamitsatziro kooya okantyakia yaviantyarori maaroni yovametairirira icharini. [12]Ikantzinakia yoka aani, ontzimatye yaanakiri isaikakairi

16. The training of a shaman apprentice. By Daniel Bernales Quillatupa (Aroshi).

ivankoki. [13]Airo ishinitajeri ijataje anta iponaanta, intsipatajiari iririntzipaye, iriri, iriniro, pashinipaye ishaninka. [14]Airo ijataje ivankoki iri: intsipatyari iyoka sheripiari iriperantzi antarikonaka, okantyakia aririka tsika ijate antamiki, ontzimatye iyometayeteri maaroni inchashipaye, okantyakia iyotantyarori apaata paitarika irora yashiteriri shirampari mantsiyaripaye. [15]Iyoyetero maaroni irora kameetsayetatsiri inchashipaye inchaparitsapaye, otaki inchato, maaroni ontzimatye iyometairi.

[16]Aririka apaata ojevatantanakiari isheripiarite pashinika

evankari: ontzimatye irakairi iroñaaka ikantaitziri "sheri." ¹⁷Ari-
rika inkotsitakero, ontzimatye ikamaranke irika shiramparika,
ontzimatye yamavitero. ¹⁸Ikantziri aani imavitaro pairani
irirori. ¹⁹Arika ontzimatye amavitero, aririka ikamarankakai
iyoka antarikona sheripiari, airo irora anariavaitatsi, irojatzita
asaikake shitamenkotsiki. ²⁰Aririka asaiki antamiki, airo anaria-
vaitanakatsi. ²¹Ikantziri aani, akimavakerorika oshonkakotana-
kai aito, *hooo*, kimitaka kipatsika airo okatziyanaja kameetsa,
oshevashevatanakityeya. ²²Asaikaki irojatzi avisantakai.
     ²³Ari irakajairori, aririka ishitovapaje kashiri. ²⁴Ikantziri
aririka ishitovachekitapaje, ari inivetarori antarikonaka ika-
marankiri evankari kovatsiri isheripiarite. ²⁵Ari okantatyeya,
arika ikamarankakiri, intakiaro iikamarankiri, ikantzi aani,
airo avanaja katyori aajatzi pochari. ²⁶Airo avajaro kaniri
kotsirintsi, ontzimatye tavakorintsi, irotaki ivaitari. ²⁷Aajatzi
airo avayetari kantavaishiyetachari yora shima. ²⁸Irokia aririka
avisanaki pashini, iyovapaje pashini kashiri, ari yampitaitajeri
ivankarika ikamarankaitajeri okantya irojatzi yaviantakiaro.
²⁹Iroñaakakia yoka antarikona sheripiari inkotsitaki osheki
oshi sheri irojatzi omitsopatsatantakia. ³⁰Itomaitakiaro kapiroki, irotaki yantsotakairiri apaata yoka evankerika. ³¹Ikantziri
aani, aririka yantsotakaitakiri sherika, omapero oshintsiperotzi,
te oshiyajantyaro aririka ikamarankaite. ³²Osheki oshintsitzi
sherika. ³³Aririka yantsotakakai tsiteni, kapicheeni intakiaro
yatsotakakai. ³⁴Iritaki opaironi irakoki okantyakia ipatyai, ipa-
tyairo maaroni iyotani, ikantakota iyotanitara isheripiaritzi.
     ³⁵Arika antsotakeri, airo osamanitanaki añaatyero oshon-
kakotanake, oshevashevatanake oka kipatsika. ³⁶Aririka oshin-
kiperotanakai, ari añaavakiri piratsipaye, marankipaye kantavaishitachari. ³⁷Aririka añaavakiri, airo akaimi, ontzimatye
ashintsite aminashityari. ³⁸Aririka impokake maranki, ari inin-
tapakai, kimitaka omaperotatya añaavakiririka. ³⁹Ari yankovi-

tapakai aitziki, kimitaka omapero maranki antaitapaintzini,
yankovitakai maaroni aitziki, avatsakipaye irojatzi antave
akintsiki.
    [40]Pokapake pashini, maaroni kantavaishiyetachari maranki,
irojatzi avisantajai iroka oshintsinka sheri ovakerakia añaavai-
taje. [41]Kantzimaitacha aanika antarikona sheripiari irojatzi
isaikake yaminakai, aririka amaperotakiro, amavetero
oshintsinka sheri.
    [42]Ari okantatyeya arika avisaki apite, mava kitaiteri, ari
yatsotakajaipashini sherika irojatzi añaantakiari kantashiyetachari yora piratsipaye: koshiri, kitairiki, pashini piratsipaye
kovenkaripaye. [43]Airo akaime, airo atsarove.
    [44]Okantya, okantya, okantya, avisaki pashiniki kashiri
iroñaaka aviantyarori. [45]Irotaki ikantantairi antarikona
sheripiari, amatakerorika, ari añaakeri yora manitzi, antari
kashekari. [46]Airotya iyora añaavetari, añaashitakiari aka
aririka ashinkitanakiaro sherika. [47]Ari añiiriri, ari anteriri
aririka impokake manitzira kovatsiri iyaimi. [48]Ontzimatye
aroka anteri, airo ashinitairi ivai. [49]Akantya, akantya, ampo-
sakeri, ikitsaravaitakai. [50]Airo akaimamaita irojatzi amakota-
kantakiari, irojatzi amishiyantakiari, irojatzi avamantakiari.
    [51]Iroñaakakia, arika avisaki iroñaaka, aritaki añaakeri manitzi
irojatzi avamantakiari. [52]Ikantakai iroñaaka antarikona
sheripiari, "Pimatakero."
    [53]Ari avisaki osheki kashiri apite, mava, irojatzi aviaperotan-
takiaro. [54]Aririka imatakero iroñaaka aajatzita ari iñaantaka-
kairo ankishokiri, aajatzi antsopairo kaariperori saikatsiri
ivatsaki yora aparoni mantsiyari. [55]Iritaki nijakairori antarikona
sheripiari, "Tsame ajataite aminaite mantsiyari anta." [56]Iritaki
nijaironi, arika yaakero sherika, intziritakiri mantsiyarika
tsikarika ikatsitzi, poñaaka yasorokamaityaro. [57]Yasorokiro,
yasorokiro irojatzi yantakiaro. [58]Imaperotakerorika

isheripiaritzi, ari intsopakairo maaroni saikantariri
mantsiyarika.

⁵⁹Okantya iroñaaka iñaakeri pashini mantsiyari ikantakai
ivametairira, "Intsitya, pamatziro avirori," irojatzi iñaantaka-
kiari ivankerika kovakerori sheripiari, irojatzi itsopantakiaro,
irojatzi yaviaperotantakiaro yaavintayeteri, ivavisakoteri
yokapayeka mantsiyaripaye.

⁶⁰Iriromakia pashini yora aririka ikaimavaitanake, iñaake-
rika maranki, piratsipaye kaariperori, ikaimavaitanake, aririka
ikamarankavaitanake, arika ishitavaitanake, okantakantziro
itsaronka, iritaki ikantziri aani, iritaki kaariperotatsiri. ⁶¹Ari
inkinanaki ishiri, ari onkinanaki nijaaki, piapaka nijaaveri
kaariperoripaye. ⁶²Iritaki aririka apaata ikisaninteri ashaninka,
iritaki pimantziriri nijaaki, irotaki ikamantari atziripaye. ⁶³Irika
eentsi ipimantakeririka, apaatziro ivanakia, airo ikisotanaki,
temakia aririka ivinkakiri ishiri anta nijaaki, ari irora ivamakeri,
ari ipiinkaki. ⁶⁴Irotakikia aririka imantsiyavaite, arika
ipimantante sheripiari kaariperori.

⁶⁵Tzimatsirika ashitanintachari, ijatashitakeri iroñaaka iriperantzi sheripiari, aririka yaminavakeri, ari iyotavakeri iriperan-
tzika. ⁶⁶Ikante, "Aja, imantsiyatantarika tzimatsi kaariperori
atziri ipimantakitziri nijaaki. ⁶⁷Pikoverika yavisakotaje, ari
irora avavisakotajeri." ⁶⁸Ikantzirika iroñaaka iyotzirora pashini
yaavintantzi, yatsotakero isherini.

⁶⁹Ikantziri aani, iñaakero irirori kimitaka airo atenatanaki,
ari añaavakia ajatanaki kimitaka omapero ajatanaki irojatzi
areetantakia intsompaikinta nijaa. ⁷⁰Ari añaapakeri atziri
saikatsiri ashitarori nijaa paitachari "tsomiri." ⁷¹Ari añaakeri
yoka eentsika inariake ara, ontzimatye aajeri ishiri iroñaaka.
⁷²Ontzimatye añaanateri yora tsomiri kaariperori nijaaveri,
okantyakia ipantavajairi eentsika. ⁷³Aririka ipakairi, irotaki
yavisakotantajiari yoka eentsi imantsiyavaitzi.

⁷⁴Ikantzi aani, maaroni saikatsiri kipatsikika tzimatsi oki, tzimatsi ovante, tzimatsi oyempita. ⁷⁵Aririka maaroni añaavai-tzika, añaaventziri aririka akishimatero kipatsi, ankishimateri inchato, maaroni tzimatsiri jaka, ari okimakai. ⁷⁶Irotaki irora ikantziri sheripiaripaye iñaaveyetarora, te onkatziyavaitashitya inchato, te osaikavaishitya nijaa, te osaikavaishitya impereta-paye, tzimatsi ashitarori. ⁷⁷Ari ikantziri aani iñaavakeri pairani, yatsotantavetakarori sheri.

⁷⁸Irotaki irora aanini pairani iñaavetari yaavintayetziri atziripaye ipokashitziri, ijatashitziri mantsiyaripaye yaavintziri. ⁷⁹Temakia irora ovakera neentsitapaki, okantzimonintyana nosampivaiteri aani. ⁸⁰Intaanikia nokimiri ikinkitsavaijeete ikaratzi yantarikonajeetzi. ⁸¹Irotakikia nantarinintanaki kapi-cheeni, nojatzi nokivantziri, irotaki ikamantakinari okaratzi iroñaaka noñaaventakerika.

⁸²Ari okaratzi noyotakonintziri ikantakota sheripiari ika-mantanari aani Kasanto.

¹Very well, now I will begin informing Elena about what she asked me, so that she could advise her fellow men over there, from where she comes from. ²I will tell about shamans from the past. ³My grandfather Kasanto told me about them when he was alive. ⁴When my fellow men wanted to be a shaman, he would go through an ordeal. ⁵The fellow man who wanted to be a sha-man had to observe a strict diet to be able to master all and gain shamanic power.

⁶My grandfather told me that this fellow man, who will trans-fer his power to the apprentice, had to be a skilled adult shaman, not someone who is a layman. ⁷My grandfather said that a bad shaman will offer the spirit of his fellow men to the master of the river, or to the master of trees, for example, lupuna, a bad tree that kills people. ⁸The shaman who didn't follow all diet re-

strictions won't master all knowledge of a good shaman who will cure people when they get sick.

⁹My grandfather said that the learner should be a good young man who will not have sexual relations with women. ¹⁰This fasting includes everything: the learner has to be celibate. ¹¹My grandfather said that the learner shouldn't accost women to be able to master everything when the elderly person trains him. ¹²My grandfather told me that the learner has to live continuously with the elderly person. ¹³He won't allow him to go home to be with his brothers, father, mother, and other kinfolk. ¹⁴He will stay with the experienced shaman in order to go to the forest, where he should teach the young man about herbs, with which he'll be able to treat sick people in the future. ¹⁵He will know all good stuff [for one's health]: plants, roots, bark—all this he has to learn.

¹⁶Later on, another direction in the young man's shamanic training is drinking tobacco. ¹⁷When tobacco leaves are prepared, the young man will vomit with the tobacco concoction, but he has to endure it. ¹⁸My grandfather said that he tried tobacco himself. ¹⁹When we are given tobacco by the old shaman, when he makes us vomit it, we shouldn't lie down on the ground but should stay on the elevated platform of the house. ²⁰When we go to the forest, we shouldn't lie on the ground. ²¹My grandfather said that we will feel that our head is spinning, ooooh, like the ground does not stay still and is moving. ²²We should stay seated until it passes.

²³We are made to drink tobacco during the time of the new moon. ²⁴He said, when the new moon appears, then it is practiced, giving tobacco to those who want to be shamans. ²⁵All this time, when the apprentice is induced to vomit with tobacco, he shouldn't eat salty or sweet food. ²⁶Boiled manioc is not eaten either, but grilled manioc, with the skin, should be eaten. ²⁷All

kinds of fish should not be consumed either. [28]After one month passes, the young man is induced to vomit again until he shows that he handles tobacco well. [29]Now the old shaman will cook a lot of tobacco leaves when they turn into a soft mass. [30]He will stuff the mass into a piece of bamboo [pipe], so that the young man could suck on it. [31]This mass is much stronger than the one the apprentice was given to induce vomiting. [32]This tobacco mass is very powerful. [33]The apprentice will begin sucking on a small amount of tobacco at night. [34]It will be handed to him in the shaman's hand, so that his power and knowledge are given to him, because then he becomes a knowledgeable shaman.

[35]After sucking on the mass, in a short time one feels that the ground is turning around and moving. [36]When he is intoxicated, he will see animals and various snakes. [37]When he sees them, he shouldn't scream, he has to remain strong and watch them. [38]When a snake comes toward him, and it wants him, it appears real. [39]It will coil around his feet, like a real snake would do, will coil around his body, and will reach his neck.

[40]Others will be coming, of different colors, until the tobacco loses its strength. [41]The old shaman will sit and watch [to see] if he handles tobacco well.

[42]As a rule, two or three days will pass, and tobacco will be administered again in order for the apprentice to see all kinds of animals: monkey, peccary, and other menacing animals. [43]He shouldn't scream, or be afraid.

[44]In this manner, months will pass to master it all. [45]If he handles it well, the old shaman says, he'll see a jaguar, a big jaguar. [46]He doesn't see the jaguar in reality, he sees it in a vision, when he is intoxicated with tobacco. [47]He sees it and fights it when the animal comes to devour him. [48]He has to keep fighting in order not to be eaten by it. [49]So he will be fighting, and it will

scratch him. ⁵⁰He shouldn't scream until it gets tired and is made to go away, until he kills him. ⁵¹Sometime later he'll see that it is killed. ⁵²The old shaman will say, "You've accomplished it."

⁵³Two or three months will pass until the apprentice becomes an expert. ⁵⁴When he's accomplished it, he'll practice spitting [on a patient] and sucking illness-causing items from the body of a sick person. ⁵⁵The old shaman will show him how to do it, "Let's go look for a sick person." ⁵⁶He will show it, when he takes tobacco and rubs it into the area of the sick person's body where there is pain, then he makes gestures as if he were extracting something. ⁵⁷He does it until he removes all harm-causing items from the body. ⁵⁸If he is a skilled shaman, he can extract all [harm-causing items] residing in the sick person.

⁵⁹Now that he [has] examined a patient, the old shaman says to the apprentice, "Well, you did it," when he sees that the young man, who wants to be a shaman, has the power to extract harmful items from the body and cure sick people.

⁶⁰In contrast, others who scream when they see a snake or horrible animals, who vomit and defecate because of fear, they are rogue [shamans], as my grandfather said. ⁶¹Their souls go to the depths of the river and transform into malevolent masters. ⁶²They are those who will sell their fellow men whom they hate to the master of the river, that's why our fellow men die. ⁶³If there is a baby who is sold [to the master of the river], he will die, he won't linger, because when his soul is submerged into the waters, he will die there, he will drown. ⁶⁴That's why if a baby gets sick, he has been sold by a rogue shaman [to the master of the river].

⁶⁵If there is a father of the family who goes to see an expert shaman, when he sees him, the expert shaman already knows. ⁶⁶He will say, "Aha, he is sick because there is a malicious per-

son who sold him [to the master of the river]. ⁶⁷If you want him to recover, we shall cure him." ⁶⁸He says this because he knows how to cure with tobacco.

⁶⁹What my grandfather said, he saw it, and he said, that one will feel like he has no weight, and [when] he goes, he will see it [in a trance] like he truly went until he arrived at the bottom of the river. ⁷⁰There he will see a person sitting, the master of the river, called *tsomiri*. ⁷¹There he will see the baby who is lying prostrate, whose soul he will have to take back. ⁷²He will have to speak to the *tsomiri*, the malevolent master of the river, so that he returns the baby. ⁷³When he gives the baby to the apprentice, then the sick baby will recover.

⁷⁴My grandfather said, everything that exists on this land has eyes, mouths, and ears. ⁷⁵When we speak, when we speak on someone's account, when we speak badly of the land, of the tree, everything that exists here will hear us. ⁷⁶That's why shamans say, because they have seen it, that a tree exists for a reason, a river exists for a reason, so do rocks, they all have masters. ⁷⁷This way my grandfather talked about what he saw long ago when he chewed tobacco.

⁷⁸This is what my deceased grandfather saw when he cured people when they would come, when the sick would come and he cured them. ⁷⁹Since I was a child, I couldn't ask my grandfather questions [about the treatments]. ⁸⁰I only heard him talk to the adults. ⁸¹When I grew up a little bit, I would come to visit with him, and he informed me about all this that I am now talking about.

⁸²This is all that I know about shamans about whom my grandfather Kasanto informed me.

FIFTY-TWO

Sheripiari Julio Quintsori

(Shaman Julio Quintsori)

Frida Thomas Huamán

[1]Nonkinkitsatavakiro pairani nosari Jurio Kinchori, sheripiari inatzi. [2]Ikantziro, isheripiata, itsotziro sheri. [3]Iinara ikantziro, "Pikotsitenaro sheri." [4]Ojiriakiro, *jiri, jiri, jiri.* [5]Oshekitakiro maaroni. [6]Airo otzirika impaniki. [7]Okotsitakiro, okotsitakiro, okantakiro, omoyakakiro, omoyakakiro. [8]Okiripitapaki, ari okiripitapaki, ari okantapitsatsitapakia sherira. [9]Irojatzita iroñaaka kapiroki isokaitakiniri, irotaki itsotziri. [10]Aisatzi yaminantantyari ninkarika katsitanaintsiri. [11]Pashini osheki pokashitziri.

[12]Ikamarankanaki eentsi, *mokoro, mokoro,* shiyapaka iniro, onkanteri, "Pinkishokavakinari notomi." [13]Yamonkotaki, yamonkotaki, yaityaro sheri, itsotakiro. Poñaashitaka inkishokakiri eentsira, *kisho, kisho,* itsotzimaintyari, *tsimimi, tsimimi, tsimimi.* [14]Iroñaaka ivanteki ikante, *ajak.* [15]Oyovatye iroñaaka tsika paita antziri eentsira. [16]Terika yantatziri shiritsi, tsika paita antziriri samakariritya. [17]Ari okanta noñaakiri aapi Jurio Kinchori.

[1]I will tell you that there was my grandfather, and he was a shaman. [2]They say, he did a shamanic job and consumed concentrated syrup of tobacco. [3]He would say to his wife, "Make me tobacco syrup." [4]She would cut tobacco leaves, *jiri jiri jiri* (action of

17. A shaman spits out the contents of his mouth, which include disease-causing items. By Daniel Bernales Quillatupa (Aroshi).

cutting plant leaves). [5]She would harvest a lot of tobacco leaves. [6]There shouldn't be sand in the leaves. [7]She would cook them and make them boil. [8]The tobacco leaves would reduce in size and turn into sticky, thick liquid. [9]Then he would put it in his pipe *mansha* [the pipe is made of hollow sugarcane]. [10]This he consumed to diagnose a sick person. [11]Many people would come to see him.

[12]When a child vomited, *mokoro mokoro* (vomiting action), his mother would run to my grandfather and say, "Spit on my son." [13]He will consume his coca leaves and drink his tobacco syrup, *tsimimi, tsimimi, tsimimi* (chewing action). [14]Then he will

spit on the child, *kisho, kisho, kisho* (spitting action). [15]Then he will say, *ahak* (loud expulsion of spittle). [16]Whatever was the cause of the boy's illness would come out from his mouth. [17]If not, the boy choked from bad air, or because someone had been annoyed with him. This is what I've seen of my grandfather Julio Quintsori.

FIFTY-THREE

Impantsakoteri isherini
(He Will Sing about His Tobacco)

Paulina García Ñate

[1]Novakotavakeri naari sheripiaripaye, ikantzi irirori ipantsa-kotziro isherini, yaviakeri irirori, ikantzi.

[2]Ñaakero, ñaakero, ñaakero *ña.*
[3]*Jomm, jomm,* koraketake manitzi, manitzi, manitzi.
[4]Oitakena sheri *na,* oitakena sheri *na,* sheri *na.*
[5]Naakataki, naakataki oitakena.
[6]Manitzipaye ipiya *na,* ipiyatakaro, ipiyatakaro isherini
  tyami, isherini *tyami.*
[7]Oshinkitakena, oshinkitakena *ma* kamarampira,
  kamarampira.
[8]Naviantyarori *ma* pisherini,
[9]Noshiyantanakiariri ashitarori manitzi, manitzi irirori *ma.*
[10]Iinantyari *ma* naari *ma* naari.
[11]Namenaiyete *na* ninkarika mantsiyatatsiniri,
  mantsiyatatsiniri.
[12]Naaka *ma* kora, naaka *ma* amenajeniri.
[13]Nayeteromatya katsitzimotakiri *na,* okatsitzimotakiri
  ivatsakipayera.
[14]Aritaki naari naakotantajiari *ma,* yavisakotantyari.
[15]Naaka, naaka sheripiari nonatzi, nonatzi naaka.

[1]I will explain what the shaman is singing about; he is saying that he will sing about his tobacco, which gives him power.

[2]You will see, you will see, you will see.

[3]*Jomm, jomm*, the jaguar, the jaguar, the jaguar is coming.

[4]He made me take tobacco, tobacco, tobacco.

[5]He made me take tobacco.

[6]The jaguar gave back his tobacco, gave back his tobacco.

[7]Ayahuasca, ayahuasca made me intoxicated, made me intoxicated.

[8]So that I manage your tobacco,

[9]So that I be equal to jaguar's master.

[10]So that I be his spouse.

[11]I will examine those who are sick.

[12]I am a medicine man who will take care of them.

[13]I will remove all that causes them pain in their flesh.

[14]I will remove it so that they recover.

[15]I am a shaman, I am.

FIFTY-FOUR

Yantavairi sheripiari

(Shaman's Work)

Moises Santos Rojas

[1]Sheripiari iyotziri irirori yatsotziro sheri. [2]Irotaki arika yantso-takiro sheri, yantsimiyakiri mantsiyari, ari onkantaki ivavisako-teri, iroma airorika aajatzita eiro okantzi ivavisakoteri. [3]Irotaki yañaantari aparoni sheripiari, intanakiaro tekirata yaminiri mantsiyarinta, yamonkotavaki. [4]Yamonkotaki, yamonkotaki, poña yantsotakiro isherinira, iroñaaka ovakira yaminiri mantsiyarira.

[5]Naari ari notzimakiri aka, ari nokimotataki, ari nantaritaki. [6]Sheripiari isaiki tonkarikinta, pairani isaikavita aka.

[7]Sheripiari, ankantero, atsotzirori sheri. [8]Arika ninkarika omantsiyatatsini, arika ijatashitakiri, inkantaiteri, "Nonintzi paavintenaro nishinto, omantsiyatatzi." [9]Sheripiari jataki yaavintero. [10]Aripaite iyoka sheripiari, oyoviri paitarika ivantekinta matsitantsi. [11]Arika oyovanaki paitarika, arika yantsotakiri mantsiyarinta, paitarika yaaitaki, isampitakero.

[12]"Tsika pivaka?" [13]"Novapainta anta. [14]Ari ipaitakinari novari, novaka anta." [15]Irotaki yaajiri yantsotapainta ivante-kinta, arika yantsotajiro mantsiyaronta.

[16]"Niroka, koñaatapaki. [17]Pinkaimiro tsikarika otzimi onki-yerota iroñaaka aka." [18]Inkiyakavaitaitero, iitamatsivaitaitero. [19]Arika aayetajiro maaroni tsikapaita okitatayetakiri, mantsiya-

ronta amatajaro, avisakotaji. ²⁰Ari okantari yantavairi
sheripiari.

²¹Onashita irori antzirika noina ochonkantzi. ²²"Airo piki-
miro," onkante, "Tsame aitamatsiteri iyokave, aitamatsitero
okave." ²³Tekatsite. ²⁴Intaani ookotziri kamari. ²⁵Iritaki antavai-
tatsini, amayetzirori mantsiyaripaye. ²⁶Ari okantari yantavai-
rinta sheripiari. ²⁷Pairani noñaaki apite sheripiari, aparoni
ipaita Kintsikovari, pashini ipaitari Piiko. ²⁸Sheripiari inatzi.
²⁹Ari okantari yañaantari aparoni sheripiari. ³⁰Atsotzirori
sheri, ari yovakaki sheri, irotaki yaavintantyari irirori. ³¹Irotaki
nokamantavakimiri ikantari aparoni sheripiari antavaite irirori.

¹Shamans know how to consume tobacco. ²When they consume
tobacco [they would spit it on the affected body part] and then
suck the tobacco off the sick person's body, so that the patient
would be able to recover, or not be able to do it. ³Such is the
shaman's life: he begins chewing the tobacco mass before he ex-
amines the sick person, he chews it. ⁴He chews and chews, and
then he sucks the tobacco [off the patient's body], when he ex-
amines him.

⁵I was born here, I grew up here, here I became an adult.
⁶Shamans are in the uplands, but in the past they lived here [in
the valley].

⁷Shamans, we'll say, suck on tobacco. ⁸When someone gets
sick, when a relative goes to see the shaman, he will say to him,
"I want you to treat my daughter, she is sick." ⁹The shaman
would go to treat her. ¹⁰When this shaman [treats her], whatever
comes out of his mouth is related to sorcery. ¹¹When something
comes out, when he sucks the tobacco paste off the sick person,
whatever he picks out [from his vomit], he will ask her questions.

¹²"Where did you eat?" ¹³[She would say,] "I ate over there.

¹⁴There I was given the food, I ate over there." ¹⁵This is what came out of his mouth, when he was sucking on this sick female.

¹⁶"Here she is, I can see her in a vision. ¹⁷Find out from her where she has it [the refuse buried], she should dig it out." ¹⁸She is brought in and identified as a witch. ¹⁹When she takes out everything that she buried in the ground, the sick person overcomes the disease and recovers. ²⁰This is shaman's work.

²¹What my wife does is healing with steam baths. ²²She will say, "Don't listen to it" [what they say], "Let's identify this man as a witch, let's identify this woman as a witch." ²³They are not witches. ²⁴It's the demon they point to. ²⁵This is the demon's work, he brings disease to the sick people. ²⁶Such is shaman's work. ²⁷Long ago I saw two shamans, one was called Kintsiko-vari, another—Piiko. ²⁸They were shamans. ²⁹Such is their way of life. ³⁰They suck on [the pipe with] tobacco paste, make the tobacco come out [from their mouths], and with this they cure. ³¹This is what I have advised you on, [namely,] what a shaman does.

FIFTY-FIVE

Sheripiari

(Shaman)

Ines Pérez de Santos

¹Noñeeri naari iyoka ikantakirika noimi iyoka sheripiari, noñaakiri naari. ²Ipaita Oshipio, ikantzija, noñiiri omantsiyataki ina. ³Okantzi, "Tsame añaakiteri pikonkiri, aanakina." ⁴Nojataki. ⁵Noñaakiri, okatsitaki ina asankini, okatsitaki oito. ⁶Itsotakiro isherini ivira aka iyapiroteki, itsotakiro, itsotakiro. ⁷Ikishokakiro ina, ikishokakiro, yaaki ovira aka kaarashi. ⁸Ikantziroja, "Yantakimi, pimontsakari shiretsi." ⁹Poña oitokika inchashi itsotakiroka aajatzita. ¹⁰Poña naminavintsatziri, nokantzi, "Tsika ikantaka?" ¹¹Itsotziro, itsotziro, poña ikantaja *ajak*, yamaki ovira aka pinitsi yoisotakotakiro oishikira ina. ¹²Ikantzirokia, "Maatsi aparoni shirampari nintavintamiri. ¹³Te pininteri, iritaki aashivaitakimiri piishika. ¹⁴Te pininteri, iroñaaka okatsitantakarika piito. ¹⁵Iroñaaka ari pamatajia."

¹⁶Noñaakiri, ijataki. ¹⁷Yaapaintzi inchashi, yaakiro oishipayenta, ikaakitakiro ina. ¹⁸Okitaitamani tzinavaitaja ina, okantzi, "Te onkatsitaji noito."

¹⁹Novakiro naari noshirikinta. ²⁰Noñaakirora ina inchashira, nojataki naminakiro, ari noñaantakiaro naari. ²¹Okatsitaki noito, ovakira navankarotapaki. ²²Nokantziro, "Ina, tsame anto. ²³Ari noñaakotakiri pavaini, yaakiro inchashi." ²⁴Naakitziro naari, nokaakitakaro, otekatsitakanakina.

²⁵Irotaki naari noviri noshiriki. ²⁶Irotaki naavintantari,

18. A healer administers eyedrops into her patient's eyes. By Daniel Bernales Quillatupa (Aroshi).

ikantzi ninkarika pokatsini, "Noito, noito, noito." [27]Naaka nochekatziro ironta okontsainta. [28]"Nompitenkakimi. [29]Ari katsinkaini." [30]Arika nompitenkakimi avirori, arika nonkan-taki, "Paakitena katsinkakini." [31]Ari ompitenkakai okikika, onkantakai katsinkakini, onkantapakai *tsinkaririri* maaroni aitokinta.

[32]Irotaki nañaantari naari ninkarika pokatsini, inkantapa-kina, "Nonintzi pinkaatena terika pisaatena." [33]Nosaatakiri, nosaatakiri, tekatsivaitanaji, jataji. [34]Irotaki nantziri naari.

[35]Iyokama sheripiarika noñaakiri ikantzirika noimi inkiya-kavaitakiro, arika intsotakiro. [36]Aayetakiro ara osheki. [37]Nami-

niro kiyavaitatsiri. ³⁸Nokantzi, "Intsitya, okimitara aakiro ovira aka, ojakiro kovenkaripaye?" ³⁹Nokantzi, "Tsika okantya osaikikia?" ⁴⁰Irotaki naari nokinkishiriapintari. ⁴¹Nokantzi, "Tsika onkantyarika onkitatantapakiarori arakia?" ⁴²Okantzikia, "Te naaka kitateroni, ipoki kamari, ikantana, 'Tsame ankitatakotero omantsiyateta onkamiita.'"

⁴³Ari okantari naari noñiiri, noñiimaintakaro anta isaikakantakanari noimi kirinka. ⁴⁴Kameetsa kooya avankaro, ari okimitamana, asaikaiyeni. ⁴⁵Yamaitakiro, ityankavaitziro, itzikiyavaitziro, yatsikavaitziro iyora amakiroriratya. ⁴⁶Poñaaka irora paitaranki ari imisaikapakiro. ⁴⁷Yaaki iroñaaka kirimini ovira oka, ipakiro, "Pinkiye!" ⁴⁸Naminamintsatziro, okiyavaitzi, okiyayetakiro.

⁴⁹Iyonta mantsiyarinta irotaintsi inkami. ⁵⁰Poñaakia nojatanaki naari, nokantziri, noñaakirira ikantaka *eej, eej*. ⁵¹Itapiyaka imotyaki, nokantakiri, "Tsika paita antakimiri?"

⁵²"Notapiyatya, okantakotakina irora naniro," ikantzi. ⁵³Poña naashitakiri irora oishi iroñaaka chochoki paitachari *guanábana*. ⁵⁴Namirokashitakiri, *miro miro*, notsipatashitakiri *paico*, naakiro, nopichovatakiniri, *pichori pichori*. ⁵⁵Nokantziri, "Intsitya, pire, omapirorika imatsikaitzimi, pikantzira matsi."

⁵⁶Noitakiri. ⁵⁷Tekira osamanini, "Tsika okanta ikimavakiro?" ⁵⁸Ikantzikiaja, "Arive, otsinkanakina pipakinariranki, naaka kantakashinintakaro. ⁵⁹Nokantakantavaitakiro naniro, iroñaaka otsinkanakina."

⁶⁰Poñaashitaka ikimavakiro otsinkanakiri, tzinanaka iroñaaka. ⁶¹Jataki, ijatashitziri pasavaitakirori iraniro. ⁶²Ikantapakiri, "Aitaki pipasavaitziro, aritaki ovirapakiari." ⁶³"Te, ikantavakirikia, te. ⁶⁴Aakotemita maaroni, airorika, airo pitekatsitaji." ⁶⁵Ikantzirikia, "Te, opapakina chookipatsainira nijaa, niravaki. ⁶⁶Tsikarika paita ovitsikashitakinari, iroñaaka otsinkanakina." ⁶⁷Arikia yookakakiri.

⁶⁸Inintavitaka iviromi avankarora, inintzi iviro. ⁶⁹Nokan-
tziri naaka, "Airo pivavaitziro, pivantyarori evankarora. ⁷⁰Pami-
navakia pañaantariki. ⁷¹Paitarika pantziri avirori? ⁷²Kameetsa-
takimirika, aritaki onkantaki piviro, airorika, airo okantzi
piviro avankarora." ⁷³Ari nokantakiriri. ⁷⁴Nookakavintakero, te
ivaitero. ⁷⁵Irotaki noñaakiri naari nosaikatzi kirinka okaratzi
yantziri sheripiari. ⁷⁶Ari ovirapakari.

¹I saw the shaman whom my husband mentioned, I also saw
him. ²His name was Eusebio, and I saw him when my mother got
sick. ³She said, "Let's go and see your uncle, I am sick."

⁴I went [to watch the shaman]. ⁵I saw that she had pain in her
heart and her head. ⁶The shaman sucked a tobacco mass of this
size through his pipe, he sucked and sucked. ⁷Then he spat on
my mother, he spat, and refuse of this size came out. ⁸He said,
"There is damage done, you are choking with bad air." ⁹Then he
removed plant leaves from her head, when he sucked with his
mouth on her head. ¹⁰I was watching and said, "How could it
be?" ¹¹He sucked and sucked and then made this sound, *ahak*
(action of loud expectoration of spittle), and removed a magic
herb of this size; it was tied up with my mother's hair. ¹²He said,
"There is a man who wants you. ¹³You don't want him. ¹⁴It was
him who took your hair with certain intent. ¹⁵You don't want
him, so you have a headache now, but you will overcome it."

¹⁶I saw him go to the forest. ¹⁷He gathered leaves of a medicinal plant and administered the herbal concoction into my
mother's eyes. ¹⁸The next day my mother got up and said, "My
head doesn't hurt me."

¹⁹I put it in my head. ²⁰Because I saw my mother's recovery
due to this herb, I went to look for it in the jungle, so that I could
test it myself. ²¹I had headaches during my periods. ²²I said to

her, "Mother, let's go over there. ²³I've seen what my uncle did: he gathered this plant's leaves." ²⁴I harvested the herb, administered its drops in my eyes, and got better.

²⁵This is what I put in my head. ²⁶With this herb I cure, when someone comes and says, "My head, my head, my head." ²⁷I cut herbs in the area where they grow like a carpet. ²⁸[I say,] "I will administer drops in your eyes. ²⁹They are cold." ³⁰I will administer the drops in your eyes, after I say, "Bring me *katsinkakini* (cold-inducing plant)." ³¹When we receive herbal drops in our eyes, we feel cold, and the drops produce a sudden stir, *tsinkaririri* (a sudden feeling of a stir), in our entire head.⁹

³²In my life, I've seen people come and say, "I want you to bathe me, or bathe me with steam." ³³I will give him a steam bath, he will recover, and will take off. ³⁴This is what I do.

³⁵In contrast, the shaman whom I've seen, whom my husband mentioned, made a woman dig into the ground, when he sucked [bad stuff from the patient]. ³⁶And she would dig out all her charms. ³⁷I looked at what she was digging out. ³⁸I said, "Well, how could she extract these dangerous things of this size? ³⁹How could it be?" ⁴⁰This is what I always thought about. ⁴¹I said, "How will she bury them in this place?" ⁴²She said, "I will not bury it, a demon comes and tells me, 'Let's bury it, so that she will get sick and die.'"

⁴³So it happened that I saw it downriver, when I lived in this place with my husband. ⁴⁴A nice girl, I see a mental image of her, like today we are sitting here. ⁴⁵She was brought in, he pushed her, kicked her, this person who brought her. ⁴⁶Then he made her sit on the ground. ⁴⁷He grabbed a plank of the chonta palm of this size and said, "Dig!" ⁴⁸From a distance, I watched her dig for a long time; she extracted many things.

⁴⁹The sick person was about to die. ⁵⁰Then I went [to see the

sick person], I said, when I saw him doing *eeh, eeh* (breathing heavily). ⁵¹His stomach was bloated, and I said to him, "What happened to you?"

⁵²He said, "I am bloated, because my daughter-in-law did it to me." ⁵³Then I gathered for him leaves of the plant called *guanábana*.¹⁰ ⁵⁴I mashed them with my hands, *miro miro* (mashing action) and mixed the mass with *paico* leaves; I took them and ground them for him, *pichori pichori* (grinding action).¹¹ ⁵⁵I said, "Well, drink it, and [we'll see] whether this is true that you are bewitched, because you say the witch [did it to you]."

⁵⁶I gave him the drink. ⁵⁷A little bit later, I asked, "Is your body responding to the medicine?" ⁵⁸He said, "Very well, I felt a stir in my body, from what you had given to me. ⁵⁹I am guilty for what happened to my daughter-in-law, now that the medicine revived me."

⁶⁰Afterward, the medicine had an effect on him, he got better and got up. ⁶¹He went to see his cousin, who was brutally beating the girl. ⁶²He said to him, "It's enough of your beating, this will be enough." ⁶³He [his cousin] said to him, "No. ⁶⁴She should extract everything; if not, you will not recover." ⁶⁵He said, "No, this little sister gave me a concoction, I drank it. ⁶⁶Whatever it was that she made for me, but now I am revived." ⁶⁷At that moment the sick person made his cousin release her.

⁶⁸His cousin wanted to kill this young girl. ⁶⁹I said to him, "Don't kill her on a whim, why are you killing her? ⁷⁰Look at your own life. ⁷¹What are you doing? ⁷²If you are without sin, then you could kill her; if not, you can't kill this young girl." ⁷³This is what I said to him. ⁷⁴He set her free, he didn't kill her. ⁷⁵This is what I saw when I lived downstream, all that the shaman did. ⁷⁶Here it ends.

FIFTY-SIX

Okantakota matsitantsi

(About Witchcraft)

Ruth Quillatupa Lopez, with Daniel Bernales Quillatupa

[1]–Ina, pinkitsatakotairo okantakota matsitantsi. [2]–Matsitantsija, tzimatsi yometairori antaroventzirori omatsitzi irori, okantero irokave, "Kameetsarini, pinkaakityaro." [3]Onkaakitakero okiki, okantya, okantya, irorija oñaakeri paitarika, kamaripaye oñaayetakiri iroñaakaja. [4]Aririka iroñaaka oyometakeroraja, okantya iroñaaka ninkarika mantsiyatanaintsini onintzirira irora omatsikeri. [5]Omishitanajero, omishitanajero tsikarika okanta onintzira onintakaro okantero.

[6]Opoñaashitakia iroñaaka pokaki iroñaaka sheripiarira, yamenakero, ikante, "Teve, irotaki ironta omatsikatziro." [7]Iroñaaka irora matsikantaintsirira impokashitakero. [8]Ikante, "Avirokataki matsikakero, tsika okantaka piyotantakarori?" [9]"Iro yometakenaro ironta, irotaki kaakitakenari." [10]"Iroñaaka tsika pikantzika avirori pivavisakotajeri?" [11]"Airo yavisakotaje, novakaniri irasankani." [12]Irojatzi ikiyakantaitakiaro iroñaaka. [13]Ikiyakaitakero otapinaki menkotsi, tsikarika isaikajeetzini, tsikarika imaajeetzini, tsikarika ivajeetani. [14]Irojatzi impasavaitaitakero, ivaitakero jenokinta, airo ipaitajero ovarite, yaaitanakero nijaaki, imitsitziyavaitero irojatzi okinkitsatantakia, "Naakataki matsikakeri, okantatyana, 'Tsame amatsikiri ayarita.'" [15]Irojatzita impasavaitaitakerorika, intsatakoitakero. [16]Terikaja, impasainavaitaitakero oitoki, itankainavaitaitakero.

¹⁷Onkantya, onkantya iyoraja aririka onintzi aakotajeri, aakotajeri omishiriki, okante, "Ari novakotakeriri." ¹⁸Iroñaaka yamaitakero, inkiyakavaitaitero. ¹⁹Aayetaki inchakipatsaini, tonkitsipaye, kaniritsakipaye, samanitonki, manirotonki, sharotonki, ikaratzi ivayetarira shinkitzinkaripayera. ²⁰Inkantya, inkantya, okante, "Ari naakotajeri, airo pipasatana." ²¹Ari yamatanintajia.

²²Inkantya, inkantya okantajero iroñaaka yometakerorira. ²³"Nokantzimi, iroñaaka, 'Tsame pimaperoteri, ayarita.'" ²⁴Iroñaaka oñaakeri tsiya yatziritzimotakero, iritaki shintsiventeroni. ²⁵Okaratzi oñaayetziri kamariperotatsirira. ²⁶Okante, "Iritaki kantana, 'Tsame piviri.' ²⁷Pipasavaitana naaka, iriro yometanarira. ²⁸Te pimpasateri, atziri inatzi, noñeeri naaka. ²⁹Iritaki kantanari, 'Tsame pantero,' naaka pipasavaishitaka. ³⁰Iriro te panteri, atziri kityonkari iitsari." ³¹Oñaanatziri tsiyara, iñaanatziro irirori, oñaanatziri irori.

³²Ari inkantya, inkantya, ikantzi, "Tsika otzimika? ³³Tsika osaikika iroñaaka yometakemirori?" ³⁴Onkante, "Ari osaiki anta." ³⁵Yaaitanakero, onkante, "Te, iritaki yometainaro," yokotavakayetara. ³⁶Imitsitziyavaitaitero nijaaki, onkiyavaite, impasavaitaitero. ³⁷Airotya kameetsa ikantaranki isampitaitero kameetsa. ³⁸Ijatashitero tsiteni, itaavaitaitero.

³⁹Aroka asaikaiyeka, iroñaaka te añeero. ⁴⁰Kimitachari paitarika avavaitanakiari, apaata imishitanakai, irora pokapaintatsiri inkaranki, tera atziriperote, matsi onatzi. ⁴¹Ari opoñiiyari. ⁴²Aririka iñiitajai, inkantaite, "Korakitaintsi matsi." ⁴³Airo ipaita paitarika ayari, arika imishitakai, ari okantari. ⁴⁴Onkantya, onkantya arika amatayetajia. ⁴⁵Aritya akoventajiri tsikarika okitatziri, ainirotayetatsi. ⁴⁶Airotya yaajaitajai kameetsa, inkantaitanakai matsi.

⁴⁷Iroñaaka aririka ivaitakero, ikante, "Tsika ikanta irorave piyometantarori?" ⁴⁸"Te, irotaki kantana nonintzi naari, noyo-

tero okaratzi pantzirira." [49]Iro kantzimaitacha te onkameentsate, inkantavaitaitai amatsitzi.

[50]Aririka ivaitakero iroñaaka irora, pairani aka notzimera,
nokantziri, Tzimashitoroki, maatsi pokayetatsiri, tekirata
ankimisantanaketa, poñaachari Oventeniki, isheninkapaye
nosarini, koñaatakotaki, ikantziri, kasorina, itaaitakero
koñaaro.

[51]Okanta opiantakari, asaikantajari kameetsa iroñaaka.
[52]Airorika itaaitziromi, irojatzi onkantyami. [53]Te ankimisantero
aroka. [54]Irora tera ankimisantero, arorija kameetsa asaiki.

[55]Kantayetacha shinkitzinkaripaye, ari ankimiri "matsi,"
"matsi," "matsi." [56]Ari ankimiri, "Korakitaintsi matsi." [57]Aririka
tsika apintsamatsitya ajate, ari imishitakai. [58]Iroñaaka aroka
amishitakavaishitya, irotakima amantsiyatanaki.

[59]Pairani ari okantari, "Korakitaintsi osaitekira, paama-
ventyaro, korakitaintsi matsi." [60]Iroñaaka ayotantajiarori
korakitaintsi, ankimavakeri tsiya, *shitzikoro, shitzikoro.*
[61]"Korakitaintsi kaariperori atziri, irotaki yavisaiyanakerika."
[62]Yovamachetapakai arorikia, ijevatakai ayamarite. [63]Airo
ipaitai avarite, amatsitatzira, amatsikapajerikari. [64]Ari okantari
pairani, nokimiri pairani.

[65]Noñaavetakaro naari irojatzi yanipichokitachana.
[66]Noñaakoventziri pairani iroñaaka yora ikantaitziri Omani.
[67]Iritaki kinkiarori irirori matsitantsi. [68]Paitarika kapicheeni,
ishaavaitanakia ireentsite, "Irotaki matsikakero. [69]Pinkiye tsika
pivakotakenaro." [70]Airorika yaanakero iroñaaka, yoisotakota-
nakero *kosta*riki, ivinkakotero nijaaki pitotsiki. [71]Isaitakero,
chak, jaikimantsataka. [72]Saikamachetaki, arima amavetakero
ayatsinkari, airo.

[73]Ikanta, ikanta, maatsi ñaaperoyetachari iroñaaka Yorina-
kira. [74]Ikantzi, tsikapaita ari ikantanaitatya irorave impokerika
aka, aroka ikantajeetai matsi. [75]"Tsametyami amateri arori."

⁷⁶Yairikajeetakerini, irojatzi isaikavetani Koshentoni. ⁷⁷Yaakeri iroñaaka iyorave Omanira, yoisoitakeri irirori, yoisoitakeri, yampitsitakeniri irako, iitzi, yaaki *kosta*ri, itetaitaki mapi, iteta-kotanakiri pitotsiki. ⁷⁸Niyanki ikimatziri, "*Vao, vao, vao,* poiso-riakotena, poisoriakotena, airo poisotakotana!" ⁷⁹Irojatzita niyanki, ivinkakotakeri. ⁸⁰Irojatzi opiantakari, kaari akiman-taja ikantaitai "matsi," "matsi."

    ⁸¹–Paitaka inkantantari *vao, vao, vao?* ⁸²Masherotanaki?

    ⁸³–Tsikama ankineka añaavaitanake nijaaki ivinkakirira? ⁸⁴Inkante, "Poisoriakotaina, airo nantamintsajeetajemi." ⁸⁵Iki-satyara irirori, itetanaitzi pitotsiki niyanki, yoipakakotakeri. ⁸⁶Imitsitziyakeri, tsitziyanakitya, itetakitzira mapi aajatzita. ⁸⁷Ari overanakari, tekatsitaki Omani. ⁸⁸Iritaki saikavetacha pairani Yorinakira.

¹–Mother, tell about sorcery.

    ²–Sorcery, there is an older person who teaches her, who is a veteran sorcerer; she will tell her, "This is good, I will adminis-ter it in your eyes." ³She will administer it in her eyes, and later on, she will see something, she will see evil spirits. ⁴When she teaches her, sometime later somebody will get sick, when she casts a spell on this person. ⁵She will see this person repeatedly in a dream, when she wants to do harm to him.

    ⁶Afterward, a shaman will come, he will see her [in his vision] and say, "She is the one who cast a spell." ⁷Now, he will come to see the one who cast spell. ⁸He will say, "You cast spell, how did you learn it?" ⁹"She taught me sorcery, she was the one who ad-ministered the concoction in my eyes." ¹⁰"Now, what are you say-ing, will you make him recover?" ¹¹"No, I ate his heart already." ¹²Then they will make her dig. ¹³They will make her dig under the elevated platform where family members sit, sleep, and eat. ¹⁴Then they will beat her up, place her on the upper level of the

house, and won't give her food; she will be taken to the river and left submerged in the water until she says, "I am the one who cast spell, because she told me, 'Let's cast spell and eat.'" ¹⁵She will be beaten up and hanged. ¹⁶Or she will be beaten in her head, and her head will split.

¹⁷If she wants to quit doing harm to this person in her dream, she will say, "I buried it here." ¹⁸She will be taken to this place and will be made to dig. ¹⁹She will extract small twigs, bones, yuca peel, bones of peccary, deer, agouti, all things that people who have feasts eat. ²⁰She will say, "I will truly quit, don't beat me." ²¹The victim will recover.

²²She will say who taught her sorcery. ²³"I am telling you, 'Let's make him worse, let's eat him.'" ²⁴She will see a demonic nocturnal hawk in human form who will force her to do harm. ²⁵She sees all kinds of evil beings. ²⁶She will say, "He told me, 'Let's kill him.' ²⁷You are beating me, but he is the one who taught me. ²⁸You didn't beat him, and he is a person, I've seen him. ²⁹He is the one who told me, 'Let's do harm,' so you punish me in vain. ³⁰Him you didn't punish, and he is a person in a red robe." ³¹She talks to the nocturnal hawk, he talks to her, she talks to him.

³²They will ask her, "Where were you born? ³³Where is the one who taught you?" ³⁴She will say, "She lives here." ³⁵They will capture her, and she will say, "No, it was her who taught me," she will identify her as a witch. ³⁶She will be submerged in the river, she will dig and will be beaten. ³⁷But they won't interrogate her thoroughly. ³⁸They will find her at night, and she will be burned.

³⁹We don't have it in this area now.⁴⁰For example, when we eat something together with someone who visited us recently, and later we see him in a dream, this person is not a good one, he's a witch. ⁴¹This is how it begins. ⁴²When someone sees us in a dream, [he will say], "A witch is coming." ⁴³He won't give us

anything to eat [next time], when he sees us in a dream, this is the way it is. ⁴⁴This person will recover little by little. ⁴⁵We will reveal to others whatever was buried, but there is always something [left in the ground]. ⁴⁶We won't be treated well, we will be treated like a witch.

⁴⁷When they kill her, they will say, "Why did you teach her?" ⁴⁸"No, she told me that she wants to know how to do harm." ⁴⁹Nonetheless, this won't do, they will treat us as witches.

⁵⁰When they killed them, in the past, where I was born, in Tzimashitoroki, there were those who had come from Oventeni, my grandfather's relatives, before our conversion to Christianity, they said, that kerosene appeared and witches were burned alive.

⁵¹So sorcery has disappeared, that's why we live well. ⁵²Hadn't witches been burned, it'd have existed. ⁵³We weren't Christians then. ⁵⁴Now that we don't practice sorcery, we live well.

⁵⁵Those who drink *masato* [non-Christians], we were called witches. ⁵⁶We will hear, "A witch is coming." ⁵⁷When we decide to go to some place, they will see us in a dream. ⁵⁸When one sees dreams, then we could get sick.

⁵⁹In the past, it was this way, "She is coming tomorrow, be careful, a witch is coming." ⁶⁰To know if a witch is coming, we will listen to the nocturnal hawk's sound, *shitzikoro, shitzikoro* (nocturnal hawk's call). ⁶¹"A bad person is coming, they have passed by [the bird, sent by the witch, and the witch]." ⁶²We leave the house against our will, because our evil spirit directs us. ⁶³We won't be given food, because we are a witch, we could cast a spell. ⁶⁴This was the way in the past, I heard it in the past.

⁶⁵I also saw it when I was a little girl. ⁶⁶I saw what they did to someone called Omani. ⁶⁷He would often mention sorcery. ⁶⁸On any occasion, [like] his son had diarrhea, "She did harm to him. ⁶⁹Dig out where you placed it [evil charms]." ⁷⁰When they capture her, they tie her up with a burlap-like material and sub-

merge her in the water in a canoe. [71]They pour water into the canoe, *chak* (action of quickly pouring water into a receptacle), until it's filled with water. [72]She sits there against her will, in case she might endure the cold, but she doesn't.

[73]He was a brave from Yurinaki. [74]He would say, whenever, all the time, he came here, he would call us all "witches." [75]"Let's handle this." [76]They grabbed him; this happened when Ko-shento lived here. [77]They grabbed him, that Omani, tied him up, folded his arms and his legs, took a bag, filled it with stones, and placed him in a canoe. [78]When it was in the middle of the river, they heard him say, "*Vao, vao, vao*, untie me, untie me, don't tie me up!" [79]In the middle of the river, they submerged the canoe [by placing in it the bag of stones]. [80]Since then, it stopped, we haven't been called witches.

[81]–Why did he say *vao, vao, vao*? [82]Did he transform into a river toad?

[83]–How could one talk in the river, when they submerged the canoe? [84]He wanted to say, "Untie me, I won't aggravate you anymore." [85]They were angry, so they put him in the canoe and let it go down in the middle of the river. [86]They drowned him, he went to the bottom of the river, because there were stones in the canoe. [87]This was the end, Omani ceased to exist. [88]He lived in Yurinaki long ago.

FIFTY-SEVEN

Ochonkiri Abdias

(She Steam-Bathed Abdias)

María Virginia Lopez, Abdias Caleb Quinchori, Bertha Rodríguez de Caleb, and Victorina Rosas de Castro

[1]–Irotaki nantziri naaka, nochonkantavaitzi kapicheeni, je, je, ari akantero aka. [2]Aka avitsikero, irotaki atsipatairori inchashipatsaini.
    [3]–Piñaavaite añaaniki.
    [4]–Pimairite, kooya.
    [5]–Airorika airo ayotzi, paita pantziri.
    [6]–Nojatzi antamiki, nayi inchashi.
    [7]–Tsika opaitaka pinchashiri?
    [8]–Iroka ashi onkisairika nijaa, arika ankimiro, ankatsivaite.
    [9]–Tema añaavintatyero, je, irotaki ari pinkanterori.
    [10]–Tera noñaavaitero naari, pishiyakantakovaitena, pinkantero.
    [11]Irotaki novantari naari. [12]Irotaki kameetsatatsiri arika onkisairika nijaa. [13]Iroka ashi eerivaiterika, peerivaitzi, panonkavaitzi. [14]Nontsonkaki. [15]Nojavaitapintzi chapinki Kiniri.
    [16]Chapinki nopoñaara, akimakotziri pishtako, itsonka ivayetakiro iroka kirinkaka. [17]Iroñaakakia arive, tekatsi. [18]Tzimatsi nijaaka, je, je, amoyakakiro nijaaka. [19]Arive, kooya, irotakitya, kooya, omapero avirori morinashi, ari okaratzi, arive.
    [20]–Nonkinkitsatakotero. [21]Paamakitaki mapi, noisashitakiro ochonkantyanari aavintantantziri. [22]Onchonkina aka noitzi-

kika. ²³Nokatsitakika, nanonkakika, te navisakote.
²⁴Ipayevitakana *doctor* aavintarontsi, tekatsi onkantena.
²⁵Maatsi aavintatzinkaro, opokaki, nokaimatziro Bertha.
²⁶Okantziro, "Paavintena," okatsivaitzi irori. ²⁷Inchashi
otetakirira ooyakira, irotaki aavintarontsira pariakairori
mantsiyarentsi. ²⁸Ankatsivaiterika, irotaki aavintakia, aritaki ompiakiro
oyatsinari. ²⁹Ari onchonkakina, notashitashitaka mapi
onchonkantyanari. ³⁰Arika omoyanaki ara kovitzikira, arika
ontetashitakena onkarate *cuatro* mapi, aritaima ompianaka
oyatsinka. ³¹Okatsitzika noitziki, maatsirika irorika, yantavairi
kamari. ³²Aritaki ompariapaki, paita katsitakakinari noitzikira. ³³Nokatsitantari, te nonkantsivaitashitya, irotaki nokin-
kitsatakotziro. ³⁴Aritaki ovinkashitakina, amenero paita
shitovatsini.

³⁵–Pimpokanake. ³⁶Tsika irora inchapatari?

³⁷–Tema piyotziro pisaatantayetzi aviroka, tsika akanteka
atevaishita inchashipaye. ³⁸Okimitarakia pivarirokia, te ayotero.
³⁹Pikimitara aviroka pivariro, terika arima ankantakimi, pin-
chonkantavaite. ⁴⁰Ayotziro akaataro inchashipatsaini, kamari-
vinkipatsaini. ⁴¹Tsonkataka novinitsitepatsaini. ⁴²Tzimataita-
tsitaima aviroka piyamarishite.

⁴³–Pairikina, akave!

⁴⁴–Itsonkapitsatakinaro novaavote ivapakanaro nokaata-
pintari. ⁴⁵Ikantavita ashi onkisai nijaa, tema te noyotero
novariro.

⁴⁶–Ari okantari, arika asaatantavaite. ⁴⁷Noñiiro naari ovakera nosaatantavaitzi, nopomirintsitakaro, osheki noñaashitakaro. ⁴⁸Mava osarentsi naviantakarori naari, ari nokantakeri
nosaantayetzi. ⁴⁹Kitaiterikipaye asheninkapaye ikimakovinta-
kina, "Osaatantavaitzi." ⁵⁰Nosaatantavaitzi naari neetsikiropai-
tenikia naviaakiro okoñaatzimotakina okantarika oshiyaro

tsika opaitaranki, noyotantajiarori arika ipaitaitziroka. [51]Arika aviamatakiro, arika tsika ipaita avia, terika sharoni, samani, ari ankimakiro ankatsinkayete, ishiyarotaima eentsiranki, arika ontzimanite. [52]Ari okantari pairani. [53]Osaikatzima, je, aritakirakia, pinkantakoteri aka, airo pipashiriakotziri. [54]Yatsipetakaro.

[55]–Opaamakitaki mapira, katsirinivee!

[56]–Incha, pinkamantero, pikantziri inkaranki, ninka ovamitakimirori, tsika ikantaitziroranki?

[57]–Tema nokantakiro inkaranki, tema ishayeni Mariayeni, ikantaitziro María Varote, irotaki opanarori pairani. [58]Nokantziro, mava osarentsi okanta naviantakarori. [59]Nopomirintsitakityaro naari. [60]Arika asaatantavaite, airo aminitaro. [61]Tsika okaratzi mapi otashitakiri? [62]Aparoni, mava, *cuatro*, apaatara tara, onkantavakimita piitziki. [63]Iroñaaka pisaikavaki, ari pinkantavakiari piitziki. [64]Pamirokavakia piitzikira.

[65]–Paamakitaki!

[66]–Tema pikantzi *cuatro*, *cuatro*, tema ari, *cuatro*, aritaki ari nonkantavakia. [67]Pamirokiro piitzira ara, pamirokiro, maaroni pitapiikira aisatzita.

[68]–Katsirinivee, katsirini, nokoviro noitziki, noitziki.

[69]–Je, tsikarika okatsitzi, aritaki pinkantyari. [70]Pinkantavajeetavakia pitapiikirakia, pitapiikira. [71]Pinkantakoperotavakia, tema opoñaari okatsitzikia.

[72]Pintetashiteri pashini mapi. [73]Poña noipiyakiro, nonchonkanakia naari. [74]Pintetashiteri pashini. [75]Aikitziroini inkimarontavakiarota. [76]Aritaki okaraki nosaatantayetzi anta aisatzi katsitatsiri, *cuatro*, aritaki inkimanintakia. [77]Kimitaka arika nompokate, ari napitapananteri.

[78]–Aviroka pinintzi pishintsivintero.

[79]–Je, aparoni airo ashitakotzi, ariajaini aroka pava. [80]Te aroka pava, pava aparoni inkantakai, ari ishitakotanajai.

[81]Iroma aroka atziri anatzi, airo okantzi avavisakotante shintsini. [82]Tema oshekini katsitayetatsiri anta otsipikonatanta, oshekini virakocha, osheki asheninka, oshekini yanesha. [83]Kantzimaintacha airo ipinatzimi. [84]Yanesha mashitsari inajeetatzi. [85]Chapinkiranki noshintotsori irori, osamanitakotaka apite kashiri osamanitaki. [86]Nopavitakaro no*terefono*te pashini yanesha, saikatsiri Sanramonki, pomirintsi nokantavitaro. [87]Nopavitakari no*terefono*te, aritaima ompokaki. [88]Tekatsi, tsonka. [89]Pamakina pivashiro.

[90]–Iroka?

[91]–Je, irove, iyamatya. [92]Tsika asaakoteroka?

[93]–Aritaki anta. [94]Airo ataairokia?

[95]–Airo.

[96]–Intakironta.

[97]–Ja, arive, ari ontaakia pivankirikavee.

[98]–Te, airo ariita, pinkinakanintakero jeñokini.

[99]–Pamakiro kostarira ovantyarori, *plástico*, terika tsika opaita.

[100]–Aavintakinaranki Virginia opaitaranki, aavintakina, ochonkakina inchashiteranki. [101]Amatakonentanajana, tekatsitajana noitziki. [102]Yaavintavetakana aavintantzinkari irirori shipatonatsipaye, tekatsi onkantena. [103]Ochonkakina inchashite, tekatsitajana noitziki. [104]Te onkemajero oyatsinka, okaratzi nokemiri novatsaki, noitziki. [105]Neeriyetaki noitziki, aavintajanaro, tekatsitajana. [106]Irotaki iroperori aavintantzinkaro inchashi ayiri ovariyiro katsitzimotairi, katsitatsiri avatsaki. [107]Omaperotatziro oyotziro aavintantsi paitachari Virginia. [108]Nokantzi, okaratzi oyotzi irori kooyara aavintantzinkaro. [109]Ari ayotantyarori aavintante, ontzimatye antzivintyaro. [110]Eero iririka, naakarika kovatsini noyote naavintante, eero noñiiro kooya, eero novaro katyori, eero novari pochari, onkantya noyotantyarori naavintante, irotaki nokantziri.

¹¹¹Nonkantavaje noverantavakiaro, nokantzi, ochonkakina Virginia, okaratzi yovapaintsiri inchapetoki *plástico*, iro okaratzi pariapaintsiri, iro saikantanari noitzikira irotaki. ¹¹²Tzimatsi iyovaitatziri ivakotakena noitziki, nokatsivaitantari. ¹¹³Ikantzi aka novankokika tzimatsi kitatarentsi, ikitatziri yovaitatsiri. ¹¹⁴Ampitajena, nonkatsivaite, aritaki aakotajena irorave okaratzi katsitzimotakenari. ¹¹⁵Irotaki noverantavakarori nokantavakeri.

¹–This is what I do, when I heal with steam a little bit, yes, we will do it this way. ²We'll arrange them, we'll combine herbs [in a pot].

    ³–Speak our language.

    ⁴–Calm down, woman.

    ⁵–If you don't speak, we will not know what you are doing.

    ⁶–I go to the forest to gather herbs.

    ⁷–What are the herbs called?

    ⁸–This herb is for preventing the water from bothering us, when we feel pain.

    ⁹–We have to make comments about it, so this is how you will do it.

    ¹⁰–Since I don't know her, tell her to take a picture of me.

    ¹¹This is how I earn my living. ¹²This herb is good when water bothers us. ¹³This herb—when we have an itch or inflammation. ¹⁴I will finish [arranging the herbs]. ¹⁵The other day I went to Kimiri.

    ¹⁶Last time, from where I came from, we heard about a *pishtako*, they killed her, this gringa.[12] ¹⁷Very well, now there aren't any more leaves. ¹⁸We have water, yes, we'll make it boil. ¹⁹Very well, woman, bring *morinashi* leaves, that's it, very well.[13]

    ²⁰–I will talk about it. ²¹The stones [in the fire] have been hot, because they started a fire to give me a steam bath. ²²She

will treat my foot here. ²³This spot causes me pain; I have an inflammation, and I do not get better. ²⁴A doctor gave me medicine, but it did nothing to me. ²⁵There is a healer, she came, and I called Bertha. ²⁶Bertha said to her, "Heal me," she had been in pain. ²⁷Those herbs that are placed in the pot, this is the medicine that will make disease come out.

²⁸When something causes us pain, we cure with this, and the pain will disappear. ²⁹So I will be treated with herbs, since they heated the stones to give me a steam bath. ³⁰When the water boils in this pot, and the heated stones, four in number, will be placed in it for me, my pain, perhaps, will disappear. ³¹The pain in my foot, what I have here that is causing me pain, is, possibly, the work of a demon. ³²It will truly come out, whatever is causing me pain in my foot. ³³The pain that I have is not accidental; this is what I am telling about. ³⁴After she steams me with herbs, we'll examine whatever will fall out [from my body during the bath].

³⁵–Come here. ³⁶Where are the planks to handle the stones?

³⁷–You know how to do steam baths, but we say, we fill the pot haphazardly with plants. ³⁸Like, you make things fall out from the body, and we don't know how to do it. ³⁹Like, hadn't you made them fall, we wouldn't have asked you to come and do a steam bath. ⁴⁰We know how to bathe with leaves, with leaves of *kamarivenki* (anti-demonic magic plant). ⁴¹My magic herbs were eaten [by turkeys]. ⁴²Maybe you have leaves of *kamarivenki*.

⁴³–Give me support, ouch!

⁴⁴–My turkeys ate all my herbs, with which I bathed myself. ⁴⁵They say, water bothers us, but I don't know how to make them fall out [pain-causing agents].

⁴⁶–This is it, when we do baths with herbs. ⁴⁷I've experienced it too, when I began doing steam baths, and I went through a

lot of difficulty and suffered a lot. [48]It took me three years to master it, so that I could steam-bathe. [49]My fellow men during those days heard about me, "She is doing steam baths." [50]When I did steam-bathing, I mastered slowly the power of making it [illness-causing objects] appear, whatever they look like, I don't know what they are called. [51]When I was practicing, when we eat something like agouti, peccary, we feel fever, similar to that when a baby is born. [52]This was the way in the past. [53]The pot with leaves is placed [in the bathing area], yes, that's right, and this is what you'll do; don't pull up the robe [so that the steam from the pot fills the enclosed space around the patient, otherwise the steam will escape]. [54]He has sensed that the heated stone is hot.

[55]–The stone is hot, it hurts!

[56]–Well, inform us about what you said before: who taught you, what is her name?

[57]–Perhaps as I said before, perhaps it was the deceased old woman María, called María Varoto, she was the one who gave it [the power to cure] to me long ago. [58]I say, it took me three years to master it. [59]I went through a lot of difficulty. [60]When we do steam baths, we shouldn't look at it [the leaves in the pot]. [61]How many stones did she heat up? [62]One, three, four, wait, while it [the steam] affects your feet. [63]Now you will sit down, this way you will do it to affect your feet. [64]Massage your feet.

[65]–It is really hot!

[66]–You say four, four stones, therefore, you have it, four, this is how I will do it. [67]Massage your feet here, massage them, and your back too.

[68]–It hurts like hell, it hurts, I want only my feet [to be worked on].

[69]–Yes, in the area where it hurts you, this is what you'll do.

[70]Massage his back. [71]Do it a little bit more, since this is where his pain originates.

[72]Put another heated stone in the pot. [73]Later on, I will reuse it, when I steam-bathe [Bertha]. [74]Place another stone. [75]Closer, so that he feels it [the heat]. [76]To do the steam-bathing of this area where it hurts him, four [stones are needed], then he will truly feel the effect. [77]It seems that when I come back, I will do his steam-bathing again.

[78]–You wanted to make her promise that she would come.

[79]–Yes, some [patients] are not going to recover, unless we are all Pava. [80]We are not Pava, only Pava can heal us, so he will cure us. [81]In contrast, we are humans, we can't cure quickly. [82]There are many sick people in Ciudadela [the indigenous community of La Merced], many Andean folks, my fellow men, and Yanesha. [83]Nevertheless, they won't pay me. [84]The Yanesha are stingy. [85]Recently, my niece had a two-month delay [in payment]. [86]Recently, I gave her [a patient] my phone in vain, I gave my telephone number to a Yanesha woman from San Ramon, and I had difficulty talking to her [pleaded with her]. [87]I gave my telephone number, maybe, she will come [and bring the money]. [88]There is no more, the treatment is over. [89]Bring me a recipient [into which the water from the pot will be emptied].

[90]–This?

[91]–Yes, very well, poor thing. [92]Where are we going to empty it?

[93]–Over there. [94]Are we going to burn it [the contents of the pot]?

[95]–No.

[96]–Go outside [the compound].

[97]–Your seedlings will die because the hot water will burn them.

[98]–No, the water won't reach the plants, go a little bit farther up [to dispose of the water].

[99]–Bring me a burlap bag to put the contents of the pot on it, or a sheet of plastic, or whatever.

[100]–I was treated by Virginia, and she cured me, she bathed me with steamed herbs. [101]I have overcome the ailment, my foot has healed. [102]I had been treated by those bearded healers [i.e., medics from a clinic], but their medicine did nothing to me. [103]She bathed me with steamed herbs, and my foot has healed. [104]I don't feel pain that I had in my foot and my body. [105]I had an inflammation in my foot, she treated me, and I have healed. [106]This is the best healer who uses herbs that take out, make fall out pain-causing things that hurt our bodies. [107]She is a good healer, she knows how to cure, the one called Virginia. [108]I say, she knows it all, this woman healer. [109]To learn how to heal, one has to diet. [110]Neither some person or me, who wants to know how to cure, will see women, eat salty or sweet foods, to be able to learn how to cure, this is what I say.

[111]I will say one last thing, I say, Virginia bathed me with steamed herbs, and came out pieces of plastic, this is what fell out, this is what had been in my foot. [112]Someone knows about them, the one who placed them in my foot, that's why it hurt me. [113]They say, there are things buried in my house, buried by someone who knows about them. [114]I will repeat the procedure, if I continue to feel pain, she will take out those things that cause it. [115]This is the last thing that I say.

FIFTY-EIGHT

Antavairi aavintantzinkaro

(Healer's Work)

Luzmila Machari Quinchori

[1]Naaka nantavaitzi notsipatari noimi, naari nantavaitzi, tsika paitaranki, ari nokaraiyeni noimi apiteroite nantavaitzi, naaka, noimi. [2]Irotaki noñaantari novantari kapicheeni. [3]Ari okaratapaki. [4]Pashini jiroka, nochonkantari apite okaratzi, notsipatairori. [5]Ari okaratzi nochonkatantzi, naaka nochontantari, novitsikakero. [6]Jiro nokantayetziro iroka. [7]Novakotakero, notashitake maapi. [8]Naakero, poñaaka nochonkero, notetakero mapi, notetakiro mapi. [9]Novanitakotakiroja, naminakero. [10]Naminero, naminero, jeroka, katsitakakimiri. [11]Ari ompariaki tsikapaitarika antajairi, tsikarika aka irora akipiyavaite, paitari antapaintaiyeni, arika irora tsikapaitaranki imatsikaitajai, ari oshitovaki ara tsipanashikika. [12]Ari ompariaki, aririka onkatsitajai aka, terika onkatsite aka aitziki, ari ompariaki katsitakajairi. [13]Aririka ompariaje, ari pishitakotaje.

[14]Naaka nochonkantzi aka, noyomoniratekika, irotaki novantari naari. [15]Aririka impoke katsivaitatsini, ipokashitena, naaka nonchonkavakeri. [16]Okantya, okantya, ishitakotaje.

[17]Naaka apaniroini, tekatsi amitakotenani. [18]Naarija iyometaitakitzinaro, iyometaitakitzinaro Bermudezki, noyotakiro Bermudezki. [19]Naaka iyometaitakinaroja Bermudezki, okantakina ashaninkaraja, "Jiroka, iroka oishika, piyotero avirori, pivavisakotantantyari irora piyomoniratekika." [20]Noyotziro

nosaatantzi, nonimotanakaro, noyotakiro. ²¹Te iyomitainaro
nosari, naaka apanironi noyotashitakaro. ²²Aka notzimi, Pum-
purianikika. ²³Tzimatsi *cuarenta cuatro años.* ²⁴Nosaatantzika
seis años, osheki pokashitzina naaka. ²⁵Naaka naayetzi oishipa-
tsaini ovaantsiki, maatsi aisatzi nayiri antamiki. ²⁶Irotaki naari
nosaatantari.

²⁷Irotaki novavisakotantari maaroni. ²⁸Opariayetzi kiravo,
kitsapi, ashiropaye, katsitakajairi, aririka imatsikaitaja, maatsi
pashini kisanintairi, arika ampankivaite, irotaki ikisanintantairi.
²⁹Tsikarika poñaayetachari, airo ayotziri tsikarika ipoña, airo
ayotziri ashaninkapaye. ³⁰Osheki naavintziri saikatsiri nonampiki, ari ishitakotaji. ³¹Aajatzi yantemi shiretsika, aririka pika-
marankavaite, nochonkakimitya. ³²Okitataitamani shitako-
tajemi, airo pikami, ari pishitakotaje. ³³Ari okaratapaki.

¹I work together with my husband, we work, the two of us, I
and my husband. ²That's why I say that we have something to
eat. ³That's all. ⁴The leaves in the pot, here, I steam-bathe with
them, the two kinds, look. ⁵I steam-bathe with them, I will arrange them in the pot, I will keep arranging them. ⁶This is how
I do it. ⁷I will place it [in the fire], and I will heat the stones. ⁸I
will take the pot [off the fire] and steam-bathe [the patient], and
I will add stones to the pot [consecutively]. ⁹I will put the pot
aside and examine its contents. ¹⁰I will look and look, here, the
thing that causes us pain. ¹¹It falls out, whatever harm was done
to us, whatever we are poisoned with, whatever typically does
harm, when we are bewitched, it will come out. ¹²So it falls out,
when it hurts here (points to her shoulder), or when it hurts here
in our foot, it falls out, the thing that causes pain. ¹³When it falls
out, you will recover.

¹⁴I steam-bathe here, in my community, with this I eat [earn
my living]. ¹⁵When someone comes, when he is in pain, he

comes to see me, and I will steam-bathe him. [16]Sometime later, he will recover.

[17]I work alone, no one helps me. [18]I was taught to steam-bathe in Puerto Bermúdez, I learned it in Puerto Bermúdez. [19]I was taught in Puerto Bermúdez, there was this fellow woman who will say to me, "Here, this leaf, with this they will recover, in your community." [20]I learned to treat [people] with herbs, I know how to do it. [21]My grandmother didn't teach me, I learned on my own. [22]I was born here, in Centro Pumpuriani. [23]I am forty-four years old. [24]I've been steam-bathing with herbs for six years, and a lot of people have come to see me. [25]I get the herbs from my *chacra* (plot of land) and from the forest. [26]I steam-bathe with them.

[27]I treat everything. [28]Nails, needles, wire fall out, the items that cause us pain, when we are bewitched, or there are those who are envious, when we harvest [abundant] crops, they have envy. [29]They [witches] come from other places, we don't know them. [30]I treat many people in my community, and the sick person recovers [after the treatment]. [31]Also, when you choke with bad air, when you vomit, I will steam-bathe you. [32]The next day, you will recover, you won't die [after my treatment], you will recover. [33]That's all.

Concluding Remarks

The concluding thoughts offered here are concerned with a possible import of this work for the studies of lowland South American indigenous societies and its envisioned resonance with the native community of Upper Perené speakers.

Being the first systematic and focused investigation of Upper Perené language and culture, the anthology's novelty lies in its incisive exploration of the themes of history, landscape, and ritual, conducted on the basis of the comprehensive documentary text corpus. Expressing the speaker-insider perspective on Upper Perené Arawaks' past and present ways of living, this anthology is anticipated to be of interest to linguistic anthropologists, descriptive linguists, and students of lowland South American indigenous societies. The collection includes fifty-eight multigenre original texts accompanied by thorough English-language translations. To meet the expectations of academic readers, a copious commentary and notes have been provided in each section of the book, as a way of giving the necessary ethnographic context and fulfilling the ethnographer's duty "of description, saying what it is others are saying" (Geertz 1986:374). The analytical commentary is based on my own observations and experiences, as well as on the body of previously published ethnographies of Kampan and other Amazonian peoples.

In theoretical terms, the proffered interpretations are aligned with the discourse-centered approach to language and culture (Sherzer and Urban 1986; Sherzer 1987; Urban 1991), drawing on the understanding that the collected texts are "an embodiment of the essence of culture," "constitutive of what the language-culture-society relationship is all about" (Sherzer 1987:297).

In particular, the texts from part 1, "History" elucidate the native notion of history, organized around two major space-time periods, *pairani* (mythic past times) and *iroñaaka* (modernity). The *pairani* period refers to the primordial times when humans, animals, plants, and other life-forms did not constitute separate worlds, when transformations of humans into nonhuman forms took place, either of the individual's own accord or at the whim of the solar divinity Pava or the Ashéninka man called Naviriri Piantzinkari (Naviriri the Transformer).

The *iroñaaka* period, or modernity, roughly begins with the mid-nineteenth-century military conquest of the Upper Perené valley, resulting in large-scale displacement and despoliation of the native population and the irrevocable spread of the colonist economy. The *iroñaaka* times are associated with the 1891 occupation of the Upper Perené land by the coffee-growing, British-owned Peruvian Corporation and the subsequent territorial delimitation led by the *intanakarori* (founding fathers) or *nocharinitepaye* (our grandfathers/ ancestors) to whom the drafting of the boundaries of the currently existing native communities and establishment of nucleated settlements are attributed. The language group's "enlightened" and "civilized" existence in modern times is typically ascribed to the evangelizing work of the U.S. Adventist missionary Fernando Stahl, likened by some to Pava, the main pagan deity of Upper Perené Arawaks.

Oral tradition indicates that the rubber-boom era and the

internal conflict involving the homegrown terrorist organizations Sendero Luminoso (Shining Path) and MRTA (Movimiento Revolucionario Tupac Amaru, the Tupac Amaru Revolutionary Movement) had a fairly minor impact on Upper Perené Arawaks' ways of living compared to the effects on other Kampan groups, which bore the brunt of the rubber-boom enslavement and/or conscription into the insurgents' armed units and labor camps.

The centrality of landscape to the Upper Perené conception of the community's historical past and speakers' ontological beliefs is brought into focus by the texts from part 2, "Landscape." As oral tradition makes clear, the language group's history is understood to be "inscribed" into its territory, with ecological landmarks serving as the ultimate "mnemonic devices" (Rappaport 1989:88). The landmarks do not constitute a chronologically continuous network of Upper Perené Arawaks' historical episodes. Rather, they mark particular events of spiritual and cultural value to native speakers. In accordance with the speakers' animistic thought, the landmarks are saturated with "immanent divinity" (Veber 2003:191), exemplified by Ashiropanko (the Iron House), an abandoned temple-forge located to the northwest of Bajo Marankiari. The landmark used to be a veneration place of the sacred fire, perceived to be manifestation of the solar divinity Pava, the most highly ranked deity among Upper Perené Arawaks.

Oral tradition maintains that the spaces of the river, the hills, rocks, caves, lakes, and other landscape features are inhabited by supremely powerful beings, unsympathetic to humans. Apart from a small pantheon of astral and stone divinities, supernatural spiritual beings include various *ashitarori~ashitariri* (masters-owners) who watch over animal and plant species and control human access to them. Others constitute a large group of deadly *kamari* (demonic beings). The habitats of masters-owners, as well as sacred dwellings and final resting places of supernatural beings, are typically named after them, revealing the preeminence of the speakers' spiritual and cultural preoccupations in landscape conceptualization. Landscape has retained memories of legendary exploits of some extraordinary ancestors endowed with supernatural powers. For example, the landmark Imoro Naviriri (the Naviriri Hole), a big indentation in the uplands of Mariscal Cáceres, now filled with water, is a redemption site where a woman put an end to her brother's lethal transformational acts by condemning him to linger forever in the bowels of earth. Her brother, called Naviriri the Transformer, posed a grave threat to Upper Perené Arawaks, gradually exterminating his own fellow men at whim.

The texts from part 3, "Ritual" present a fascinating window into native ways of interaction with the riverine and forest ecologies, revealing a system of sophisticated ritual behavior previously reported to be impoverished and incoherent (e.g., Weiss 1974:399, 1975:513). Although a sweeping introduction of Christianity has altered the dynamic of Upper Perené ritual behavior in that the publicly conducted ritual ceremonies have gradually faded away, the low-key affliction rites have persisted and are still being regularly practiced on an individual basis. From the public ceremonies, two calendrical rites were of significance, known as *mavira* (the arrow flower festival), a December event, and *shimashiripaite*, the cannibalistic feast held in June, during the flowering period of the *shimashiri* tree (*pino chuncho*). In addition, community-wide ritual festivities were regularly conducted to honor two astral deities, Ooriatsiri (alternatively, Tasorentsi or Pava), the sun, and Kashiri, the moon. The festivities typically followed a familiar script involving singing accompanied by panpipe music, dancing, and manioc beer drinking.

The texts convincingly demonstrate the spiritual nature of

the communal celebrations, which were seen by the celebrants as a requisite offering to omnipotent ill-disposed beings. Offerings to divinities and masters-owners in the form of prayers, panpipe music, dancing and singing, first fruits, traditional drink, or stimulants were widely practiced. Ridiculed by their mestizo neighbors and local Adventist believers as odd relics of the "uncivilized" past, public rites and festivities have been dormant for decades.

Affliction rites have been accorded significant attention in the anthology due to their critical import for the everyday existence of Upper Perené Arawaks. Affliction rites are rituals meant to neutralize a potential threat to a person's psychosomatic health or redress harm already done to the body. Upper Perené Arawaks' disease ontology postulates that the illness-causing agent is either a human or nonhuman *kamari* (demonic being) who could be identified and disposed of in the course of a ritual intervention conducted by a shaman or, with less effect, by a steam bath specialist. In both shamanistic and herbal ritual interventions, restoration of psychological and physical health is achieved through the purification of the afflicted body, when the disease-causing items are sucked out and then spit out by a shaman or fall out as the result of a steam bath treatment by an herbal specialist. In addition, to inoculate the body against a potential attack by a *kamari*, an individual takes recourse to the available prophylactic means: ritual blowing, spitting, abstinence, induced vomiting, use of ritual formulas, and application of magic herbs (see Anderson 2000; Weiss 1975).

The anthology was created with the Ashéninka Perené community's needs in mind. For the native community, this publication is of paramount importance due to its comprehensive coverage of various discourse genres and topics in the native language, with the texts' spelling being in conformity with the phonemic inventory of Ashéninka Perené. To native readers, the book constitutes an invaluable resource in the context of a rapidly shrinking speaker base, limited domains of native-language use, and lack of reading materials in the language. Literate middle-aged parents and grandparents anticipate the book to adequately serve the didactic goals of home and public schooling. For example, Victorina Rosas de Castro of Bajo Marankiari, one of the project's main language consultants and the mother of six children, stressed to me that this book is her ultimate hope. She plans to use it as reading and discussion material with her youngest child and grandchildren.

The collection of Upper Perené texts, spanning the period from the primordial mythic times to the contemporary era, also fulfils an important task of addressing the contributors' quest "to explain . . . [people's] fate" (Lévi-Strauss 1978:41). What the fifty-eight bilingual texts reveal, thus making this publication so significant to the contributors and the native community, is that the Upper Perené Ashaninkas managed to retain control of their destiny and preserve their sociocultural identity, in spite of the group's long history of being a frontier community and long-standing interaction with powerful indigenous neighbors and outsiders. Tellingly, during my conversations with members of the local non-native elite, paternalistic comments were made about modern Upper Perené Ashaninkas' gradual loss of their identity under the pressure of the market economy and their current state of disorientation and uncertainty about finding direction in life. However, my observations and conversations with language speakers and this text collection assert otherwise.

The group's contemporary reality, from the narrators' perspective, is constituted by the conscious actions of its members. In a way, the texts presented here convincingly "describe people who clearly shaped their fates" (Basso 1995:304). Similar to the stories of Brazilian Kalapalo (Cariban) from lowland Amazonia, which "describe experiences of individuals taking chances, exploring alternatives to their lives, making strategic choices when conditions forced them into new and untried situations" (Basso 1995:304), texts by Upper Perené Ashaninkas demonstrate the "historical agency" of this Kampan people, contrary to the non-native characterization of them as "play-things in the grip of the all-powerful logic of State and Capital" (Viveiros de Castro 1996:193).

The triumphant force of Upper Perené Ashéninka agentive power is illustrated by Fredi Miguel Ucayali's words: "Hadn't our ancestral grandfathers been warriors, we wouldn't live here today. We should thank our grandfathers who defended our land, that's why we have a place to live" (*Yookantapakairi virakocha* [How the Whites Threw Us Out], text 7). Although some look back at the *pairani* (old times) as an idyllic time of order, social harmony, and physical and moral purity, the contemporary Upper Perené pursuit of a better life aims at creatively and doggedly adapting the native society to modernity, through participation in market relations, political and religious institutions, and elected offices of *comunidad nativa* (native community).

Similar to other lowland South American societies, Upper Perené Arawaks have been engaged in the process of "authentically remaking" their contemporary social identity (Clifford 2004:20). In this historic process of identity transformation, intertwined with the colonial and postcolonial development of the Peruvian nation-state (see Whitehead 1992), Upper Perené Ashéninkas are making use of their oral tradition, including texts from this anthology. The purpose is to maintain the tradition of "ritually powerful" performances of chanting, orating, and singing (Hornborg and Hill 2011:17).

Regarding the native concern about the cracks appearing in

the Upper Perené Ashéninka sociocultural identity, primarily centered on the erosion of the speaker base, it may be too premature to predict the group's linguistic and cultural demise in view of the society's surprising imperviousness to the pressures of mainstream Peruvian culture. A plausible explanation lies in both the Kampan character of impregnable self-assurance and the unshakeable foundation of animistic ontological beliefs about their universe (Lenaerts 2006a:554). Overall, Arawak societies' shared "cultural repertoire . . . has proved [to be] highly resilient to . . . external intrusions" (Whitehead 2002:72), as contemporary ethnogenesis studies of lowland South American indigenous peoples have indicated (Hornborg and Hill 2011).

That Upper Perené Arawaks have preserved intact their metaphysical categories of being and the world in spite of the massive implantation of Christian religion is eminently obvious in the majority of recorded texts. Although the influential Adventist Church, which has a monopoly in the Upper Perené area, regards shamanism, sun and sacred fire worshipping, polygyny, coca chewing, and *masato* drinking as "demonic" (Narby 1989:85–86), the Ashéninka Perené still hold onto the ancestral beliefs. Like Achuar (Jivaroan), an Amazonian group of Ecuador and Peru that has been heavily missionized by Catholic and Protestant clergymen, the Ashéninka tend "to keep to themselves" (Lenaerts 2006a:544), with the native "superficial conversion" to Christianity being merely "a façade" (Descola 1996:31). In the text *Ikantakota sheripiari pairani* (About Shamans Who Existed in the Past; text 51), Daniel Bernales Quillatupa affirms his allegiance to sentient nature's immanence, stressing the point of the interconnectedness of the entire universe. The narrator invokes his grandfather's authority while stating, "My grandfather said, everything that exists on this land has eyes, mouths, and ears. When we speak, when we speak on someone's account, when we speak badly of the land, of the tree, everything that exists here will hear us. That's why shamans say, because they have seen it, that a tree exists for a reason, a river exists for a reason, so do rocks, they all have masters."

During my exchanges with Upper Perené language speakers, they recognized with the usual Kampan candidness that the vitality of the language, spoken essentially by the older adults, and of certain rituals, such as initiation rites and the *mavira* festival, are in a woeful need of revitalization. They also acknowledged the irreversible loss of the institution of local shamanism and the abandonment of native religion. However, place rituals and especially affliction rites continue to occupy center stage in the cultural life of Upper Perené Ashaninkas, as the text *Ochonkiri Abdias* (She Steam-Bathed Abdias; text 57) illustrates. The narrator Abdias Caleb Quinchori, who suffers from what looks like severe rheumatism, pins hope for his recovery on the healer's ritual divination, as part of the post–steam bath treatment: "The pain in my foot, what I have here that is causing me pain, is, possibly, the work of a demon. It will truly come out, whatever is causing me pain in my foot. The pain that I have is not accidental; this is what I am telling about. After she steams me with herbs, we'll examine whatever will fall out [from my body during the bath]."

It is envisioned that this collection of directly recorded native texts, with accompanying commentary, will provide ample insights into Upper Perené Arawaks' ways of speaking and thinking about their historical past and present, the society's ontologies of landscape and ritual practices, and the continuous struggle of "ethnic self-fashioning" (Whitehead 2011:356) in the context of the multicultural Peruvian nation-state (Kymlicka 2003).

APPENDIX

Ideophones Used by the Narrators

aaaa: A macaw parrtot's call
ajak ajak: Action of loud expectoration of spittle
apishoi shoi ta: Rapidly coiling around an entity
chak: Action of quickly pouring water into a receptacle
chee: Jumping action, making a big leap
chenki: Action of striking a match
jao jao-jau jau: Sound of a barking dog
jemm jemm: Sound of a water sprite
jiri jiri jiri: Action of cutting a soft substance
jomm jomm: Sound of a jaguar's roar or the bone spirit's call
jojoo: Sound of female laughter
joo: Sound of a big splash
joo joo: Sound of a howler monkey
jooo jooo: Sound made by a human calling a dog
kin kin: Sound of a crying baby snake
kisho kisho: Spitting action
miro miro: Crushing a soft substance with hands
mokoro mokoro: Vomiting action
morok morok: Penetrating a hard substance
motok: Quick entry and disappearance
muu muu: Sound of a cow
oorioo: Sound of a rooster
petak petak: Fanning action, moving an object up and down
pichori pichori: Action of pounding a soft substance
pok pok: Falling of a light object
shepi(k): Grabbing an object in the air

shiririri: Slow-motion action

shi shi: Making grimaces caused by pain

shitzikoro shitzikoro: Nocturnal hawks call

shoi shoi ta: Action of making circular movements

shoki shoki shoki: Grinding action

tek tek: Hitting action, without deep penetration

terempiri terempiri: Movement in a curved trajectory

teroo teroo teroo: Call of the teroni, a macaw species

te te te: Sound of a bubbling whirlpool

tin tin tin: Sound of a tambor

tonka tonka: Action of going up a hill

too(k): Sound of a discharged gun

tsapok: Shallow splash produced by the fall of a light object

tsapon: Splash produced by the fall of a heavy object

tsimimi tsimimi: Chewing action

tsinkaririri: Sudden feeling of a stir inside the body

tyak tyak: Hitting action

tzinik: Static, frozen state; lack of movement

varok: A startle reaction in response to sudden stimuli, such as
    a noise or touch

NOTES

INTRODUCTION

1. Identification of plant and animal species is based on Denevan 1971; Weiss 1975; Johnson 2003; Rojas Zolezzi 1994, 2002; Shepard 2002; Gavin 2002; Pinedo 2008.

PART 1. HISTORY

1. Recently published indigenous oral accounts, brought to light by a language activist from the Upper Perené area, Enrique Casanto Shingari (Macera and Casanto 2009), and by the anthropologist Hanne Veber (2009), present additional materials about the mestizo rebel and his cadre. On the basis of the Casanto family's stories and interviews with five elders from various corners of the Ashaninka-speaking territory, conducted in the 1980s and 1990s, Casanto contends that Apinka was mortally wounded in combat, lingered for some time, and later died in the presence of his family and entourage in Metraro (Macera and Casanto 2009:63, 68). This refutes rumors of his ascension in smoke and a Yanesha myth about Apinka's death being inflicted by his classificatory brother during a game (see, e.g., Ortiz 1974:174; Lehnertz 1974:148; Santos-Granero 2004a:113). Apinka's widow, Martina Márquez Zumaeta, who reportedly is from the Rio Tambo area, assumed leadership on her husband's behalf. Years later she died with her sons in one of the battles with Spaniards (Macera and Casanto 2009:70).

   The rest of the Apinka story is interwoven with mythological strands involving bodily transformations of the Spanish enemy

and Apinka's companions (Macera and Casanto 2009:68–70). To
avenge the death of the *korakona* (supreme leader; of Quechua
origin, kora-kona [headman-AUG]), the warriors Shampakitzi
and Sharivoiri led two military raids on the Kimiri mission and
the San Ramon garrison. They also asked shamans to convert
the approaching Spaniards into nonhuman form, in order to prevent the Spanish soldiers from advancing into the Perené valley.
At this point, Naviriri the Transformer volunteered his services
and turned the intruders into stones. Weiss (1975:314–15) also
mentions transformations of Caucasians by Naviriri.

In addition, Casanto collected stories about Apinka's and his
son's comrades, totaling seventy warriors in number. According to those accounts, none of Apinka's military leaders died of
natural causes. They all ended up transformed into nonhuman
entities, in line with the canons of the old times. Such transformations were either effected by shamans or other warriors or
happened due to unknown causes. For example, the warrior Taa-
vantzi, from the present-day Pampa Whaley area of the Upper
Perené River, notorious for his heavy drinking, self-converted
into a bird of the species that carries his name (Macera and
Casanto 2009:208, 247).

In contrast, an interview with the famous Upper Perené
leader Miqueas Mishari Mofat, now deceased, who was born and
raised in Kishitariki (Mariscal Cáceres), indicates that Apinka
had a little son who died early from an unidentified disease
and that, according to local lore, after his son's death Apinka
became depressed and "only drank *masato* every day, until he
got gravely ill and died" (Veber 2009:138). Miqueas Mishari's
account says nothing of "fantastic" events that are often attributed to Apinka's life and death, while it emphasizes the leader's
organizational acumen ("organized warriors well"), his knowledge of local languages ("he also spoke various languages, like

Yanesha"), and his charisma ("he was a charismatic man") (Veber 2009:136).

2. Weiss characterizes Pajonal Campas as "traditional enemies of the River Campas." He points out that "the enmity has been both continuous and long-standing, in contrast to the relatively short-lived animosities and feuds that have prevailed at different times within either of the two groups" (1975:237).

3. Present-day Metraro is a sleepy mestizo village, having been abandoned by Ashaninka families in the late 1930s due to high mortality rates among its Adventist mission's population (Paz-Soldán and Kuczynski-Godard 1939:130–48).

PART 2. LANDSCAPE

1. Elias Meza Pedro's recollections neatly overlap with the reminiscences of Miqueas Mishari Mofat, another longtime Kishitariki resident, who depicts in detail the ceremonial life of the Kishitariki fire divinity temple (Veber 2009:131).

2. Among the sites of ritual gatherings, the Cerro de la Sal (the Salt Hill), located at the headwaters of the Perené River, was by far the most effective mechanism in the construction of a cohesive Campa identity and the maintenance of interethnic solidarity. The hill's sacred status was acknowledged, according to Santos-Granero (2004a:107–8), by ritual offerings of coca leaves, *chamairo*, and lime to the Salt person by "visiting miners," on-site ritual specialists who "performed sacred ceremonies" on one of the salt hills. The Upper Perené documentary corpus does not contain evidence of this sort.

3. The complexity and comprehensiveness of Upper Perené Arawaks' hydrological and topographic landscape terms and place names suggest that their culture was as much "hydrocentric" as it was montane. In contrast, many Arawak-speaking tribal for-

mations, e.g., Piro (Gow 1991:72–73), are reported to have a pre-
ponderance of hydrological vocabulary, possibly associated with
their "pervasive" hydrocentric ethnolinguistic identity (Hornborg and Hill 2011:10).

4. The existence of secret landscape names is corroborated by
Augusto Capurro Mayor, the former chief of Pampa Michi, who
states that shamans "discovered and gave names to hills, brooks,
trees" (Veber 2009:191). Narby's Ashéninka Pichis language consultant pointed out to him that once a shaman takes ayahuasca
and arrives "in an unknown place, a place he does not know, his
person being transformed into a jaguar, in his vision," he "sees"
in his vision that the place is named such-and-such, without
even asking questions (Narby 1989:269).

5. Among Campas, disfiguring an enemy by crushing the body
with a heavy stone was not uncommon in the old times. For
example, the 1674 conflict between the Pichana mission's
Ashaninka convert called Mangoré and the missionary Father
Izquierdo ended in the death of the father and his two companions, who were first shot with arrows and then crushed
with clubs. Amich (1854:61–65) describes the Indian attackers
"grinding and crushing the bones" of the victims before trussing
up the corpses, dragging them to the river, and dumping them
there. Mangoré was killed by his own sister when he entered
the Kimiri mission a few days later, intending to incite a rebellion among the Indian converts. Mangoré's sister was reported
to have "repeatedly hit her brother's head [with a large stone] so
many times that his brain splashed out" (Amich 1854:65).

6. According to Payne (1980:48), *kaviniri* is a tree in the genus *Cinnamomum*; its bark is used as a whistle to scare away demons
(Kindberg 1980:26). Weiss (1975:264, 276) describes its leaves as
a tobacco-like substance that produces "beautiful dreams" when
ingested. Among Upper Perené Arawaks, the *kaviniri* plant's

master-owner is feared due to the tree's highly destructive, apocalyptic power. When the plant's leaves are thrown into the river or it is cut down or even merely touched, Armageddon-like events may follow, including lightning, thunder, floods, earthquakes, and annihilation of those living in the plant's habitat.

PART 3. RITUAL

1. The *ivenki* plant does not grow in the wild and is propagated by bulbs. There are over two hundred *ivenki* plants, each having a certain name (Anderson 1996:81). Due to the strict sex-based prescription as to who is allowed to handle a plant, men and women each have their own magic plant, *ivenki* for men and *ovenki* for women.

2. *Ivenki* are often used in combination with the medicinal plant *pinitsi* (*tila* species; Spanish *pusanga*), although *pinitsi* can be used on its own to treat various medical conditions, e.g., erectile dysfunction, enlarged prostate, or an infant's colic (when a baby cries inconsolably and persistently for no reason). The plant is known as a sexual charm, believed to have magic properties of helping to seduce a person of the opposite sex. In the past, a warrior treated with *pinitsi* would turn into a frenzied individual exhibiting unbridled pugnaciousness. *Pinitsi* can be drunk as a potion, rubbed onto the injured area, used to bathe a person, or squeezed into the eyes as a liquid.

3. Rojas Zolezzi (1994:147) mentions a similar calendrical rite, celebrated by Upper Perené Arawaks in January, when *savoro* (wild cane) blossoms at the peak of the wet season. Although no reminiscences of this event were recorded for this collection, the indigenous contributors agree that the festival might have taken place, in spite of their lack of direct knowledge of the ritual. According to Rojas Zolezzi, the nocturnal festival took place in

the Pichanaki area of the Perené River, at the intersection of the old intertribal trails. The symbolic meaning of the calendrical event was to mark the end (death) of the year and the beginning of a new life (resurrection), in the hope of everyone's survival in the new year (Gaster 1950). The festival's leader wore a headdress made of the plumes of *savoro* and directed nonstop dancing. The festival's rule was to stay awake all night, since "the one who fell asleep, would die this year" (Rojas Zolezzi 1994:147).

4. The data collected in this volume contradict Hornborg and Hill's observation about ritual flute music being "absent among Arawak speakers of eastern Peru," except for Yanesha (2011:17, 20). The Upper Perené documentary corpus provides evidence of the widespread use of flute music on festive occasions.

5. In addition to the solar and lunar divinities, the fire divinity *paamari* (Spanish, *dios de la candela*) was arguably venerated during the annual three-day festival "for thousands of years" (*desde hacia miles de años*) in Kishitariki, present-day Mariscal Cáceres (Veber 2009:131). According to the testimony of Miqueas Mishari Mofat, now deceased, the nocturnal festival was held at the dedicated site, called *carapa* (communal house for males, including shamans and others, committed to the service of the fire divinity). The ritual consisted of priestly prayers, vigils, singing, and *masato* drinking. The festival's objective was to hear the divine message for the next year, received through the medium of "the voice" of the fire divinity. The vigil was conducted by the temple's shamans, who would communicate the message to the tribal chiefs, e.g., about bountiful harvest or poor outcomes of fishing trips. The "ritual grammar" of the upland Kishitariki festival offerings of singing, dancing, and manioc beer is quite similar to that of the calendrical festivals and the sun- and moon-honoring celebrations of the riverine Pampa Michi and Bajo Marankiari populations of Upper Perené Arawaks.

6. The practice of "sacred fire" worship is corroborated by Weiss, who cites his consultant Shariti's words about "sacred fires [which] were formerly everywhere among the Campas (in the Perené region at least, we should add), although they are now forgotten; . . . they are kept aflame continuously in a house without walls, and a good person could hear the voice of *Pavá*, the Sun, in the flames" (1975:470).

7. Glenn Shepard, a medical anthropologist who studied the Machiguenga, a closely-related Kampan group, succinctly summarizes the native rationale for the pubescent girls' hair cutting: "Long hair is a spiritual burden, a breeding ground for lice, and if it falls into the wrong hands [i.e., the hands of a *matsi*], a magical weapon against its owner" (2002:212).

8. The juice of *huito* fruit (*Genipa americana*) is used for body painting. Rojas Zolezzi (1994:120) states that before the community-wide manioc beer party that was held on the occasion of her reaching her new social status, the girl's body was painted to make her unattractive in the eyes of young men. Otherwise they would have dreams about having sexual relations with the girl, and sexual dreams were believed to weaken the men and even make them sick.

9. Herbal eyedrops are commonly used among Kampan peoples to cure "headaches, fevers, nightmares, sadness, anger, and extramarital passions, as well as to improve the aim of hunters." The eye medicine (*Rubiaceae* sp.) has a blinding effect when squeezed into the eyes and induces a bout of tears. The tears are understood to cleanse the eyes of "harmful apparitions," to produce a "symbolic release of repressed tears or sorrow," or to purify the soul (Shepard 2002:219).

10. The juice of the *guanábana* fruit (soursop; from the tree *Annona muricata*), is a diuretic and helps with hepatic illnesses. The tea made with the leaves has antispasmodic and sedative properties.

356

11. In folk medicine, the juice of *paico* leaves, or wormwood (*Chenopodium ambrosioides*), is used to treat intestinal worms and parasites.

12. The *pishtaco* is an Andean folk character called a "throat-cutter." Accounts of sightings of *pishtacos* in the Perené valley are found in numerous sources (e.g., Anderson 2000:234–35; Santos-Granero 1998:137–38; Veber 2009:284). Endowed with supernatural powers, *pishtacos* have the physical appearance of gringos and attack only lonely travelers in remote locations. The purpose of the killings is allegedly to extract indigenous body fat, to be used in treatments for white people's diseases or as fuel for cars and planes.

13. Leaves of the *morinashi* plant (unidentified) are commonly used by Upper Perené Arawaks in steam baths and herbal baths.

GLOSSARY

aavintantzinkaro: A female native healer who treats sick people
with herbs and steam baths. The word consists of the verb root
aavint (cure), the customary suffix -*ant*, and the nonmasculine
nominalizer -*tzinkaro*. See *Antavairi aavintantzinkaro* (Healer's
Work), by Luzmila Machari Quinchori, text 58.

afuu: A ritual formula whose articulation results in the targeted
entity's transformation. This utterance may be accompanied by a
ritual act of blowing. Naviriri, the cultural hero of Upper Perené
Arawaks, used this formula in his transformational exploits. See
Naviriri Piantzinkari.

Amaisha: Yanesha, also known as Amuesha (Aikhenvald 1999:64;
2012:5). The name of the Arawak neighbors of Ashéninka Perené,
located to the east and northeast of the Perené valley. The term is
considered offensive by native speakers. See map 1.

Amuesha: See Amaisha.

anchoveta: A small fish species (*Knodus breviceps*), called *shiva* in
Ashéninka Perené.

antyaviari: An expert shaman. See sheripiari.

Apinka: Apu Inca or Seer Inca, a cultural hero and an itinerant
divinity who introduced Ashéninka Perené to natural resources,
native occupations, and underground burials; also, a brutal headman from the uplands of Metraro. Native mythic thought and oral
tradition associate Apinka with Juan Santos Atahualpa. See *Pava
Apinka* (God Apinka), by Luis Mauricio Rosa, text 4; *Apinka*, by
Bertha Rodríguez de Caleb and Abdias Caleb Quinchori, text 5;
and *Apinka*, by Elías Meza Pedro, with Gregorio Santos Pérez and
Livia Julio de Quinchori, text 6.

Apontsiki: A dwarf-like demonic divinity, a sidekick of Apinka. See
Pava Apinka (God Apinka), by Luis Mauricio Rosa, text 4.

Ashaninka: "Our fellow" (Heise et al. 2000:27), the self-
denomination of Upper Perené Arawaks. When parsed into mean-
ingful units, *a-* (our) is the possessive prefix, the root *shan* or *shen*
means "be same, of the same group," and *-inka* is the nominalizer.
In the Spanish writing tradition, the root vowel is marked with
the acute accent (′).

Asheninka: Same as Ashaninka, but less frequently used among
Upper Perené Arawaks as a self-designation label, in comparison with Ashaninka. In Spanish orthography, the root vowel is
marked with the acute accent (′).

Ashiropanko: The Iron House, a historical landmark. It functioned
as a temple-forge in which sacred fire was venerated. The landmark is located a few kilometers downstream from Bajo Marankiari. See map 3.

ashitarori~ashitariri: Masters-owners of animals, plants, and places.
See atsityopi(ni); kiatsi; nijaaveri; Tsamirimenta.

atsityopi(ni): A mythical armadillo-like or anaconda-like creature,
also called *kiatsi*, that inhabited the Perené River in the vicinity of
present-day Pampa Michi. See kiatsi; nijaaveri; and map 2.

carachama: A small fish species (*Aphanotorulus unicolor*), called
jetari in Ashéninka Perené. This suckermouth catfish is caught
with bare hands during the dry season. See jetari.

catahua: The sandbox tree (*Hura crepitans*), called *kavana* in Ashéninka Perené, whose caustic sap is used to poison arrows and
stupefy fish; its leaves are used in ethnomedicine. See *Tsika
okanta noñaakoventakiri matsipaye* (How I Witnessed Events
Involving Witches), by Bertha Rodríguez de Caleb, text 15.

Cerro de la Sal: The Salt Hill, a historical landmark in the Upper
Perené landscape, located not far from the confluence of the
Chanchamayo and Paucartambo Rivers. The Cerro de la Sal con-

sisted of three salt hills that were mined during the dry season. The salt mines constituted a commercial center of pan-Kampan trading networks. See map 3.

chacra: A plot of land, called *novani* (my land) in Ashéninka Perené.

chamairo: Refers to the liana (*Mussatia hyacinthina*). When *chamairo* is mixed with dried coca leaves, it sweetens the bitter taste of coca. See coca.

chonta: A palm species (*Juania australis*), called *kirii* in Ashéninka Perené. Mythic thought attributes its origin to Kirii, Naviriri's grandson, who self-transformed into a chonta palm after his death (Veber 2009:287–88; Mihas 2011:40). Its wood is used to make bows; its palm hearts are eaten raw.

chori: Andean Quechua-speaking highlanders and people of mixed origin (Spaniards and Andean highlanders). The terms *chori*, *mestizos*, and *colonos* (colonists) are often used interchangeably, although the latter is also applied to colonists of European descent. When referring to females, the word's ending changes from *-ri* to *-ra, chora*. Some Ashéninka Perené speakers elongate the middle vowel, articulating *choori* (male highlander) or *choora* (female highlander). See mestizo.

chorina: A palm species (*Oenocarpus mapora*) known for its tasty fruit, which is cooked in boiled water and then eaten. Its leaves are used in ethnomedicine.

chupadora: A small fish species, called *shima* in Ashéninka Perené. See shima.

coca: A stimulant; the leaves of the coca plant (*Erythroxylum coca*) are commonly masticated to maintain an adequate energy level. Coca was a traditional offering to divinities, together with *chamairo* and powdered lime. See chamairo; ishiko.

cushma: A traditional cotton robe.

Gran Pajonal: An elevated area of great grasslands with multiple open savannahs, called *kishii* in Ashéninka Perené and *pajo-*

nales in Spanish (Hvalkof 1989; Denevan 1971). This rugged area, located to the northwest of the Upper Perené valley, is occupied by speakers of Pajonal Ashéninka, called *kishiisatzi*. See kishiisatzi; map 1.

illocutionary force (of an utterance): Refers to the speaker's intention to accomplish a particular goal while articulating a given sentence. The utterance "could you open the window please" is intended to be a request, that is, it has the illocutionary force of a request. The Upper Perené ritual formula *afuu* (be it) has the illocutionary force of a command aimed at transforming one life-form into another.

Imoro Naviriri: A large indentation in the uplands of Metraro where Naviriri Piantzinkari (Naviriri the Transformer) found his end. Mythic tradition contends that his own family members conspired against him to stop his uncontrollable transformational exploits. His sister Savoro (some sources say her name was Piyoro) pushed Naviriri into a big hole that had been dug by her husband, Ashoshi (armadillo), from which he was unable to get out. See Naviriri Piantzinkari; savoro; piyoro.

ishiko: Lime. Burned lime in powdered form is used with dried coca leaves as a sweetening agent. An outcrop of lime deposits is located halfway between Ashiropanko and Manitzipanko. In the past, it was customary to travel to this location to mine lime. See coca; map 3.

ivenki: Native magic plants (*Cyperus piripiri*), grown in people's house gardens. The plants have specialized uses; out of fear of contamination, *ivenki* are handled only by males and *ovenki* only by females. See kamarivenki; masontovenki.

jetari: See carachama.

Juan Santos Atahualpa: A Peruvian cultural icon, a mestizo rebel from Cuzco who managed to establish multiethnic alliances with lowland and highland natives in the present-day area of Selva

Central and who expelled Spaniards from the area in the middle of the eighteenth century. As the result of this resounding victory, colonization of the Perené valley was stopped and resumed only a century later. See Selva Central; Apinka.

kamarampi: Ayahuasca (*Banisteriopsis caapi*), the hallucinogenic drug taken by expert shamans, which is believed to put them in direct contact with spirits.

kamari: A demonic creature. See matsi; peyari; shiretsi.

kamarivenki: A magic herb. The word consists of *kamari* (demon) and *venki* (magic plant). Either the magic herb is drunk or the person is bathed with it to counteract the illness inflicted by an encounter with a demon. See *Iñaaventa kamari Kovatsironi* (Speaking with Regard to the Demon from Kovatsironi), by Ines Pérez de Santos, text 29.

kamenantsi: A discourse genre, translated as "traditional advice." It can be performed publicly, for example, by a tribal chief during a marriage ceremony, or privately, for example, by a parent instructing a child in mundane tasks. See *Kamenantsi* (Traditional Advice), by Daniel Bernales Quillatupa, text 36.

Kampan: A contemporary version of the term "Campa," given to a subgroup of the ten genetically related Arawak languages of lowland Peru, including five varieties of Ashéninka/Asháninka (Perené, Apurucayali, Ucayali-Yurúa, Pichis, Pajonal, and Tambo-Ene), Kakinte (also spelled Caquinte), Machiguenga, Nomatsiguenga, and Nanti. The word "Campa" is considered derogatory and offensive by Ashaninkas.

kaniri: The staple crop of sweet manioc (*Manihot esculenta*), also called cassava or yuca.

kapok tree: The lupuna tree (*Ceiba pentandra*), called *shina* in Ashéninka Perené. The gigantic tree is believed to have a master-owner, a miniature female whose nocturnal songs are known to attract single males. If a man listens to the songs, his soul can be captured, and he will have to be treated with a special kind of *ivenki, shinavenki*, to get his soul back. See shina.

Kashiri: The lunar divinity.

katonkosatzi: A dweller of the upriver area, the Upper Perené self-denomination term. The noun is composed of *katonko* (upriver) and the nominalizing suffix *-satzi*. To indicate nonmasculine gender, *-sato* is used, *katonkosato* (a female dweller from upriver).

kaviniri: A sacred plant of the *Cinnamomum* genus that grows in the uplands of the Upper Perené valley. If it is cut down or merely touched, the plant is believed to produce lightning, thunder, floods, earthquakes, and destruction of those living in its habitat. As Ines Pérez de Santos reports in *Iñaaventa kamari Kovatsironi* (Speaking with Regard to the Demon from Kovatsironi), text 29, long ago on the orders of shamans, *kaviniri* leaves were placed in the Perené River and caused a total destruction of the area around the Kovatsironi River (present-day Santa Ana).

kiatsi: A malevolent mythic creature, the master-owner of the Perené River, which combined features of an armadillo and an anaconda. Other names of the river owners are *nijaaveri, tsomiri*, and *atsityopini*. See atsityopini; nijaaveri; tsomiri.

Kishiisatzi: Ashéninka-speaking inhabitants of Gran Pajonal (Great Grasslands). Kishiisatzi were known for their mastery of the bow and arrow and their ruthlessness toward the enemy. The noun is composed of *kishii* (grassland) and the nominalizer *-satzi*. To indicate nonmasculine gender, *-sato* is used: *kishiisato* (a female dweller from the grasslands). See Gran Pajonal; Pajonalino.

kompatziri: Ashéninka Perené for *compadre*, a godfather of ego's baptized or initiated child. The *kompatziri* relationship is comparable to that of a partnership, roughly translated as "trading partner" or even "friend" (*amigo* in Spanish), someone with whom a person spends time socially and does business.

kompiro: The ivory palm (*Phytelephas macrocarpa*), *humiro* or *yarina* in Spanish. It is typically used as construction wood.

koñapi: Vegetable poison, *barbasco* (*Lonchocarpus nicou*). *Koñapi* is used to stupefy fish in dammed streams and self-contained lakes during communal or family fishing expeditions. The plant's crushed roots and leaves are emptied into the water and within half an hour the stupefied fish float to the surface, ready to be picked up and loaded into baskets. See vakoshi.

korakona: A supreme chief; *kura* means "strongman," and *kona* indicates plurality or augmentation in Quechua. The terms were in circulation among the Upper Perené population as forms of address and reference to tribal chiefs. *Korakona* was the supreme chief, exemplified by Apinka; *pinkatsari* was second in rank, of regional stature; and *jevari* was a local chief, the lowest rank in the leadership hierarchy (Macera and Casanto 2009:15). See Apinka; pinkatsari.

Mangoré: A converted Ashaninka strongman from the Franciscan mission of Pichana who in 1674 executed the mission's priest and his two companions and later was killed by his own sister when he tried to incite a rebellion in the mission of Kimiri (Amich 1854:61–65).

maninkaro: An immortal invisible woman, master-owner of the local hills in the Upper Perené valley. A hunter is lost forever in the hills once a *maninkaro* woman takes him as her husband. See *Maninkaroite* (The Invisible Women), by Moises Santos Rojas, text 31.

manioc: See kaniri.

manitzi: A jaguar. Oral tradition attributes to native shamans an ability to transform into jaguars in their dreamy flights.

Manitzipanko: The Jaguar House, or La Boca del Tigre, a historical landmark located a dozen kilometers downstream from Bajo Marankiari (see map 3). According to native lore, a predatory jaguar-shaman was shut away in the cave whose aperture slit is seen in the towering cliff on the left side of the Perené River. See *Manitzipanko* (The Jaguar House), by Ruth Quillatupa Lopez, text 21.

Marinkama: A cultural hero, a skilled and fearless warrior from Gran Pajonal who reportedly fought against the Peruvian military in the Perené valley in the mid-nineteenth century. Also, Marinkama is believed to be the founder of the temple-forge Ashiropanko. See Ashiropanko; *Natsitonini* (The Stream of Bones), by Manuel Rubén Jacinto, text 8.

masato: A traditional fermented drink made of manioc roots. See kaniri; piarentsi.

masontovenki: An *ivenki* plant rubbed onto a person's body to make the enemy, for example, a *matsi* or a policeman, unresponsive to this person's appearance and actions. The word consists of two nominal roots, *masonto* (being in a confused mental state) and -*venki* (magic plant). See ivenki; matsi.

matsi: Human witches who are thought to receive training from non-human demonic teachers in a dream. To cast a spell on the victim, they secretly bury the victim's personal items (hair, bones of animals and fish the victim consumed, other refuse) in the ground. The *matsi* are believed to regularly feed on the victim's flesh in his or her sleep, making the afflicted person progressively sick. The intervention is conducted by a shaman or a healer. In a tobacco-induced séance, the shaman can identify the witch and order her execution or expulsion from the village. Alternatively, during a steam bath treatment, the healer makes the offending charms fall out from the afflicted person's body. See sheripiari; aavintantzin-karo.

mavira: The festival that marks the beginning of the season of scarcity, or *kiarontsi* (the wet season), understood to be the beginning of a new year. The festival was held when *savoro* (wild cane) begins to blossom. *Mavira* is an assimilated loan from Spanish, the original word being *navidad* (Christmas). Despite its name, the festival has nothing to do with the birth of Christ. The festival's aim was to celebrate life in the hope of staying alive in the next year. See *Mavira*, by Ines Pérez de Santos and Moises Santos Rojas, text 44.

mestizo: People of mixed origin, descendants of Spaniards and Andean highlanders. In Ashéninka Perené, they are called *chori*. See chori. Generally, mestizo is defined as "the term for the result of the hybrid mixing of Spanish and other Europeans with Africans or Native Americans (sometimes in some places only between Spanish and indigenous people of the Americas)" (Whitten and Whitten 2011:28).

Metraro: A historic landmark, an upland settlement founded by Apinka in the mid-eighteenth century (See map 3). The village is strategically located at the intersection of old trails, halfway between the Yanesha territory and Gran Pajonal. Metraro became the site of the first Seventh-day Adventist mission post in the Perené valley, established by Fernando Stahl, a North American missionary, in 1922. See Gran Pajonal; Apinka; Stahl, Fernando.

nampitsi: A settlement. The word consists of *nampi* (be abundant) and -*tsi*, the nominal suffix that appears on nonpossessed nouns. *Nonampi* is "my settlement"; alternatively, the Spanish loan word *comunidad* (community) is used, for example, *noyomonirateki* (in my community).

Naviriri Piantzinkari: Naviriri the Transformer, a trickster and cultural hero who possessed mystic transformational powers that allowed him to convert humans into other life-forms at whim. Naviriri was lured by his sister Savoro (some say her name was Piyoro) into a big hole, which was dug out by his brother-in-law Armadillo, and disappeared into the bowels of earth. See Imoro Naviriri.

nijaaveri: A water sprite, master-owner of the Perené River. See kiatsi.

Ooriatsiri: The sun. Also means "solar divinity," often interchangeably used with "Pava" (father) and Tasorentsi (the one who blows [blesses]). See Pava.

ovantzinkari: "Those who exist to kill" or "killers." The term applied to Panoan and Arawak-speaking Piro raiders, traditional enemies of Kampan peoples. See map 1.

ovayeri: "Those who kill" or "warriors." The term does not have a negative connotation, in comparison with *ovantzinkari*.

Pachaka(ma): A stone divinity, venerated by Upper Perené Arawaks before the penetration of Seventh-Day Adventist missionaries. Other known names are Yompiri and Paatsiri. See *Atziri yamaniri mapi poña paamari* (People Were Worshipping Stone and Fire), by Elías Meza Pedro, with Gregorio Santos Pérez, text 17.

Pajonalino: Spanish for a dweller of Gran Pajonal. See Gran Pajonal; kishiisatzi.

Panoans: Neighboring tribes of Cashibo, Shipibo, and Conibo, whose settlements are located on the Ucayali River. See map 1.

pantsantsi: A song, distinguished as a distinct genre in native discourse.

pareni(ni): A river; the designation of one of the main rivers of Chanchamayo Province, called Perené in Spanish.

parenisatzi/parenisatzo: One who dwells along the Perené River. The root *pareni* (river) is combined with the nominalizer *-satzi* (masculine) or *-sato* (nonmasculine).

Pava: The solar divinity, the highest-ranking divinity among Upper Perené Arawaks.

Perené Colony: A British-owned coffee-producing company established in the area of Selva Central in 1891. It received five hundred thousand hectares of land in the Chanchamayo and Perené valleys

as part of the Peruvian national debt settlement. It is called La
Colonia del Perené in Spanish. See Selva Central.

performative utterance: Refers to a sentence by which a speaker
does something, for example, "You are under arrest," "I baptize
thee," or "I do" are, respectively, acts of detention, baptism, and
promise.

Peruvian Corporation: A British company, known in Spanish as
La Peruvian, that received over two million hectares of land in
lowland Peru in 1891 (Barclay 1989:44). It ran a low-profit coffee-
producing company, the Perené Colony, in the Chanchamayo and
Perené valleys until its withdrawal in 1965. See Perené Colony.

peyari: A bony, deer-like demonic creature with an enlarged penis
who seeks males to satisfy his sexual desire. Also known as *manironari* (deer-like). See *Peyari* (The Bone Spirit), by Gregorio Santos
Pérez, text 28.

piarentsi: A fermented, beer-like traditional drink made from boiled
and mashed sweet manioc. Pounded maize is often added to the
fermented mass. The drink is also called *ñoño* or *oviari*. See kaniri;
masato.

pinitsi: A magic plant, of the same species as *tilo* (*Justicia pectoralis*),
pusanga in Spanish, commonly used as a sexual charm. It can also
be used to treat various medical conditions. See *Tsika okantakota
ovayeritantsi* (About the Craft of War), by Daniel Bernales Quillatupa, text 9.

pinkatsari: A regional chief. See korakona.

pish(i)tacos: Legendary throat-cutters who purportedly kill natives
to extract their body fat. They look like white people and lurk in
remote locations along the highway, La Merced-Satipo, attacking
solitary passersby.

piyoro: A flowering tree, called *ocuera blanca* in Spanish (*Cordia* sp.).
The tree's white blossoms, which appear in August, signaled the

peak of the trading season, when Ashaninka and non-Ashaninka households would travel to the Cerro de la Sal and other places to exchange their goods. For example, Pajonal Ashéninka traded their arrows and the clay-like substance called *tsiri*, Perené Ashéninka bartered baby slings, Pichis Ashéninka traded their *cushmas*, and Panoans, their pottery (Bodley 1973; Rojas Zolezzi 1994:145–47). In the mythic times, Piyoro was believed to be Naviriri Piantzinkari's sister, transformed by her brother into a tree. See Cerro de la Sal; Naviriri Piantzinkari.

Poiyotzi: A gray-headed child, also called Kirii, a never-growing grandson of Naviriri Piantzinkari (Naviriri the Transformer), whom the latter constantly carried on his shoulders (see Naviriri Piantzinkari; chonta). Poiyotzi was blamed for annoying his grandfather with questions that the child would blurt out each time he saw something while being carried. Upper Perené lore contends that to avoid the task of explaining things to his overly inquisitive grandson, the irritated Naviriri would transform the object in question into something else. Poiyotzi was also avoided because of his power to turn people's hair gray at the moment a person would look at the child.

reality status: A grammatical category referring to realis events, which are perceived to have happened or be happening, and events that belong to the realm of thought, that is, irrealis events, which didn't happen (Dixon 2012:472–73).

savoro: Wild cane, or *caña brava* in Spanish (*Gynerium sagittatum*). The time of the plant blossoming, December–January, was associated with the onset of the season of scarcity, the wet season, and the beginning of the new year, which was celebrated at a festival near the present-day villages of San Jeronimo de Yurinaki (Rojas Zolezzi 1994:147), Pampa Michi, and San Miguel Centro Marankiari. See mavira.

Selva Central: The lowland territory of the eastern Andean foothills

of Peru, composed of the Chanchamayo, Oxapampa, and Satipo
Provinces. The area is "a traditional homeland of Yanesha and
Ashaninka" (Santos-Granero and Barclay 1998:15).

sheri: Tobacco (*Nicotiana tabacum*). Its syrup is used in massive doses by shamans, together with *kamarampi* (ayahuasca)
(*Banisteriopsis caapi*), to communicate with spirits of malevolent
shamans and *matsi*, dead humans, and creatures inhabiting the
forests and rivers. See matsi; kamarampi.

sheripiari: A shaman, the central figure of the Upper Perené social
organization in the past (Varese 2002:162). During treatment of
sick patients, shamans resolved social conflicts and tensions. Since
the native theory of disease is "grounded in relationships, . . . in
conscious or unconscious aggressiveness," shamans fulfilled the
task of "social management" and restoration of social harmony
by explicitly identifying the disease-causing aggressor (Lenaerts
2006c:12).

shima: Fish; also designates one of the important subsistence fishes
in the Upper Perené valley, called *boquichico* in Spanish (*Prochilodus nigricans*). Also known as *chupadora*. See chupadora.

shimashiri: A flowering tree, Pino chuncho (*Schizolobium amazonicum*). When the yellow blossoms of the *shimashiri* tree appeared
in July–August, at the peak of the dry season, the *shimashiripaite*
feast was held, as reported in *Shinavaite ovariri atziri* (*Shinavaite
Who Ate People*), by Abdias Caleb Quinchori, text 41. Shimashiri
is also believed to be one of Naviriri's sisters. See Naviriri Piantzinkari.

Shimirentsi: Piro (Yine), in Ashéninka Perené (see map 1). In the
past, Piro raiders were traditional enemies of the Perené Ashaninka. The enmity toward Piro is expressed in the label given to
them, *ovantzinkari* (killers). See ovantzinkari.

shina: The kapok or lupuna tree, known for its gigantic size. Its wood
is used for making dugout canoes, and its bark and leaves are used

for medicinal purposes. In mythic thought, *shina* has a malevolent master-owner. See kapok tree.

shiretsi: The human soul or spirit, or a demonic dead person's spirit. The living person's soul is referred to by a possessed form, for example, *noshiri* (my soul), but the dead person's spirit is referred to by a nonpossessed form, *shiretsi*.

shiringa: A rubber or *caucho* tree (*Hevea brasiliensis*).

shoviri: A single-pipe flute, *quena* in Spanish. It is made from bamboo, *kapiro* in Ashéninka Perené.

sonkari: A panpipe, *antara* in Spanish. Typically it has six to ten tubes made from wild cane.

Stahl, Fernando: The North American Adventist missionary who is credited with massive conversion of Upper Perené Arawaks into the Adventist strain of Christianity in the 1920s (Stahl 1932). As a result of his evangelical work among Upper Perené Ashaninka, Adventist mission centers, organized around a school and a church, were established in Metraro, Cascadas, Sotziki, Kivinaki, and Sotani in the 1920s and 1930s (Santos-Garnero and Barclay 1998:238–39). See Metraro.

Tsamirimenta: The Curassow Crest Stone, a historical landmark, located a few miles downstream from Pucharini (see map 3). The rock outcrop on the left side of the Perené River was believed to be "owned" by the master of curassows, called *iriri tsamiri* (father of curassows). See *Tsamirimenta* (The Curassow Crest Stone), by Moises Santos Rojas, text 30.

Tzivi: Salt. In mythic thought, Salt was a person in the old times who restlessly traveled in the Upper Perené area. At some point, the Salt person decided to end her life by asking her husband (some say her brother) to crush her head with a log of the light balsa wood, as she wanted to be transformed into an ephemeral, dust-like substance. However, he killed her with a stone, which allegedly made the tiny salt beads heavy. The place of her transformation is called Tziviariki (The Salt Place), known in Spanish as the Cerro de la Sal. Accordingly, the adjacent river is called Tziviarini, the Salt River. See Tziviarini.

Tziviarini: The Salt River. See Tzivi; Cerro de la Sal.

vakoshi: Vegetable poison, *huaca* in Spanish (*Clibadium remotiflorum*), which is used in communal fishing during the dry period. To stupefy fish, the milky liquid obtained from the crushed roots of the plant is distributed into the dammed areas of streams, small ponds, and lakes. See koñapi.

vishiriantsi: A song sung by more than one person. Native communal singing is akin to chanting, since it involves repetitive singing of a few lines with pivotal words altered, yet the meaning of the altered words is easily understood from the context (Beier 2002).

REFERENCES

Aikhenvald, Alexandra Y. 2013. Amazonia: Linguistic History. In *The Encyclopedia of Global Human Migrations*, ed. Immanuel Ness, 1:334–91. Chichester: Wiley-Blackwell.

————. 2012. *The Languages of the Amazon.* Cambridge: Cambridge University Press.

————. 1999. The Arawak Language Family. In *The Amazonian Languages*, ed. R. M. W. Dixon and Alexandra Y. Aikhenvald, 65–106. Cambridge: Cambridge University Press.

Amich, José. 1854. *Compendio histórico.* Paris: Libreria de Rosa y Bouret.

Anderson, Ronald J. 2000. *Ashéninka Stories of Change.* Publications in Sociolinguistics 4. Dallas: SIL International.

————. 1996. The Magical *Ivenki* Plant in Asheninka War and Hunting Stories. In *Beyond Indigenous Voices: LAILA/ALILA's 11th International Symposium on Latin American Literatures (1994)*, ed. Mary H. Preuss, 75–81. Culver City CA: Labyrinthos.

————. 1991. Clasificación de la flora y la fauna segun los Asheninca. *Revista Latinoamericana de Estudios Etnolingüísticos* 6:95–112.

Austin, John L. 1962. *How to Do Things with Words.* Cambridge MA: Harvard University Press.

Baer, Gerhard. 1992. The One Intoxicated by Tobacco: Matsigenka Shamanism. In *Portals of Power: Shamanism in South America*, ed. E. Jean Matteson Langdon and Gerhard Baer, 79–100. Albuquerque: University of New Mexico Press.

Barclay, Frederica. 1989. *La colonia del Perene.* Iquitos, Peru: Centro de Estudios Teológicos de la Amazonia.

Basso, Ellen B. 1995. *The Last Cannibals.* Austin: University of Texas Press.

———. 1987. *In Favor of Deceit: A Study of Tricksters in an Amazonian Society.* Tucson: University of Arizona Press.

———. 1985. *A Musical View of the Universe: Kalapalo Myth and Ritual Performances.* Philadelphia: University of Pennsylvania Press.

Beier, Christine. 2002. Creating Communities: Feasting and Chanting among the Nantis of Peruvian Amazonia. In *Texas Linguistic Forum*, vol. 45, ed. Inger Mey, Ginger Pizer, His-Yao Su, and Susan Szmania, 1–10. Proceedings of the Symposium about Language and Society—Austin (SALSA). Accessed November 28, 2012. studentorgs.utexas.edu/salsa/proceedings/2002.htm.

Bell, Catherine. (1997) 2009. *Ritual: Perspectives and Dimensions.* Oxford: Oxford University Press.

Benavides, Margarita, ed. 2006. *Atlas de comunidades nativas de la Selva Central.* Lima: Instituto del Bien Común.

———. 1986. La usurpación del dios tecnológico y la articulación temprana en la selva peruana: Misioneros, herramientas y mesianismo. *Amazonia Indígena: Boletín de Análisis COPAL–Solidaridad con los Grupos Nativos* 6(12):30–35.

Bender, Barbara, ed. 1993. *Landscape: Politics and Perspectives.* Providence RI: Berg.

Bloomfield, Leonard. 1927. Literate and Illiterate Speech. *American Speech* 2(10):432–39.

Bodley, John Henry. 1973. Deferred Exchange among the Campa Indians. *Anthropos* 68(3/4):589–96.

———. 1972. A Transformative Movement among the Campa of Eastern Peru. *Anthropos* 67(1/2):220–28.

———. 1970. Campa Socio-economic Adaptation. Doctoral thesis, University of Oregon.

Brown, Mario P. 1974. Cosmovisión de los Ashaninkas (Campas). In *Amazonia: ¿Liberación o esclavitud?*, ed. Juan Marcos Mercier,

Gaston Villeneuve, and Equipo de Misioneros y Nativos de la Selva, 55–60. Lima: Ediciones Paulinas.

Brown, Michael. 1991. Beyond Resistance: A Comparative Study of Utopian Renewal in Amazonia. *Ethnohistory* 38(4):388–413.

Brown, Michael E., and Eduardo Fernandez. 1992. Tribe and State in a Frontier Mosaic. In *War in the Tribal Zone: Expanding States and Indigenous Warfare*, ed. R. Brian Ferguson and Neil L. Whitehead, 175–97. Santa Fe NM: School of American Research Press.

Buchillet, Dominique. 1992. Nobody Is There to Hear: Desana Therapeutic Incantations. In *Portals of Power: Shamanism in South America*, ed. E. Jean Matteson Langdon and Gerhard Baer, 211–30. Albuquerque: University of New Mexico Press.

Chevalier, Jacque M. 1982. *Civilization and the Stolen Gift: Capital, Kin, and Cult in Eastern Peru.* Toronto: University of Toronto Press.

Clifford, James. 2004. Looking Several Ways: Anthropology and Native Heritage in Alaska. *Current Anthropology* 45(1):5–30.

Connerton, Paul. 1989. *How Societies Remember.* Cambridge: Cambridge University Press.

Daignealt, Anna Luisa. 2009. An Ethnolinguistic Study of the Yanesha (Amuesha) Language and Speech Community in Peru's Andean Amazon, and the Traditional Role of Ponapnora, a Female Rite of Passage. Master's thesis, Université de Montreál. Accessed November 25, 2012. https://papyrus.bib.umontreal.ca/jspui/bit stream/1866/4055/4/Daigneault_Anna_L_2010_memoire.pdf.

Danielsen, Swintha. 2007. *Baure: An Arawak Language of Bolivia.* Leiden, Netherlands: CNWS Publications.

Demmer, Ulrich, and Martin Gaenszle, eds. 2007. *The Power of Discourse in Ritual Performance: Rhetoric, Poetics, Transformations.* Berlin: LIT Verlag.

Denevan, William M. 1971. Campa Subsistence in the Gran Pajonal, Eastern Peru. *Geographical Review* (New York) 61(4):496–519.

Descola, Philippe. 1996. *In the Society of Nature: A Native Ecology in Amazonia.* Cambridge: Cambridge University Press.

———. 1992. Societies of Nature and the Nature of Society. In *Conceptualizing Society,* ed. Adam Kuper, 107–26. London: Routledge.

Dixon, R. M. W. 2012. *Basic Linguistic Theory. Further Grammatical Topics.* Vol. 3. Oxford: Oxford University Press.

Eliade, Mircea. (1959) 1987. *The Sacred and the Profane: The Nature of Religion.* Trans. Willard R. Trask. Orlando: Harcourt.

Elick, John William. 1969. An Ethnography of the Pichis Valley Campa of Eastern Peru. Doctoral thesis, University of California, Los Angeles.

Fishman, Joshua A. 1991. *Reversing Language Shift: Theoretical and Empirical Foundations of Assistance to Threatened Languages.* Clevedon UK: Multilingual Matters.

García Salazar, Gabriela Victoria. 1997. Generalidades de la morfología y fonologia del Ashéninca del Ucayali. *Revista Latinoamericana de Estudios Etnolingüísticos* 9.

Gaster, Theodor Herzl. 1950. *Thespis: Ritual, Myth, and Drama in the Ancient Near East.* New York: Henry Schuman.

Gavin, Michael C. 2002. An Assessment of Forest Use Value in the Northern Peruvian Amazon. Doctoral thesis, University of Connecticut.

Geertz, Clifford. 1986. Making Experiences, Authoring Selves. In *The Anthropology of Experience,* ed. Victor W. Turner and Edward M. Bruner, 373–80. Urbana: University of Illinois Press.

Gibson, James Jerome. 1979. *The Ecological Approach to Visual Perception.* Boston: Houghton-Mifflin.

Gow, Peter. 1995. Land, People, and Paper in Western Amazonia. In *The Anthropology of Landscape: Perspectives on Place and Space,* ed. Eric Hirsch and Michael Hanlon, 43–62. Oxford: Clarendon Press.

————. 1991. *Of Mixed Blood: Kinship and History in Peruvian Amazonia.* Oxford: Clarendon Press.

Graham, Laura R. 1995. *Performing Dreams: Discourses of Immortality among the Xavante of Central Brazil.* Austin: University of Texas Press.

Grimes, Ronald L. 1985. *Research in Ritual Studies: A Programmatic Essay and Bibliography.* London: Scarecrow Press.

Heise, María, David Payne, Judith Payne, and Elsa Vilchez. 2000. *Diccionario escolar Ashaninka/Asheninka.* Lima: Ministerio de Educacíon.

Henrich, Joseph. 1997. Market Incorporation, Agricultural Change, and Sustainability among the Machiguenga Indians of the Peruvian Amazon. *Human Ecology* 25(2):319–51.

Hill, Jonathan D. 2011. Sacred Landscapes as Environmental Histories in Lowland South America. In *Ethnicity in Ancient Amazonia: Reconstructing Past Identities from Archaeology, Linguistics, and Ethnohistory,* ed. Alf Hornborg and Jonathan D. Hill, 259–77. Boulder: University Press of Colorado.

————. 1993. *Keepers of the Sacred Chants: The Poetics of Ritual Power in an Amazonian Society.* Tucson: University of Arizona Press.

————. 1989. Ritual Production of Environmental History among the Arawakan Wakuénai of Venezuela. *Human Ecology* 17(1):1–25.

Hirsch, Eric. 1995. Introduction: Landscape: Between Place and Space. In *The Anthropology of Landscape: Perspectives on Place and Space,* ed. Eric Hirsch and Michael Hanlon, 1–30. Oxford: Clarendon Press.

Hornborg, Alf, and Jonathan D. Hill. 2011. Introduction: Ethnicity in Ancient Amazonia. In *Ethnicity in Ancient Amazonia: Reconstructing Past Identities from Archaeology, Linguistics, and Ethnohistory,* ed. Alf Hornborg and Jonathan D. Hill, 1–27. Boulder: University Press of Colorado.

Hualde, José Ignacio. 2005. *The Sounds of Spanish.* Cambridge: Cambridge University Press.

Hvalkof, Søren. 1989. The Nature of Development: Native and Settler Views in Gran Pajonal, Peruvian Amazon. *Folk* 31:125–50.

Illius, Bruno. 1992. The Concept of *Nihue* among the Shipibo-Conibo of Eastern Peru. In *Portals of Power: Shamanism in South America,* ed. E. Jean Matteson Langdon and Gerhard Baer, 63–77. Albuquerque: University of New Mexico Press.

Johnson, Allen. 2003. *Families of the Forest: The Matsigenka Indians of the Peruvian Amazon.* Berkeley: University of California Press.

Killick, Evan. 2008. Creating Community: Land Titling, Education, and Settlement Formation among the Ashéninka of Peruvian Amazonia. *Journal of Latin American and Caribbean Anthropology* 13(1):22–47.

Kindberg, Lee. 1980. *Diccionario Asháninca.* Yarinacocha, Peru: Instituto Lingüístico de Verano.

Kindberg, Willard, Ronald Anderson, Janice Anderson, and Larry Rau. 1979. *Leyendas de los Campa Asháninca.* Lima: Instituto Lingüístico de Verano.

Kymlicka, Will. 2003. Estados multiculturales y ciudadanos interculturales. In *Realidad multilingüe y desafío intercultural: Ciudadanía, política, y educación,* ed. Roberto Zariquiey, 49–81. Lima: Pontificia Universidad Católica del Peru.

La Cerna Salcedo, Juan Carlos. 2012. *Misiones, modernidad y civilización de los Campas: Historia de la presencia Adventista entre los Ashaninkas de la Selva Central peruana (1920–1948).* Lima: Universidad Nacional Mayor de San Marcos.

Lagrou, Els. 2007. Cashinahua Poetics: Metaphors of Sociality and Personhood in Ritual Song. In *The Power of Discourse in Ritual Performance: Rhetoric, Poetics, Transformations,* ed. Ulrich Demmer and Martin Gaenszle, 174–200. Berlin: Verlag.

Lathrap, Donald W. 1970. *The Upper Amazon*. London: Thames and Hudson.

Lehnertz, Jay Frederick. 1974. Lands of the Infidels: The Franciscans in the Central Montaña of Peru, 1709–1824. Doctoral thesis, University of Wisconsin.

Lenaerts, Marc. 2006a. "Le jour où Páwa, notre Père à tous, a abandonné la terre . . .": Le bricolage religieux chez les Ashéninka de l'Ucayali. *Anthropos* 101(2): 541–58.

———. 2006b. Ontologie animique, ethnosciences et universalisme cognitif: Le regard Ashéninka. *L'Homme* 179:113–39.

———. 2006c. Substances, Relationships and the Omnipresence of the Body: An Overview of Ashéninka Ethnomedicine (Western Amazonia). *Journal of Ethnobiology and Ethnomedicine* 49. Accessed November 25, 2012. http:www.ethnobiomed.com/content/2/1/49.

Lévi-Strauss, Claude. 1978. *Myth and Meaning*. London: Routledge.

———. (1964) 1992. *The Raw and the Cooked: Introduction to a Science of Mythology*. Vol. 1. Trans. John Weightman and Doreen Weightman. London: Penguin Books.

———. 1963. *Structural Anthropology*. Trans. Claire Jacobson and Brooke Grundfest Schoepf. New York: Basic Books.

———. 1955. The Structural Study of Myth. *Journal of American Folklore* 68(270): 428–44.

Lewis, M. Paul, Gary F. Simons, and Charles D. Fennig, eds. 2013. *Ethnologue: Languages of the World*. 17th ed. Dallas: SIL International.

Luziatelli, Gaia, Marten Sørensen, Ida Theilade, and Per Mølgaard. 2010. Asháninka Medicinal Plants: A Case Study of the Native Community of Bajo Quimiriki, Junín, Peru. *Journal of Ethnobiology and Ethnomedicine* 6(21). Accessed November 12, 2012. http://www.ethnobiomed.com/content/6/1/21.

Macera, Pablo, and Enrique Casanto. 2009. *El poder libre Asháninka*. Lima: Universidad de San Martin de Porres.

Martel Paredes, Víctor Arturo. 2009. Cambios semanticos en el léxico relacionado a la cosmovisión Asháninka del Bajo Perené generados por el doctrinamiento de la iglecia Adventista. Bachelor's thesis, Universidad Nacional Mayor de San Marcos. Accessed October 13, 2012. http://cybertesis.unmsm.edu.pe/handle /cybertesis/947.

Métraux, Alfred. 1942. A Quechua Messiah in Eastern Peru. *American Anthropologist* 44:721–25.

Michael, Lev. 2008. Nanti Evidential Practice: Language, Knowledge and Social Action in an Amazonian Society. Doctoral thesis, University of Texas.

Mihas, Elena. 2013. Composite Ideophone-Gesture Utterances in the Ashéninka Perené "Community of Practice," an Amazonian Arawak Society from Central-Eastern Peru. *Gesture* 13(1):28–62.

———. 2012. Ideophones in Alto Perené (Arawak) from Eastern Peru. *Studies in Language* 36(2):300–343.

———. 2011. *Añaani katonkosatzi parenini / El idioma del Alto Perené*. Milwaukee: Clark Graphics.

Narby, Jeremy. 1989. Visions of Land: The Ashaninca and Resource Development in the Pichis Valley in the Central Jungle. Doctoral thesis, Stanford University.

Navarro, Manuel. 1924. *La tribu Campa: Prefectura apostólica de San Francisco Ucayali*. Lima: Imprenta del Colegio de Huérfanos San Vicente.

Nuckolls, Janis. 1995. Quechua Texts of Perception. *Semiotica* 103(1/2):145–69.

———. 1992. Sound-Symbolic Involvement. *Journal of Linguistic Anthropology* 2(1):51–80.

Oakdale, Suzanne. 2007. *I Foresee My Life: The Ritual Performance of*

Autobiography in an Amazonian Community. Lincoln: University of Nebraska Press.

Ortiz, Dionisio. 1974. *El Pachitea y el Alto Ucayali: Vision historica de dos importantes regiones de la selva peruana.* Vol. 1. Lima: Imprenta Editorial San Antonio.

Payne, David. 1980. *Diccionario Asheninka-Castellano.* Yarinacocha, Peru: Instituto Lingüístico de Verano.

Paz-Soldán, Carlos E., and Máxime Kuczynski-Godard. 1939. *La selva peruana: Sus pobladores y su colonización en seguridad sanitaria.* Lima: Instituto de Medicina Social de la Universidad de San Marcos.

Peralta, Percy A., and Karen A. Kainer. 2008. Market Integration and Livelihood Systems: A Comparative Case of Three Ashaninka Villages in the Peruvian Amazon. *Journal of Sustainable Forestry* 27(1–2):145–71.

Pinedo, Danny. 2008. La orfandad de los peces: Uso consuetudinario de los recursos pesqueros en la cuenca del río Pichis, Perú. In *El manejo de las pesquerías en los ríos de Sudamérica,* ed. Danny Pinedo and Carlos Soria, 75–142. Ottawa: Instituto del Bien Común.

Rappaport, Joanne. 1989. Geography and Historical Understanding in Indigenous Colombia. In *Who Needs the Past? Indigenous Values and Archeology,* ed. Robert Layton, 84–94. London: Unwin Hyman.

Reeve, Mary-Elizabeth. 1993–94. Narratives of Catastrophe: The Zaparoan Experience in Amazonian Ecuador. *Schweizerische Amerikanisten-Gesellschaft Bulletin* 57–58:17–24.

———. 1985. Identity as Process: The Meaning of Runapura for Quichua Speakers of Curaray River, Eastern Ecuador. Doctoral thesis, University of Illinois, Urbana-Champaign.

Reichel-Dolmatoff, Gerardo. 1975. *The Shaman and the Jaguar.* Philadelphia: Temple University Press.

Renard-Casevitz, France-Marie. 1992. História kampa, memória Asha-
    ninca. In *Historia dos índios no Brasil,* ed. Manuela Carneiro da
    Cunha, 197–212. São Paulo: Companhia das Letras.
Roe, Peter G. 1988. The Josho Nahuanbo Are All Wet and Under-
    cooked: Shipibo Views of the Whiteman and Incas in Myth,
    Legend, and History. In *Rethinking History and Myth: Indigenous
    South American Perspectives on the Past,* ed. Jonathan D. Hill,
    106–35. Urbana: University of Illinois Press.
Rojas Zolezzi, Enrique. 2002. Las clasificaciones Ashaninka de la
    fauna del piedemonte central: Un caso de diferentes niveles de
    aproximación. *Bulletin de l'Institute Français d'Etudes Andines*
    31(2):185–212.
———. 1994. *Los Ashaninka: El pueblo tras el bosque.* Contribución
    a la Etnología de los Campa de la Selva Central Peruana. Lima:
    Pontificia Universidad Católica del Peru.
Romani Miranda, Maggie Mabell. 2004. Toponimia en el Gran Pajo-
    nal con especial atención a los topónimos de afiliación Ashaninka.
    Master's thesis, Universidad Nacional Mayor de San Marcos.
Santos-Granero, Fernando. 2009a. Hybrid Bodyscapes: A Visual His-
    tory of Yanesha Patterns of Cultural Change. *Current Anthro-
    pology* 50(4):477–512.
———. 2009b. *Vital Enemies: Slavery, Predation, and the Amer-
    indian Political Economy of Life.* Austin: University of Texas Press.
———. 2004a. Arawakan Sacred Landscapes. Emplaced Myths,
    Place Rituals, and the Production of Locality in Western Ama-
    zonia. In *Kultur, Raum, Landschaft: Zur Bedeutung des Raumes
    in Zeiten der Globalität,* ed. Ernst Halbmayer and Elke Mader,
    93–122. Frankfurt am Main: Brandes and Apsel Verlag.
———. 2004b. The Enemy Within: Child Sorcery, Revolution, and
    the Evils of Modernization in Eastern Peru. In *In Darkness and
    Secrecy,* ed. Neil L. Whitehead and Robin Wright, 272–305. Dur-
    ham NC: Duke University Press.

———. 2002a. The Arawakan Matrix: Ethos, Language, and History in Native South America. In *Comparative Arawakan Histories: Rethinking Language Family and Culture in Amazonia*, ed. Jonathan D. Hill and Fernando Santos-Granero, 25–50. Urbana: University of Illinois Press.

———. 2002b. Saint Christopher in the Amazon: Child Sorcery, Colonialism, and Violence among the Southern Arawak. *Ethnohistory* 49(3):507–43.

———. 1998. Writing History into the Landscape: Space, Myth, and Ritual in Contemporary Amazonia. *American Ethnologist* 25(2): 128–48.

———. 1988. Templos y herrerías: Utopía y re-creación cultural en la Amazonia peruana (siglos XVIII–XIX). *Bulletin de l'Institute Français d'Etudes Andines* 17(2):1–22.

Santos-Granero, Fernando, and Frederica Barclay. 1998. *Selva Central: History, Economy, and Land Use in Peruvian Amazonia*. Trans. Elisabeth King. Washington DC: Smithsonian Institution Press.

Sarmiento Barletti, Juan Pablo. 2011. Kametsa Asaiki: The Pursuit of the 'Good Life' in an Ashaninka Village (Peruvian Amazonia). Doctoral thesis, University of St. Andrews. Accessed November 20, 2012. http://hdl.handle.net/10023/2114.

Schama, Simon. 1995. *Landscape and Memory*. London: Harper Collins.

Shepard, Glenn H., Jr. 2002. Three Days for Weeping: Dreams, Emotions, and Death in the Peruvian Amazon. *Medical Anthropology Quarterly* 16(2):200–229.

———. 1997. Noun Classification and Ethnozoological Classification in Machiguenga. *Journal of Amazonian Languages* 1(1):31–59.

Sherzer, Joel. 2004. *Stories, Myths, Chants, and Songs of the Kuna Indians*. Austin: University of Texas Press.

———. 1990. *Verbal Art in San Blas: Kuna Culture through Its Discourse*. Cambridge: Cambridge University Press.

———. 1987. A Discourse-Centered Approach to Language and Culture. *American Anthropologist* 89(2):295–309.

Sherzer, Joel, and Greg Urban, eds. 1986. *Native South American Discourse.* Amsterdam: Mouton de Gruyter.

Smith, Richard Chase. 1977. Deliverance from Chaos for a Song: A Social and a Religious Interpretation of the Ritual Performance of Amuesha Music. Doctoral thesis, Cornell University.

Stahl, Ferdinand Anthony. 1932. *In the Amazon Jungles.* Mountain View CA: Pacific Press.

Tibesar, Antonine S. 1952. San Antonio de Eneno: A Mission in the Peruvian Montana. *Primitive Man* 25(1/2):23–39.

———. 1950. The Salt Trade among the Montana Indians of the Tarma Area of Eastern Peru. *Primitive Man* 23(4):103–8.

Torre López, Fernando. 1966. Fenomenología religiosa de la tribu Anti o Campa. *Folklore Americano* (Lima) 14.

Turner, Victor. 1969. *The Ritual Process: Structure and Anti-structure.* Chicago: Aldine.

———. 1968. *The Drums of Affliction: A Study of Religious Processes among the Ndembu of Zambia.* Oxford: Clarendon Press.

———. 1967. *The Forest of Symbols: Aspects of Ndembu Ritual.* Ithaca NY: Cornell University Press.

Urban, Greg. 1991. *A Discourse-Centered Approach to Culture: Native South American Myths and Rituals.* Austin: University of Texas Press.

Uzendoski, Michael A., and Edith Felicia Calapucha-Tapuy. 2012. *The Ecology of the Spoken Word: Amazonian Storytelling and Shamanism among the Napo Runa.* Urbana: University of Illinois Press.

Vansina, Jan. 1985. *Oral Tradition as History.* Madison: University of Wisconsin Press.

Varese, Stefano. 2002. *Salt of the Mountain: Campa Asháninka His-*

tory and Resistance in the Peruvian Jungle. Norman: University of Oklahoma Press.

——. 1996. The Ethnopolitics of Indian Resistance in Latin America. *Latin American Perspectives* 23(2):58–71.

Veber, Hanne. 2009. *Historias para nuestro futuro / Yotantsi Ashi Otsipaniki: Narraciones autobiográficas de líderes Asháninkas y Ashéninkas.* Copenhagen: Grupo Internacional de Trabajo Sobre Asuntos Indígenas.

——. 2003. Asháninka Messianism: The Production of a "Black Hole" in Western Amazonian Ethnography. *Current Anthropology* 44(2): 183–211.

Vilaça, Aparecida. 2005. Chronically Unstable Bodies: Reflections on Amazonian Corporalities. *Journal of the Royal Anthropological Institute* 11:445–64.

Vilchez, Elsa. 2008. Léxico y discurso de los Asháninka. Paper presented at the Congreso de Lexicografía, Lima, April 18–23.

Viveiros de Castro, Eduardo. 1998. Cosmological Deixis and Amerindian Perspectivism. *Journal of the Royal Anthropological Institute* 4(3):469–88.

——. 1996. Images of Nature and Society in Amazonian Ethnology. *Annual Review of Anthropology* 25:179–200.

Weiss, Gerald. 1975. The World of a Forest Tribe in South America. *Anthropological Papers of the American Museum of Natural History* 52(5): 219–588.

——. 1974. Campa Organization. *American Ethnologist* 1(2):379–403.

——. 1973. Shamanism and Priesthood in Light of the Campa Ayahuasca Ceremony. In *Hallucinogens and Shamanism,* ed. Michael J. Harner, 40–47. New York: Oxford University Press.

Whitehead, Neil L. 2011. Afterword: Ethnicity in Ancient Amazonia. In *Ethnicity in Ancient Amazonia: Reconstructing Past Identities from Archaeology, Linguistics, and Ethnohistory,* ed. Alf Hornborg and Jonathan D. Hill, 349–58. Boulder: University Press of Colorado.

———. 2002. Arawak Linguistic and Cultural Identity through Time: Contact, Colonialism, and Creolization. In *Comparative Arawakan Histories: Rethinking Language Family and Culture in Amazonia,* ed. Jonathan D. Hill and Fernando Santos-Granero, 51–73. Urbana: University of Illinois Press.

———. 1992. Tribes Make States and States Make Tribes: Warfare and the Creation of Colonial Tribes and States in Northeastern South America. In *War in the Tribal Zone: Expanding States and Indigenous Warfare,* ed. R. Brian Ferguson and Neil L. Whitehead, 127–50. Santa Fe NM: School of American Research Press.

Whitehead, Neil L., and Robin Wright, eds. 2004. *In Darkness and Secrecy.* Durham NC: Duke University Press.

Whitten, Norman E., Jr. 1985. *Sicuanga Runa: The Other Side of Development in Amazonian Ecuador.* Urbana: University of Illinois Press.

———. 1978. Ecological Imagery and Cultural Adaptability: The Canelos Quichua of Eastern Ecuador. *American Anthropologist* 80(4):836–59.

Whitten, Norman E., Jr., and Dorothea Scott Whitten. 2011. *Histories of the Present: People and Power in Ecuador.* Urbana: University of Illinois Press.

Wilbert, Johannes, and Karin Simoneau, eds. 1992. *Folk Literature of South American Indians: General Index.* Los Angeles: UCLA Latin American Center.

Zucchi, Alberta. 2002. A New Model of the Northern Arawakan Expansion. In *Comparative Arawakan Histories: Rethinking Language Family and Culture in Amazonia,* ed. Jonathan D. Hill and Fernando Santos-Granero, 199–222. Urbana: University of Illinois Press.

INDEX

Page numbers in italics signify photographs or drawings.